Seoul

"All you've got to do is decide to go and the hardest part is over.

So go!"

TONY WHEELER, COFOUNDER – LONELY PLANET

THOMAS O'MALLEY, PHILLIP TANG

Contents

COVID-19

We have re-checked every business in this book before publication to ensure that it is still open after the COVID-19 outbreak. However, the economic and social impacts of COVID-19 will continue to be felt long after the outbreak has been contained, and many businesses, services and events referenced in this guide may experience ongoing restrictions. Some businesses may be temporarily closed, have changed their opening hours and services, or require bookings; some unfortunately could have closed permanently. We suggest you check with venues before visiting for the latest information.

(left) **Deoksugung p82** Daily changing of the guard ceremony

(right) **Changdeokgung p60** Secret Garden pavilion

Right:
Gyeongbokgung (p58)

PRASIT PHOTO/GETTY IMAGES ©

WELCOME TO
Seoul

Seoul sparkles with design magic. I'm bewitched by the fancy threads of Apgujeong, with its perfect angles; but the real heart-stealer is the city's knack for fashioning a hanok *into a modern* makgeolli *hang-out, or a palace into a moonlit dining hall serving royal cuisine. I'll peer across Gangnam's skyscrapers from a sky-high temple, or scoff kimchi tacos in green spaces converted from old oil tankers, which might suggest NYC or Tokyo; yet every temple eave,* hotteok *and K-Indie tune reminds me, I'm in Seoul.*

By Phillip Tang, Writer
For more about our writers, see p256

Seoul's Top Experiences

1 STEP BACK IN TIME

The history of Korea is palpable at ground level in Seoul. Monumental palaces and their vast courts are unmissable, as are the neighbourhoods of traditional wooden houses, royal statues staking their place on the street and the colourful silken flutter of the changing of the guards. Visible too are the fingerprints of the country's encounters with the West and China, in the architecture of temples, train stations, food markets and the everyday lives of Seoulites.

Make Like Royalty

Peek into the lives of Korean royalty at the five grand palaces of Seoul. A fairy-tale land of secret gardens, elegant greenhouses, throne halls, stone-bridge ponds and exquisite Joseon architecture awaits. p58

Royal guards at Gwanghwamun gate, Gyeongbokgung

Walk Through an Ancient Korean Town

Get lost wandering the labyrinthine streets, in an age of craftsmanship when Seoulites lived in one-storey wooden *hanok*, with graceful tiled roofs and internal courtyard gardens. Nestled between two major palaces and rising up the foothills, Bukchon Hanok Village (pictured above and left) is the largest neighbourhood, with 900 fascinating real homes. p61

DMZ

The tension at the heavily guarded border splitting North and South Korea is palpable along the Demilitarized Zone (DMZ), a symbol of the Cold War, now turned surreal tourist draw. Observation points along the DMZ peek into the secretive North. p152

2 BOTTOMLESS *BANCHAN*

There are tasty thrills everywhere in Seoul. Restaurants and street stalls serve all budgets, from sticky street snacks to sumptuous royal banquets with endlessly delightful *banchan* side-dishes. Join young Seoulites taste-testing fusion food in cafes; or embrace the market buzz where cooks prepare fresh kimchi and traditional Korean dishes before your eyes (and nose).

Fine Dining

Dining in Seoul is best in groups of two or 20, some dishes are not served to solo diners. Fine dining pairs wine and *soju* with dishes, but the real fun is at a royal court banquet. A procession of small dishes appears continuously at your table, like a traditional tasting menu fit for a Joseon Dynasty emperor, complete with musical performances. p36

Tasting Your Way Through Seoul's Snacks

If you can stick it on a skewer for standing and eating shoulder to shoulder with locals, you'll find it in Seoul. Quick thrills include hot sticky, spicy rice cake *tteokbokki, odeng* (fish cakes), kimchi *mandu* (dumplings) and taste bud-thrilling Korean takes on corndogs, tacos and fried chicken. At Gwangjang Market, alleys of vendors create street eats like stewed pig trotters, and *bindaetteok* (mung-bean pancakes). p181

Left: Gwangjang Market (p137); Above left: *Bindaetteok* (mung-bean pancakes); Above right: Myeong-dong street-food stall (p85)

3 DESIGN OF THE FUTURE

For a city rich in serious history, Seoul has a forward-looking, free-spirited attitude to its architecture. Glass and steel are forged into very human curves, taking into consideration the surrounding trees and waterways. The buildings of the city are a peek into the future, at what a slick modern metropolis will look like. Sometimes it's quirky, but there is always an element of that Korean cool.

Seoul City Hall

This giant glass wave (pictured below), designed by Kerl Yoo, is a modern reinterpretation of the traditional curved eaves found on palaces and temple roofs in Korea. Inside, the towering vertical garden gives hints of a future where thoughtful architecture meets nature. p85

T.DALLAS/SHUTTERSTOCK ©

Dongdaemun Design Plaza & Park

Designed by the late Zaha Hadid, the neo-futuristic DDP cultural complex (pictured above) is an undulating aluminium and concrete landmark. p135

Leeum Samsung Museum of Art

Korea's premier art gallery (pictured right) balances contemporary and traditional art, and features a rusted stainless-steel structure designed by French architect Jean Nouvel. p110

4 K-POP, K-DRAMA AND K-BEAUTY

Go all in on *Hallyu* (the Korean Wave), the global cultural force that is Korean pop music, gaming, soap operas and beauty products. Seoul is the epicentre of interactive K-Pop experiences and famous locations from K-Drama series; here you can develop an obsession for that slick Korean way of flaunting a Gangnam-style life.

Get Some Gangnam Style

Gangnam is the home of K-Pop record labels and SMTown coexartium (pictured above) – a five-level interactive museum and store dedicated to K-Pop idols such as Girls' Generation and Exo. p124

K-Drama

Choong Ang High School (p69) is an attractive early-20th-century complex that featured as a location in the hit Korean TV drama *Winter Sonata*, while Sanmotoonge (p147) featured as the cafe in the drama *Coffee Prince*.

K-Beauty

Seoul is cosmetics heaven – local boutiques and chains sell top-quality, inexpensive products, many made famous by K-Pop and K-Drama idols. Apgujeong Rodeo Drive is ritzy, while the young congregate in Hongdae. p46

5 DRINK & BE MERRY

Seoulites are serious about having fun. They tend to let their guard down, and even get a little wild, at their world-famous mega clubs and many traditional festivals. If quiet reflection is more your style, simply sitting sipping tea is especially pleasurable at an atmospheric teahouse.

PATCHAN_HK/SHUTTERSTOCK ©

KOBBY DAGAN/SHUTTERSTOCK ©

Teahouses

Healing teas are at the centre of Korea's ancient culture. Teahouses (pictured, top) are elegant places to sip green tea and herbal, fruit or toasted-rice-and-barley brews. p40

Lotus Lantern Festival

The lively celebrations for Buddha's birthday (pictured above left), in May, last for weeks. Some nights culminate in a dazzling lantern parade. p24

Makgeolli & *Maekju*

Start or finish your night at a German-inspired *maekju* (beer) hall serving Korean draught and fried chicken. Try the *makgeolli* (pictured above), a milky alcoholic brew made from unrefined fermented rice. p41

6 FINDING TRANQUILITY

JON HICKS/GETTY IMAGES ©

Inwangsan Guksadang

Shamans once performed exorcisms here, though today you might only spot one performing a blessing. Yet Seoul's most famous shamanist shrine, Inwangsan Guksadang, in its lofty mountain position, feels almost mythical. p144

Bongeun-sa

Experience traditional Korean Buddhist life through a temple-life day at Bongeun-sa (pictured below left). Monks will lead you through a tea ceremony and tour of the 1200-year-old complex. Copying Buddhist sutras, brush-stroke by brushstroke, is a highlight. p123

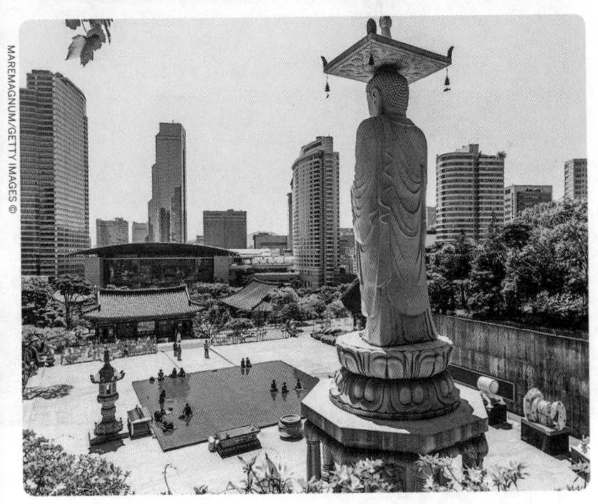

MAREMAGNUM/GETTY IMAGES ©

The metropolis of Seoul has a release valve for all the urban activity: its temples and shrines are places anybody can seek out when they need to slow down. You can even tap into the rhythm of daily life there through a Temple Life program; it's an experience you are unlikely to forget. The fact that so many of these ancient buildings are so monumentally gorgeous is a bonus.

Top: Jogye-sa (p63)

7 WILD CITY

Nature is never far away in Seoul, where a regal mountain watches over the city. The metropolis weaves waterways and narrow parks through its streets, giving urban explorers a breather. The sound of birdcall has returned to a running stream that once was a highway, and when you really want to escape the city, there are spectacular hikes for all levels of fitness in easy reach, with historic monuments shining through swathes of green.

TRABANTOS/SHUTTERSTOCK ©

SIMON RICHMOND/LONELY PLANET ©

KEITMA/SHUTTERSTOCK ©

Hike the Old City Wall

Namsan is the most central of the city's four guardian mountains. Locals actively patronise the 109-hectare park and hiking paths to the summit, including one that follows the line of the old Seoul City Wall (pictured above right). p83

Follow a River Through the City

Cheong-gye-cheon (pictured above left) is a riverside park and walking course that cuts through the city, bringing greenery, heron, small fish and a calm respite from the surrounding commercial hubbub. p64

Gyeongui Line Forest Park

The Gyeongui Line Forest Park (pictured above) is a narrow green space that runs along the discarded railroad tracks through youthful Hongdae. Within are nooks for reading, grassy picnic areas, exercise equipment and more. p94

What's New

Seoul is a megacity with a population boom. For the first time ever, more than 50% of the country's people live in the capital, so it's lucky that the city is on track to expanding its bike and e-scooter lanes to handle the movement of all its folk.

Frieze Seoul Art Fair

There was a buzz in the international art scene when it was revealed that in 2022, Seoul would be the first Asian city to host a Frieze Art Fair, joining other hosts New York, Los Angeles and London. Frieze is one of the largest art fairs in the world, and Frieze Seoul is staged in collaboration with about 100 local galleries. Fair dates vary each year, but will happen around September at COEX Exhibition Centre in Gangnam.

Seongsu-dong

Dubbed the 'Brooklyn of Seoul', Seongsu-dong's hip factor has taken off with plenty of new bars, restaurants and art spaces converted from shoe warehouses in the east of Seoul.

Night Markets

Summer night markets bring food trucks, gift stalls and live music. Riverside Banpo Romantic Moonlight Market (p126) is next to the Banpo Bridge Rainbow Fountain. The Oil Tank Culture Park Forest Picnic Market (p102) happens in abandoned oil tanks converted into an art centre.

Seoul Olympic Museum

Revamped again in 2021, the Seoul Olympic Museum (p121) is now interactive with VR headset games and includes all highlights, history and loads of memorabilia from the Pyeongchang 2018 Winter Olympics, 1988 Seoul Olympics and international games.

Augmented Reality Apps

The Seoul Metropolitan Government's official 'i Tour Seoul+' app has been

LOCAL KNOWLEDGE

WHAT'S HAPPENING IN SEOUL

Phillip Tang, Lonely Planet writer

The role of the church in Seoul and South Korea as a whole is a topic that every Seoulite on the street seems to have an opinion on. The pandemic sparked a local backlash against conservative Christian churches for ignoring government demands aimed at controlling the spread. Over a thousand Covid-19 cases were linked to defiant members of the fundamentalist Sarang Jeil Church, who attended anti-government rallies in Seoul and refused to get tested. This might have all faded away if they didn't have so much political clout. The church rose in popularity in 2019, but after being accused of spreading false health advice, they then lost a lot of political influence over the 2022 presidential elections. Conservative politicians have since distanced themselves from Sarang Jeil Church to dodge getting caught up in the fallout.

updated with augmented reality. Point the camera at your surroundings for an overlay of nearby sights and restaurants. Similarly Changdeokgung, the most beautiful of Seoul's five palaces, takes its good looks to augmented reality. The 'Changdeok AR-irang' app lets you visualise (and photograph) yourself dressed in the outfits of the royal era, as well see royal dances overlaid on the palace grounds where they once took place.

Free, Fast Wi-fi Everywhere

In 2020 the government upgraded and expanded its 'Kkachi On' free public wi-fi network to cutting edge Wi-Fi 6 technology. This means the world's fastest (and most secure) wi-fi is now available for free to all Seoulites and visitors in every major public street, park, market and public building (such as libraries), as well as on every bus.

Cycling and E-Scooters

The government has given cycling and e-scooters a boost with 23.3km of new bicycle lanes. The cycle paths run alongside the waterways of Cheong-gye-cheon, connecting with Seoul Forest and Olympic Park. Riders are completely separated from motorists; and a new law at the end of 2020 means e-scooters are classified as bicycles and can use bike paths.

Drink Trends

Bars are moving beyond serving strong *soju* and into sippable Korean wines. Wine makers are branching out beyond traditional grape varieties and into wild grapes and even Korean apples, plums and berries. Bars serving handcrafted cocktails and *makgeolli* (fermented rice alcohol) also continue to spring up across the city in areas such as Hongdae, Itaewon and Gangnam. Coffee consumption has spiked in popularity, despite lockdowns in recent times. Seoulites have turned to home delivery or homemade for their caffeine fix.

BTS Museum

A new museum dedicated to top K-pop groups, including the world's largest K-pop act BTS, has opened in Yongsan in Seoul. The 4,700 m2 Hybe Corporation label (formerly Big Hit Entertainment) museum displays BTS memorabilia such as outfits and microphones touched by the boy band.

LISTEN, WATCH & FOLLOW

For inspiration and up-to-date news, visit https://www.lonelyplanet.com/south-korea/articles.

Seoulistic (www.seoulistic.com) Excellent and highly detailed blog from a Seoul local committed to sharing the best of his city.

The Soul of Seoul (www.thesoulofseoul.net) Comprehensive travel blog by an American woman married to a Korean.

What's Han Your Mind (https://anchor.fm/whatshanyourmind) Weekly podcast sharing anecdotes on life in Seoul through one word.

I Seoul U (www.instagram.com/iseoulu) Inspiring snaps from the official Seoul City Instagram account.

FAST FACTS

Food trend Royal palace-era recipes

South Korean population living in greater Seoul Over 50%

Women under 50 with cosmetic procedures 20%

Population 9.96 million

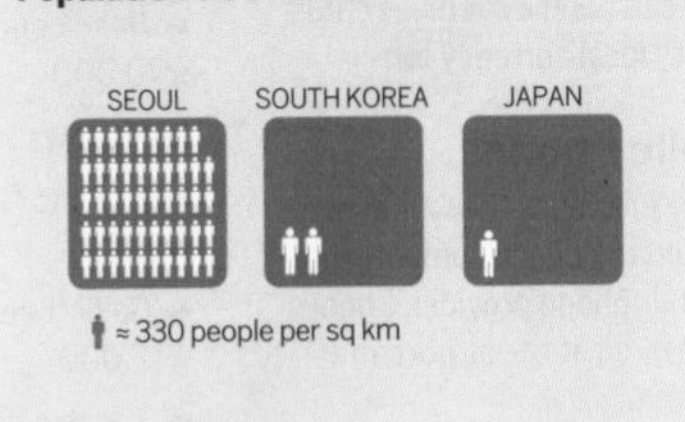

Tourist Visas

Korea now requires most visitors to apply for an electronic travel authorisation before travel, similar to the USA's ESTA and Canada's eTA. The Korea Electronic Travel Authorization (K-ETA) costs ₩10,000 and is valid for two years. Eligible visitors are generally those who would have been on the permit-on-arrival list in the past, such as citizens from the UK and USA. Apply and pay online, at least 24 hours before travel, through the official K-ETA website (www.k-eta.go.kr).

Need to Know

For more information, see Survival Guide (p205)

Currency
Korean won (₩)

Language
Korean, English

Visas
Australian, UK, US and most western European citizens receive a 90-day entry permit on arrival.

Money
ATMs are widely available, and credit cards are accepted by most businesses, although not everywhere can handle overseas cards, so carry local currency too.

Mobile Phones
South Korea uses the CDMA digital standard; check compatibility with your phone provider. Phones can be hired at the airport and elsewhere.

Time
GMT/UTC plus nine hours. No daylight saving.

Tourist Information
KTO Tourist Information Center (Map p232, E7; ☎02-1330; www.visitkorea.or.kr; 2nd fl, 40 Cheonggyecheon-ro; ⊙9am-8pm; 👪; Ⓢ Line 1 to Jonggak, Exit 5) Knowledgeable staff, free internet, brochures and maps, and free experiences including cooking and craft classes.

Daily Costs

Budget: Less than ₩100,000
- Dorm bed: ₩20,000
- Street food: ₩1000–5000
- Local beer: ₩3000
- Hiking up Namsan: free
- Entry to many museums: free
- Subway ticket: ₩1400

Midrange: ₩100,000–300,000
- *Hanok* guesthouse: ₩70,000
- Food walking tour: ₩60,000
- Entry to Gyeongbokgung: ₩3000
- *Galbi* (beef ribs) per person: ₩12,000
- Theatre ticket: ₩40,000

Top End: More than ₩300,000
- Hotel room: ₩200,000
- Royal Korean banquet: ₩70,000
- Scrub and massage at top-notch spa: ₩60,000
- DMZ tour: ₩100,000

Advance Planning

Two months before Start learning *hangeul* (Korean phonetic alphabet) and train for hiking up mountains. Book for Starlight Tours of Gyeongbokgung (March to April), or Moonlight Tours of Changdeokgung (April, May or August to October).

Three weeks before Plan your itinerary, check for festivals and events, book a DMZ tour and templestay program.

One week before Make reservations at top-end restaurants, buy tickets to concerts.

Useful Websites

Visit Seoul (www.visitseoul.net) The official government site to everything about the city.

Seoul (www.magazine.seoulselection.com) Online version of the monthly magazine with its finger on the city's pulse.

Lonely Planet (www.lonelyplanet.com/seoul) Destination information, hotel reviews, traveller forum and more.

WHEN TO GO

Spring and autumn are uniformly pleasant; summer sweltering and muggy; winters nasty and long. Typhoons are a possibility from late June to September.

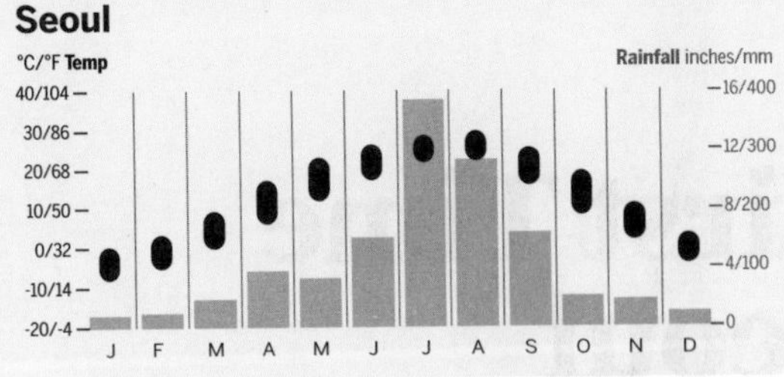

Arriving in Seoul

Incheon International Airport A'rex express trains to Seoul station ₩9000 (43 minutes from Terminal 1, 51 minutes from Terminal 2); all-stop trains ₩4150 from Terminal 1 (55 minutes), ₩4950 from Terminal 2 (one hour). Bus to city-centre hotels from ₩9000 (one hour); taxi around ₩65,000.

Gimpo International Airport A'rex trains run to Seoul Station (₩1300, 15 minutes) or take the subway (₩1450, 35 minutes). Buses (from ₩5000) and taxis (around ₩35,000) will be slower – around 40 minutes to an hour, depending on traffic.

Seoul Station Long-distance trains arrive at this centrally located terminal; a taxi ride to most central hotels will be under ₩5000.

For much more on **arrival** see p206

Getting Around

You'll definitely want to purchase a T-Money card (also called CITYPASS+) for discounts on bus, subway, taxi and train fares as well as for general convenience. Handy apps for interactive mapping and real-time journey planning across Seoul's transport network include **Subway Korea, Kakao Metro/Kakao Bus** and **Seoul Topis** (http://topis.seoul.go.kr).

Subway The best way to get around, with an extensive network, frequent services and inexpensive fares.

Bus Handy for routes around Namsan and Northern Seoul, and for short hops in bad weather.

Taxi Best for short trips; the basic fare starts at ₩3000 for the first 2km.

Bicycle Seoul Bike, the city's public-bike scheme, can be used by visitors.

Car hire Useful only for long trips out of the city; budget from ₩80,000 per day.

For much more on **getting around** see p208

Sleeping

Seoul offers the lot, from no-frills guesthouses to *hanok* (traditional wooden homes) homestays to five-star palaces, but reserve well in advance, especially if visiting during busy travel periods such as Chinese New Year and Japan's Golden Week holidays (usually the end of April or early May). Note that many hotels raise their rates at weekends, and some quote without the 10% government tax added.

Useful Websites

Lonely Planet (www.lonelyplanet.com/south-korea/seoul/hotels) Reviews for all kinds of accommodation in Seoul.

Korean Hotel Reservation Center (www.khrc.com) Check for low rates on top-end hotels.

Homestay Korea (www.homestaykorea.com) If you wish to stay with a Korean family.

Best Guesthouse in Seoul (www.guesthouseinseoul.org) Reviews of Seoul guesthouses.

Nicerent (www.nicerent.com) Good for longer-term stays of a month or more.

For much more on **sleeping** see p165

First Time Seoul

For more information, see Survival Guide (p205)

Checklist

- Make sure your passport is valid for at least six months past your arrival date
- Book limited tickets to Starlight Tours at Gyeongbokgung, or Moonlight Tours at Changdeokgung, and for the popular USO DMZ tours
- Reserve a month ahead at high-end restaurants such as Jungsik
- Inform your debit-/credit-card company you're heading away
- Arrange for appropriate travel insurance

What to Pack

- South Korea electrical adapter, the same as the plug used in most of Europe
- Hand sanitiser, deodorant and tampons – surprisingly hard to find or with little variety
- Good walking shoes – there are plenty of mountain paths to climb
- Extra luggage – Seoul is a shopper's paradise

Top Tips for Your Trip

- Most museums are closed Monday, so plan other activities.
- The last Wednesday of the month is Culture Day. Many museums offer free admission.
- Walk between Insadong, Ikseon-dong and Myeong-dong. It's more interesting than the subway, which involves changing a couple times.
- Stroll along the Cheong-gye-cheon stream to sights alongside or nearby, such as Deoksugung, Insadong and Gwangjang Market.
- Buy a reloadable T-money transport card. It's easier than buying a ticket each trip, plus you can switch bus or subway within half an hour with little additional cost.
- Most restaurants close for 'break time' from about 3pm to 5pm.
- Free wi-fi is everywhere; subway platforms offer a T-mobile connection by selecting 'Use network as is', disconnecting and reconnecting, and then clicking the 'Free Wifi' button.

What to Wear

Young Seoulites are fashion-conscious but stick to current trends, even in the hippest of bars. Any kind of outdoor activity, even walking up Namsan, sees many an older Korean in brightly coloured jackets and outdoor gear, so you are unlikely to look out of place similarly dressed. Shorts and flip-flops will make you stand out as a foreigner, even on hot days; locals tend to stick to loose fitting clothing rather than baring skin. Spring days can be warm with sudden drops in temperature at night, when a light jacket comes in handy. Summer is hot and humid so avoid bright colours and grey, which tend to reveal perspiration. Wear waterproof shoes if going in June or July.

Be Forewarned

- Motorists can be impatient with pedestrians, so take extra care when crossing the road.
- Police in full riot gear, carrying shields and batons, are a not-uncommon sight in central Seoul. Student, trade-union, anti-American, environmental and other protests can occasionally turn physical. Keep well out of the way of any confrontations.

Seoul Addresses

Korea's address system was updated in 2011 to consist of logically numbered buildings on named streets. However, locals still sometimes don't know the new street names, and old-style addresses are still used on some business cards and websites.

Taxes & Refunds

Goods and services sold in Seoul include 10% value-added tax (VAT). If you spend more than ₩30,000 at participating tax-free shops, you can receive a partial refund on some items (between 5% and 7%). Be sure to collect the special receipt, which can be used to obtain a tax refund in the airport or, increasingly, in locations in and around Seoul's malls and shopping areas.

Seoul also has a growing number of duty-free shops and malls where goods are sold tax-free on the spot, but you'll need to show your passport.

Tipping

Tipping is neither required nor expected in South Korea.

Bargaining

Acceptable at markets and some shops. If you are buying more than one item, it's also OK to ask for a discount – use your judgement.

Language

Korean is the common language. It's relatively easy to find English-speakers in Seoul, but learning the writing system, *hangeul*, and a few key phrases will help you in being able to decode menus and timetables. Nearly all the street signs are in Korean and English.

Do you have a Western-style room?
서양식 방 있나요? sŏ·yang·shik pang in·na·yo

Smaller lodgings may only have Korean-style rooms (with floor mattresses). If you want a 'proper' bed, check ahead.

Please bring a fork/knife.
포크/나이프 가져다 주세요. p'o·k'ŭ/na·i·p'ŭ ka·jŏ·da ju·se·yo

In Korean restaurants the spoon is meant for rice and soup, and chopsticks are for everything else; ask if you need other utensils.

Can you make it less spicy?
덜 맵게 해 주시겠어요? tŏl maep·ké hae·ju·shi·gess·ŏ·yo

Korean food is an enthusiastic assault on the senses, often spicy enough to trigger off sweat or tears – you may want to play it safe.

Where can I find a steam-room?
찜질방 어디에 있나요? jjim·jil·bang ŏ·di·é in·na·yo

Generally open 24 hours, these facilities at public baths are perfect when you need some down time – whether to watch TV, read, just relax or even sleep overnight.

5 Please call the tourist interpreting service.
통역 서비스에 전화해 주세요.
t'ong·yŏk sŏ·bi·sŭ·é chŏn·hwa·hae·ju·se·yo

To ensure that you get to the right place, Korean taxi drivers have a number to call to hook you up with someone who will translate directions for you.

Etiquette

There are several social rules that Koreans stick to, although they will generally make allowances for foreigners. Even so, follow these tips to avoid faux pas.

➡ **Meetings and greetings** A quick, short bow is most respectful for meetings and departures. Give or receive any object using both hands – especially name cards (an essential feature of doing business in Korea), money and gifts.

➡ **Shoes** Remove your shoes on entering a Korean home, guesthouse, temple or Korean-style restaurant.

➡ **Eating and drinking** Pour drinks for others and use both hands when pouring or receiving. Use chopsticks or a spoon to touch food and don't leave either sticking up in a bowl of rice.

➡ **Loss of face** Potentially awkward remarks or scenes should be quickly smoothed over, and if you sense someone trying to change the subject, go with the flow. An argument or embarrassing situation should be avoided at all costs.

erfect Days

One

nghwamun & Jongno-gu (p56)

Start your tour of **Gyeongbokgung** at the palace's expertly restored main Gwanghwamun, where you can watch ıgeantry of the changing of the guard e hour. Explore the winding streets of **hon Hanok Village** and **Insa-dong**, ng for refreshments at a cafe or tea- in between browsing the equally ubiq- s art galleries and craft stores in these . If you finish early, continue on to the onverted *hanok* cafes of **Ikseon-dong**.

Lunch Try the legendary meat dumplings at Koong (p71).

nghwamun & Jongno-gu (p56)

Join the afternoon tour of **Changdeokgung**, which also includes luwon (Secret Garden). Explore the wood- ounds of the venerable shrine **Jongmyo**, ing the spirit tablets of the Joseon kings queens.

Dinner Sample Korean street food at Gwangjang Market (p137).

eong-dong & Jung-gu (p79)

Take your seat at a fun nonverbal show such as **Nanta** or **Jump**. Be zled by the bright lights and retail over- l of **Myeong-dong** and neighbouring **ndaemun Market**, where the stalls stay n all night.

Day Two

Itaewon & Yongsan-gu (p106)

Survey centuries of Korean history and art by selectively dipping into the vast collection of the **National Museum of Korea**. Shuttle over to the west side of Yongsan-gu to enjoy the contemporary art and architecture at the splendid **Leeum Samsung Museum of Art**.

Lunch Tuck into Southern American barbecue at Linus' BBQ (p112).

Myeong-dong & Jung-gu (p79)

Wander the lively, multicultural lanes around Itaewon and the more boutiquey Hannam-dong, then for a post-lunch workout, hike up **Namsan** to **N Seoul Tower**. It's not a difficult climb, but if you don't have the energy there's a cable car or a bus. It's very romantic watching the sunset from atop this central mountain as the night lights of Seoul flicker to life. Freshen up with a steam in the saunas and a soak in the tubs at the **Dragon Hill Spa & Resort**.

Dinner Savour delicious bibimbap at Mokmyeoksanbang (p86).

Itaewon & Yongsan-gu (p106)

Explore **Itaewon** after dinner for a fun night of hopping between cafes, bars and dance clubs.

RUNPHOTO/GETTY IMAGES ©

Gyeongbokgung (p58)

MANFRED GOTTSCHALK/GETTY IMAGES ©

Namdaemun Market (p86)

Day Three

Northern Seoul (p141)

Reflect on the struggles and sacrifices of Koreans to overcome colonialism and create a modern country at **Seodaemun Prison History Hall**. Afterwards, hike up nearby **Inwangsan** along **Seoul City Wall** for fabulous views of the city, surreal rock formations and the otherworldly shamanistic rituals of **Inwangsan Guksadang**.

Lunch Fuel up on elegant *mandu* (dumplings) at Jaha Sonmandoo (p147).

Northern Seoul (p141)

Keep on shadowing the **Seoul City Wall** down to Buam-dong and over **Bukaksan** and to Seongbuk-dong, a hike of around two hours. Catch your breath and rest your feet in the beautiful teahouse **Suyeon Sanbang**, and the equally serene surrounds of the temple **Gilsang-sa**.

Dinner Gorge on cheap and tasty rice-cake at I Love Sindangdong (p137).

Dongdaemun & Eastern Seoul (p133)

If your hiking legs haven't given out, it's only another hour or so following the City Wall over **Naksan** and down to **Dongdaemun**, where the night market will just be starting to crank up (alternatively, take the subway). Admire the 21st-century architectural styling of **Dongdaemun Design Plaza & Park**, then trawl the market stalls for a new outfit.

Day Four

Western Seoul (p92)

Both contemporary art and panoramic views up and down the Han can be enjoyed at **63 Sky Art Gallery** on Yeouido. Hire a bicycle in Hangang Riverside Park and pedal out to **Seonyudo Park** on an island in the Han River.

Lunch Pick your own seafood for cooking at Noryangjin Fish Market (p98).

Western Seoul (p92)

If you're interested in contemporary architecture, then **Ewha Womans University's** stunning entrance building and **KT&G SangsangMadang** in Hongdae are both worth seeing. Hongdae and neighbouring Sangsu-dong and Yeonnam-dong are brimming with hip hang-outs; if it's Saturday you can shop for quirky, original craft souvenirs at the **Free Market** or **Dongjin Market**. A late-afternoon visit to the atmospheric Buddhist temple **Bongeun-sa** can segue nicely into browsing the boutiques of **Apgujeong**, **Cheongdam** or **Garosu-gil**.

Dinner Treat yourself to neo-Korean cuisine with a booking at Jungsik (p127).

Gangnam & Southern Seoul (p119)

After dinner pitch up at the **Banpo Hangang Park** by 9pm to see the day's last floodlit flourish of the **Banpo Bridge Rainbow Fountain** off the Banpo Bridge.

Month By Month

TOP EVENTS

Jongmyo Daeje, May

Seoul Fringe Festival, July or August

Sajik Daeje, September

Seoul Lantern Festival, November

January

Wrap up well against very chilly weather as temperatures in Seoul can drop to below -10°C (14°F). It's a good time for trips to nearby ski resorts.

Seollal (Lunar New Year)

Seoul empties out as locals visit hometowns to honour ancestors and eat traditional foods over this three-day national festival (www.visitseoul.net). Events in Seoul are held at the major palaces and folk villages. Celebrations start 1 February 2022, 21 January 2023 and 9 February 2024.

April

It can still be cold and wet in spring, so come prepared. Nature determines the exact timing, but early April is generally when parts of Seoul turn pink in a transient flurry of delicate cherry blossoms.

Yeongdeungpo Yeouido Spring Flower Festival

One of the best places to experience the blossoming trees and flowers is Yeouido (www.ydp.go.kr). Other good spots include Namsan and Ewha Womans University, and Jeongdok Public Library in Samcheong-dong.

Royal Wedding Ceremony of King Gojong and Empress Myeongseong

A re-enactment of the royal wedding ceremony of King Gojong, the last king of the Joseon dynasty, and Empress Myeongseong (Queen Min), is held on the third Saturday in April at Unhyeongung, where the original ceremony took place on 21 March 1866 (www.unhyeongung.or.kr).

Festival Bom

Bom means spring in Korean and that's when this city-wide festival of the arts (www.festivalbom.org) occurs. Both local and international artists take part and performances range from dance and drama to music and installations.

May

Buddha's birthday brings a kaleidoscope of light and colour, as rows of delicate paper lanterns, lit at dusk, are strung along the main thoroughfares and in temple courtyards. Night markets begin in earnest.

Jongmyo Daeje

Held on the first Sunday of the month, this ceremony (www.jongmyo.net) honours Korea's royal ancestors. It involves a solemn costumed parade from Gyeongbokgung through downtown Seoul to the royal shrine at Jongmyo, where spectators can enjoy traditional music and an elaborate, all-day ritual.

Lotus Lantern Festival

Seoul's Buddhist temples, such as Jogye-sa and Bongeun-sa, are the focus of this celebration of Buddha's birthday (celebrated on 8 May 2022, 26 May 2023 and 15 May 2024). The preceding weekend,

Seoul celebrates with a huge daytime street festival and evening lantern parade (www.llf.or.kr).

Seoul World DJ Festival

Dozens of DJs from all over Korea and the world descend upon an outdoor arena for two nights and three days of nonstop partying (www.worlddjfest.com).

Seoul International Cartoon & Animation Festival (SICAF)

Half a million animation geeks pack auditoriums in Seoul each year to see why the city is an epicentre of animated craftsmanship (fans of *The Simpsons* have Korean artists to thank). See www.sicaf.org for details.

June

The hot weather and period before the rains of July mean this is a great time to enjoy Seoul's outdoors.

Korean Queer Cultural Festival

Seoul's LGBTIQ+ community emerges from the shadows for a series of citywide events, including a parade, street party and film festival (www.kqcf.org).

Dano Festival

Held according to the lunar calendar (on the 5th day of the 5th month), this festival features shamanist rituals and mask dances at several locales, including Namsangol Hanok Village and the National Folk Museum of Korea.

July

Pack heavy-duty rain gear and waterproof shoes, as this is when Seoul experiences a month of monsoon-like rains.

Bucheon International Fantastic Film Festival (BiFan)

Held in Bucheon, just outside of Seoul, BiFan (www.bifan.kr) is a feast of the best in movie sci-fi, fantasy and horror. Theatres are within walking distance of Songnae Station (Line 1, towards Incheon).

August

The rain abates and is replaced by sweltering humidity. Cool off in Seoul's parks and public areas: there are free outdoor concerts most nights in Seoul Plaza and many free events held in the parks along the Han River.

Seoul Fringe Festival

One of Seoul's best performing-arts festivals (wwweng.seoulfringefestival.net); local and international artists converge on the Hongdae area to flee the mainstream.

September

You can catch a rerun of the royal wedding ceremony at Unhyeongung on the third Saturday of the month.

Sajik Daeje

Held at Sajikdan on the third Sunday of the month, the 'Great Rite for the Gods of Earth and Agriculture' is one of Seoul's most important ancestral rituals. Ceremonies, including offerings of fresh meat, are performed in traditional costumes to music by a court orchestra.

Chuseok

The Harvest Moon Festival is a major three-day holiday when families gather, eat crescent-shaped rice cakes and visit their ancestors' graves to make offerings of food and drink, and perform *sebae* (a ritual bow). Begins 10 September in 2022, 28 September 2023, and 17 September in 2024.

Seoul Drum Festival

Focusing on Korea's fantastic percussive legacy, this three-day international event (www.seouldrum.go.kr) in Seoul Plaza brings together all kinds of ways to make a lot of noise.

October

Autumn is a great time to visit Seoul, particularly if you like hiking, as this is the season when the mountains run through a palette of rustic colours.

Seoul International Fireworks Festival

Best viewed from Yeouido Hangang Park, this festival sees dazzling fireworks displays by both Korean and international teams (www.hanwhafireworks.com).

Asia Song Festival

This mega K-Pop event (www.asiasongfestival.com) at Jamsil Stadium includes performances by star *hallyu* bands and singers (meaning ones that have become popular outside of Korea), such as Girls' Generation and Super Junior.

Korea International Art Fair

Held at COEX, KIAF is one of the region's top art fairs and a good opportunity to get a jump on the country's hottest new artists (www.kiaf.org)

November

Seoul Lantern Festival

Centred on the Cheong-gye-cheon, this festival sees the stream-park illuminated by gigantic, fantastic lanterns made by master craftsmen (www.seoullantern.com).

(Top) Seoul International Fireworks Festival
(Bottom) Cheong-gye-cheon (p64) during the Lotus Lantern Festival

TAWATCHAIPRAKOBKIT/GETTY IMAGES ©

SIHO/SHUTTERSTOCK ©

With Kids

Seoul is a safe, family-friendly city with lots of kid-friendly museums (including several devoted to kids themselves), as well as amusement parks, playgrounds and fun events that will appeal to all age groups. Lonely Planet's Travel with Children is good for general family-travel advice.

K-Pop Rules

Thanks to the global appeal of local pop culture, little ones are likely to be more au fait with contemporary Korean pop culture than their parents. Be prepared to search out shops stocking BTS or Big Bang posters, DVDs of Korean TV soap operas, or *manhwa* (Korean comics and graphic novels). Kyobo Bookshop (p76) is a good place to start.

Educational Experiences

Museums and other traditional culture centres don't need to be boring. The National Museum of Korea (p108) and the National Folk Museum (p59) have fun, hands-on children's sections, and the War Memorial of Korea (p109) has outdoor warplanes and tanks that make for a popular playground. Various events, some involving dressing up in traditional costumes or having a go at taekwondo, happen at Namsangol Hanok Village (p83). Older kids and teenagers will likely want to visit places such as the Seoul Animation Center (p85) to learn more about local animated TV series and films, or Samsung D'Light (p124) to play with the latest digital technology. Nonverbal shows such as Nanta and Jump (p90) are great family entertainment.

Park Life

At theme parks such as Lotte World (p122) and Everland (p157), family entertainment comes in mega-sized portions. Easier on the wallet are the scores of free open spaces that constitute Seoul's wealth of city-managed parks – places such as Seoul Forest (p136), Olympic Park (p121), Children's Grand Park (p137) and the string of bicycle-lane-connected parks that hug the Han River's banks (p95). Each summer six big outdoor-pool complexes open in the Han River parks, too.

Need to Know

Sleeping & Eating Korean-style *ondol* rooms are family-friendly, as everyone sleeps on a *yo* (floor mattress) in the same space. Children are welcome in restaurants, though few will have kids' menus. High chairs aren't common.

Babysitting Some top hotels and residences can arrange babysitting.

Festivals Children's Day (5 May) sees special events for kids across Seoul.

Korea 4 Expats.com (www.korea4expats.com) Child-related information.

For Free

You don't need a wallet packed with won to enjoy Seoul. Many of the best things you can do – hiking around the city's ancient city walls, enjoying the pageant of the changing of the guard at the palaces, or watching traditional dance at Insa-dong Outdoor Stage – cost nothing at all.

JULY7TH/GETTY IMAGES ©

Namsangol Hanok Village (p83)

Go for a Hike

Join the legions of locals who take full advantage of Seoul's mountainous topography. All four of the city's guardian mountains – Bukaksan, Naksan, Namsan and Inwangsan – have hiking routes; the really keen can summit them all by following the remains of the Seoul City Wall. The panoramic city views are your reward for the effort.

The city government has also spent enormous sums to create pleasant waterside parks both along the Han River and in central Seoul, where the long-buried-over Cheong-gye-cheon (p64) now sparkles in the light of day. More urban green strips have been developed with the Gyeongui Line Forest Park (p94) in Hongdae, and crossing over train lines and highways with the Seoullo 7017 (p83) pedestrian overpass park, plus the short and sweet Deoksugung Stone Wall Road (p83). Seoul Forest (p136) is another major reforestation project, as is the creation of a beautiful landscaped park from an old water-filtration plant on the Han River island of Seonyudo (p96).

Architectural Treasures

Admission to most royal palaces is not costly and usually includes free guided tours. Additionally, it costs nothing to enjoy the changing of the guard ceremonies at Gyeongbokgung (p58), Deoksugung (p82) and the Bosingak bell tower pavilion (p70). Impressive religious architecture is freely on show at the Buddhist temples Jogye-sa (p63), Bongeun-sa (p123) and Gilsang-sa (p146). You can also view aristocratic *hanok* (traditional one-storey wooden houses) for free at Namsangol Hanok Village (p83), or clusters of still-lived-in, more modest traditional homes in Bukchon, Seochon and Ikseon-dong (p54).

Those with more contemporary architectural tastes will want to get an eyeful of the sinuous lines of both Dongdaemun Design Plaza (p135) and City Hall (p85), as well as a host of stylish structures in Gangnam such as Daniel Libeskind's Tangent building (p124).

Museums & Galleries

The list of museums with no entrance fee is pretty extensive and includes the National Museum (p108), Seoul Museum of History (p65) and Seoul Museum of Art (p84). The last Wednesday of the month is Culture Day, with many museums, such as MMCA Seoul (p69), offering free admission. You don't need to be a buyer to drop by the scores of free art-gallery shows in areas such as Insa-dong and Samcheong-dong (p67). There are thousands of interesting outdoor sculptures scattered across Seoul, with over 200 of them alone in Olympic Park (p121). And for fun, inventive street art, wander the alleys of Ihwa-dong and Mullae Arts Village (p96).

MMCA Seoul (designed by Hyunjun Mihn; p69)

Festivals & Events

Not a week goes by without a free festival or event happening somewhere in the city. Seoul's government often puts on free shows in Seoul Plaza (p84) in front of City Hall, and there's the lit-up fountain (p125) gushing off Banpo Bridge in the warmer months.

Like a Local

Prepare for Seoul's cultural divide. Bukchon and Seochon (both north of the Han River) are the city's historical heart, where courtly palace culture meets pre- and post-colonial commerce. South of the Han, nouveau-riche Gangnam is stacked with top-end boutiques, restaurants and bars.

Round-the-Clock Shopping

Whichever side of the river they live on, Seoulites love (or is that live?) to shop. For all the city's headlong rush into the 21st century, sprawling all-night markets, such as those at Dongdaemun (p139) and Namdaemun (p86), confirm more traditional and time-worn images of Asian commerce. This impression is further reinforced by the bazaars devoted to herbal medicines at Seoul Yangnyeongsi (p139) and to antiques at Dapsimni (p139); plus the sprawling Yongsan Electronics Market (p118) and a whole floor of secondhand phones at I'Park Mall (p117). A fascinating insight into local life can also be gleaned from what people sell off at flea markets, the biggest of which is the Seoul Folk Flea Market (p140). If the old and secondhand aren't to your taste, contemporary fashions and fads can be gauged on trips to mercantile hubs such as Hongdae, Myeong-dong, Apgujeong, Cheongdam and Garosu-gil.

Keeping Fit

Going hiking in and around Seoul can be a frightening business. This is not so much because of the precariousness of the mountain trails (quite the opposite – these are usually well marked and seldom short of small armies of hikers), but because you will almost certainly feel under-dressed. Seoulites are super avid walkers and few would even think of venturing out without being kitted head to toe in the latest hi-tech and invariably brightly coloured gear. A trip to Dongdaemun Market or a shopping mall to purchase an outfit of local brands, such as Blackyak or the Redface, should have you breathing a little easier.

Hiking is not the only popular keep-fit pastime. The cycle lanes running alongside the Han River (p95) are also actively patronised, as are the free outdoor gyms located in many parks.

Bang-ing Around

The old expat playground of Itaewon has become a much more multicultural affair, appealing to worldly Koreans and their curious brethren. The adjacent areas of Hannam-dong, Haebangchon (aka HBC) and Gyeongridan have an equally, if not more, happening vibe.

However, to really take Seoul's relaxation pulse, a nocturnal visit to hip Hongdae, Sinchon and Daehangno – both major hubs for students and the young – is recommended. Here you'll encounter the highest concentrations of Seoul's various versions of the *bang*. Meaning 'room', *bang* come in the shape of karaoke rooms *(noraebang)*, private DVD screening rooms (DVD *bang*) popular with cuddling teens, and online-game rooms (PC *bang*).

Finally, if you really want to sample local life, get naked! Stripping off and sweating at a *jjimjilbang* (luxury sauna) is a very popular way for Seoulites to steam off their stresses.

Courses & Tours

Helping you know your hansik *(Korean food) from your* hanbok *(traditional clothing), a variety of courses and tours will put you on the fast track to understanding Korean culture. Some are very popular, so they're worth booking well in advance, particularly the USO trip to the DMZ.*

RAKER/SHUTTERSTOCK ©

Dongdaemun Market (p86)

Courses

Templestays & Meditation

Templestay Information Center (p63) Here you can book overnight stay programs at beautiful temples in Seoul, including Bongeun-sa (p123), Jogye-sa (p63) and Gilsang-sa (p146), and around Korea. No attempt will be made to convert you to Buddhism during these inexpensive and relaxing programs, which are a brilliant way to learn a little about Korean Buddhism, meditation and crafts, such as how to make paper lanterns and prayer beads.

International Seon Center (p103) Come here for English lectures on Buddhist teaching every Saturday from 2pm to 4pm and for the Templelife program that runs every afternoon from 2pm to 5pm, which includes a chat with a monk over tea. You'll find the centre on the 2nd floor of the round theatre to the left of the campus inner gate (Hyehwamun).

Food, Drink & Culture

Seoul Eats Food Tours (☎010-6706 7769; www.seouleats.com; per person ₩80,000, for custom group tours ₩375,000) Expert foodie tours with bespoke or fixed itineraries by Korean-American Dan Grey, who regularly works with visiting TV chefs.

O'ngo (p77) Well-run cooking classes and food tours around the city are offered here. The beginners class lasts two hours and you can choose a variety of different dishes to learn about including *haemul pajeon* (seafood pancake), *sundubu* (soft tofu stew), *bulgogi* (marinated beef) and the many types of kimchi.

Sool Company (MMPKorea, Makgeolli Mamas & Papas; Map p238, E2; www.thesoolcompany.com; 343 Samil-Daero) Well-qualified brewing instructors offer hands-on courses that provide all you need to know about *makgeolli* (a mildly alcoholic drink made from rice, water and *nuruk*, a wheat-based mix of yeasts, enzymes and moulds) and how to make it. The introductory courses let you go home with your own batch of *makgeolli* ready to drink in about a week.

Gastro Tour Seoul (www.gastrotourseoul.com; tours from ₩99,000) Culinary and culture tours run by local Veronica Kang. Itineraries include tours around Insa-dong and Bukchon, Seoul's Little Tokyo in Ichon-dong, and a trip to a winery at Anseong in the Gyeonggi-do.

Korean Language

YBM Sisa (p78) Korean classes (maximum 10 people) for all ability levels cover grammar, writing and conversation. Private tuition (₩50,000 per hour for one person) can also be arranged here.

Yonsei University (p103) The university runs part- and full-time Korean language and culture classes for serious students.

Tours

Seoul City Tour Bus (p78) Comfortable tour buses circuit top tourist attractions north of the Han River, allowing you to see a lot in a short time. Hop on and off anywhere along the two routes, one on a single-decker bus covering the palaces and sights on the downtown area, the other on a double-decker bus in a wider loop including Hongdae and Yeouido. Buy tickets on the bus, which can be caught outside Donghwa Duty Free Shop at Gwanghwamun. Check the website for details of night tours, which zigzag across the Han River so you can view the illuminated bridges, and for trips on the trolley-like buses in Gangnam.

Seoul City Walking Tours (☎02-6925 0777; http://dobo.visitseoul.net; admission free) FREE Reserve three days in advance for one of 23 different free walking tours offered by the city in association with volunteer guides. Themes take you on tours around the palaces, Bukchon, Cheong-gye-cheon, Namsan fortress and Seoul City Hall.

Koridoor Tours (p209) Apart from running the very popular DMZ/JSA tour for the USO (United Service Organizations), this company also offers city tours; trips to out-of-town destinations, such as Suwon and Incheon; paragliding, scuba diving and deep-sea fishing tours; and ski trips to local resorts in the winter.

ARTYOUKAN/SHUTTERSTOCK ©

Seoul City Tour bus

Royal Asiatic Society (p77) Organises enlightening walking and bus tours to all parts of South Korea, usually on weekends; check the website for the schedule. Nonmembers are welcome to join. The reasonably priced tours are led by English speakers who are experts in their field. The society also organises lectures several times a month in Seoul.

Hiking Around Seoul

With several mountains and hills within its boundaries, and even more a short journey away, Seoul is a fantastic place to plan some hiking. Trails are well marked and vary from relatively easy strolls of a few hours to a 10-day hiking challenge running 157km around the city.

JIPEN/SHUTTERSTOCK ©

Namhan Sanseong Provincial Park (p34)

Seoul City Wall

Initially built in 1396, Seoul's original **fortress wall** (www.seoulcitywall.seoul.go.kr) runs for 18.6km, connecting the peaks of Bukaksan (342m), Naksan (125m), Namsan (262m) and Inwangsan (338m), all north of the Han River. It was punctuated by four major gates and four sub-gates, of which six remain.

Over time parts of the wall were demolished, but in its multiple attempts to have the entire structure designated by Unesco as a World Heritage site, the city has been restoring some of the missing sections. Today at least 70% (12.8km) is in place and it's relatively easy to follow a hiking route beside and, in several cases, atop the walls.

The circuit can be accomplished in a day (exhausting), but is better split over two; or just choose a section or two, should you prefer to take your time and do some sightseeing. Start at Heunginjimun (Dongdaemun), near to which is the Seoul City Wall Museum (p136), and walk in an anticlockwise direction – this way you'll get the steepest section up and down Bukaksan done in the morning and could linger on Namsan later in the afternoon.

Seoul Dulle-gil

More ambitious hikers can tackle part or all of the **Seoul Dulle-gil** (Seoul Trail; www.gil.seoul.go.kr), which runs for 157km around the city's outskirts. Each of the eight sections starts and finishes beside a subway station and goes over a mountain (sometimes two), through forests and parks and alongside streams.

Section 1 Suraksan and Bulamsan (18.6km, 8¾ hours; start: Dobongsan, finish: Taereung)

Section 2 Yongmasan (12.6km, 5¼ hours; start: Taereung, finish: Gwangnaru)

Section 3 Godeoksan and Iljasan (26.1km, nine hours; start: Gwangnaru, finish: Suseo)

Section 4 Daemosan and Umyeonsan (17.9km, eight hours; start: Suseo, finish: Sadang)

Section 5 Gwanaksan (12.7km, 5¾ hours; start: Sadang, finish: Seoksu)

Section 6 Anyangcheon stream (18km, 4½ hours; start: Seoksu, finish: Gayang)

Section 7 Bongsan and Aengbongsan (16.6km, 6¼ hours; start: Gayang, finish: Gubapal)

Section 8 Bukhansan (34.5km, 17 hours; start: Gubapal, finish: Dobongsan)

Bukaksan

The tallest of Seoul's four guardian peaks, **Bukaksan** (북악산; Bugaksan; Baegaksan; www.bukak.or.kr; admission free; ⌚9am-3pm Apr-Oct, from 10am Nov-Mar; Ⓢ Line 3 to Gyeongbokgung, Exit 3) FREE was off limits to the public for 38 years following a dramatic assassination attempt by North Korean agents on then-President Park Chung-hee in 1968. Security remains tight along this spectacular 2.5km section of the Seoul City Wall that rises steeply from Changuimun (p145), the old subgate in Buam-dong. The trail hops over the peak above **Cheongwadae** (청와대, Blue House; Map p232, C1; ☎02-737 5800; www.president.go.kr; 1 Cheongwadae-ro; admission free; ⌚tours 10am, 11am, 2pm & 3pm Tue-Sat; Ⓢ Line 3 to Gyeongbokgung, Exit 5) FREE to the Malbawi Information Center near **Sukjeong-mun**, the main north gate, which can also be accessed from Samcheong Park (p146).

This section of the fortress wall is open only during daylight hours and photography is permitted at designated spots only, such as **Baekakmaru**, the summit viewpoint. You're also required to show your passport at Changuimun in exchange for a pass, which must be worn at all times. The wall is in excellent condition, and with plenty of soldiers and CCTV cameras, there's a vivid sense of its original purpose as the city's last line of defence.

Inwangsan

Though it lacks the grim-faced soldiers found on Bukaksan, the section of Seoul City Wall snaking up and down **Inwangsan** (인왕산; Ⓢ Line 3 to Gyeongbokgung, Exit 3) offers even more spectacular views, no restrictions on what you can shoot (photographs, that is), and the enigmatic **Seonbawi** (Zen Rocks) near the summit. The views from the top present a complete panorama of Seoul, with several palaces visible as well as the Seoul City Wall flowing over Bukaksan, Naksan and Namsan. You can clearly see how the old city nestled inside its guardian mountains. The hike, with some sheer stepped sections, is best started just south of Changuimun, finishing at a lower elevation east of Dongnimmun. Along the way you can detour to the shamanistic shrine Inwangsan Guksadang (p144).

Ansan

At 295.9m **Ansan** (안산; Ⓢ Line 3 to Dongnimmun, Exit 5) is a relatively easy mountain to climb and is topped with **bongsudae**, a set of the smoke-signal beacons used during the Joseon dynasty. You can also take a very pleasant walk around Ansan through woodlands following the **Ansan Jarak-gil**, a broad, generally level path partly made up of wooden decking. Access this by walking uphill from Seodaemun Prison History Hall (p145) and looking for direction signs behind the military compound there.

Other Hiking Options

Namhan Sanseong Provincial Park This park, 25km southeast of Seoul, is famous for its beautiful pine and oak forests, wildflowers and the World Heritage–listed remains of a fortress, parts of which dates back to the 7th century.

Bukhansan National Park (p160) North of the city, this park is studded with granite peaks which provide sweeping vistas, and are covered in pine and maple trees, with gushing streams and remote temples.

Above: A stretch of Seoul's City Wall on Bukaksan (p33)

Right: Sunrise from Bukhansan (p160)

CJ NATTANAI/SHUTTERSTOCK ©

Bibimbap (literally 'mixed rice'; p18

Dining Out

Sampling the many varied delights of Korean cuisine is one of Seoul's great pleasures. Restaurants, cafes and street stalls are scattered throughout every neighbourhood with options to suit all budgets and tastes – whether that's simple rice and vegetables, a DIY barbecue blowout or the procession of banchan *(side dishes) that makes up a royal court banquet.*

What's Hot

Though Korean tastebuds lean towards their own highly developed cuisine, young Seoulites gobble up global food trends, with the result that Seoul's restaurant scene now rivals those of Hong Kong and Shanghai as the most dynamic in Asia.

Ongoing trends include anything Americana (the more regional the better), whether that's New York–style pizza, Maine lobster or Alabama brisket. Thai and Vietnamese are hot, and KoMex (Korean-Mexican fusion) continues to reign with its kimchi tacos and other fusion fare.

Diners are prepared to queue for hours for the chance to eat (and photograph) the hottest new trends. Social media is one of the reasons why presentation has become all-important – in Seoul, food has to look as good as it tastes.

Restaurants & Cafes

Most Korean-style restaurants offer a table-and-chairs option, but in some traditional places customers sit on floor cushions at low tables. Few staff speak English, but most restaurants have at least some English on the menu.

In Seoul, eating out is a group activity. A number of Korean meals are often not available for solo diners.

Convenience Stores & Street Stalls

Street stalls and *pojangmacha* (tent bars) are great options for inexpensive meals, and some of them open long after most restaurants close. Areas in Insa-dong, Myeong-dong and markets at Gwangjang, Namdaemun and Dongdaemun are the best spots to dig in with locals.

For cheap eats on the go, convenience stores sell snack foods such as *gimbap* (rice and veggies wrapped in seaweed) and instant noodles. Some have seating.

Vegetarians & Vegans

Though vegetarian and vegan travellers generally have a tough time elsewhere in Korea, Seoul offers much greater choice. As well as Korean dishes such as *bibimbap* (order it without meat, or egg), tofu dishes and vegetable *pajeon* (savoury fried pancakes), and of course the ever-present kimchi, you'll find several traditional restaurants that specialise in 100% vegetarian Buddhist temple food. Western-style vegetarian/vegan restaurants are becoming more common, and you can find traditionally vegetarian international cuisine such as Indian and Middle Eastern.

Website **Happy Cow** (www.happycow.net/asia/south_korea/seoul) is a good resource.

NEED TO KNOW

Opening Hours

Restaurants and cafes 11am to 11pm

Convenience stores 24 hours

Price Ranges

$ less than ₩12,000

$$ ₩12,000–25,000

$$$ over ₩25,000

Reservations

It's generally not necessary to book unless you want your own private room or are in a large group.

Guides & Blogs

ZenKimchi (www.zenkimchi.com)

Seoul Eats (www.seouleats.com)

What's Stewin (https://whatsstewin.blogspot.hk)

A Fat Girl's Food Guide (www.afatgirlsfoodguide.com)

Eating by Neighbourhood

➡ **Gwanghwamun & Jongno-gu** (p70) The full gamut of Korean gastronomy, from *kimchi-jjigae* (kimchi stew) to *banchan* (side dishes) banquets.

➡ **Myeong-dong & Jung-gu** (p85) Choose between late-night *pojangmacha* (street tents) and long-established Korean restaurants.

➡ **Western Seoul** (p97) University districts feature cafe-bakeries, comfort food and Korean BBQ; Noryangjin Fish Market for seafood lovers.

➡ **Itaewon & Yongsan-gu** (p111) Thai, Turkish, Texan – whatever international tastes you're craving, you'll find them here.

➡ **Gangnam & Southern Seoul** (p126) Expense-account restaurants abound in Apgujeong and Cheongdam, with more casual hang-outs in Garosu-gil.

➡ **Dongdaemun & Eastern Seoul** (p137) Home to throwback North Korean restaurants and snack-filled Gwangjang Market.

BONCHAN/SHUTTERSTOCK ©

Above: Noryangjin Fish Market (p98)

Left: *Pajeon* (Korean savoury pancake; p185)

Lonely Planet's Top Choices

Jungsik (p127) Neo-Korean fine dining at affordable prices.

Noryangjin Fish Market (p98) Super-fresh fish dinners at Korea's largest seafood market.

Congdu (p87) Subtle, contemporary takes on classic Korean dishes.

Samwon Garden (p128) The quintessential *galbi* experience.

Gwangjang Market (p137) Delicious, cheap street food in a bustling covered market.

Onion (p137) Delectable baked goods and coffee in Seoul's hippest cafe.

Best by Budget

₩

Tongin Market Box Lunch Cafe (p70) Old-school market arcade.

Myeong-dong Gyoja (p85) Hand-pulled-noodle soup with dumplings.

Chang Hwa Dang (p72) Kaeseong-style dumplings.

Namdaemun Market (p86) Fresh and tasty market dishes.

I Love Sindangdong (p137) *Tteokbokki*-based comfort food.

₩₩

Hongik Sutbul Galbi (p98) Fine cuts of pork and beef cooked over real charcoal.

Min's Kitchen (p127) Fresh, delicate Korean flavours in dishes like shrimp *bibimbap*.

Linus' BBQ (p112) Authentic Alabama brisket and pulled-pork platters in Itaewon.

Samarkand (p138) Uzbekistan eatery grilling tasty lamb shashlik.

₩₩₩

Ogawa (p71) Upmarket sushi restaurant that won't break the bank.

GastroTong (p71) Sophisticated Swiss-European cuisine.

N.Grill (p87) Incredible views and French cuisine cooked by a Michelin-starred chef.

Best by Cuisine

Traditional Korean

Korea House (p87) Traditional banquet and performance.

Hanmiri (p71) Modern take on traditional cuisine overlooking the Cheong-gye-cheon.

Jaha Sonmandoo (p147) Dumplings on the slopes of Bukaksan.

Tosokchon (p71) Ginseng-chicken stew that's worth the wait.

International

Linus' BBQ (p112) Alabama-style barbecue.

Ciuri Ciuri (p99) Savour Sicilian dishes in Hongdae.

Vatos (p112) Mexican street tacos with Korean flavours.

Samarkand (p138) Uzbekistan lamb shashlik and bread.

Menya Sandaime (p98) Slurp up delicious bowls of ramen.

Tuk Tuk Noodle Thai (p97) Uncompromising flavours at a top Thai restaurant.

Potala (p86) Authentic dishes from the Himalayan region.

Best Vegetarian & Vegan

Balwoo Gongyang (p73) Buddhist vegetarian feasts overlooking Jogye-sa.

Plant Cafe & Kitchen (p111) Vegan mains and baked goods in Itaewon.

Osegyehyang (p72) Insa-dong hideaway that keeps it vegan.

Rogpa Tea Stall (p70) Fair-trade Tibetan dishes in a charming teahouse.

Best Bakeries, Desserts & Cafes

Passion 5 (p111) Glitzy arcade with gourmet baked goods and patisserie.

Seoureseo Duljjaero Jalhaneunjip (p71) Time travel to the '70s while enjoying red-bean porridge.

Fell & Cole (p98) Uniquely flavoured ice creams.

Scoff (p147) Sweet British baked treats in Buam-dong.

Tartine (p111) The best American-style pecan pies this side of the Pacific.

Onion (p137) Artisanal baked goods in Seongsu-dong, 'Seoul's Brooklyn'.

Soju (local vodka)

Bar Open

From antique teahouses and coffee roasters to craft-beer pubs and cocktail bars, Seoul offers an unbelievable number of places to relax over a drink. No-frills hof *(pubs) are everywhere, and don't miss that quintessential Seoul nightlife experience:* soju *(local vodka) shots and snacks at a* pojangmacha *(street tent bar).*

Teahouses & Cafes

Korea's centuries-old tea culture can be appreciated in quaint teahouses in Seoul's traditional neighbourhoods. These places major in herbal, fruit, roasted rice and barley teas, many of which have medicinal properties and don't actually contain tea, though it's of course possible to sip green, black and other fermented teas.

Koreans have taken to coffee in a big way, with many home-grown chains as well as artisan third-wave roasters, though you'll quickly suss out that a quality brew is not cheap. For a low-priced caffeine hit, most convenience stores sell fresh-brewed coffee for around ₩1200.

But while a coffee or tea can cost the the equivalent of a whole Korean meal, you're also paying for the space – Seoul has some of the most beautifully designed cafes in the world – so don't feel bad about lingering all day. In fact, many venues encourage you to do so by creating designer environments and packing them with books, art – even cats to cuddle or sheep to pet.

Hof & Bars

Drinking, and drinking heavily, is a big part of Korean socialising; many a night out starts and finishes in a *hof*. Inspired by German beer halls, the term generally means anywhere that primarily serves draught Korean beer, with the requisite plate of fried chicken and other *anju* (snacks commonly eaten when drinking). Always check whether a bar requires you to buy a plate of *anju* before drinking; places that don't are called 'one-shot' bars.

If you're looking for something more sophisticated, there are plenty of craft-beer bars, cocktail bars and quirky drinking dens in Itaewon, Hongdae, Sinchon and Gangnam.

Tent Bars & Convenience Stores

Beloved by Seoulites, *pojangmacha* are humble, blue-tarp shelters scattered across the city's streets, serving food thought to pair well with booze; after enough *soju*, you may feel brave enough for *takbal* (chicken feet).

While *poja* are both cheap and atmospheric, for the truly budget-conscious drinker, nowhere competes with the seating area of a 24-hour convenience store, where you can park up and knock back cheap *soju* and beer to your heart's (and liver's) content.

Drinking Trends

Makgeolli, a milky alcoholic brew popular among the older generation, is now a hit with the young and trendy. Made from unrefined fermented rice, *makgeolli* clocks about 5% to 8% ABV. Seoul has several bars where a range of varieties can be savoured, often along with *pajeon* (Korean savoury pancakes), said to be the perfect pairing.

Until recently *maekju* (beer) was limited to cheap local brands, all lagers, including Cass, Max and Hite. The craft-beer revolution has well and truly hit, though, with microbreweries and brewpubs producing local ales, and imported beers available in many bars and restaurants.

Clubbing

Gangnam is home to Seoul's world-famous clubbing scene, while Itaewon and Hongdae have decent choices, too. Most clubs don't get busy until midnight and only start pumping after 2am, with Friday and Saturday nights the busiest. Dress codes are generally not too strict, but it's a good idea to bring your passport for age checks.

NEED TO KNOW

Opening Hours

Bars noon to 2am

Clubs 10pm to 5am Wed–Sun

How Much?

- Local beer ₩3000 to ₩5000
- Craft beer ₩5000 to ₩12,000
- Cocktail ₩7000 to ₩18,000
- Coffee ₩2500 to ₩8000
- Tea ₩6000 to ₩9000

Cover Charges

At clubs, the entry charge of ₩10,000 to ₩30,000 usually includes a free drink.

Drinking Water

In restaurants and cafes you'll usually be served chilled, filtered water upon sitting (or asked to help yourself from a fridge).

Drinking Etiquette

Out drinking with Koreans, the custom is to always pour for those older than you, never to pour for yourself and to use both hands to hold your glass while it's being filled.

LGBTIQ+ Scene

LGBTIQ+-friendly areas include Itaewon (gay and trans bars and clubs), Nagwon-dong near Insa-dong (gay and tent bars) and Hongdae and Edae (mainly lesbian bars).

Drinking & Nightlife by Neighbourhood

- **Gwanghwamun & Jongno-gu** (p73) Teahouses and cafes in Insa-dong and Samcheong-dong, Bukchon and Tongui-dong; tent bars (many gay-friendly) and gay bars in Nagwon-dong.
- **Western Seoul** (p99) Hongdae, Sangsu-dong and Yeonnam-dong for cool, youth-orientated bars, cafes, dance and live-music clubs.
- **Itaewon & Yongsan-gu** (p113) Expat-friendly bars and clubs; gay-friendly 'Homo Hill; craft beers in Gyeongridan.
- **Gangnam & Southern Seoul** (p128) Chic, pricey cocktail bars in Apgujeong and Cheongdam; megaclubs with top DJs.
- **Dongdaemun & Eastern Seoul** (p147) Hip, industrial-chic cafe culture in Seongsu-dong.

Lonely Planet's Top Choices

Sik Mool (p74) Sophisticated *hanok* cafe-bar in new 'it' 'hood Ikseon-dong.

Southside Parlor (p114) Easy-going, Texas-style mixology.

Suyeon Sanbang (p147) Charming teahouse in a heritage *hanok* in the hills.

Grand Ole Opry (p114) Throw-back honky-tonk GI bar – go before it's gone.

Club Octagon (p128) Regarded as one the world's best.

Cakeshop (p113) Fun-lovin', dive-y club in Itaewon.

Best Tea

Dawon (p74) Traditional tea-house in the heart of Insa-dong set around a spacious courtyard.

Cha Masineun Tteul (p74) Enjoy steamed pumpkin cake and lovely views.

Dalsaeneun Dalman Saeng-gak Handa Classic Insa-dong teashop hideaway.

Tea Therapy (p75) Brews for whatever ails you.

Madang Flower Cafe (p74) Flower-based brews in a con-verted Ikseon-dong *hanok*.

Best Coffee

Steamers Coffee Factory (p129) Third-wave coffee-roasting champs.

Club Espresso (p149) Single-origin beans from around the world.

Anthracite (p99) Top independ-ent coffee roaster and cafe in happening Sangsu.

Kopi Bangasgan (p75) Arty *hanok* cafe in Samcheong-dong.

Hakrim (p149) Little has changed here since the 1950s.

The Bread Blue (p99) Superb soy lattes in Sinchon.

Best Cocktails & Wine

Southside Parlor (p114) Artisan cocktails by hipster mixologists.

Fox Wine Bistro (p101) Top selection of wines in Hongdae.

N.Grill (p87) Open-air bar with amazing views from N Seoul Tower.

Namsan Winery (p114) Low-key Itaewon venue with well-priced Iberian wines.

Best Cafe-Bars

Daelim Changgo (p138) Huge, industrial-chic cafe-bar with hip interior styling.

Café Sukkara Rustic lovely on the edge of Hongdae.

Baker's Table (p113) Friendly brunch spot with real German beers on tap.

Best Microbrew Bars

Magpie Brewing Co (p116) One of Seoul's originals pour-ing a range of celebrated craft ales.

Booth (p116) Another big player, with brewpubs across the city.

Pongdang (p129) Korean brewers who know their stuff.

Amazing Brewing Co (p139) Hip local microbrewery in Seongsu-dong.

Best Traditional Alcoholic Beverages

Mowmow (p116) Itaewon *makgeolli* dive off the busy bar strip.

Moon Jar (p129) Smart and rustic bar with a good menu.

Baekseju-maeul (p75) *Makgeolli* bar run by big brewer, Kooksoondang.

Blue Star Pub (p75) Brass kettles full of *makgeolli* served in a dive-y hang-out.

Muldwinda (p88) Most stylish bar for sampling fine-grade *makgeolli*.

Best Clubbing

Club Octagon (p128) Gangnam megaclub regarded as one of the world's best.

M2 (p101) Huge underground space for parties in Hongdae.

Soap (p114) Itaewon basement club pulling in world-class DJs.

NB2 (p100) Huge, underground space for partying in Hongdae.

Best LGBTIQ+ Bars & Clubs

Barcode (p74) Cosy, convivial gay cocktail bar in Nagwon-dong.

Shortbus (p75) Spacious hang-out serving good cocktails.

Club MWG (p100) Grungy Hongdae club hosting regular LGBTIQ+ events.

Labris (p101) One of Seoul's few lesbian bars.

Queen (p115) Popular bar on Itaewon's 'Homo Hill'.

Hongdae (p101)

Showtime

Don't worry too much about the language barrier: Seoul offers an intriguing and surprisingly accessible menu of traditional music, dance, drama, comedy and K-pop at performing-arts centres and venues across the capital.

Classical & Traditional

Seoul is the best place in Korea to enjoy traditional music and dance performances. Some shows may include half a dozen different styles. Expect a broad range of international offerings too, from world-class visiting orchestras to contemporary dance troupes.

Jazz, Rock & Pop

From the glossy, manufactured K-Pop industry to the underground indie scene, Seoul offers an eclectic assortment of live music.

Hongdae is *the* place for Seoul's K-Indie scene, where intimate venues host local indie, punk, metal and hip-hop acts. Live jazz venues of all sizes can be found throughout the city.

Concerts by visiting megastars are held at arena venues such as YES 24 Live Hall (p139), while touring bands and K-Pop acts often perform at the Olympic Stadium or Gymnastic Stadium at Olympic Park (p121).

Bang Culture

Bang are complexes of rooms designed for groups to rent by the hour, where you make your own entertainment in a variety of ways, including playing computer games or watching movies. In *noraebang* (karaoke rooms) you can sing along to well-known songs, including plenty with English lyrics.

Theatre & Cinema

Theatre, except for drama festivals, is usually performed in Korean, though musicals and nonverbal performance shows, such as Nanta

NEED TO KNOW

Tickets

Interpark (http://ticket.interpark.com) Theatre, concerts and sporting event tickets.

KTO Tourist Information Center (p214) Sells daily discount tickets for shows.

Daehangno Information Center (p149) Tickets for shows staged at the dozens of venues around Daehangno.

Information

Korea Gig Guide (www.koreagigguide.com)

Groove Korea (www.groovekorea.com)

10 Magazine (www.10mag.com)

CineinKorea (www.cineinkorea.com)

(p88), can be enjoyed even if you don't understand the language.

Non-Korean films are screened in their original language with subtitles. Certain cinemas show Korean films with English subtitles at off-peak times – check the expat-oriented website **www.cineinkorea.com** to find out where, and for complete Seoul cinema listings.

Spectator Sports

BASKETBALL

Seoul's two professional basketball teams, Samsung Thunders and SK Knights, play in the 10-team **Korean Basketball League** (www.kbl.or.kr) from October to April. Thunders play at Jamsil Arena, while the Knights are at Jamsil Students' Gymnasium, both in Seoul Sports Complex (p132).

BASEBALL

Introduced in 1905 by American missionaries, baseball is Korea's favourite sport. There are three Seoul teams in the **Korean Baseball Organization** (http://eng.koreabaseball.com) and two of them – Doosan Bears and LG Twins – play at Jamsil Baseball Stadium at the Seoul Sports Complex; the Nexen Heroes play at **Mokdong Stadium** (목동종합운동장; ☎02-2640 3808; http://stadium.seoul.go.kr; 939 Anyangcheon-ro; Ⓢ Line 5, Omok-gyo, Exit 4). Matches take place from April to October (except for the summer break) and are well attended, with a lively boozy atmosphere and plenty of off-field entertainment. Games generally start at 6.30pm, with the occasional earlier start. Ticket prices start at ₩10,000.

SOCCER

In the 12-team professional **K-League** (www.kleague.com; tickets from ₩15,000) Division 1, FC Seoul plays from March to November at the World Cup Stadium (p102). Crowds are bigger and there's more atmosphere when the national team is playing at the stadium, cheered on by the Red Devil supporters. South Korea famously reached the semi-finals of the World Cup in 2002 when they were joint hosts along with Japan.

TAEKWONDO

While taekwondo is not popular with locals as a spectator sport, those interested in Korea's national martial art can head to Kukkiwon Stadium (p132) to catch a tournament, training session or tourist demonstration by some of taekwondo's best. Otherwise there are displays staged at Namsangol Hanok Village (p83) at 1pm and 3pm daily from May to June and September to October. Expect to see graceful movements, spectacular pine-board breaking and acrobatic high kicking.

Music Festivals

Pentaport Rock Festival (www.pentaportrock.com) Major rock festival held in Incheon province in late July.

Seoul Jazz Festival (www.seouljazz.co.kr) Multi-day event in May featuring world-class musos.

Greenplugged Seoul (www.gpsfestival.com) Two-day, riverside festival featuring local bands in May.

Ultra Korea (www.umfkorea.com) Three-day electronic musical festival in June that attracts global superstar DJs.

HBC Festival (www.hbcfest.com) Local bands take over Haebangchon venues at this one-day event in May and October.

Entertainment by Neighbourhood

➡ **Myeong-dong & Jung-gu** (p88) Nonverbal theatre is king here; see traditional shows at the Korea House and Namsangol Hanok Village.

➡ **Western Seoul** (p101) Hongdae is the hub of Seoul's vibrant indie music scene; or see free movies at Cinemateque KOFA.

➡ **Itaewon & Yongsan-gu** (p117) Seoul's most international 'hood is a good place for live jazz.

➡ **Gangnam & Southern Seoul** (p130) Home to the Seoul Arts Center and LG Arts Center.

➡ **Northern Seoul** (p149) Daehangno is a performing-arts hub with scores of venues.

Lonely Planet's Top Choices

Nanta Theatre (p102) The original and best of Seoul's wide selection of nonverbal shows.

National Theater of Korea (p88) Home to the national drama, *changgeuk* (Korean opera), orchestra and dance companies.

Korea House (p87) Intimate theatre for a quality variety show of traditional performing arts.

National Gugak Center (p130) Traditional Korean classical and folk music, and dance.

Su Noraebang (p99) Stylish karaoke venue in the heart of Hongdae.

Best for K-Pop

K-Wave Experience (p125) Get the full K-Pop makeover and photo op.

K-Star Road (p126) Take a stroll down the 'Hallyuwood' Walk of Fame.

Seoul Global Cultural Center (p91) K-Pop dance classes to learn all the latest moves.

SMTown coexartium (p124) Party with K-Pop holograms at this five-storey shrine.

Best for K-Indie

FF (p101) Come early to hear local indie bands banging out their sets.

DGBD (p102) Standing room only at this legendary rock venue.

KT&G SangsangMadang (p101) Catch top indie bands in Hongdae.

Best for Jazz

Club Evans (p101) Evergreen Hongdae jazz haunt.

All that Jazz (p117) Long-established, well-respected Itaewon venue.

Jazz Story (p149) Live sets in a striking bar.

Best for Theatre & Dance

Seoul Arts Center (p130) Opera, concert and recital performances.

Sejong Center for the Performing Arts (p76) Big musicals and intimate classical concerts are staged here.

LG Arts Center (p130) Slick theatre space hosting quality productions.

ArkoPAC (p149) Theatre company specialising in dance performances.

Jeongdong Theater (p88) Modern traditional Korean theatre.

Best for Movies

Cinemateque KOFA (p102) Free screenings of classic and contemporary Korean films.

Cinematheque/Seoul Arts Cinema (p75) A chance to catch local arthouse films with subtitles.

Megabox COEX (p130) Cineplex with 17 screens and 4000 seats.

Best Arts Festivals

Seoul Performing Arts Festival (www.spaf.or.kr) Month-long theatre, dance and music festival held in September.

International Modern Dance Festival (www.modafe.org) May event featuring a variety of performances from ballet to contemporary dance.

Seoul Fringe Festival (www.seoulfringefestival.net) Each August this major performing-arts festival takes over Hongdae.

Seoul International Dance Festival (www.sidance.org) Large-scale contemporary dance festival held every October since 1998.

Best Mixed Events

Mudaeruk (p101) Electronica, films and art in the basement of the Lost Continent of Mu.

Café BBang (p102) Indie artists and bands as well as film, art exhibitions and parties.

Indie Art-Hall GONG (p102) All kinds of cool goings on in part of a steel factory south of the Han.

Treasure Hunt

With endless markets, multistorey department stores and glitzy malls, shopping is a 24-7 pursuit in consumerist Seoul. Whether it's for hanbok *(traditional clothing) or* hanji *(handmade paper), art-and-design pieces, cut-price cosmetics or K-Pop souvenirs, chances are slim that you will leave empty-handed.*

Always in Fashion

For clothing, shoes, and accessories, Dongdaemun Market and the surrounding high-rise malls offer the city's biggest selection, though the area is sprawling and much of it is geared up for wholesale and fabrics. The narrow, brightly lit streets of Myeong-dong are more shopper-friendly and stock plenty of local brands. Larger sizes in clothes and shoes, souvenir T-shirts, leather jackets and tailor-made clothing can be found in Itaewon, where English is widely understood.

Outfits by hot local K-designers – such as Lie Sang Bong, Kathleen Kye, fleamadonna, Doii Lee and Misung Jung – are best sourced in major department stores or the boutiques of Myeong-dong, Apgujeong and Cheongdam. For high-end fashion the ritzy Apgujeong Rodeo Drive in Gangnam district is a must. As well as local K-designers, all the big-name luxury brands such as Louis Vuitton, Gucci and Prada are here, and it's an experience that offers all the glamour and posturing fashionistas you'd find in LA's Beverly Hills; it's worth having a prowl even if you're not splashing the cash.

Shirts or blouses made of lightweight, see-through *ramie* (cloth made from pounded bark) make for an unusual fashion gift; the quality is usually high, but as with naturally dyed *hanbok,* such clothes are pricey. Everyday *hanbok* is reasonably priced, but formal styles, made of colourful silk and intricately embroidered, are objects of wonder and cost a fortune.

Cosmetics are a big attraction for shoppers visiting Seoul. Myeong-dong is ground zero for local boutiques and chains selling top-quality, inexpensive skin and makeup products, many of which are organic. An item that proves particularly popular with locals and international visitors is BB (blemish balm) cream, a two-in-one moisturiser and makeup – made famous by its popularity with *hallyu* (Korean Wave) film and pop stars.

Antiques & Crafts

Traditional souvenirs such as embroidery, patchwork wrapping cloths *(bojagi),* handmade paper *(hanji),* wooden masks, fans, painted wooden carvings and lacquerware boxes inlaid with mother-of-pearl *(najeon chilgi)* can be found at craft and souvenir shops throughout Insa-dong, the city's best shopping area for Seoul-inspired goodies to take home. For a more limited, albeit cheaper, selection of souvenirs, check out Buildings C and D at Namdaemun Market (p86). You'll also find kitchen and tableware areas where you can buy traditional Korean stone bowls, *bangjja* bronzeware, tea-sets and chopsticks.

More expensive items include pale-green celadon pottery (best bought at the source in **Icheon Ceramic Village** (이천 도예촌; www.icheon.go.kr; Gwango-dong; ⊙10am-5pm; 🚌114, 24-7, 20-4)), reproduction Joseon dynasty furniture, and contemporary art from Seoul's multitude of commercial galleries.

Antique-lovers should hit up the Dapsimni arcades (p139), which specialise mainly in Joseon-era items such as pottery,

Buddhist statues and furniture. The street running south from Itaewon subway is lined with beautiful antique shops selling mostly Western furniture and objets d'art, while the Seoul Folk Flea Market (p140) has mountains of mid-century ephemera, old cameras and instruments, and other retro junk.

Food & Drink

Gim (dried seaweed) is a popular purchase; get it in larger sheets to have a go at rolling your own *gimbap* back home. The many types of health-giving Korean tea are a good buy, as are rice wines such as *makgeolli* and *baekseju,* and local liquors such as *soju*. Ginseng, the wonder root, turns up everywhere. Sold raw, dried or steamed, you can chew it, eat it, drink it or bathe in it to benefit from its health-giving properties.

Electronics

While Seoul is home to some of the world's largest electronic companies such as Samsung and LG, don't come here expecting low prices on the latest Korean-made gadgets, which can cost more than the same models shipped overseas.

However, Seoul is a decent place to pick up cheap, second-hand phones and other used tech at the I'Park Mall (p117) above Yongsan Station and the sprawling Yongsan Electronics Market (p118) next door. Note that any cellphones purchased in Seoul come with a few quirks, including a loud camera shutter, which you can't deactivate (you can perhaps guess why the government introduced this regulation).

Located within the building of Samsung's world headquarters, Samsung D'Light showcases all the new releases, plus exhibitions on technology and innovation.

NEED TO KNOW

Opening Hours

Shops 10am to 9pm; some close Sunday

Department stores 10am to 8pm

Markets Times vary, but some stalls may stay open even on days when a market is generally closed.

Bargaining

Acceptable at markets and some shops. If you are buying more than one item, it's also OK to ask for a discount – use your judgement.

Tax Refunds

If you spend more than ₩30,000 at participating tax-free shops, you can receive a partial refund on some items (between 5% and 7%) of the 10% value-added tax (VAT). Be sure to collect the special receipt, which can be used to obtain a tax refund at the airport or, increasingly, in locations in and around Seoul's malls and shopping areas.

Seoul also has a growing number of duty-free shops and malls where goods are sold tax-free on the spot, but you'll need to show your passport.

Shopping by Neighbourhood

➡ **Gwanghwamun & Jongno-gu** (p76) Insadong and Samcheong-dong are packed with art galleries, traditional craft shops and quirky boutiques; Seochon, west of the palace, is worth a look too.

➡ **Myeong-dong & Jung-gu** (p90) Best for department stores, fashion outlets and cosmetics, with all-night shopping at Namdaemun Market.

➡ **Western Seoul** (p102) Youth fashion trends are serviced in Hongdae and, increasingly, Yeonnam-dong.

➡ **Itaewon & Yongsan-gu** (p117) Itaewon is handy for expat-sized clothing, shoes and tailors, while Hannam-dong is developing a rep for designer boutiques.

➡ **Gangnam & Southern Seoul** (p130) Luxe retail in Apgujeong and Cheongdam; more affordable boutiques in Garosu-gil; one-stop shopping megamalls COEX and D Cube City.

➡ **Dongdaemun & Eastern Seoul** (p139) Sprawling markets and high-rise malls for serious shopaholics and bulk buyers.

Lonely Planet's Top Choices

Insa-dong Maru (p76) Slick showcase for local crafts, fashion and homewares.

KCDF Gallery (p77) Gorgeous design emporium embracing traditional crafts with a contemporary slant.

10 Corso Como Seoul (p130) Beautifully curated high-fashion and lifestyle store in classy Cheongdam.

Namdaemun Market (p86) Haggle for bargains at this sprawling city-centre warren of stalls selling all life's essentials.

Shinsegae (p90) The 'Harrods' of Seoul is the city's classiest department store.

Best Markets

Namdaemun Market (p86) Korea's largest and most atmospheric market.

Gwangjang Market (p137) Most famous for food, but also has vintage clothing and textiles.

Dongdaemun Market (p139) Energetic 24-hour shopping and good market food.

Seoul Folk Flea Market (p140) Fantastic place to sift through trash and treasure.

Seoul Yangnyeongsi Herb Medicine Market (p139) Take in wonderful fragrances at Asia's largest herbal market.

Best for Fashion

10 Corso Como Seoul (p130) High-end fashion by international and local designers.

Lab 5 (p131) Good spot to seek out the latest in K-design.

Åland (p90) Excellent selection of streetwear for men and women.

Boon the Shop (p132) Designer boutiques and clothing in ritzy Apgujeong.

Gentle Monster (p103) Edgy shades and frames as worn by Korean stars.

Jilkyungyee (p77) Tastefully designed *hanbok* for both sexes.

Best Department Stores & Malls

COEX Mall (p130) A shiny, modern megamall and Asia's largest underground shopping precinct.

Shinsegae (p90) Korea's first department store has local designers and a lovely roof garden.

Galleria (p130) Haute couture along Apgujeong Rodeo Drive.

Lotte Department Store (p91) Several branches across the city, including at Lotte World Tower, Korea's tallest skyscraper.

Mecenatpolis Mall (p103) One of Seoul's best-designed malls.

Hyundai Department Store (p131) Luxury brands by local and international designers.

Best Books, CDS & DVDs

Seoul Selection (p76) Best choice of books and DVDs about Korea.

What the Book (p118) Good selection of novels, second-hand books, magazines and guidebooks.

Kyobo Bookshop (p76) Great range of English-language books, Korean CDs and stationery.

K-Wave Experience (p125) Has a decent stock of K-Wave CDs and DVDs.

Vinyl & Plastic (p117) Warehouse-styled vinyl and CD emporium with cafe attached.

Best for Design

Market m* (p90) Wooden furniture, bags, storage and stationery from Korea and Japan.

Jonginamoo (p77) Beautiful traditional furniture and home decor.

Dongdaemun Design Plaza & Park (p135) A scatter of design shops, markets and exhibitions.

Gallery Art Zone (p77) Contemporary Korean design from portable speakers to ceramics.

Millimetre Milligram (p117) Designer accessories, furniture and art books.

Object Recycle (p103) Great selection of recycled and upcycled designer goods from across Korea.

Best for Crafts & Souvenirs

Ssamziegil (p77) Insa-dong complex for quirky fashion, accessories or souvenirs.

Free Market (p102) Weekly creative market in Hongdae.

Namdaemun Market (p86) Selection of traditional handicrafts at wholesale prices.

Key (p103) Affordable, exclusive items, from jewellery to paintings.

Korea House (p87) Elegant selection of crafts.

Yongsan Crafts Museum (p117) High-quality traditional crafts by local designers.

GUITAR PHOTOGRAPHER/SHUTTERSTOCK ©

Sunrise from Baegundae (p160)

Active Seoul

Hiking is popular year-round (see p33), while skiing and ice skating take over in winter. For something a little more relaxing, locals like to sweat and soak the day away in a jjimjilbang *(Korean spa).*

24-Hour Spas

The best *jjimjilbang* offer a variety of communal baths (they might be green tea or ginseng) and saunas (mugwort, pine or jade). The etiquette is to get fully naked for spas, hence men and women are always separate in the bath area. But saunas, napping rooms and other facilities may be mixed; in these areas wear the robes or shorts and T-shirts provided. Most spas are open 24 hours. The basic entry fee covers up to 12 hours of unlimited use of all the baths and saunas; treatments like body scrubs cost extra.

Baseball & Golf Practice

Private golf courses are usually for members only, but there are driving ranges in top-end hotels and elsewhere, including Gangnam.

Baseball batting cages can be found in locations such as Sinchon and Insa-dong.

Cycling

Seoul's bike-sharing scheme, like similar civic ventures in London and Paris, can be used by visitors. The green-and-white bikes and their matching docking stations can be found at over 150 locations across the city. To use, first purchase a voucher at www.bikeseoul.com to

NEED TO KNOW

Information

Adventure Club (www.adventurekorea.com) Contact for details of caving, rock climbing, white-water rafting, paintball games and other adventurous outdoor activities.

Seoul Hiking Group (https://seoulhiking.com) Heads off hiking at least once a week.

Korea4Expats.com (www.korea4expats.com) Listings for community groups and different activities, with good info on cycling too.

Costs

Baseball/soccer tickets ₩8000 to ₩20,000.

Jjimjilbang ₩7000 to ₩13,000 entry, depending on the level of facilities.

obtain an unlock code, which is then keyed in on the bike itself (selecting the 'Foreign Tourist' option).

The bikes cost ₩1000 per hour for up to two hours, and ₩1000 every half hour after that. A deposit of ₩50,000 is taken from your credit card and refunded within 24 hours of the bike being redocked.

Cycleways run along both sides of the Han River past sports fields and picnic areas where there are also plenty of bike-hire stalls (₩3000 per hour, open 9am to 8.30pm March to November), as well as free rental close by the subways at Okso (Exit 4), Eungbong (Exit 1), Gongneung (Exit 4), Yeongdeungpo-gu Office (Exit 2), Sanggye (Exit 1), Gangbyeon (Exit 1) and Jamsil (Exit 2) – which can vary from two hours to all day. Bring your own padlock, and leave a driving licence or other ID.

Swimming

Outdoor pools open in July and August in the Han River parks.

Winter Sports

From December to February a handful of ski resorts open that are within an hour of Seoul by bus. Many of the resorts closest to the city run free shuttle buses from Seoul's main stations, making it possible to do a day-long ski excursion and return to Seoul at night. If you'd like to stay overnight or for the weekend, travel-agency package deals are a good bet, as they include transport, accommodation, ski-equipment hire and lift passes. Check out:

Bears Town Ski Resort (베어스타운리조트 스키장; ☎031 540 5000; www.bearstown.com; 27 Geumgang-ro 2536beon-gil, Naechon-myeon, Pocheon-si; 1-day lift passes ₩75,000; 👪)

Jisan Forest Resort (지산 포레스트 리조트; ☎031 644 1200; www.jisanresort.co.kr; lift tickets per day adult/child ₩69,000/46,000)

Yangji Pine Resort (양지파인리조트 스키장; www.pineresort.com; 112 Nampyeong-ro, Yangji-myeon; lift tickets per day adult/child ₩70,000/48,000; 👪).

Winter is also the time when Seoulites like to skate under the stars at the magical, inexpensive ice-skating rink that appears on Seoul Plaza (p91) outside City Hall. Swimming pools along the Han River are also turned into skating rinks, as are the pools at the Grand Hyatt Seoul (p172) and Banyan Tree Club & Spa (p170). Lotte World's indoor ice-skating rink (p132) is open all year.

Taekwondo Courses

While taekwondo is not popular with locals as a spectator sport, those interested in Korea's national martial art can head to Kukkiwon Stadium (p132) where training sessions can be arranged. Consult the website (www.kukkiwon.or.kr) for more details.

ul Plaza Ice Skating Rink (p91)

Lonely Planet's Top Choices

Bukhansan National Park (p160) Hiking opportunities abound in this national park reachable by Seoul's subway.

Inwangsan (p34) Seoul's 18.6km City Wall can be hiked in its entirety over two days, but this stretch offers the best views.

Dragon Hill Spa & Resort (p118) The best of Seoul's inner-city *jjimjilbang* experiences.

Seoul Plaza Ice Skating Rink (p91) Get your skates on at this outdoor rink set up each winter.

Seoul Global Cultural Center (p91) Classes in anything from *hanji* (handmade paper) craft to painting and calligraphy.

Best Skiing

Bears Town Ski Resort (p50) Located 50 minutes northeast of Seoul. USO, the American troops' activities organisation, runs ski tours to this resort, and anyone is welcome to join.

Jisan Forest Resort (p102) Fifty-six kilometres south of Seoul and a 40-minute bus ride from Gangnam.

Yangji Pine Resort (p50) Around a 40-minute drive southeast of Seoul.

Best Spas & Jjimjilbang

Dragon Hill Spa & Resort (p118) Complex of pools, saunas and spas, including some infused with cedar or ginseng.

Spa Lei (p132) Classy women-only spa in Gangnam.

Happy Day Spa (p171) A reasonably good 24-hour sauna and *jjimjilbang* in the Marigold Hotel.

Explore Seoul

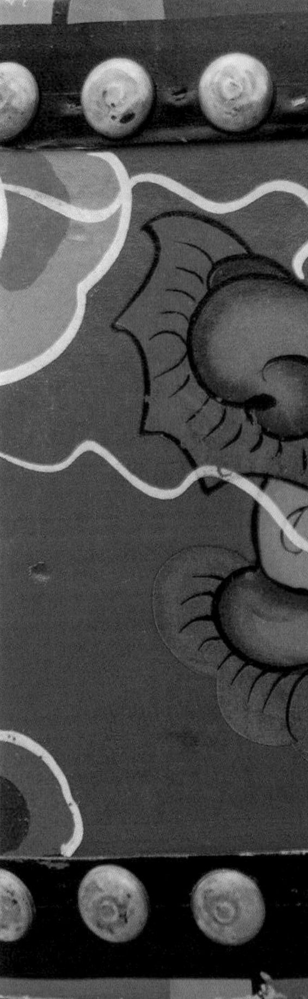

SEOUL'S TOP SIGHTS

Neighbourhoods at a Glance

❶ Gwanghwamun & Jongno-gu p56

The centuries-old heart of Seoul revolves around these once-regal palace quarters. Between Gyeongbokgung and Changdeokgung, Bukchon covers several areas, including Samcheong-dong, and Gahoe-dong, famous for its traditional *hanok* (wooden homes). West of Gyeongbokgung, Seochon is increasingly popular for its galleries, cafes and boutiques. South of Bukchon are maze-like and gallery-filled Insa-dong, and hip *hanok* area Ikseon-dong.

❷ Myeong-dong & Jung-gu p79

Seoul's retail world bursts forth in the brightly lit, packed, noisy streets of Myeong-dong – Seoul's equivalent of London's Oxford St or NYC's Fifth Ave, with a massive, 24-hour mar-

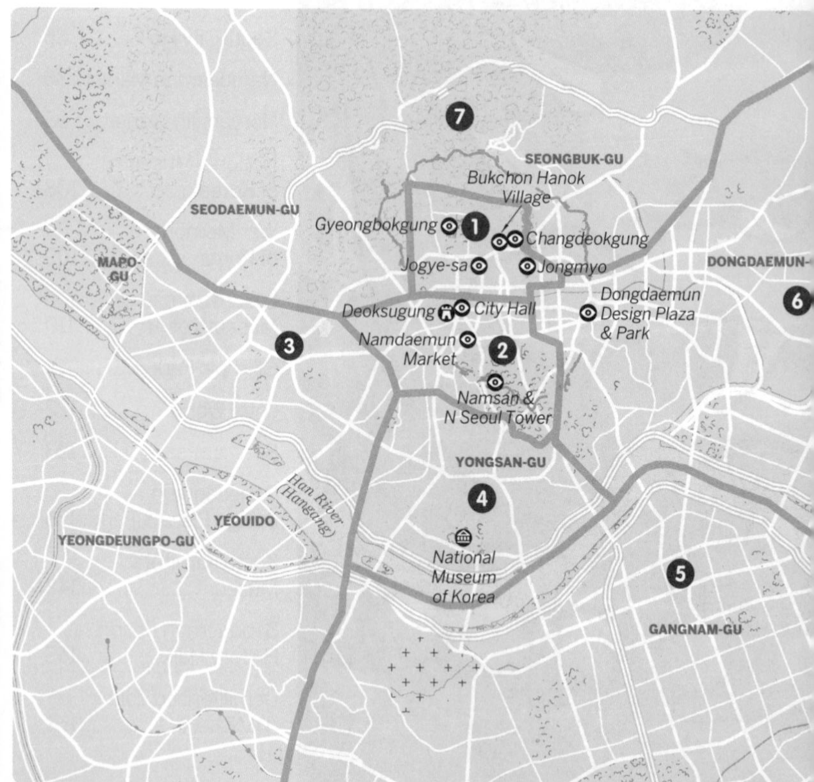

ket (Namdaemun) thrown in. Looming over the commercial frenzy are the peaceful and tree-clad slopes of Namsan.

3 Western Seoul p92

Seoul's principal student quarter is home to Hongdae (around Hongik University), Edae (around Ewha Womans University) and Sinchon (between Yonsei and Sogang Universities). These are youthful, creative districts short on traditional sights, but big on modern-day diversions and entertainments. South of Hongdae across the Han River, the island of Yeouido has several places of interest, all easily visited if you hire a bike at its riverside or central park.

4 Itaewon & Yongsan-gu p106

Defined by the off-limits US army base that eats up a chunk of Yongsan-gu, this area has long been Seoul's 'foreign' hangout for hamburgers, hookers and everything else. Nowadays, Itaewon (and adjacent 'hoods Hannam-dong, Haebangchon and Gyeongridan) boasts one of the most dynamic restaurant scenes in Asia, with a new global food trend emerging every five minutes. The diversity extends to the nightlife, with craft beer, underground clubs and something for every sexual persuasion. The area also has several major museums you won't want to miss.

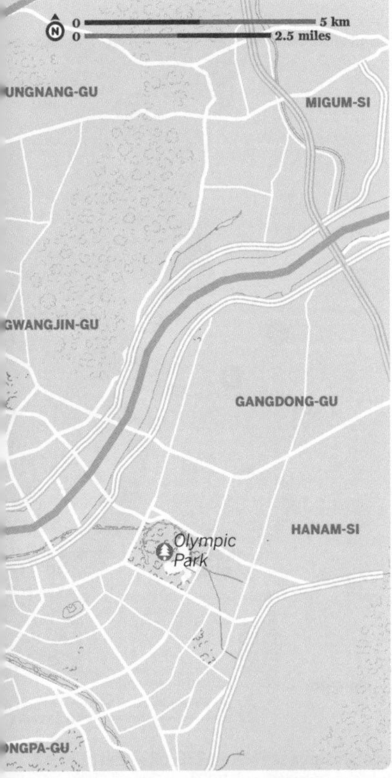

5 Gangnam & Southern Seoul p119

Gangnam (meaning South of the River) is booming with new luxury high-rises bisected by broad highways. Expansive areas of greenery figure, too, in the shape of Olympic Park, the strip of recreation areas along the Han River, and Seonjeongneung Park, home to royal tombs. Luxury label boutiques are clustered in Apgujeong and Cheongdam. You'll also find several major performance-arts centres across the district.

6 Dongdaemun & Eastern Seoul p133

Home to high-rise malls and labyrinthine covered markets, the 24-hour retail frenzy of Dongdaemun attracts suitcase-wheeling shoppers from all over Asia. It's mostly clothing and fabrics, but you can also find Seoul's busiest street-food arcades in Gwangjang Market. Further east the couture gives way to antiques, flea-markets and herbal medicines. Dramatic contemporary architecture is provided by Zaha Hadid's Dongdaemun Plaza & Park, while up-and-coming Seongsu-dong, an old shoemaking district being touted as Seoul's answer to Brooklyn, is awash with industrial-chic cafes and hip boutiques.

7 Northern Seoul p141

Some of Seoul's most charming neighbourhoods are clustered across three of the city's guardian mountains. To the east, beside Naksan, you'll find student and performing-arts hub Daehangno. At Bukaksan is Seongbuk-dong, an affluent residential district with excellent museums. Buam-dong further west is the starting point for hikes along the City Wall, while the slopes of Inwangsan are home to the city's most famous shamanist shrine. Continuing south is a park dedicated to Korea's independence, at Seodaemun.

Gwanghwamun & Jongno-gu

GWANGHWAMUN & AROUND | INSA-DONG | BUKCHON | SAMCHEONG-DONG | IKSEON-DONG

Neighbourhood Top Five

❶ **Gyeongbokgung** (p58) Admiring the scale and artistry of the largest of Seoul's palaces, fronted by the grand gateway Gwanghwamun, where you can watch the changing of the guard.

❷ **Changdeokgung** (p60) Discovering Huwon, the serene traditional garden secreted behind the most beautiful of Seoul's five main palaces.

❸ **Bukchon Hanok Village** (p61), Stepping back in time in the picturesque maze of the city's densest cluster of traditional-style homes.

❹ **Jogye-sa** (p63) Learning about Buddhism at one of Seoul's most active temples and epicentre of the spectacular Lotus Lantern Festival in May.

❺ **Arario Museum in SPACE** (p66) Browsing an impressive collection of contemporary art.

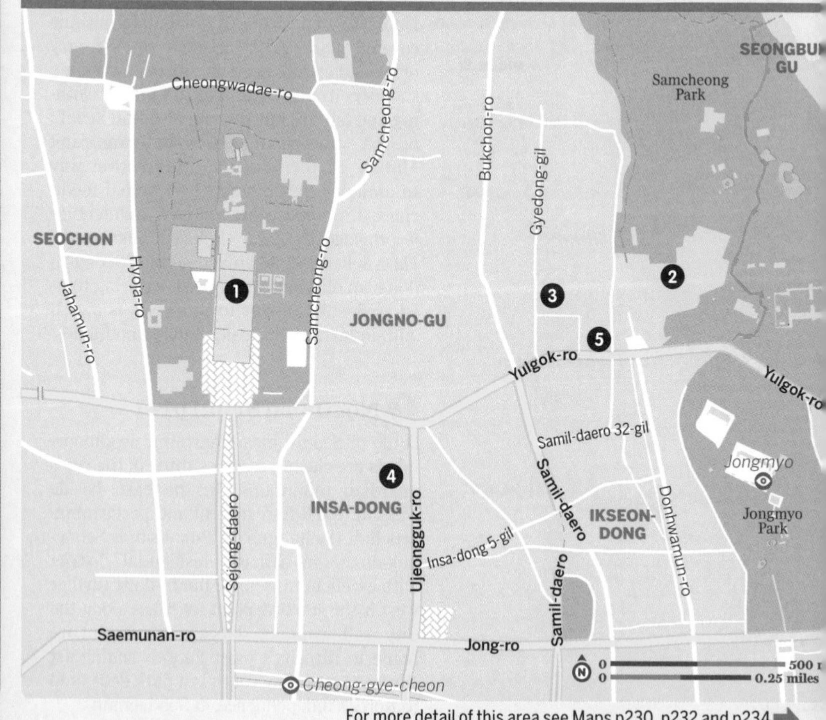

For more detail of this area see Maps p230, p232 and p234

Explore Gwanghwamun & Jongno-gu

The focus of the area – and for many visitors, of the whole city – is Seoul's royal palace compounds, which need at least half a day each to do them justice. Although their size and splendour have been greatly reduced from their heyday in the 18th century, the compounds, in the district of Jongno-gu, provide a glimpse of what it was like to live at the powerful heart of the old city. Save for the odd painted screen and altar, the large palace buildings are mostly empty, allowing you to appreciate the Confucian ideals of frugality, simplicity and separation of the sexes in the architecture as well as the gardens. The area is referred to as Gwanghwamun after the majestic gate to the main palace of Gyeongbokgung and the elongated square in front of it.

If you want to see *hanok* (traditional Korean houses) in a real-life neighbourhood, Bukchon, the area between Gyeongbokgung and Changdeokgung, makes for a pleasant hour, or more if you stop off in a teahouse. Centuries ago this is where the *yangban* (aristocrats) lived but most estates were divided into plots in the early 20th century to create the smaller *hanok* you can now view around Gahoe-dong. For more clusters of *hanok* in a trendy setting head to Seochon west of Gyeongbokgung; or to Inkseon-dong, one of Seoul's most tourist-friendly areas, for a compact maze of small streets filled with traditional teahouses, restaurants, galleries and craft stores.

Local Life

➡ **Teatime** Take a breather from sightseeing over a beverage in one of Insa-dong, Bukchon, Seochon or Ikseon-dong's charming traditional teahouses or contemporary cafes.

➡ **Jongmyo Square** The park in front of this venerable shrine (p62) is a daily gathering spot for Seoul's senior set, who come to natter, play board games such as *baduk* and *janggi* and sometimes dance to *trot* (traditional electro-pop music).

➡ **Streamside wanders** Stroll along the landscaped paths either side of the Cheong-gye-cheon (p64); if the weather's fine, cool your heels in the stream.

Getting There & Away

➡ **Subway** Lines 1, 3 and 5 all have stations in this area; Anguk is best for Insa-dong and Bukchon, Jongno 3-ga Exit 4 for Ikseon-dong, and Exit 3 for the gay bars.

➡ **Tour bus** The Seoul City Tour Bus has stops around the palaces and Insa-dong.

Lonely Planet's Top Tip

If you plan to visit all four of Seoul's palaces – **Gyeongbokgung** (p58), **Changdeokgung** (p60), **Changgyeonggung** (p144) and **Deoksugung** (p82) – and the shrine **Jongmyo** (p62), you can save some money by buying a combined ticket (₩10,000) valid for up to three months. The ticket is sold at each of the palaces and also covers entry to Huwon at Changdeokgung.

Best Places to Eat

➡ Balwoo Gongyang (p73)

➡ Ogawa (p71)

➡ Ikseon Dimibang (p72)

For reviews, see p70.➡

Best Places to Drink

➡ Sik Mool (p74)

➡ Dawon (p74)

➡ Blue Star Pub (p75)

For reviews, see p73.➡

Best Shopping

➡ KCDF Gallery (p77)

➡ Insa-dong Maru (p76)

➡ Kyobo Bookshop (p76)

For reviews, see p76.➡

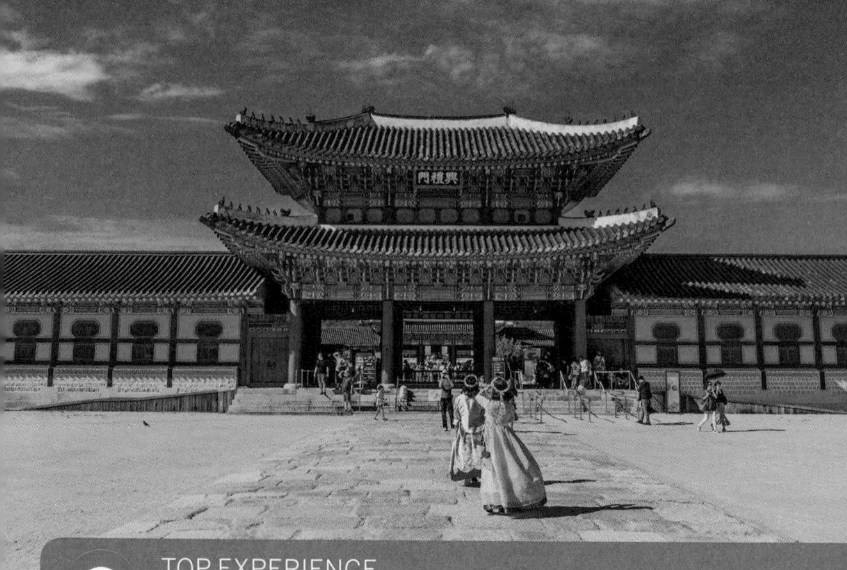

TOP EXPERIENCE
DISCOVER ICONIC GYEONGBOKGUNG

Seoul's largest royal palace is an icon of the city and attracts the lion's share of visitors. The grand buildings once housed scholars, eunuchs, concubines, soldiers and servants. Today the museums and dramatic changing-of-the-guard ceremony make for an absorbing afternoon or full day.

Palace History

Originally built by King Taejo in 1395, Gyeongbokgung served as the principal royal residence until 1592, when it was burnt down during the Japanese invasion. It lay in ruins for nearly 300 years until Heungseon Daewongun, regent and father of King Gojong, started to rebuild it in 1865. Gojong moved in during 1868, but the expensive rebuilding project bankrupted the government.

During Japanese colonial rule, the front section of the palace was again destroyed in order to build the enormous Japanese Government General Building. This was itself demolished in the 1990s to enable Gwanghwamun to be rebuilt in the form you see today.

Palace Layout

The palace's impressive main gate, **Gwanghwamun** (광화문), restored in 2010, is flanked by stone carvings of *haechi,* mythical lion-like creatures traditionally set to protect the palace against fire; they never really did work and, appearances to the contrary, are superfluous today as the gate is now a painted concrete rather than wood structure.

Moving across the palace's broad front courtyard, you pass through a second gate, **Heungnyemun**, and over a small artificial stream (for good feng shui a palace should

DON'T MISS

- Gwanghwamun
- Geunjeongjeon
- Gyeonghoeru
- National Folk Museum
- National Palace Museum

PRACTICALITIES

- 경복궁; Palace of Shining Happiness
- Map p232, D3
- www.royalpalace.go.kr
- 161 Sajik-ro
- adult/child ₩3000/1500
- 9am-5pm Wed-Mon Nov-Feb, to 6pm Mar-May, Sep & Oct, to 6.30pm Jun-Aug
- S Line 3 to Gyeongbokgung, Exit 5

have water in front and a mountain to the rear, which in this case is Bukaksan) to face the ornate two-storey **Geunjeongjeon**. In this impressive throne hall kings were crowned, met foreign envoys and conducted affairs of state.

West of Geunjeongjeon is **Gyeonghoeru**, a large pavilion resting on 48 pillars and overlooking an artificial lake with two small islands. State banquets were held inside and royals went boating on the pond.

Living Quarters & Gardens

A series of smaller meeting halls precede the king's living quarters, **Gangyeongjeon**, behind which are **Gyotaejeon**, those of the queen. Next you'll come to the terraced garden, **Amisan**; the red-brick chimneys decorated with longevity symbols on the garden's top terrace were used to release smoke from the palace's *ondol* (underfloor heating) system.

Symbolically located on the eastern side of the grounds (where the sun rises) is **Donggun**, the living quarters for the crown prince. To the rear, King Gojong built more halls for his own personal use and an ornamental pond with **Hyangwonjeong**, an attractive hexagonal pavilion on an island.

Museums Within the Palace

The **National Palace Museum of Korea** (국립고궁박물관; ☎02-3701 7500; www.gogung.go.kr; 12 Hyoja-ro; ⏲9am-6pm Tue-Fri, to 7pm Sat & Sun) FREE, to the left just inside Gwanghwamun, has royal artefacts that highlight the wonderful artistic skills of the Joseon era – royal seals, illustrations of court ceremonies, and the gold-embroidered *hanbok* (traditional clothing) and exquisite hairpins worn by the queens and princesses. Note this museum closes on a different day to the palace.

In a separate section in the northeast of the grounds is the excellent **National Folk Museum of Korea** (국립민속박물관; ☎02-3704 3114; www.nfm.go.kr; 37 Samcheong-ro; free with Gyeongbokgung; ⏲9am-6pm Wed-Mon Mar-Oct, to 5pm Wed-Mon Nov-Feb; S Line 3 to Anguk, Exit 1) FREE. It has three main exhibition halls covering the history of the Korean people, the agricultural way of life and the life of *yangban* (aristocrats) during the Joseon era. Among the many interesting exhibits is an amazingly colourful funeral bier – these were used to give the deceased a great send-off.

On the approach to the museum is an **open-air exhibition** of historical buildings and structures, including a street of buildings styled as they would have been in the early 20th century. Also here is the separate National Children's Museum (p65) and play area.

TOURS & CEREMONIES

An audio commentary and a free guided tour (in English at 11am, 1.30pm and 3.30pm) are available to learn more about the palace. At the National Folk Museum of Korea the English guided tours start at 10.30am and 2.30pm, while at the National Palace Museum of Korea, the tour is at 3pm. Changing of the guard ceremonies beside Gwanghwamun occur every hour, on the hour between 10am and 4pm.

In the early hours of 8 October 1895, Gyeongbokgung was the scene of a dramatic moment in Korean history. Japanese assassins broke into the palace and murdered Empress Myeongseong (Queen Min), one of the most powerful figures at that time in Korea. She was targeted because of her attempts to modernise Korea and protect its independence. After her body was burnt, it is said only one finger survived the fire. Later 56 individuals were arrested but not one was convicted for the murder.

TOP EXPERIENCE

EXPLORE THE BEAUTY OF CHANGDEOKGUNG

The most beautiful of Seoul's four main palaces, World Heritage–listed Changdeokgung was originally built in the early 15th century as a secondary palace to Gyeongbokgung. Following the destruction of both palaces during the Japanese invasion in the 1590s, Changdeokgung was rebuilt and became the primary royal residence until 1872. It remained in use well into the 20th century.

Palace Layout

Enter through the imposing gate **Donhwamun** (dating from 1608), turn right and cross over the stone bridge (built in 1414) – note the guardian animals carved on its sides. On the left is the beautiful main palace building, **Injeongjeon**. It sits in harmony with the paved courtyard, the open corridors and the trees behind it.

Next door are the government office buildings, including one with a blue-tiled roof. Further on are the private living quarters of the royal family. Peering inside the partially furnished rooms, you can feel what these Joseon palaces were like in their heyday – bustling beehives buzzing round the king, full of gossip, intrigue and whispering.

Round the back is a terraced garden with decorative *ondol* chimneys. Over on the right is something completely different – **Nakseonjae**, built by King Heonjong (r 1834–49) in an austere Confucian style using unpainted wood. Royal descendants lived here until 1989.

DON'T MISS

- Huwon
- Injeongjeon
- Nakseonjae
- Ongnyucheon

PRACTICALITIES

- 창덕궁
- Map p230, F5
- http://eng.cdg.go.kr/main/main.htm
- 99 Yulgok-ro
- adult/child ₩3000/1500, incl Huwon ₩8000/4000
- 9am-6pm Tue-Sun Feb-May, Sep & Oct, to 6.30pm Jun-Aug, to 5.30pm Nov-Jan, Huwon closes 1hr earlier
- S Line 3 to Anguk, Exit 3

The Secret Garden

Walk through the dense woodland and suddenly you come across a serene glade. The **Huwon** (Secret Garden) is a beautiful vista of pavilions on the edge of a square lily pond, with other halls and a two-storey library. The board out the front, written by King Jeongjo, means 'Gather the Universe'. Joseon kings relaxed, studied and wrote poems in this tranquil setting.

Further on are a couple more ponds and **Yeongyeongdang**, originally built in 1828 as a place for the crown prince to study. **Ongnyucheon** is a brook at the back of the garden where there's a huge rock, **Soyoam**, with three Chinese characters inscribed on it by King Injo in 1636 – *ong-nyu-cheon,* which means 'jade flowing stream' – and a poem composed in Chinese characters by King Sukjong in 1690.

Visiting the Palace

All visits are by one-hour guided tours that run in English at 10.15am and 1.15pm; if you just want to see the sights, tours in Korean are at 9.30am, 11.30am and 3.30pm. To also see the palace's Secret Garden, Huwon, join English tours at 10.30am, 11.30am and 2.30pm (also 3.30pm February to November). Come early (or reserve online) as the Huwon tours are restricted to 50 people at a time.

Try to book well ahead for the worthwhile monthly **Moonlight Tours** (April to May, and August to October), limited to 100 people and costing ₩30,000. Buy tickets online at **Auction** (www.ticket.auction.co.kr) or call 02-1566 1369 (English).

TOP EXPERIENCE
GET LOST IN BUKCHON HANOK VILLAGE

Bukchon (North Village), covering the area between Gyeongbokgung and Changdeokgung, is home to around 900 *hanok*, Seoul's largest concentration of these traditional Korean homes. Although super-touristy in parts, the streets here are a pleasure to aimlessly wander and get lost in, admiring the buildings' patterned walls and tiled roofs contrasting with the modern city in the distance.

Bukchon Information & Events

To find out more about the area head first to the **Bukchon Traditional Culture Center** (북촌문화센터; 02-2171 2459; http://bukchon.seoul.go.kr/eng/exp/center1_1.jsp; 37 Gyedong-gil; 9am-6pm Mon-Sat) FREE, which has a small exhibition about *hanok* and is housed, appropriately enough, in a *hanok*.

With three days' advance notice you can arrange a free guided tour of the area with a volunteer from Seoul City Walking Tours (p209). Free maps and leaflets about the area can also be picked up from **Bukchon Tourist Information Center** (Map p230; 02-2148 4161; cnr Bukchon-ro & Bukchon-ro 4-gil; 9am-6pm).

Note that massed tour groups swamp Bukchon every weekend, particularly during the middle hours of the day; avoid the crowds by visiting early in the morning or later in the evening.

DON'T MISS

- Bukchon Traditional Culture Center
- Simsimheon
- Gahoe Minhwa Workshop
- Dong-Lim Knot Workshop

PRACTICALITIES

- 북촌한옥마을
- Map p230, D5
- http://hanok.seoul.go.kr
- Bukchon-ro
- admission free
- 24hr
- S Line 3 to Anguk, Exit 3

Inside the Hanok

Given the throng of tourists and the number of *hanok* that now house commercial businesses, it's easy to overlook the fact that this region was once a residential area and still remains so in parts.

For a critical take on the contemporary history and development of Bukchon see www.kahoidong.com. The site is run by David Kilburn, who lives with his wife in one of the most traditional of *hanok* in Gahoe-dong, the most picturesque – and thus busiest – part of Bukchon.

Despite being zoned as a residential area, several *hanok* here are open to the public. Simsimheon (p69), meaning 'House Where the Heart is Found', is a modern *hanok* that was rebuilt using traditional methods on the site of two older ones. Entry includes tea, which is sipped overlooking the internal garden. It's also possible to stay in a family home turned guesthouse.

Craft & Art Museums & Workshops

There are several places in Bukchon where you can learn about the traditional crafts still practised in this area or view private collections of arts and crafts.

Gahoe Minhwa Workshop (가회민화공방; www.gahoemuseum.org; 17 Bukchon-ro 8-gil; adult/child ₩2000/1000; 10.30am-6pm Tue-Sun, to 5pm Dec-Feb; S Line 3 to Anguk, Exit 2) is both a *hanok* museum and cultural centre with a treasure trove of amulets and folk paintings. You can attend workshops in traditional painting and take away your efforts as a print or a T-shirt.

If traditional knotting techniques are your thing, then attend classes to make ornaments such as tassels and thread jewellery at the *hanok* of the Dong-Lim Knot Workshop (p78).

TOP EXPERIENCE

EXAMINE ROYAL ARTEFACTS AT JONGMYO

As interesting for the dense woodland as for its royal artefacts, World Heritage–listed Jongmyo contains the 'spirit tablets' of the Joseon kings and queens and loyal government officials. Special holes bored into the wood tablets are said to house the royal spirits. The Confucian shrine is equally famous for its ceremony Jongmyo Daeje, considered the oldest complete ceremony in the world.

Near the entrance to Jongmyo are two ponds, both square (representing earth) with a round island (representing the heavens). In the middle of the main path you'll notice triple stone paths; one is for the king, the other for the crown prince and the raised middle section for the spirits.

The main shrine, **Jeongjeon**, constructed in 1395, is fronted by a large stone-flagged courtyard. Inside are 49 royal spirit tablets in 19 small rooms that are usually locked.

On the right-hand side of the main entrance is **Gonsindang** (http://jikimi.cha.go.kr) FREE, which houses the spirit tablets of 83 meritorious subjects. They served their kings well and were rewarded with their spirit tablets sharing the royal compound – the highest honour they could hope for. On the left side are shrines to Chilsa, the seven gods who aid kings.

The smaller shrine, **Yeongnyeongjeon** (Hall of Eternal Peace), built in 1421, has 34 spirit tablets of lesser kings in six rooms. These include four ancestors of King Taejo (the founder of the Joseon dynasty) who were made kings posthumously. Behind this building a footbridge leads over to Changgyeonggung (p144).

On the first Sunday in May, known as **Jongmyo Daeje** (www.jongmyo.net/english_index.asp) FREE, the Yi clan, descendants of the Joseon kings, make lavish offerings of food and drink to the spirits of their royal ancestors. Starting at 11.30am with a procession from Gwanghwamun Sq to the shrine, the ceremony culminates seven hours later at the main shrine Jeongjeon.

DON'T MISS

- Jeongjeon
- Gonsindang
- Yeongnyeongjeon

PRACTICALITIES

- 종묘
- Map p234, H3
- 02-2174 3636
- http://jm.cha.go.kr
- 157 Jong-ro
- adult/child ₩1000/500
- 9am-5pm Wed-Mon Feb-May, Sep & Oct, to 6.30pm Jun-Aug, to 5.30pm Nov-Jan
- S Line 1, 3 or 5 to Jongno 3-ga, Exit 11

TOP EXPERIENCE

LEARN ABOUT BUDDHISM AT JOGYE-SA

The headquarters of the Jogye Order of Korean Buddhism has the largest hall of worship in Seoul, decorated with murals from Buddha's life and carved floral latticework doors. The temple compound, always a hive of activity, really comes alive during the city's spectacular Lotus Lantern Festival (p24) celebrating Buddha's birthday in late April or May, and is a great place to learn a little about Buddhist practice.

DON'T MISS

- Daeungjeon
- Beomjongru
- Temple Life program

PRACTICALITIES

- 조계사
- Map p234, A3
- ☎02-768 8600
- www.jogyesa.kr/user/english
- 55-Ujeongguk-ro
- ⏲24hr
- Ⓢ Line 3 to Anguk, Exit 6

Buddha Triad

Inside **Daeungjeon** (대웅전; Worship Hall) at Jogye-sa are three giant gilded Buddha statues: on the left is Amitabha, Buddha of the Western Paradise; in the centre is the historical Buddha, who lived in India and achieved enlightenment; on the right is the Bhaisaiya or Medicine Buddha, with a medicine bowl in his hand. The small 15th-century Buddha in the glass case was the main Buddha statue before he was replaced by the much larger ones in 2006. On the right-hand side is a guardian altar with lots of fierce-looking guardians in the painting behind, and on the left side is the altar used for memorial services.

Believers who enter the temple bow three times, touching their forehead to the ground – once for Buddha, once for the *dharma* (teaching) and once for the *sangha* (monks), 20 of whom serve in this temple.

Other Buildings

Behind Daeungjeon is the modern **Geuknakjeon** (Paradise Hall) dedicated to Amitabha Buddha; funeral services, *dharma* talks and other prayer services are held here.

On the left side of the compound is the octagonal 10-storey **stupa** in which is enshrined a relic of Buddha brought to Korea in 1913 by a Sri Lankan monk.

Beomjongru (Brahma Bell Pavilion) houses a drum to summon earthbound animals, a wooden fish-shaped gong to summon aquatic beings, a metal cloud-shaped gong to summon birds and a large bronze bell to summon underground creatures. The bell is rung 28 times at 4am and 33 times at 6pm.

Also within the grounds is the **Central Buddhist Museum** (☎02-2011 1960; ⏲9am-6pm Tue-Sun) FREE displaying regularly changing exhibitions relating to the religion. Attached to the museum is a tea shop and gift shop. There is also a small diner at the rear of the grounds serving very simple vegetarian dishes.

Temple Life Programs

Near the main entrance, the **Jogye-sa Information Center for Foreigners** (☎02-732 5292; ⏲10am-5pm) is staffed by English-speaking guides. Drop by here to make a booking for the **Temple Life program** (₩30,000; 1pm to 4pm Saturday), which includes a temple tour, meditation practice, lotus-lantern and prayer-bead making, woodblock printing, painting and a tea ceremony. An overnight templestay can also be arranged here.

To find out more about Buddhism or book a Templestay program elsewhere in Seoul or Korea, the **Templestay Information Center** (☎02-2013 2000; www.templestay.com; ⏲9am-7pm) is just across the street from Jogye-sa. Along the street you'll also find many shops selling monks' robes, prayer beads, lanterns and the like.

TOP EXPERIENCE

WANDER ALONG CHEONG-GYE-CHEON

This stream cutting through the city is a rare sight in the metropolis and one that instantly relaxes Seoulites with its greenery, and places to stop alongside landscaped walkways to enjoy the trickling water, whisper sweet nothings or hop across footbridges. There are a variety of public artworks, such as murals and the oversized pink-and-blue shell entitled Spring in Cheong-gye Plaza.

Walking beside the stream is a useful, peaceful way to move between sights such as Gwangjang Market, Dongdaemun and Insa-dong.

Roughly US$384 million was spent to remove a neglected raised highway and reveal the stream underneath. What seems like the original clear waters of the 5.8km of this beautiful stream is actually liquid pumped in at great expense from upstream, making it a not-so environmentally friendly water feature.

Between the Gwang-gyo and Jangton-gyo bridges is a 192m **wall mural** of painted tiles depicting King Jeongjo visiting his father's tomb in Hwaseong (Suwon) in 1785. Continue on past Dongdaemun and you'll eventually reach the Cheong-gye-cheon Museum.

For a fortnight in November, both banks of the Cheong-gye-cheon are illuminated by a fantastical array of lanterns made by master craftspeople for the **Seoul Lantern Festival** (서울빛초롱축제; www.seoullantern.com) FREE.

DON'T MISS

- Cheong-gye Plaza
- Mural of King Jeongjo's royal parade
- Walking beside the stream

PRACTICALITIES

- 청계천
- Map p232, D7
- 02-2290 6803
- www.cheonggyecheon.or.kr
- 110 Sejong-daero
- 24hr
- Line 5 to Gwanghwamun, Exit 5

SIGHTS

Use the imposing Gyeongbokgung as your point of reference. To its east are contemporary galleries and traditional Bukchon filled with *hanok* (wooden homes). Further east is Changdeokgung, while south are the small streets of Insa-dong, a traditionally gallery-filled area.

Gwanghwamun & Around

GYEONGBOKGUNG PALACE
See p58.

CHEONG-GYE-CHEON RIVER
See p64.

DAELIM CONTEMPORARY ART MUSEUM GALLERY
Map p232 (02-720 0667; www.daelimmuseum.org; 21 Jahamun-ro 4-gil; 10am-6pm Tue, Wed, Fri & Sun, to 8pm Thu & Sat; ; Line 3 to Gyeongbokgung, Exit 5) Daelim specialises in exhibitions on photography, design and fashion. The building, which was originally a family house, was remodelled by French architect Vincent Cornu and has a lovely garden to the rear and a cheap cafe and events hall in a separate building to the right of the main gallery. Admission charge varies with exhibitions.

NATIONAL MUSEUM OF KOREAN CONTEMPORARY HISTORY MUSEUM
Map p232 (02-3703 9200; www.much.go.kr; 198 Sejong-daero; 10am-6pm Tue, Thu, Fri & Sun, to 9pm Wed & Sat; Line 5 to Gwanghwamun, Exit 2) FREE The last century has been a tumultuous time for Korea, the key moments of which are memorialised and celebrated in this museum charting the highs and lows of that journey. The displays are modern, multilingual and engaging, as well as proof of how far the country has come in the decades since its almost total destruction during the Korean War. Bring ID if you'd like to use a free audio-tour guide in English.

Head to the roof garden for a great view of Gyeongbokgung and Gwanghwamun Sq.

SEOUL MUSEUM OF HISTORY MUSEUM
Map p232 (서울역사박물관; 02-724 0274; www.museum.seoul.kr; 55 Saemunan-ro; 9am-8pm Tue-Fri, to 7pm Sat & Sun, to 6pm Sat & Sun Nov-Feb; P; Line 5 to Gwanghwamun, Exit 7) FREE To gain an appreciation of the total transformation of Seoul down the centuries, visit this fascinating museum, which charts the city's history since the dawn of the Joseon dynasty. Outside is one of the old tram cars that used to run in the city in the 1930s, as well as a section of the old Gwanghwamun gate. Inside there's a massive scale model of the city you can walk around, plus donated exhibitions of crafts and photographs.

There may be charges for special exhibitions. Classical-music concerts are sometimes staged here.

NATIONAL CHILDREN'S MUSEUM MUSEUM
Map p232 (02-3704 4540; www.kidsnfm.go.kr; 137 Samcheong-ro; 9am-6pm Mar-May, Sep & Oct, to 6.30pm Jun-Aug, to 5pm Nov-Feb; ; Line 3 to Anguk, Exit 1) FREE Advance reservations are recommended for this interactive and guided museum for kids, as walk-in visitors are limited in number daily.

On Saturdays and Sundays from May to August, the museum stays open a little longer, to 7pm.

UNHYEONGUNG PALACE
Map p234 (운현궁, Cloud Hanging over the Valley Palace; 02-766 9090; www.unhyeongung.or.kr; 464 Samil-daero; 9am-7pm Tue-Sun Apr-Oct, to 6pm Tue-Sun Nov-Mar; Line 3 to Anguk, Exit 4) FREE This palace has a modest, natural-wood design reflecting the austere tastes of Heungseon Daewongun (1820–98), King Gojong's stern and conservative father. Rooms are furnished and mannequins display the dress styles of the time. It's also possible to try on *hanbok* (₩1000), and various artistic events are staged here throughout the year, including traditional music and dance concerts, usually on Friday at noon.

Heungseon Daewongun policies included massacring Korean Catholics, excluding foreigners from Korea, closing Confucian schools and rebuilding Gyeongbokgung (p58). Gojong was born and raised here until 1863, when he ascended the throne aged 12 with his father acting as regent.

GYEONGHUIGUNG PALACE
Map p232 (경희궁; Palace of Shining Celebration; 02-724 0274; 55 Saemunan-ro; 9am-6pm Tue-Sun; P; Line 5 to Gwanghwamun, Exit 1)

FREE The Palace of Shining Celebration, completed in 1623, used to consist of a warren of courtyards, buildings, walls and gates spread over a large area. But it was destroyed during the Japanese annexation and a Japanese school was established here. Only the main audience hall, **Sungjeongjeon**, and the smaller official hall behind it along with a few paved courtyards, walls and corridors have been restored.

The impressive entrance gate, **Heunghwamun**, has toured around Seoul, and was moved to its present site in 1988. To the left before you reach the palace buildings is the **SeMA Gyeonghuigung Museum of Art** (02-723 2491; http://sema.seoul.go.kr/global/eindex.jsp; 45 Saemunan-ro; 10am-6pm Tue-Sun) FREE hosting regularly changing art exhibitions of a variable quality and interest.

GWANGHWAMUN SQUARE SQUARE

Map p232 (광화문광장; Sejong-daero; S Line 5 to Gwanghwamun, Exit 4) This broad, elongated square provides a grand approach to Gyeongbokgung (p58) and is used for various events (as well as protests). Giant statues celebrate two national heroes: **Admiral Yi Sun-sin**, 1545–98, who stands atop a plinth at the square's southern end; and **King Sejong**, 1397–1450, who sits regally on a throne in the middle of the square. An entrance at the base of the King Sejong statue leads down to an **underground exhibition** (The Story of King Sejong; 10.30am-10pm Tue-Sun) FREE with sections on both the men.

King Sejong is revered as a scholar king of unmatched abilities. Admiral Yi Sun-sin designed new types of metal-clad warships called *geobukseon* (turtle boats), and used them to help achieve a series of stunning victories over the much larger Japanese navy that had attacked Korea at the end of the 16th century.

SEJONG GALLERY GALLERY

Map p232 (02-399 1111; www.sejongpac.or.kr; 175 Sejong-daero; 10am-5pm; S Line 5 to Gwanghwamun, Exit 8) FREE The regularly changing exhibitions at the gallery in the Sejong Center (p76), the largest cultural complex in Seoul, are generally worth a look for an insight into what's going on in the local contemporary-art scene. The sculpture garden behind the complex is also a pleasant place to hang out with some interesting pieces.

SAJIKDAN SHRINE

Map p232 (사직단; www.jongno.go.kr; Sajik Park, 89 Sajik-ro; 24hr; S Line 3 to Gyeongbokgung, Exit 5) FREE This impressive stone altar in a tranquil park surrounded by low stone walls and ornate wooden gates dates back to 1395 and King Taejo, founder of the Joseon dynasty. It was used to pray to the gods for good harvests. No access inside the altar.

CHEONGWADAE SARANGCHAE MUSEUM

Map p232 (청와대 사랑채; www.cwdsarangchae.kr; 45 Hyoja-ro 13-gil; 9am-6pm Tue-Sun; S Line 3 to Gyeongbokgung, Exit 4) FREE Much more interesting than the tour of Cheongwadae (p34) itself is this exhibition hall opposite the exit from the presidential compound. Inside are displays promoting Korea and Seoul as well as the work of past presidents and some of the gifts they have been given by international visitors. It's all very nicely put together and in one section you have a photo op with a digitised image of the president on Cheongwadae's front lawn.

There's also a pleasant cafe next to which **cooking classes** are run for overseas tourists (₩10,000, for groups of 10 or more); make a reservation through the website.

Insa-dong, Bukchon, Samcheong-dong & Ikseon-dong

CHANGDEOKGUNG PALACE

See p60.

BUKCHON HANOK VILLAGE AREA

See p61.

JONGMYO SHRINE

See p62.

JOGYE-SA TEMPLE

See p63.

ARARIO MUSEUM IN SPACE MUSEUM

Map p230 (02-736 5700; www.arariomuseum.org; 83 Yulgok-ro; adult/youth/child ₩15,000/9000/6000; 10am-7pm Tue-Sun; S Line 3 to Anguk, Exit 3) Korean business magnate and contemporary-art collector Kam Chang-il has found the perfect home for jewels from his collection at this ivy-clad brick building that's considered a seminal piece of early-1970s architecture. The building's

GALLERIES GALORE

Seoul's eclectic contemporary-art scene is clustered either side of Gyeongbukgong, in Samcheong-dong, Tongui-dong and Insa-dong. The many commercial galleries here put on regularly changing shows of both local and international artists, which unless otherwise mentioned are free to browse. Useful resources include the free monthly art magazine *ArtnMap* (www.artnmap.com) and *Seoul Art Guide* (in Korean).

Samcheong-dong

Kukje (Map p230; ☎02-735 8449; www.kukjegallery.com; 54 Samcheong-ro; ⊙10am-6pm Mon-Sat, to 5pm Sun; S Line 3 to Anguk, Exit 1) Kukje's two main gallery spaces are found off the main road, behind its restaurant building, which has the running woman sculpture by Jonathan Borofsky on its roof. It's a leading venue for international artists to exhibit, with Damien Hirst, Anish Kapoor and Bill Viola all having had shows here. Admission varies.

Artsonje Center (Map p230; ☎02-733 8949; www.artsonje.org; 87 Yulgok-ro 3-gil; adult/child ₩3000/1000; ⊙noon-7pm Tue-Sun; S Line 3 to Anguk, Exit 1) Founded in 1998, Artsonje supports experimental art, runs workshops and has lectures as well as an annual Open Call for new works. Also here is a cafe and arthouse cinema. It is also the Seoul outpost for the fascinating **Real DMZ Project** (www.realdmz.org), an annual show with artworks based on research carried out in the DMZ.

Gallery Hyundai (Map p230; ☎02-287 3500; www.galleryhyundai.com; 8 Samcheong-ro; ⊙10am-6pm Tue-Sun; S Line 3 to Anguk, Exit 1) The trailblazer for Korea's contemporary commercial-gallery scene, Hyundai has been going strong since 1970 and represents some of the giants of the scene including Lee Joong-seop and Paik Nam June. As well as this exhibition space it has another branch nearby at 14 Samcheong-ro.

Hakgojae (Map p230; ☎02-720 1524; www.hakgojae.com; 50 Samcheong-ro; ⊙10am-7pm Tue-Sat, to 6pm Sun; S Line 3 to Anguk, Exit 1) This elegant gallery is easily spotted by the robot sculpture on the roof of its modern section. Entry is via the converted *hanok* building, which neatly symbolises the gallery's aim 'to review the old to learn the new'.

Tongui-dong

Jean Art Gallery (Map p232; ☎02-738 7570; www.jeanart.net; 25 Hyoja-ro; ⊙10am-6pm Tue-Fri, to 5pm Sat & Sun; S Line 3 to Gyeongbokgung, Exit 3 or 4) Pioneer of the Tongui-dong gallery scene and specialising in representing contemporary Korean and Japanese artists, such as Naru Yoshitomo and Yayoi Kusama: one of Yayoi's 2m-tall dotted pumpkin sculptures stands in a courtyard outside one of the gallery's buildings.

Artside (Map p232; ☎02-725 1020; www.artside.org; 15 Jahamun-ro 6-gil; ⊙10am-6pm Tue-Sun; S Line 3 to Gyeongbokgung, Exit 3 or 4) Since 1999, Artside has taken a leading role in artistic exchange between Korea and China by regularly staging exhibits by contemporary Chinese artists such as Zhang Xiaogang.

Gallery Simon (갤러리 시몬; Map p232; ☎02-549 3031; http://gallerysimon.com; 20 Jahamun-ro 6-gil; ⊙10am-6.30pm Tue-Sun; S Line 3 to Gyeongbokgung, Exit 3 or 4) Exhibitions include sculptures and interesting installations. Has a chic top-floor cafe with views over *hanok* roofs.

Ryugaheon (류가헌; Map p232; ☎02-720 2010; www.ryugaheon.com; 10-3 Hyoja-ro 7-gil; ⊙11am-6pm Tue-Sun; S Line 3 to Gyeongbokgung, Exit 5) Based in a restored *hanok*, Ryugaheon specialises in photography exhibitions, but you may also see other types of art here such as canvases of embroidered flowers. There are two display spaces and a small library of art books you're welcome to browse.

Insa-dong

Sun Art Center (Map p234; ☎02-734 0458; www.sungallery.co.kr; 8 Insa-dong 5-gil; ⊙10am-6pm Tue-Sun; S Line 3 to Anguk, Exit 6) One of Seoul's longest running commercial-art galleries, in business since 1977, Sun Art specialises in early-20th-century Korean art and awards an annual prize to the most promising local artist.

Neighbourhood Walk Bukchon Views

START ANGUK STATION, EXIT 3
END ANGUK STATION, EXIT 1
LENGTH 3KM; TWO HOURS

Take in views across Bukchon's tiled *hanok* (traditional wooden homes) roofs on this walk around the area between Gyeongbokgung and Changdeokgung. This walk is best done in the early morning or early evening (or even on a moonlit night) to avoid the daytime crowds.

From the Anguk station subway exit turn left at the first junction and walk 200m to **1 Bukchon Traditional Culture Center** (p61), where you can learn about the area's architecture. Continue to head north up Gyedong-gil, an attractive street lined with cafes, boutiques and *hanok* guesthouses; at the T-junction at the top of the hill is the entrance to **2 Choong Ang High School**, an attractive early-20th-century educational complex that featured as a location in the hit Korean TV drama *Winter Sonata*.

Wind your way back downhill from here past the **3 Gahoe Minhwa Workshop** (p61) and the **4 Dong-Lim Knot Workshop** (p78) to emerge on the major road Bukchon-ro. Cross over and locate the start of **5 Bukchon-ro 11-gil**; follow this narrow street uphill towards the parallel set of picturesque streets lined with *hanok* in Gahoe-dong. To see inside one of the *hanok* pause at **6 Simsimheon** (p69).

Turn left and go a few blocks west towards the chimney stack to Bukchon-ro 5na-gil; to the right is a **7 viewing spot** across Samcheong-dong. Head south down the hill, perhaps pausing for tea at **8 Cha Masineun Tteul** (p74).

Carry on downhill and turn left after the **9 World Jewellery Museum** and then right at the junction. On the corner by a tourist information booth, walk up to **10 Jeongdok Public Library**; the small, quiet park in front of the building is a prime spot for viewing cherry blossoms in spring and the yellowing leaves of ginkgo trees in autumn.

Return to the subway station via Yunposeon-gil.

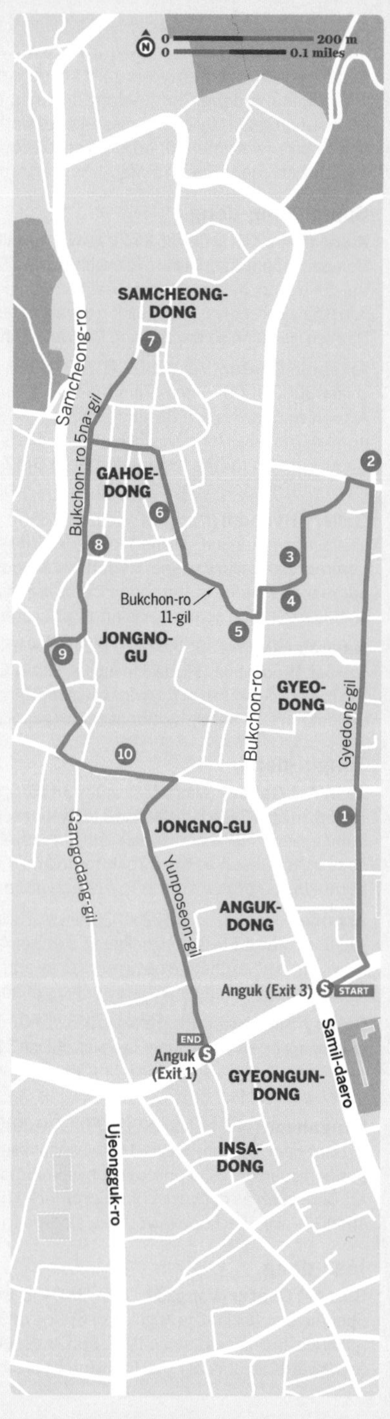

compact, low-ceilinged rooms and labyrinthine layout fit the conceptual pieces like a glove, including works by Nam June Paik, Koo Kang, Lee Ufan, Tracey Emin, Damien Hirst and Sam Taylor-Johnson – you never know what artistic wonder lies around the next corner.

Also part of the building are a *hanok* and a five-storey glass annexe (added in 1997) – both are used as cafes and restaurants.

MMCA SEOUL MUSEUM

Map p230 (☎02-3701 9500; www.mmca.go.kr; 30 Samcheong-ro; ₩4000, last Wed of month free; ⏲10am-6pm Tue-Thu, to 9pm Fri & Sat; ⓈLine 3 to Anguk, Exit 1) Combining architectural elements from several centuries of Seoul's history, this branch of the city's premier contemporary-art museum is an impressive melding of spacious gallery buildings with the art deco buildings of the former Defense Security Command compound. The MMCA tries to stay contemporary, with new modes of presenting pieces in a space that includes a gallery theatre and multipurpose hall.

In a garden to the rear of the main gallery buildings you'll find **Jongchinbu**, the office of royal genealogy during the Joseon dynasty, restored to its original site after a spell spent up the road next to Jeongdok Library. This traditional structure is a nice contrast to Park Ki Won's *Flash Wall*, a set of wire-wool candy-floss gateways also in the garden.

A free shuttle bus runs four times a day between the other branches of the MCCA in Gwacheon and Deoksugung.

TTEOK & KITCHEN UTENSIL MUSEUM MUSEUM

Map p234 (떡박물관; ☎02-741 5447; www.tkmuseum.or.kr; 71 Donhwamun-ro; adult/youth ₩3000/2000; ⏲10am-6pm; ⓈLine 1, 3 or 5 to Jongno 3-ga, Exit 6) For those interested in the local sweet culture, this two-room museum at the Institute of Traditional Korean Food offers displays of rice cakes in different colours, flavourings, shapes and sizes, plus the utensils to make them. Reserve two days in advance for '*Tteok* Experience' (₩20,000) tasting plates. *Tteok*-making classes also available.

STONE PAGODA OF WONGAK-SA MONUMENT

Map p234 (원각사지십층석탑; 99 Jong-ro, Jongno-gu; ⓈLine 1, 3 or 5 to Jongno 3-ga, Exit 1 or 5) FREE This 10-tier, 12m-high monument in Tapgol Park once graced Wongak-sa, a Buddhist temple that stood here but was destroyed in 1504 on the orders of the Confucian king. Buddhists were forced out of the cities into the mountains, where most of Korea's great temples still stand today. The pagoda, encased in a glass box, is decorated with wonderful carvings.

SIMSIMHEON ARCHITECTURE

Map p230 (심심헌; ☎02-763 3393; www.simsimheon.com; 47 Bukchon-ro 11-gil; ₩15,000; ⏲9am-6.30pm Mon-Sat; ⓈLine 3 to Anguk, Exit 2) This modern *hanok* was rebuilt using traditional methods on the site of two older ones to create a home with museum grandeur that gives a rare opportunity to see inside a (splendid) residential property in the heart of Bukchon. Entry includes tea, which is sipped overlooking the internal garden. The private body National Trust of Korea manages Simsimheon, meaning 'House Where the Heart is Found'. Reservations required.

TAPGOL PARK PARK

Map p234 (탑골 공원; 99 Jong-ro; ⏲6am-8pm; ⓈLine 1 or 5 to Jongno 3-ga, Exit 1 or 5) FREE Seoul's first modern-style park, opened in 1897, stands on the precincts of Wongak-sa, a Buddhist temple destroyed in 1504. Left behind was its remarkable 10-tier, 12m-high marble pagoda, which today is encased in a glass box at the rear of the park. Decorated with highly detailed carvings it's a beautiful and rare piece of art.

The park is also a symbol of Korean resistance to Japanese rule. Ten murals on the wall behind the pagoda depict scenes from the heroic but unsuccessful struggle of the Samil (1 March) Movement against Japanese colonisation in the early 20th century.

On 1 March 1919, Son Byeong-hui and 32 others signed and read aloud a Declaration of Independence (a copy in English can be read on the memorial plaque). All were arrested and locked up in the notorious Seodaemun Prison. A torrent of protest against Japan followed in Seoul and throughout Korea, but the Samil Movement was ruthlessly suppressed. Hundreds of independence fighters were killed and thousands arrested.

CHOONG ANG HIGH SCHOOL ARCHITECTURE

Map p230 (중앙고등학교; 164 Changdeokgung-gil; ⓈLine 3 to Anguk, Exit 3) FREE The Gothic-style early-20th-century buildings of this campus are recognised as part of Seoul's built cultural heritage and provide a nice contrast with the surrounding traditional *hanok* architecture of Bukchon. It was used as a location in the hit Korean TV drama *Winter Sonata*.

CHEONDOGYO TEMPLE TEMPLE

Map p234 (천도교 중앙대교당; ☎02-732 3956; www.chondogyo.or.kr; 11-4 Insa-dong 10-gil; ⏲9am-6pm; Ⓢ Line 3 to Anguk, Exit 6) Cheondogyo means 'Religion of the Heavenly Way', and this temple is the hall of worship for a home-grown faith containing Buddhist, Confucian and Christian elements that gathered momentum in the 1860s. Designed by a Japanese architect and completed in 1921, this is a handsome baroque-style, red-brick and stone building with a tower. Inside, the wood panelling, lines of chairs and plain decoration create an impression of a lecture theatre, although there are stained-glass windows.

BOSINGAK TOWER

Map p234 (보신각; ☎02-2148 1825; 54 Jong-ro; ⏲24hr; Ⓢ Line 1 to Jonggak, Exit 4) FREE Contrasting with the modern **Jongno Tower** (종로 타워; Map p234; 51 Jung-ro; Ⓢ Line 1, 3 or 5 to Jonggak, Exit 3) opposite, this ornate pavilion houses a recent copy of the city bell – the original, forged in 1468, is in the garden of the National Museum of Korea. Costumed guardsmen patrol around the bell and ring it 12 times at noon (the ceremony runs from 11.20am to 12.20pm Tuesday to Sunday).

EATING

The small laneways of Ikseon-dong are lined with *hanok* converted into hip restaurants and casual cafes; Insa-dong has grander *hanok* restaurant conversions aimed at tourists, as well as dumpling joints and street food. The Bukchon area has European and fast-food choices aimed at visitors resting between the traditional houses and the palaces.

Gwanghwamun & Around

ROGPA TEA STALL VEGETARIAN $

Map p232 (사직동 그 가게; ☎070-4045 6331; www.rogpa.com; 18-1 Sajik-ro 9-gil; mains ₩7000-11,000; ⏲noon-8pm Tue-Sun; ; Ⓢ Line 3 to Gyeongbokgung, Exit 1) You'll feel whisked to the Himalayas at this charming fair-trade cafe that raises awareness about Tibet (Rogpa is Tibetan for 'friend and helper'). Everything is freshly made, beautifully presented and rather delicious. All but the chicken curry are vegetarian. Dig into a tofu curry followed by a sweet *dosa* (crispy lentil pancake) and soy-milk chai.

It also runs the shop next door, selling handicrafts made by Tibetans exiled in India.

GWANGHWAMUN JIP KOREAN $

Map p232 (광화문집; ☎02-739 7737; 12 Saemunan-ro 5-gil; kimchi stew ₩7000; ⏲9am-10pm; ; Ⓢ Line 5 to Gwanghwamun, Exit 8) Following the same recipe since the 1980s, Gwanghwamun Jip is one of the most famous kimchi *jiggae* (stew) restaurants in South Korea. The homey interior is cramped but the food is truly fabulous. Its stew perfectly combines fermented kimchi with fatty pork for a spicy, refreshing taste. For an extra ₩5000, add a large rolled omelette on the side.

CHOSUN GIMBAP KOREAN $

Map p230 (조선김밥; ☎02-723 7496; 68 Yulgok-ro 3-gil; gimbap from ₩4500; ⏲11am-2.30pm & 3.30-8pm; ; Ⓢ Line 3 to Anguk, Exit 1) Right behind the National Museum of Modern and Contemporary Art, Chosun Gimbap is a rare cheap eat in the area. Its signature dish, the *chosun gimbap,* is packed with freshly prepared Korean root vegetables and feels more like a proper meal than most other *gimbap* (seaweed rice rolls). The space is small, so be prepared to wait to be seated.

TONGIN MARKET BOX LUNCH CAFE KOREAN $

Map p232 (통인시장; www.tonginmarket.co.kr; 18 Jahamun-ro 15-gl; meals ₩5000; ⏲11am-4pm Tue-Sun; Ⓢ Line 3 to Gyeongbokgung, Exit 2) For a fun lunch, buy 10 brass coins (₩5000) at the cafe about halfway along this old-school covered market. You'll be given a plastic tray with which you can then go shopping in the market. Exchange your coins for dishes such as savoury pancakes, *gimbap* (seaweed covered rice rolls) and *tteokbokki* (spicy rice-cake stew).

You can buy more coins, if needed, and use them (or cash) to pay for rice and soup (₩1000 each, kimchi is free) back at the cafe.

TOSOKCHON KOREAN **$$**

Map p232 (토속촌; ☎02-737 7444; http://tosokchon.com; 5 Jahamun-ro 5-gil; mains ₩16,000-24,000; ⏲10am-10pm; Ⓢ Line 3 to Gyeongbokgung, Exit 2) Spread over a series of *hanok,* Tosokchon is so famous for its *samgyetang* (ginseng chicken soup) that there is always a long queue waiting to get in, particularly at weekends. Try the black chicken version, which uses the silkie breed with naturally black flesh and bones.

EURO GOURMET DELI **$$**

Map p232 (www.eurogourmet.co.kr; 23 Tongui-dong, Jongno-gu; mains ₩15,000-22,000; ⏲10am-10pm; 📶; Ⓢ Line 3 to Gyeongbokgung, Exit 3) Delightful Euro-style deli-cafe specialising in sandwiches, pasta and baguette-style pizza made with premium ingredients, such as camembert and rocket panini or gorgonzola eggplant bake.

GWANGHWAMUN DDUCKAM KOREAN **$$**

Map p232 (광화문 뚝감; ☎02-722 5894; 21 Saemunan-ro 3-gil, Dangju-dong; gamjatang ₩24,000-40,000, dduckam ₩8000; ⏲24hr; ❄; Ⓢ Line 5 to Gwanghwamun, Exit 1) One of the best *gamjatang* (pork-bone soup) joints in Seoul, this 24-hour restaurant bustles with office workers at lunch. Its version of the spicy, bubbling stew has soft, tender pork that falls off the bone and is topped with perilla leaves. For a single serving in a stone pot, order the *dduckam* (뚝감).

SONG'S KITCHEN KOREAN **$$**

Map p232 (☎02-725 1713; 35-3 Pirundae-ro; mains ₩10,000-25,000; ⏲11.30am-2.30pm & 4.30-10pm Tue-Sun; Ⓢ Line 3 to Gyeongbokgung, Exit 2) In an artfully styled *hanok,* interesting dishes to share are offered (such as *tteokbokki* served in a carved-out squash), alongside western cuisine including pizza and fried-rice-filled omelettes. There's a good wine and drinks list, making it a pleasant spot to linger in the evening.

GASTROTONG SWISS, EUROPEAN **$$$**

Map p232 (가스트로통; ☎02-730 4162; www.gastrotong.com; 10 Jahamun-ro 8-gil; set course lunch/dinner from ₩30,000/50,000; ⏲11.30am-3pm & 5.30-10.30pm; 📶; Ⓢ Line 3 to Gyeongbokgung, Exit 3) Swiss-German chef Roland Hinni and his wife Yong-Shin run this charming gourmet restaurant that blends sophistication with traditional European cooking. The set lunches are splendid deals, including appetiser, soup or salad, dessert and drinks as well as a wide choice of main courses. It's small, so booking is essential.

HANMIRI KOREAN **$$$**

Map p232 (한미리; ☎02-757 5707; www.hanmiri.co.kr; 2nd fl, Premier Place, 8 Cheonggyecheon-ro; lunch/dinner from ₩34,000/56,000; ⏲11.30am-3pm & 6-9.30pm; Ⓢ Line 5 to Gwanghwamun, Exit 5) Sit on chairs at tables for this modern take on royal cuisine as you work your way through multiple dishes such as *yukhoe* (Korean steak tartare) and *kujolpan* (nine-dish crêpe wraps); book a table with windows overlooking the Cheonggye-cheon. It's gourmet, foreigner-friendly and a popular spot for business lunches and family visitors. There's another branch in Gangnam.

OGAWA JAPANESE **$$$**

Map p232 (오가와; ☎02-735 1001; 19 Saemunan-ro 5-gil; set menu lunch/dinner ₩50,000/70,000; ⏲noon-2.30pm & 6-10.30pm Mon-Fri; Ⓢ Line 5 to Gwanghwamun, Exit 1) In the basement of the Royal Building, Ogawa's expert chefs craft sushi and sashimi, piece by piece, and serve it directly over the kitchen counter – in the best Japanese style, although still with Korean twists. Extra dishes, such as udon and abalone porridge, mean you certainly won't leave hungry. Booking is essential as space is limited.

Insa-dong, Bukchon, Samcheong-dong & Ikseon-dong

★KOONG DUMPLINGS **$**

Map p234 (궁; ☎02-733 9240; www.koong.co.kr; 11-3 Insa-dong 10-gil; dumplings ₩11,000-14,000; ⏲11.30am-9.30pm; Ⓢ Line 3 to Anguk, Exit 6) Koong's traditional Kaeseong-style dumplings are legendary and more than a mouthful. Only order one portion, unless you're super hungry, or enjoy them in a flavourful soup along with chewy balls of rice cake. In summer the *pyeonsu* (flower-shaped zucchini-and-leek stuffed dumplings) are a lighter option.

SEOURESEO DULJJAERO JALHANEUNJIP DESSERTS **$**

Map p230 (서울서둘째로잘하는집; ☎02-734 5302; 122-1 Samcheong-ro; desserts ₩5000; ⏲11am-9pm Tue-Sun; Ⓢ Line 3 to Anguk, Exit 1)

Little has changed at 'Second Best Place in Seoul', a tiny tea and dessert cafe, since it opened in 1976. Apart from the medicinal teas, it serves wonderful thick *danpatjuk*, red-bean porridge with ginseng, chestnut and peanuts.

CHANG HWA DANG DUMPLINGS $

Map p234 (창화당; ☎070-8825 0908; www.changhwadang.com; 23 Supyo-ro 28-gil; dumplings ₩10,000; ⏰11.30am-2.30pm & 4-9.30pm Mon-Fri, 11.30am-9.30pm Sat & Sun; ; Ⓢ Line 1, 3 or 5 to Jongno 3-ga, Exit 4) Crowds come to Ikseon-dong to be transported to old Seoul, and half of them seem to queue at Chang Hwa Dang, where the furniture and decor hark to a lost Korea of the 1980s. Four types of fried *mandu* (Korean-style dumplings) come on a mixed plate. The charcoal-meat dumplings are the most flavourful and pair well with the house *tteokbokki* (rice cakes in a sweet and spicy sauce).

From the subway exit, head down the opposite laneway into Ikseon-dong and take the first right.

GOGUNG KOREAN $

Map p234 (고궁; ☎02-736 3211; www.gogung.co.kr; 44 Insa-dong-gil; meals from ₩8000; ⏰11am-10pm; Ⓢ Line 3 to Anguk, Exit 6) In the basement of Ssamziegil (p77) is this smart and stylish restaurant, specialising in Jeonju (capital of Jeollabuk province) bibimbap, which is fresh and garnished with nuts, but contains raw minced beef. The *dolsot* bibimbap is served in a stone hotpot. Both come with side dishes. Also try the *moju*, a sweet, cinnamon homebrew drink.

JIRISAN KOREAN $

Map p234 (지리산; ☎02-723 4696; 30 Insa-dong 14-gil; mains from ₩10,000; ⏰noon-10pm; Ⓢ Line 3 to Anguk, Exit 6) A great place to try *dolsotbap* (hotpot rice) in an authentic *hanok* atmosphere in Insa-dong. Various ingredients are added to the rice, and you mix it all up in a separate bowl with the sauces and side dishes – a do-it-yourself bibimbap.

Pour the weak burnt-rice tea from the kettle into the stone pot and put the lid on, then drink it at the end of the meal.

OSEGYEHYANG VEGAN $

Map p234 (오세계향; ☎02-735 7171; www.go5.co.kr; 14-5 Insa-dong 12-gil; meals from ₩7000; ⏰noon-3pm & 4.30-9pm; ; Ⓢ Line 3 to Anguk, Exit 6) Run by members of a Taiwanese religious sect. Sit cross-legged for vegan food that combines all sorts of mixtures and flavours. The barbecue-meat-substitute dish is flavoursome.

★IKSEON DIMIBANG EUROPEAN $$

Map p234 (익선디미방; ☎02-747 3418; www.instagr.am/ikseon_dimibang; 17-27 Supyo-ro 28-gil; set lunch ₩18,000, mains ₩18,000-26,000; ⏰noon-3pm & 5-10pm; Ⓢ Line 1, 3 or 5 to Jongno 3-ga, Exit 4) The converted *hanok* that houses this chic bistro in the revamped old neighbourhood of Ikseon-dong is obviously Korean, but the dishes are contemporary European. Excellent scorched prawn risotto is served on bright metal plates to match the sleek copper furniture. Fusion touches are seen in seafood pasta with chillis from Cheongyang. Good-value weekday set lunches include a main, salad and drink.

From the subway exit, walk north into the opposite street into Ikseon-dong to the end. Look for its logo – a silhouette of a man in a tall hat.

NEWIJO KOREAN $$

Map p234 (뉘조; ☎02-730 9310; www.newijo.com; 27 Insa-dong 14-gil; set lunch/dinner from ₩18,000/27,500; ⏰11am-10pm; ; Ⓢ Line 3 to Anguk, Exit 6) Traditional *jeonsik* meals that tend towards vegetarian Buddhist-style cuisine are served on rustic pottery in this *hanok*. The food is fresh and has a pleasing mixture of textures.

DEJANGJANGI HWADEOGPIJAJIP PIZZA $$

Map p230 (대장장이 화덕피자집; ☎02-765 4298; 42-4 Bukchon-ro; pizza ₩14,000-24,000; ⏰11.30am-9.30pm; ; Ⓢ Line 3 to Anguk, Exit 2) *Daijangjangi* means 'blacksmith', and that is exactly what the owner Lee Jae-Sung is. Some of his metal creations adorn the quirky interior of this *hanok* turned pizzeria. The pizza is authentic and the service friendly.

WOOD AND BRICK BAKERY $$

Map p230 (02-747 1592; www.woodnbrick.com; 14 Bukchon-ro 5-gil; baked goods ₩5000-10,000, mains ₩19,000-40,000; cafe 8am-10pm; Line 3 to Anguk, Exit 2) The terrace seating at this combined bakery, cafe and restaurant is a great spot from which to watch the comings and goings of Bukchon. Its baked goods, sandwiches and European-deli-style eats are top-notch.

★BALWOO GONGYANG VEGETARIAN $$$

Map p234 (발우공양; 02-2031 2081; http://eng.balwoo.or.kr; 5th fl, Templestay Information Center, 56 Ujeongguk-ro; set lunch ₩30,000, dinner ₩45,000-95,000; 11.40am-3pm & 6-8.50pm; ; Line 3 to Anguk, Exit 6) Reserve three days in advance for the fine temple-style cuisine served here. Take your time to fully savour the subtle flavours and different textures of the vegetarian dishes, which range from rice porridge and delicate salads to dumplings and fried shiitake mushrooms and mugwort in a sweet-and-sour sauce.

For less fancy vegetarian food **Balwoo Gongyang Kong** on the building's 2nd floor offers a buffet (₩9000), or simple noodle and rice dishes for around ₩4000.

DRINKING & NIGHTLIFE

Teahouses can be found in Insa-dong and Bukchon Hanok Village. Ikseong-dong and surrounds have small hip bars, craft-beer pubs and intimate, friendly gay bars. This area is not really home to clubs.

Gwanghwamun & Around

★COBBLER COCKTAIL BAR

Map p232 (코블러; 02-733 6421; www.facebook.com/BarCobbler; 16 Sajik-ro 12-gil; drinks from ₩20,000; 7pm-3am Mon-Sat; ; Line 3 to Gyeongbukgung, Exit 7) This high-end bar is located inside a *hanok* within a nest of lonesome alleyways. Owned by Robin Yoo (a pioneer in Korea's cocktail scene), it has no menu; instead, the bartender recommends some excellent cocktails, such as gin sour with lavender notes, or something from a wide range of whiskies. Everybody is given a piece of cobbler pie upon entrance.

A well-known name thanks to his first Hongdae bar, Robin's Square, Yoo renovated a broken-down *hanok*, piecing together Cobbler's interior one stick of vintage furniture at a time.

DAEO SOCHOM CAFE

Map p232 (대오서점; 010 570 1349; 55 Jahamun-ro 7-gil, Jongno-gu; 11am-10pm Tue-Sun; Line 3 to Gyeongbokgung, Exit 2) Opened as a bookstore in 1951 by Mrs Kwong and her husband Mr Cho, this charming, ramshackle cafe is still run by the same family and oozes bygone-days atmosphere with lots of memorabilia and quirky decor. Entry is ₩5000, which includes a choice of drink.

The vintage cafe gained some modern fame by the 2016 visit of lead singer RM of K-Pop group BTS.

MK2 CAFE

Map p232 (02-730 6420; 17 Jahamun-ro 10-gil; noon-10pm; ; Line 3 to Gyeongbokgung, Exit 5) The name indicates the style of this cafe, which is tastefully furnished with mid-century modern pieces. It's a good pit stop for coffee and snacks while exploring Seochon.

Insa-dong, Bukchon, Samcheong-dong & Ikseon-dong

★SIK MOOL BAR

Map p234 (식물, Plant Cafe; 02-747 4858; www.fb.me/plantcafebar; 46-1 Donhwamun-ro 11da-gil; 11am-midnight Sun-Thu, to 1am Fri & Sat; Line 1, 3 or 5 to Jongno 3-ga, Exit 6) Four *hanok* were creatively combined to create this chic designer cafe-bar that blends old and new Seoul. Clay-tile walls, Soviet-era propaganda posters, mismatched modern furniture and

LOCAL KNOWLEDGE

NAGWON-DONG & DONUI-DONG GAY BARS

Itaewon's 'Homo Hill' is not the only place in Seoul with gay bars. Far more popular with Korean *iban* (the local word for gays) no longer in their 20s are the scores of LGBTIQ+-run bars around Jongno 3-ga subway station. However, not all are welcoming of foreigners, and others will expect patrons to pay a hefty cover charge for *anju* (snacks).

Alternatively, the outdoor *pojangmacha* food stalls east of the Nakwon Musical Instruments Arcade, where you can sink cheap bear, *soju* (local vodka) and snacks, are prime hang-outs for the gay community.

'One-shot bars' are places where you can drink without a cover charge.

contemporary art surround a young crowd sipping cocktails, coffee and wine and nibbling on house-made pizza. Sik Mool and its creator, fashion photographer Louis Park, are often credited as spearheading Ikseon-dong's popularity.

★DAWON TEAHOUSE

Map p234 (다원; ☎02-730 6305; 11-4 Insa-dong 10-gil; teas ₩7000; ⏰11am-9.50pm; Ⓢ Line 3 to Anguk, Exit 6) The perfect place to unwind under the shady fruit trees in a courtyard with flickering candles. In colder weather sit indoors in *hanok* rooms decorated with scribbles or in the garden pavilion. The teas are superb, especially *omijacha hwachae* (fruit and five-flavour berry punch), a summer drink.

Small exhibition spaces surround the courtyard.

★CHA MASINEUN TTEUL TEAHOUSE

Map p230 (차마시는뜰; ☎02-722-7006; 26 Bukchon-ro 11na-gil; ⏰10am-10.30pm; Ⓢ Line 3 to Anguk, Exit 1) In the Bukchon Hanok Village area overlooking Samcheong-dong and Gwanghwamun is this lovely *hanok* with low tables arranged around a courtyard. It serves traditional teas, and a delicious bright-yellow pumpkin rice cake fresh from the steamer.

BARCODE GAY

Map p234 (☎02-3672 0940; 41-1 Donhwamun-ro; ⏰7pm-4am; Ⓢ Line 1, 3 or 5 to Jongno 3-ga, Exit 3) Run by friendly English-speaking Kim Hyoung-Jin, this stylish one-shot bar is on the 2nd floor – look for the English sign as you come out of the subway.

ALEDANG CRAFT BEER

Map p234 (에일당; ☎070-7766 3133; www.instagr.am/alepub; 33-9 Supyo-ro 28-gil, Ikseon-dong; beer ₩6800-15,000; ⏰noon-11pm; Ⓢ Line 1,3 or 5 to Jongno 3-ga, Exit 4) The courtyard of this converted *hanok* in Ikseon-dong makes the craft beers here extra special. A four-beer sampler includes citrusy light Punk IPA, and brews by Seoul's Magpie Brewing. There's also pizza, coffee, classic rock and even a disco ball.

BREW 3.14 BAR

Map p234 (☎070-4178 3014; www.facebook.com/brew314; 39 Donhwamun-ro 11-gil; ⏰4pm-midnight; Ⓢ Line 1, 3 or 5 to Jongno 3-ga, Exit 6) Along with sibling operation Brew 3.15 across the road, Brew 3.14 has carved a name for itself with its great selection of local craft beers, delicious pizza (which it calls by the American name 'pie') and moreish fried chicken. Both bars are quiet, convivial places to hang out over pints and eats.

MADANG FLOWER CAFE TEA GARDEN

Map p234 (마당플라워카페; ☎02-743 0724; 33-12 Supyo-ro 28-gil; ⏰7.30am-11pm; 📶; Ⓢ Line 1, 3 or 5 to Jongno 3-ga, Exit 4) Perhaps the most photographed spot in Ikseon-dong, and with a fantasyland of exuberant blooms and cutesy gardenware in every space of this converted corner *hanok*, it's easy to see why. Having coffee, tea or brunch (bagels, pasta) in the white-cloth-covered (for soft lighting, of course) courtyard is akin to a chic picnic.

COMICS SHOP CAFE

Map p234 (만홧가게; ☎02-741 1339; 33-7 Supyo-ro 28-gil; ₩2000 to sit, ₩500 for every 10 minutes, coffee ₩4500; ⏰11am-11pm; 📶👪; Ⓢ Line 1, 3 or 5 to Jongno 3-ga, Exit 4) A modern-style *manhwa-bang* (comic-book cafe) in a renovated *hanok*, Comics Shop lets you explore its library in a private capsule, including everything from old-school Japanese manga to copies of *Mad* magazine. Though there are only a few English-language titles and you have to pay for the space, it's a great sneak peek into local culture.

CAFFE THEMSELVES CAFE

Map p234 (www.caffethemselves.com; 388 Samil-daero; coffee ₩5500; ⏲10am-11pm; 📶; Ⓢ Line 1 to Jonggak, Exit 12) A worthy stop for those who take their coffee seriously. Baristas here know how to do a decent single-origin espresso, slow drip or cold brew. They roast their own beans, which they sell by the bag, as well as having ready-made samples to try.

TEA THERAPY TEAHOUSE

Map p230 (☎02-730 7507; http://teatherapy.com; 74 Yunposun-gil; ⏲10am-10pm; 📶; Ⓢ Line 3 to Anguk, Exit 2) Teas and herbal infusions for whatever ails you. Ask for the handy chart in English to aid you in your selection from the wide range of concoctions available (also sold packaged to take away). It's a retro-stylish kind of place with free foot baths outside the front door.

BLUE STAR PUB BAR

Map p234 (푸른별 주막; ☎02-734 3095; 17-1 Insa-dong 16-gil; ⏲3pm-midnight; Ⓢ Line 3 to Anguk, Exit 6) Owned by a stage actor, this rustic hang-out, plastered with posters, is an atmospheric place to sample *makgeolli* (rice wine) served out of brass kettles into brass bowls. Flavours include mulberry leaf, green tea and taro. Order slices of its homemade organic tofu and kimchi to eat as you drink.

From the subway exit, it's down the first laneway.

BAEKSEJU-MAEUL BAR

Map p234 (백세주마을; ☎02-720 0055; www.ksdb.co.kr; 10 Ujeongguk-ro 2-gil; ⏲5pm-1am; Ⓢ Line 2 to Jonggak, Exit 4) There is an excellent range of traditional rice wines available at this drinking and dining outlet for brewer Kooksoondang; see the website for full descriptions. From the floor seating area there's a dress-circle view of the Bosingak pavilion.

KOPI BANGASGAN CAFE

Map p230 (커피 방앗간; ☎02-732 7656; 8-11 Bukchon-ro 5ga-gil; coffee ₩4500; ⏲8.30am-10pm; Ⓢ Line 3 to Anguk, Exit 1) Based in a *hanok*, 'Coffee Mill' is a charming spot decorated with retro pieces and the quirky, colourful artworks of owner Lee Gyeong-hwan, whom you're likely to spot painting at the counter. Apart from various coffees it also serves waffles.

SHORTBUS GAY

Map p234 (☎02-741 0036; http://korea-shortbus.wix.com/shortbus; 3rd fl, 45 Donhwamun-ro; ⏲7.30pm-5am; Ⓢ Line 1, 3 or 5 to Jongno 3-ga, Exit 3) This wine-and-cocktail, one-shot bar is appealing and spacious, and the English-speaking bartenders mix a mean mojito. The homely atmosphere and diva classics attract an older gay clientele. Look up for an English sign.

ENTERTAINMENT

INSA-DONG OUTDOOR STAGE TRADITIONAL MUSIC

Map p234 (Naminsa Madang; 63-2 Insa-dong, Jongro-gu; ⏲performances 11.30am-12.40pm, 1-3pm & 3-5pm Sat; 👪) FREE This outdoor plaza at the southern entrance to Insa-dong-gil hosts interesting traditional music and dance performances every Saturday. It's on the corner adjacent to the South Insadong Tourist Information Center.

CINEMATHEQUE CINEMA

Map p234 (Seoul Arts Cinema; ☎02-741 9782; www.cinematheque.seoul.kr; 4th fl, Nagwon Arcade, 428, Samil-daero; tickets ₩6000; Ⓢ Line 1, 3 or 5 to Jongno 3-ga, Exit 5) Catch independent and foreign films (with subtitles in Korean) at this arts cinema where you'll also find Hollywood golden oldies screening at the Silver Cinema. Some Korean films may have English subtitles but it's best to check first. Various film festivals and retrospectives are held here including the Korea Queer Film Festival in June.

MUSICAL CHEF PERFORMING ARTS

Map p234 (☎02-766 0815; www.musicalchef.net; CineCore Building B2, 386 Samil-daero; tickets ₩40,000-60,000; ⏲8pm Mon, 5pm & 8pm Tue-Sun; Ⓢ Line 1 to Jonggak, Exit 12) A non-verbal theatrical production that involves a comedic *Iron Chef*–style contest, stirring beatbox and a cappella into the mix. It's an update to the show previously known as Bibap.

SEJONG CENTER FOR THE PERFORMING ARTS THEATRE
Map p232 (세종문화회관; ☎02-399 1114; www.sejongpac.or.kr; 175 Sejong-daero; Ⓢ Line 5 to Gwanghwamun, Exit 1 or 8) One of Seoul's leading arts complexes, with several performance and exhibition spaces, puts on major drama, music and art shows – everything from large-scale musicals to fusion *gugak* (traditional Korean music) and chamber orchestras.

SHOPPING

Insa-dong has been an area of art since the Joseon Dynasty (1392–1910) and still is a place to pick up artwork, brushes and tools. You'll also find tea, designer accessories, traditional clothing and quirky items such as metal bowls and cutlery, as well plenty of souvenirs.

Gwanghwamun & Around

★KYOBO BOOKSHOP BOOKS, MUSIC
Map p232 (☎02-3973 5100; www.kyobobook.co.kr; B1, Kyobo Bldg, 1 Jong-ro; ⊙9.30am-10pm; Ⓢ Line 5 to Gwanghwamun, Exit 4) Kyobo's flagship branch sells a wide range of English-language books and magazines (you'll find them on the left from the main entrance), as well as stationery, electronics, CDs and DVDs in its excellent Hottracks (www.hottracks.co.kr) giftware section.

SEOUL SELECTION BOOKS
Map p232 (☎02-734 9565; www.seoulselection.com; 6 Samcheong-ro; ⊙9.30am-6.30pm Mon-Fri; Ⓢ Line 3 to Anguk, Exit 1) Staff speak English here and can recommend titles published by Seoul Selection as well as a wide range of other publishers' books on Korean culture in English, along with Korean CDs and Korean movies and drama series on DVD (with English subtitles). The website has an excellent monthly newsletter about what's on in Seoul.

Ask about English-language walking tours of Bukchon that run on Saturday (₩30,000).

YUIMARU GIFTS & SOUVENIRS
Map p232 (유이마루; ☎02-3446 4603; www.yuimaru.co.kr; 3 Sajik-ro 9ga-gil; ⊙noon-6.30pm Mon-Fri, to 6pm Sat & Sun; Ⓢ Line 3 to Gyeongbokgung, Exit 1) The black cat Curo is the superstar character in hundreds of costumes and disguises – everything from Darth Vader to Marilyn Monroe – at this creative stationery and gifts store. Her multiple personalities appear printed on cards, stickers, bags and T-shirts.

SEJONG ART MARKET SOSO MARKET
Map p232 (www.sejongpac.or.kr; 175 Sejong-daero; ⊙noon-6pm 1st & 3rd Sat May-Oct; Ⓢ Line 5 to Gwanghwamun, Exit 1 or 8) The attractive sculpture garden behind the Sejong Center is the location of this spring-to-early-autumn, twice-monthly market, where you can buy a wide variety of works from up-and-coming artists and designers.

MONO COLLECTION ARTS & CRAFTS
Map p232 (www.monocollection.com; 17 Jahamun-ro 10-gil; ⊙9.30am-6.30pm Mon-Fri; Ⓢ Line 3 to Gyeongbokgung, Exit 5) Chang Eung Bong creates and sources exquisite fabrics used for fashion and soft furnishings, including gorgeous quilts, pillows and contemporary spins on *hanbok*. Browse the collection in the studio above MK2 (p73) cafe.

Insa-dong, Bukchon, Samcheong-dong & Ikseon-dong

★INSA-DONG MARU ARTS & CRAFTS
Map p234 (인사동마루; ☎02-2223 2500; www.insadongmaru.co.kr; 35-4 6 Insa-dong-gil; ⊙stores 10.30am-8.30pm, cafes & restaurants to 10pm; Ⓢ Line 3 to Anguk, Exit 6) Around 60 different Korean designer shops selling crafts, fashion and homewares are gathered at this slick complex. Spread over several levels, the complex surrounds a central rest area where a piano invites passers-by to give impromptu concerts.

Shops to look out for here include the monochrome accessories of 4T (www.4ourt.co.kr), and the handmade shoes of Le Cordonnier (www.ucnehandworks.co), where the master cobbler Yun Hongsik shares a space with his watch-designer daughter's brand Metal et Linnen (www.metaletlinnen.com).

★KCDF GALLERY ARTS & CRAFTS
Map p234 (☎02-736 0088; www.kcdf.kr; 44 Insa-dong gil; ⊙10am-8.30pm; Ⓢ Line 3 to Anguk, Exit 6) The Korean Craft and Design Founda-

tion's gallery showcases some of the finest locally made products, including woodwork, pottery and jewellery. It's the ideal place to find a unique, sophisticated gift or souvenir.

JILKYUNGYEE FASHION & ACCESSORIES

Map p234 (질경이; ☎02-732 5606; www.jilkyungyee.co.kr; 14-1 Insa-dong; ⏰9am-6pm; Ⓢ Line 3 to Anguk, Exit 6) Lee Ki-Yeon trained as an artist in the late 1970s when she became interested in natural dyeing and traditional Korean fashion. She went on to establish this fashion brand selling tastefully designed *hanbok* (traditional), everyday and special-occasion clothing for both sexes. The styles are easy to wear and are often more contemporary in their design than you'll find elsewhere.

MIK JEWELLERY

Map p230 (☎02-704 0124; www.m-mik.com; 118 Gyedong-gil; ⏰10am-6pm Wed-Mon; Ⓢ Line 3 to Anguk, Exit 3) You're likely to find Lim Dong Wook, the designer of these original unisex shirt-button covers, at this, his atelier and showroom. These pieces of jewellery are a neat replacement for a tie or brooch and range in price from ₩20,000 for simple designs to ₩268,000 for ones made from silver.

SSAMZIEGIL ARTS & CRAFTS

Map p234 (www.ssamzigil.com; 42 Insa-dong-gil; ⏰10.30am-8.30pm; Ⓢ Line 3 to Anguk, Exit 6) An arty four-storey complex built around a courtyard that's a popular stop for one-off clothing, accessories and household goods as well as a fair amount of cheap trinkets.

In the basement look for **Cerawork** (Map p234; ☎02-7200143; www.cerawork.co.kr; B1 Ssamziegil, 42 Insa-dong-gil; ⏰10.30am-8.30pm; Ⓢ Line 3 to Anguk, Exit 6), where you can paint your own design onto pottery for a unique souvenir.

YIDO HOMEWARES

Map p230 (☎02-722 0756; www.yido.kr; 191 Changdeokgung-gil; ⏰10am-7pm; Ⓢ Line 3 to Anguk, Exit 2) Tastefully designed, natural glazed pottery for daily and decorative use are artfully displayed on the ground floor of this complex that includes a gallery, a basement cafe and an academy where you can learn to throw or hand mould pots.

KUKJAE EMBROIDERY ARTS & CRAFTS

Map p234 (☎02-732 0830; www.suyeh.co.kr; 41 Insa-dong-gil; ⏰10am-8.30pm; Ⓢ Line 3 to Anguk, Exit 6) Exquisite traditional embroidery pieces, including handbags, cushions and pillows, from Kukjae have often been presented as official gifts by Korean presidents to visiting dignitaries. You'll also find *bojagi* patchwork cloths here used for gift wrapping or display.

JONGINAMOO HOMEWARES

Map p230 (종이나무; ☎02-766 3397; http://jonginamoo.com; 3 Bukchon-ro 5-gil; ⏰10am-10pm Mon-Sat, from noon Sun; Ⓢ Line 3 to Anguk, Exit 2) Selling beautiful traditional-style furniture and decorative pieces for your home, including a variety of lamps with shades made of *hanji* (handmade paper).

DOLSILNAI FASHION & ACCESSORIES

Map p234 (돌실나이; ☎02-737 2232; www.dolsilnai.co.kr; 35 Insa-dong-gil; ⏰10am-8pm; Ⓢ Line 3 to Anguk, Exit 6) Come here for beautifully designed, casual *hanbok* (traditional Korean clothing) made from natural fabrics in a variety of soft natural and pastel colours. There's always a selection of garments for men and women that are discounted.

There are also branches in Sinchon and Daehangno.

GALLERY ART ZONE GIFTS & SOUVENIRS

Map p230 (www.mmca.go.kr; MMCA Seoul, 30 Samcheong-ro; ⏰10am-6pm Tue, Thu, Fri & Sun, to 9pm Wed & Sat; Ⓢ Line 3 to Anguk, Exit 1) For consumers of contemporary Korean art and design, these five gallery spaces at the MMCA showcase some of the best of what's on offer, from fashion and electronic goods to ceramics and stationery.

SPORTS & ACTIVITIES

ROYAL ASIATIC SOCIETY WALKING

(www.raskb.com; tours from ₩25,000) Organises enlightening walking and bus tours to all parts of South Korea, usually on weekends; check the website for the schedule. Nonmembers are welcome to join. The reasonably priced tours are led by English speakers who are experts in their field. The society also organises lectures in Seoul on topics such as 'LesBiTrans Migrant Life in South Korea'.

O'NGO COOKING

Map p234 (☎02-3446 1607; www.ongofood.com; 12 Samil-daero 30-gil; courses from ₩65,000, tours from ₩47,000; Ⓢ Line 1, 3 or 5 to Jongno 3-ga, Exit 5)

Well-run cooking classes and food tours around the city are offered here. The beginners' class lasts two hours and you can choose a variety of different dishes to learn about including *haemul pajeon* (seafood pancake), *sundubu* (soft tofu stew), *bulgogi* (marinated beef) and the many types of kimchi.

SEOUL CITY TOUR BUS BUS

Map p232 (☎02-777 6090; www.seoulcitybus.com; tours from adult/child ₩18,000/12,000; ⌚half-hourly 9am-7pm Tue-Sun; Ⓢ Line 5 to Gwanghwamun, Exit 6) Comfortable tour buses run between Seoul's top tourist attractions, allowing you to see a lot in a short time. You can hop on and hop off anywhere along the one course: Course A covers the palaces and sights downtown; Course B traverses a wider loop including Hongdae and Yeouido; Course C covers Gangnam (p132), south of the Han River.

Buy tickets on the bus, which can be caught outside Donghwa Duty Free Shop at Gwanghwamun. Check the website for details of night tours, which zigzag across the Han River so you can view the illuminated bridges, and for trips on the trolley-like buses.

DONG-LIM KNOT WORKSHOP ART

Map p230 (www.shimyoungmi.com; 10 Bukchon-ro 12-gil; classes ₩7000-10,000; ⌚10am-6pm Tue-Sun; Ⓢ Line 3 to Anguk, Exit 2) Enter this *hanok* to find out about traditional knotting techniques and to attend classes on how to make tassels, jewellery and other ornaments from threads.

YBM SISA LANGUAGE

Map p234 (☎02-2278 0509; http://kli.ybmedu.com; 104 Jong-ro; courses from ₩132,000; ⌚6.30am-9pm Mon-Fri, 9am-4pm Sat & Sun; Ⓢ Line 1, 3 or 5 to Jongno 3-ga, Exit 15) Korean classes (maximum size 10) for all ability levels cover grammar, writing and conversation. Private tuition (₩55,000 per hour for one person) can also be arranged here.

Myeong-dong & Jung-gu

Neighbourhood Top Five

❶ **N Seoul Tower** (p81) Climbing or riding the cable car up Namsan, topped by the 262m central city peak, is a leafy retreat from Myeong-dong's commercial throng.

❷ **Namsangol Hanok Village** (p83) Learning about traditional Korean houses and culture, then catching a taekwondo display.

❸ **Seoullo 7017** (p83) Walking high above the city on a pedestrian overpass park while pondering art exhibitions and train lines.

❹ **Deoksugung** (p82) Enjoying the colourful changing of the guard outside the palace by day, and wandering between the lit-up buildings by night.

❺ **Namdaemun Market** (p86) Haggling day and night with vendors at this mammoth market, and continuing the spree in neon-lit Myeong-dong.

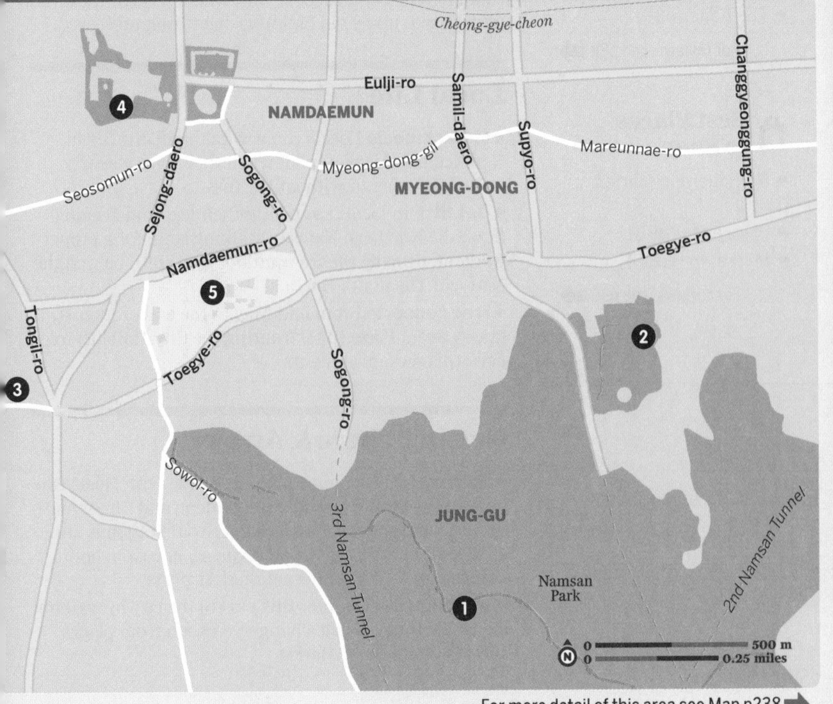

For more detail of this area see Map p238

Lonely Planet's Top Tip

On the roof of the original Shinsegae building is Trinity Garden, dotted with sculptures by Henry Moore, Joan Miró and Jeff Koons among others; there's also a cafe, or you could enjoy a picnic of goodies bought from the department store's food hall.

Best Places to Eat

- Gosang (p87)
- Congdu (p87)
- Korea House (p87)

For reviews, see p85.

Best Places to Drink

- Muldwinda (p88)
- Neurin Maeul (p88)
- The Edge (p88)

For reviews, see p88.

Best Places to Shop

- Namdaemun Market (p86)
- Shinsegae (p90)
- Market m* (p90)

For reviews, see p90.

Explore Myeong-dong & Jung-gu

Branding itself the city's belly button, Jung-gu (www.junggu.seoul.kr) stretches from the southern city gate of Sungnyemun (p84) and Namdaemun Market (p86) towards the eastern gate of Heunginjimun. Dominating the district's heart is the youth-fashion shopping area of Myeong-dong. Myeong means 'light' – apt for an area where Seoul's commercial razzle-dazzle reaches its apogee.

Myeong-dong's streets and alleyways are invariably teeming with shoppers. Masses of commercial stores cater to a repetitive set of fashion trends and a desire for cheap beauty products, along with plenty of cafes, restaurants and high-rise shopping malls. Chinese visitors in particular adore it and you'll often hear shop and stall vendors address the crowd in that language. The mass of humanity, noise and visual stimulation can become overwhelming, but don't let that put you off spending some time soaking up the electric atmosphere and indulging in retail therapy.

Tranquillity can be regained on nearby Namsan (p84), downtown Seoul's green lung, its hiking trails, parkland and old City Wall spruced up. From nearby Hoehyeon station and Namdaemun Market, the park overpass Seoullo 7017 (p83) provides some peace and good views above the highways. It exits in the deserted area west of Seoul Plaza and City Hall in Deoksugung (p82), a lovely palace around which early missionaries built Seoul's first churches and schools, and where foreign legations were based; many old buildings have been preserved.

Local Life

- **Market meals** Locals come to Cutlassfish Alley in Namdaemun Market (p86) when they want a hearty grilled-fish spread without the fuss.
- **Get fit** Join locals stretching their legs and keeping fit on the Northern Namsan walking trail; for a proper workout, drop by the free outdoor gym (p81) behind the National Theater of Korea.
- **Free concerts** From mid-May to the end of August, grassy Seoul Plaza (p84) fronting the City Hall has free performances most nights.

Getting There & Away

- **Subway** Line 4 connects Seoul Station with Hoehyeon (for Namdaemun Market), Myeongdong and Chungmuro for the Namsangol Hanok Village. Seoul Station is also a stop on the A'REX (Airport Express) line from both Incheon and Gimpo International Airports.
- **Walking** You can enter this part of the city by walking alongside the pleasant Chang-gye-cheon from places such as Gwangjang Market.

TOP EXPERIENCE
ESCAPE TO NAMSAM

Beloved by locals as a place for exercise, peaceful contemplation and hanging out with loved ones, Namsan was a sacred shamanistic spot when the Joseon ruler Taejo ordered the construction of a fortress wall across this and Seoul's three other guardian mountains. The mountain is protected within a 109-hectare park and crowned by one of the city's most iconic features: N Seoul Tower.

DON'T MISS

- N Seoul Tower
- Bongsudae
- Seoul City Wall
- Northern Namsan Circuit

PRACTICALITIES

- Map p238, E6
- 02-3455 9277
- www.nseoultower.com
- Namsan
- adult/child ₩10,000/8000
- 10am-11pm Sun-Fri, to midnight Sat
- shuttle bus 2, 3 or 5

Historic Structures

Sections of the original **Seoul City Wall** still snake across Namsan (남산); near the summit you can also see the **Bongsudae** (Mongmyeoksan Beacon; 5-6 Yejang-dong) FREE, a communications system used for 500 years to notify the central government of urgent political and military information. A traditional lighting ceremony is held here between 3pm and 4pm Tuesday to Sunday.

In the 1920s the Japanese built a Shinto shrine on the mountain, removing the shamanist prayer hall Guksadang from Namsan's summit in the process (it was rebuilt on Inwangsan).

Northern Namsan Circuit

Over the last few years the city has been restoring parts of the City Wall and parks and trails on the mountain. Along the Namsan Northern Circuit, a pedestrian path that snakes for 3km from the lower cable-car station to the National Theater, you'll find the beautifully ornate and peaceful **Waryongmyo** (와룡묘; 91-6 Sopa-ro; 8am-4pm) FREE. Built in 1862, this Buddhist/Taoist/shamanist shrine is dedicated to Zhuge Liang (AD 181–234), a Chinese statesman and general.

Further along is the archery practice ground for the Korea Whal Culture Association (p91) where you can practice firing arrows; lessons are 10am Saturday. Nearby is a free **outdoor gym** with proper weights and equipment.

Southern Namsan Circuit

The Southern Namsan Circuit has a pedestrian path and a road used by buses. It cuts through the old City Wall. Accessed from the Southern Namsan Circuit or via a pedestrian bridge over the road from near the Grand Hyatt is the Namsan Botanical Garden (p84). Paths lead from here through more wooded sections of Namsan Park, where you'll find a firefly habitat.

Modern Attractions

The iconic N Seoul Tower, the geographical centre of Seoul, is visible for miles around from its lofty position on Namsan. The panoramic views of the metropolis from its observation deck are immense. Aim to come as day becomes night to witness Seoul's city lights sparkle into view, challenging the light of the stars. Starry-eyed lovers have made it a tradition to scribble locks with their names and attach them to the railings.

It's a straightforward, easygoing walk up Namsan, though riding the **cable car** (Map p238; www.cablecar.co.kr; 1-way/return adult ₩6000/8500, child ₩3500/5500; 10am-11pm; S Line 4 to Myeongdong, Exit 3) provides even more great city views. Shuttle buses run from 7.30am to 11.30pm from various subway stations around the mountain.

TOP EXPERIENCE
MARVEL AT DEOKSUGUNG BY NIGHT

Deoksugung (meaning Palace of Virtuous Longevity) is one of Seoul's five grand palaces built during the Joseon dynasty, but is unique for allowing visitors to come at night to see the lit-up buildings. Deoksugung's other peculiarity is its fusion of architecture, in some parts using traditional Korean structures and in others a neoclassical western style.

Palace History

King Seonjo turned Deoksugung into a palace in 1593 after Japanese invaders destroyed all of Seoul's other palaces. From 1615 Deoksugung became a secondary palace, until 1897 when King Gojong moved in to keep near where foreign legations were concentrated in the city at the time. Despite being forced by the Japanese to abdicate 10 years later, the palace remained Gojong's residence until his death in 1919.

Palace Buildings

Deoksugung is a mix of contrasting architectural styles. **Junghwajeon**, the palace's main throne hall, is adorned with dragons and has golden window frames. It was reserved for ceremonial events such as coronations.

Head behind it to the grand **Seokjojeon**, completed in 1910 in neoclassical-style by British architect GR Harding. Today it houses the **Daehan Empire History Museum** (☎02-751 0753; free with admission to Deoksugung; ⏲9.30am-5pm Tue-Sun), displaying the opulent interior of the mansion. You can only visit as part of a 45-minute tour, best booked online (though it's not in English), or otherwise chance your luck upon arrival; tours depart approximately every half-hour until 5pm. Also majestic, the western wing was designed by a Japanese architect in 1938 and now is MMCA Deoksugung (p84), housing contemporary art.

Behind Gojong's living quarters, **Hamnyeongjeon**, is the interesting fusion pavilion **Jeonggwanheon** designed by Russian architect Aleksey Seredin-Sabatin as a place for the emperor to savour coffee and entertain guests. Gojong developed a taste for the beverage while holed up for a year in the Russian legation following the assassination of Queen Min. The pavilion's pillars, a veranda and metal railings are decorated with deer and bats – both auspicious creatures.

Daily Events

The **changing of the guards** is an impressive ceremony involving 50 participants, who dress up as Joseon-era soldiers and bandsmen. It happens at the Daehanmun main gate at 11am, 2pm and 3.30pm Tuesday to Sunday.

Free guided tours of the palace (in English) take place at 10.45am and 1.30pm. Otherwise, you can pick up a detailed guide for ₩500.

DON'T MISS

- Changing of the Guard
- Jeonggwanheon
- Junghwajeon
- Seokjojeon

PRACTICALITIES

- 덕수궁
- Map p238, B2
- www.deoksugung.go.kr
- 99 Sejong-daero
- adult/child/under 7yr ₩1000/500/free
- ⏲9am-9pm Tue-Sun
- Ⓢ Line 1 or 2 to City Hall, Exit 2

SIGHTS

N Seoul Tower & Namsan is the central attraction, literally, with Namsangol Hanok Village at its base and the shopping spectacle of Myeong-dong nearby. To the west of Namsan, Seoullo 7017 is a green walkway that is worth a look if you are near the Namdaemun Market as it is quite short and lit up beautifully at night. To the north of the market are the glassy curves of the City Hall building with one of the world's largest living plant walls inside.

N SEOUL TOWER & NAMSAN — TOWER

See p81.

DEOKSUGUNG — PALACE

See p82.

★NAMSANGOL HANOK VILLAGE — CULTURAL CENTRE

Map p238 (남산골한옥마을; ☎02-2264 4412; www.hanokmaeul.or.kr; 28 Toegye-ro 34-gil; ⏲9am-9pm Tue-Sun, to 8pm Nov-Mar; Ⓢ Line 3 or 4 to Chungmuro, Exit 4) FREE Located in a park at the foot of Namsan, this peaceful village is a wonderful spot to encounter traditional Korean culture. It features five differing *yangban* (upper class) houses from the Joseon era, all relocated here from different parts of Seoul. Also here is a traditional theatre, Seoul Namsan Gugakdang (p90).

On the right of the entrance gate is an office that provides free hour-long guided tours around the village in English (noon Thursday to Sunday, and 2pm Tuesday, Wednesday, Saturday and Sunday).

Here you can also partake in cultural programs including wearing *hanbok* (traditional costumes), calligraphy, making traditional paper *(hanji)*, kites and masks, and sipping traditional teas at Davansa Teahouse (p88).

From May to June and September to October, displays of the traditional Korean martial art **taekwondo** are staged daily in the village at 1pm and 3pm.

Look out for the circular sci-fi-looking **time capsule** with everyday items buried in 1994 to mark Seoul's 600th anniversary. It's not to be opened until the year 2394!

SEOULLO 7017 — PARK

Map p238 (서울로7017; http://seoullo7017.seoul.go.kr; 432 Cheongpa-ro; ⏲24hr; 👪🐾; Ⓢ Line 4 to Hoehyeon, Exit 5) FREE This overpass-turned-park is a green space in the heart of the city. About 24,000 plants are grown here, including various types of flowers and trees, all labelled. Seoullo 7017 provides an interesting, airy (though sun-exposed) view of the city centre, its highways and architecture. Cross-country locomotives snake across a web of train tracks, then at night the old Seoul Station glows and the overpass itself is lit up in moody colours.

The overpass was built in 1970, but in 2014 it was deemed unfit for automobiles and the 17m-high road was refitted as a green space for pedestrians based on the High Line in New York. Seoullo (sounding like 'Seoul Road' in English) opened in 2017, giving meaning to the numbers 7017 alongside the original build year.

A handful of cafes and galleries are located along its length and there are sometimes art exhibitions, concerts, and activities for kids, including trampolines. Free day and night walking tours of the park are provided by the Seoul city government; reserve at www.visitseoul.net.

Seoullo 7017 can be entered from various points, starting on Toegye-ro at Nomdaemun Market gate 5 (which is also Hoehyeon station, Exit 5), where there is a dedicated **information booth** (⏲10am-10pm) with maps. The midpoint entrance is at Seoul Station, Exit 8 and the overpass ends just after Cheongpa-ro.

DEOKSUGUNG STONE WALL ROAD — PLAZA

Map p238 (덕수궁 돌담길; www.deoksugung.go.kr; Deoksugung-gil; ⏲24hr; Ⓢ Line 1 or 2 to City Hall, Exit 2) Outside to the left of Deoksugung's main gate, the palace's stone southern wall creates a curved path shaded by 130 trees with benches where locals stop and rest to whisper sweet nothings or take selfies. It's a pleasant path that connects City Hall (p85) to the Seoul Museum of Art (p84).

NAMSAN PARK — MOUNTAIN

Map p238 (남산공원; 231 Samil-daero; 🚌2, 3 and 5) FREE Beloved by locals as a place for exercise, peaceful contemplation and hanging out with loved ones, Namsan was a sacred shamanistic spot when the Joseon ruler Taejo ordered the construction of a fortress wall across this and Seoul's three other guardian mountains. The mountain is protected within a 109-hectare park and crowned by one of the city's most iconic features: N Seoul Tower (p81).

Shuttle buses (7.30am to 11.30pm) run here from various subway stations around the mountain; normal bus fares apply.

CITIZENS HALL CULTURAL CENTRE

Map p238 (☎02-739 7733; http://english.sfac.or.kr/?page_id=1508; basement, City Hall, 110 Sejong-daero; ⏱9am-9pm Tue-Sun; Ⓢ Line 1 or 2 to City Hall, Exit 5) FREE Head down to City Hall's basement to reach Citizens Hall, a multipurpose space with an interesting mix of multimedia art exhibitions, design shops and a fair-trade cafe. There's also a 21st-century version of Speakers Corner and Media Wall where locals can express their views. Pick up a map and guide from its information desk.

Also here is **Gungisi Relics Exhibition Hall** FREE, a glassed-in archaeological site displaying items dating from the Joseon dynasty unearthed during excavation of the complex.

MMCA DEOKSUGUNG GALLERY

Map p238 (National Museum of Modern & Contemporary Art; www.mmca.go.kr; Deoksugung, 99 Sejong-daero; ⏱10am-7pm Tue-Thu, to 9pm Fri-Sun; Ⓢ Line 1 or 2 to City Hall, Exit 2) This branch of MMCA is within a grand colonial building inside the Deoksugung (p82) complex. It has several galleries exhibiting its permanent modern-art collection and temporary shows.

CULTURE STATION SEOUL 284 ARCHITECTURE, GALLERY

Map p238 (www.seoul284.org; 426 Cheongpa-ro; ⏱10am-7pm Tue-Sun; Ⓢ Line 1 or 4 to Seoul Station, Exit 2) FREE Formerly part of Seoul Station, this grand 1925 building with a domed roof has been beautifully restored inside and out and made into a cultural-arts space staging a variety of free events. The number 284 refers to the station's historic site number.

SEOUL MUSEUM OF ART GALLERY

Map p238 (서울시립미술관, SEMA; ☎02-2124 8800; http://sema.seoul.go.kr; 61 Deoksugung-gil; ⏱10am-8pm Tue-Fri, to 7pm Sat & Sun, to 6pm Sat & Sun Mar-Feb; Ⓢ Line 1 or 2 to City Hall, Exit 2) FREE Hosting world-class exhibitions that are always worth a visit, SEMA has ultramodern, bright galleries inside the handsome brick-and-stone facade of the 1928 Supreme Court building. For some special exhibitions, an entrance fee is charged.

NAMSAN BOTANICAL GARDEN GARDENS

(남산 야외식물원; 772-12, Hannam-dong) FREE Accessed from the Southern Namsan Circuit or via a pedestrian bridge over the road from near the Grand Hyatt is the Namsan Botanical Garden. The 59m2 are divided into 13 themed gardens including wildflowers, herbal medicine, azaleas and a garden for the blind. Paths lead from here through more wooded sections of Namsan Park, where you'll find a firefly habitat.

BANK OF KOREA MONEY MUSEUM MUSEUM

Map p238 (한국은행 화폐박물관; ☎02-759 4881; www.museum.bok.or.kr; 39 Namdaemun-ro; ⏱10am-5pm Tue-Sun; 👪; Ⓢ Line 4 to Hoehyeon, Exit 7) FREE Built in 1912, and an outstanding example of Japanese colonial architecture, the old Bank of Korea now houses a reasonably interesting exhibition on the history of local and foreign currency. There are plenty of interactive displays for kids, such as pressing their own coin or testing for counterfeit notes.

SEOUL PLAZA PLAZA

Map p238 (110 Sejong-daero; Ⓢ Line 1 or 2 to City Hall, Exit 5) Seoul Plaza, fronting City Hall, is the scene for events and free performances most nights during summer, as well as an outdoor ice-skating rink for a couple of months each winter.

SEOUL METROPOLITAN LIBRARY LIBRARY

Map p238 (http://lib.seoul.go.kr; 110 Sejong-daero; ⏱9am-9pm Mon-Fri, to 6pm Sat & Sun; Ⓢ Line 1 or 2 to City Hall, Exit 5) FREE Opened in 2012, the Seoul Metropolitan Library is within the original City Hall's Renaissance-style building, constructed in 1926, that's fronted by a clock. As well as a public library, there are photography exhibitions relating to Seoul's history. At the main desk you can pick up a self-guided tour with map, or book online at www.visitseoul.net for the English guided 'Tong Tong' tours at 10am Tuesday to Friday, 10.30am and 3pm Saturday and 10.30am and 2.30pm Sunday.

SUNGNYEMUN GATE

Map p238 (남대문; Namdaemun; 40 Sejong-daero; ⏱9am-6pm Tue-Sun; Ⓢ Line 4 to Hoehyeon, Exit 5) FREE Standing alone on an island (in direct contrast to the mayhem around it), Seoul's picturesque Great South Gate, Sungnyemun, is one of the capital's original four main gates built in the 14th

TOP EXPERIENCE
STEP INSIDE SEOUL CITY HALL

The Seoul City Hall is a monumental piece of stylish architecture outside – with its tsunami inspired curves – and in, with its wall of living plants. Redeveloped in 2013, the glass and steel 'wave' design resembles eaves found on palaces and temple roofs sheltering the handsome old City Hall, which was built in 1926 from stone.

Step inside to walls of living plants that make up the **Green Wall**, a vertical garden towering seven storeys and covering 1516m^2 – formerly the largest of its kind in the world according to Guinness World Records in 2013.

Adjacent to the verdant walls are the contorted lines of white balloons forming the art installation **'Metaseosa Seobeol'**, representing Seoul's 2000-year turbulent history.

In the basement is **Citizens Hall**, a mulitpurpose space exhibiting multimedia art and housing design shops and a fair-trade cafe. You'll also find something akin to a Speakers Corner and Media Wall where locals can air their opinions. The information desk has a map and guide.

Also here is a glassed-in display of an archaeological site from the Joseon dynasty in the Gungisi Relics Exhibition Hall. It was unearthed during excavation of City Hall. Items include arrowheads and firearms.

DON'T MISS

- Citizens Hall
- Green Wall
- Metaseosa Seobeol

PRACTICALITIES

- 서울시청사
- Map p238, C2
- http://english.seoul.go.kr
- 110 Sejong-daero
- admission free
- 7.30am-6pm Mon-Fri, from 9am Sat & Sun
- S Line 1 or 2 to City Hall, Exit 5

century. Its arched brick entrance, topped by a double-storey pavilion, is accessed by pedestrian crossing from Gate 1 of Namdaemun Market (p86).

It's been reconstructed a number of times over the years following damage under Japanese occupation and during the Korean War, and most recently after an arson attack in 2008.

SEOUL ANIMATION CENTER MUSEUM
Map p238 (서울애니메이션센터; www.ani.seoul.kr; 126 Sopa-ro; 9am-5.50pm Tue-Sun; S Line 4 to Myeongdong, Exit 1 or 3) FREE Up the hill on the way to the cable car you'll find this museum and cinema devoted to cartoons and animation from Korea and beyond. It's part of a whole strip dubbed 'Cartoon Street', with comics-and-animation-related stories and murals.

MYEONG-DONG CATHOLIC CATHEDRAL CHURCH
Map p238 (명동성당; 02-774 1784; www.mdsd.or.kr; 74 Myeong-dong-gil; Mass 9am Sun; S Line 4 to Myeongdong, Exit 6) FREE Go inside this elegant, red- and grey-brick Gothic-style cathedral, consecrated in 1898, to admire the vaulted ceiling and stained-glass windows. The cathedral provided a sanctuary for student and trade-union protestors during military rule, becoming a national symbol of democracy and human rights. Its sleek modern plaza entrance adds an intriguing 21st-century touch, with designer shops and cafes.

EATING

There's an excellent choice of street food cooked up by vendors within Myeong-dong's shopping district and, despite its tourist appearances, is often a better choice than the mediocre restaurants in the area. Eating in the food alleys of Namdaemun Market is a highlight.

★MYEONG-DONG GYOJA NOODLES $
Map p238 (명동교자; www.mdkj.co.kr; 29 Myeong-dong 10-gil; noodles ₩8000; 10.30am-9.30pm; S Line 4 to Myeongdong, Exit 8) The special *kalguksu* (noodles in a meat, dumpling and vegetable broth) is famous, so it's busy, busy, busy. Fortunately, it has multiple levels and a nearby branch to meet the demand.

DONGWON JIP KOREAN **$**

Map p238 (동원집; ☎02-2265 1339; 2 Eulji-ro 11-gil; mains from ₩8000; ⏱8am-10pm Mon-Sat; ❄; Ⓢ Line 3 to Euljiro 3-ga, Exit 4) A rowdy watering hole with excellent food, this restaurant and bar is famous for its *gamja-guk* (pork-back soup). Open since 1987, the restaurant boils its broth overnight and tenderises the meat for three hours before serving. Its *soondae* (Korean blood sausage) is also immensely popular. Even on the coldest winter nights, Dongwon Jip has lines out the door.

MOKMYEOKSANBANG KOREAN **$**

Map p238 (목멱산방; ☎02-318 4790; http://mmmroom.com; 627 Namsangongwon-gil; mains ₩7000-17,000; ⏱11am-9pm; Ⓢ Line 4 to Myeongdong, Exit 3) The delicious and beautifully presented bibimbap here is made with only natural seasonings, befitting its surrounds on the Northern Namsan Circuit. The traditional wooden house in which the restaurant is based is named after the ancient name for Namsan (Mokmyeok); it also serves Korean teas and *makgeolli* (milky rice wine) in brass kettles. Order at the till.

POTALA TIBETAN, INDIAN **$$**

Map p238 (☎02-318 0094; www.potala.co.kr; 4th fl, 32-14 Myeong-dong 2-ga; mains ₩9000-20,000; ⏱11am-10pm; 🌶; Ⓢ Line 4 to Myeong-dong, Exit 8) Books about Tibet and colourful crafts and pictures adorn this restaurant where you can sample the cuisine of the high Himalaya plateau, including *momo* (dumplings) cooked by Nepali chefs. While not exclusively vegetarian, there are plenty of vegie options.

CHUNG-JEONG-GAK ITALIAN **$$**

(충정각; ☎02-313 0424; Chungjeong-ro; mains from ₩15,000, set menu from ₩22,000; ⏱11am-10pm Mon-Sat; 📶; Ⓢ Line 2 or 5 to Chungjeongno, Exit 9) Housed in an attractive red-brick, western-style building from around 1910 with white-wood wrap-around verandah, this restaurant is a fragment of Seoul's past. The Italian food is delicious and, across from Nanta Theatre (p102), it's a good spot for a pre- or postshow meal. Inside it also has an art gallery. From the subway exit turn right and it's on your right.

TOP EXPERIENCE
HAGGLE AT NAMDAEMUN MARKET

At this sprawling, round-the-clock market you can find pretty much anything, from food and flowers to spectacles and camera equipment. It can be a confusing place; get your bearings from the numbered gates on the periphery. Its helpful **tourist information centre** (☎02-752 1913; Gate 5 or 7; ⏱10am-7pm) has a good map.

Haggling is the mode of business. Different sections have different opening hours and some shops open on Sunday, although that's not the best time to visit.

The food alleys are the definite highlights of the market. Small stalls selling *sujebi* (dough and shellfish soup), homemade *kalguksu* noodles and bibimbap for around ₩5000 are clustered on **Kalguksu Alley** near Gate 5, where you will also find **Cutlassfish Alley** for grilled mackerel sets (₩8000) and claypots of *galchi* (cutlassfish). **Haejangguk Alley**, between Gates 2 and 3, is also good for Korean eateries.

If you are looking for the souvenirs you saw in Insa-dong but at a discounted price, head to the wholesale handicrafts section at the top of Joongang **Building C and D** (p91). Also in the market is traditional Korean cookware, perfect for those dinner parties back home. Camera shops are clustered near Gate 1.

DON'T MISS

- Kalguksu, Cutlassfish and Haejangguk food alleys
- Joongang Building C and D
- Haggling for your wares

PRACTICALITIES

- Map p238, C3
- www.namdaemunmarket.co.kr
- 21 Namdaemun-sijang 4-gil
- ⏱24hr
- Ⓢ Line 4 to Hoehyeon, Exit 5

HADONGKWAN KOREAN $$

Map p238 (하동관; ☎02-776 5656; www.hadongkwan.com; 12 Myeongdong 9-gil; soup ₩12,000-15,000; ⏰7am-4pm Mon-Sat; Ⓢ Line 4 to Myeongdong, Exit 8) In business since 1935, this popular pit offers big bowls of wholesome beef broth and rice either in the regular version with a mere four slices of meat or the more expensive one with added tripe. Add salt and masses of sliced spring onions to taste.

YEONG-YANG CENTRE KOREAN $$

Map p238 (영양센터; ☎02-776 2015; 52 Myeongdong 2-gil; mains ₩10,00-22,500; ⏰10.30am-10.30pm; Ⓢ Line 4 to Myeongdong, Exit 6) A Myeong-dong institution since 1960, this is fast food Korean-style: the tasty deep-fried chicken comes in various portion sizes or there's *samgyetang* (ginseng chicken soup). A good set lunch (₩10,000) with salad, soup, bread and pickled radish is available until 4pm on weekdays, 2pm on weekends.

ANDONG JJIMDAK KOREAN $$

Map p238 (안동찜닭; ☎02-310 9233; Myeongdong 2-ga; mains ₩20,000-28,000; ⏰11am-11.30pm; 📶; Ⓢ Line 4 to Myeongdong, Exit 7) A convivial young crowd comes here for the *jjimdak* experience, a very spicy concoction of chicken, noodles, potatoes and vegetables that comes on a platter meant for sharing.

★GOSANG KOREAN $$$

Map p238 (고상; ☎02-6030 8955; 67 Suha-dong; lunch/dinner set course ₩39,800/58,000; ⏰11.30am-3pm & 5.30-10pm Mon-Fri, to 9pm Sat & Sun; 🌶; Ⓢ Line 2 to Euljiro 1-ga, Exit 4) One worth dressing up for, this classy restaurant specialises in vegetarian temple dishes that date from the Goryeo dynsasty. It's all set-course, traditional-style banquets here, and there's also a meat option. It's in a posh food court in the basement of the Center 1 Building.

★KOREA HOUSE KOREAN $$$

Map p238 (한국의집; ☎02-2266 9101; www.koreahouse.or.kr; 10 Toegye-ro 36-gil; set menu lunch ₩29,000-47,000, dinner ₩68,200-150,000, performances ₩50,000; ⏰lunch noon-2pm Mon-Fri, dinner 5-6.30pm & 7-8.30pm, performances 6.30pm & 8.30pm except 3rd Mon, shop 10am-8pm; Ⓢ Line 3 or 4 to Chungmuro, Exit 3) Scoring a hat trick for high-quality food, entertainment and shopping is Korea House. A dozen dainty, artistic courses make up the royal banquet. The *hanok,* the *hanbok*-clad waitresses, the *gayageum* (zither) music, and the platters and boxes the food is served in are all part of the experience.

The intimate theatre stages two, hour-long dance and music performances. Put on by a troupe of top musicians and dancers, the shows have some English commentary on a screen. The show includes elegant court dances, *pansori,* a spiritual shamanist dance, *samullori* (a folk dance) and *samgomu* (acrobatic female drummers each banging on three drums). There's a 30% discount on tickets if you're here for dinner.

Rounding out the experience is Korea House's shop, which stocks quality design goods, traditional crafts and books – including *Eumsik Dimibang,* a Joseon-era cookbook dating from 1670.

★CONGDU KOREAN $$$

Map p238 (콩두; ☎02-722 7002; 116-1 Deoksugung-gil; set course lunch/dinner from ₩29,800/49,800; ⏰11.30am-3pm & 5.30-10pm; Ⓢ Line 5 to Gwanghwamun, Exit 6) Feast on artfully plated, contemporary twists on Korean classics, such as pinenut soup with soy milk *espuma* (foam) or raw blue crab, at this serene restaurant tucked behind the British embassy. Meals come as set menu only and dessert includes delicious *yuja* (citrus fruit) ice cream with Korean biscuit 'gravel'. The main dining room becomes an open roof terrace in good weather.

N.GRILL INTERNATIONAL $$$

Map p238 (☎02-3455 9297; www.nseoultower.co.kr; N Seoul Tower, Namsan; set lunch/dinner from ₩50,000/95,000; ⏰11am-2pm & 5-11pm; Ⓢ Line 4 to Myeongdong, Exit 3 then cable car) Led by Michelin-starred British chef Duncan Robertson, this upmarket revolving restaurant sits up top the iconic N Seoul Tower (p81). Views are amazing, as is its French-style cooking mixed with Korean influences. Reservations are essential. Downstairs, the open-air N Terrace is a good spot for a cocktail with a view.

DRINKING & NIGHTLIFE

This area lacks the cool for great bars, though the guesthouse area south of Myeongdong station has some cosy drinking options. The restaurant at the top of Namsan has knockout views for a cocktail.

★MULDWINDA BAR

(물뛴다; ☎02-392 4200; www.facebook.com/muldwindakr; 43 Kyonggidae-ro; ⏲5pm-midnight Mon-Thu, 11am-2pm & 5-11pm Sat & Sun; Ⓢ Line 2 or 5 to Chungjeongno, Exit 7) Seoul's most sophisticated *makgeolli* bar is a place for connoisseurs of Korean liquors and those who'd like to learn a bit more about the depths and breadths of local tipples. Set up by graduates from the nearby Susubori Academy (where you can learn how to make *makgeolli*), it serves good food and is decorated with class.

THE EDGE COCKTAIL BAR

Map p238 (디엣지; ☎010 3596 4049; www.facebook.com/theedgeseoul; 2F, 8 Eulji-ro 12-gil; drinks from ₩5000; ⏲noon-midnight Tue-Thu, to 1am Fri, 2-8pm & 10pm-3am Sat & Sun; 📶; Ⓢ Line 2 or 3 to Euljiro 3-ga, Exit 10) The Edge is half record store and half cafe and bar. The venue focuses on selling records by day, but invites DJs and sells drinks after dark. On Saturdays there is a DJ night featuring hip-hop, soul and electronic music. Space is limited but cocktails are decent and affordable.

NEURIN MAEUL BAR

Map p238 (느린마을, Slow Brew Pub; ☎02-6030 0999; www.slowbrewpub.com; 2nd fl, Center 1, 26 Eulji-ro 5-gil; ⏲11am-11pm; Ⓢ Line 2 to Euljiro 1-ga, Exit 3 or 4) Top-quality *makgeolli* and other traditional Korean alcoholic drinks are brewed on-site at this huge branch of Slow Brew Pub. There's another branch in Gangnam (p129).

WALKABOUT BAR

Map p238 (☎010 6785 5847; www.fb.me/walkaboutnu; 49 Toegye-ro 20-gil; ⏲4pm-midnight Mon-Sat, to 10pm Sun; 📶; Ⓢ Line 4 to Myeongdong, Exit 3) Amid Myeong-dong's guesthouse enclave leading up to Namsan, this travel-themed bar is run by a couple of young travel nuts who serve Korean craft beers on tap. There is also good Thai food.

COFFEE LIBRE CAFE

Map p238 (☎02-774-0615; www.coffeelibre.kr; Myeong-dong Cathedral, 74 Myeong-dong-gil; ⏲11am-8pm; Ⓢ Line 4 to Myeongdong, Exit 4) A tiny branch of this speciality coffee roaster with a somewhat bizarre location within the Myeong-dong Cathedral complex, but it makes for a good pit stop to refuel on single-origin pour overs, aeropress or espressos.

DAVANSA TEAHOUSE TEAHOUSE

Map p238 (Namsangol Hanok Village, 28 Toegye-ro 34-gil; ⏲10am-6pm; Ⓢ Line 3 or 4 to Chungmuro, Exit 4) A traditional teahouse within the Namsangol Hanok Village.

CAFE THE STORY CAFE

Map p238 (Namsan; ⏲8am-7pm Mon-Fri, 9am-3pm Sat; 📶; Ⓢ Line 4 to Myeongdong, Exit 1) Myeong-dong isn't short on chain cafes, but for something with more individual character hike up to this hidden gem on the lower slope of Namsan, next to its library.

☆ ENTERTAINMENT

★NANTA THEATRE JUNG-GU PERFORMING ARTS

Map p238 (Myeongdong Nanta Theatre, 명동난타극장; ☎02-739 8288; www.nanta.co.kr; 3rd fl, Unesco Bldg, 26 Myeong-dong-gil; tickets ₩40,000-60,000; ⏲5pm & 8pm Mon-Thu, 2pm, 5pm & 8pm Fri-Sun; Ⓢ Line 4 to Myeongdong, Exit 6) Running since 1997, with no end in sight, is Korea's most successful nonverbal performance. Set in a kitchen, this high-octane, 90-minute show mixes magic tricks, *samulnori* folk music, drumming, kitchen utensils, comedy, dance, martial arts and audience participation. It's top-class entertainment that has been a hit wherever it plays. There's another venue (p102) in Hongdae.

★NATIONAL THEATER OF KOREA THEATRE

Map p238 (☎02-2280 4114; www.ntok.go.kr; 59 Jangchungdan-ro; Ⓢ Line 3 to Dongguk University, Exit 6) The several venues here are home to the national drama, *changgeuk* (Korean opera), orchestra and dance companies. Free concerts and movies are put on in summer at the outdoor stage. Walk 10 minutes here or hop on bus 2 at the stop behind Exit 6 of the subway.

★JEONGDONG THEATER THEATRE

Map p238 (☎02-751 1500; www.jeongdong.or.kr; 43 Jeongdong-gil; tickets from ₩40,000; ⏲4pm & 8pm Tue-Sun; Ⓢ Line 1 or 2 to City Hall, Exit 2) Most famous for its critically acclaimed musical *Miso,* this theatre company also produces a number of traditional nonverbal musicals.

OH! ZEMIDONG CINEMA

Map p238 (www.ohzemidong.co.kr; Chungmuro B1; ⏲11am-8pm Mon-Sat; Ⓢ Line 4 or 3 to Chungmuro)

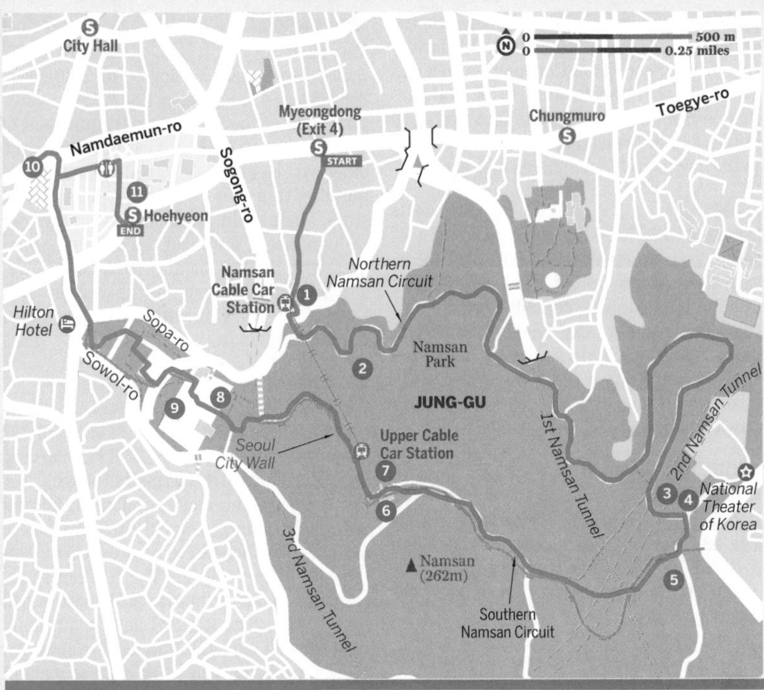

Neighbourhood Walk
Namsan Circuit

START Ⓢ LINE 4 TO MYEONGDONG, EXIT 4
END HOEHYEON STATION
LENGTH 6KM; THREE HOURS

Following pedestrian pathways and parts of the Seoul City Wall, this hike takes you around and over Namsan, providing sweeping city views and a chance to enjoy the mountain's greenery and fresh air. It's best done early in the morning, but leafy trees do provide some shade most of the way.

From the subway exit walk up to the **1 cable car station** (p81); just before you reach it you'll see steps leading up the mountainside to the pedestrian-only Northern Namsan Circuit.

Walk left for five minutes, and pause to look around the shrine **2 Waryongmyo** (p81), before following the road as it undulates gently around the mountain, past routes down to Namsangol Hanok Village and Dongguk University, until you reach the **3 outdoor gym** (p81; uphill from the National Theater of Korea) where you might catch older locals outpacing the younger folk.

You can cut out the next bit by hopping on one of the buses that go to the peak from the **4 bus stop** near here. Otherwise, turn right at the start of the Southern Namsan Circuit road and you'll soon see the **5 Seoul City Wall**, what remains of the original fortress wall of the capital. A steep set of steps shadows the wall for part of the way to the summit; at the fork continue on the steps over the wall and follow the path to **6 N Seoul Tower** (p81) and the **7 Bongsudae** (p81) signal beacons.

Grab some refreshments to enjoy at the geological centre of Seoul, before picking up the Seoul City Wall trail down to pretty **8 Joongang Park**. On the left is **9 Ahn Jung-geun Memorial Hall**.

The park continues over a road tunnel down towards the Hilton Hotel with reconstructed sections of the Seoul City Wall. Finish up taking a look at the reconstruction of **10 Sungnyemun** (p84), Seoul's picturesque Great South Gate, then browsing **11 Namdaemun Market** (p86) for a snack or a bargain.

FREE Occupying a corridor of rooms on the upper level of Chugmuro station, this facility run by the Seoul Film Corporation includes a free library of books and DVDs, both Korean and international. There are five viewing booths but you'll need to get there early in the day to grab one. There's also a gallery.

JUMP PERFORMING ARTS

Map p232 (02-722 3995; www.hijump.co.kr; 22 Jeong-dong; tickets ₩40,000-60,000; hours vary, check website; S Line 5 to Gwanghwamun, Exit 6) A long-running comedy performance that features a wacky Korean family all crazy about martial arts. The nonverbal show mixes Korean taekwondo and *taekkyeon* with slapstick and doesn't require any Korean-language knowledge.

SEOUL NAMSAN GUGAKDANG TRADITIONAL MUSIC

Map p238 (02-2261 0512; Namsangol Hanok Village, 28 Toegye-ro 34-gil; tickets from ₩20,000; closed Tue; S Line 3 or 4 to Chungmuro, Exit 4) Traditional music concerts are staged here most evenings.

SHOPPING

The largest market in Korea – Namdaemun Market (p86) – is here, selling souvenirs, luggage and knock-off clothing for half of what you might pay elsewhere. For more organised and international brands and chain stores, the neon-lit stores of Myeong-dong have you covered and are worth visiting if you enjoy night-time buzz. Head to old-world department stores for the charm as much as the luxury goods.

SEOUL SHOWTIME

Seoul has a number of long-running shows that fuse martial arts, slapstick comedy, magic, dance and audience participation. The nonverbal shows don't require any Korean knowledge, making them appealing to all ages and language levels.

There is also traditional Korean music, *changgeuk* (Korean opera, similar to Western opera), orchestra and dance on offer.

★SHINSEGAE DEPARTMENT STORE

Map p238 (신세계백화점; 02-2026 9000; www.shinsegae.com; 63 Sogong-ro; 10.30am-8pm; S Line 4 to Hoehyeon, Exit 7) Wrap yourself in luxury inside the Seoul equivalent of Harrods. It's split over two buildings, the older part based in a gorgeous 1930 colonial building that was Seoul's first department store, Mitsukoshi. Check out local designer fashion labels, and also the opulent supermarket in the basement, with a food court.

Another food court is up on the 11th floor of the building with an attached roof garden to relax in.

STYLENANDA PINK HOTEL FASHION & ACCESSORIES

Map p238 (스타일난다 핑크호텔; 02-752 4546; www.stylenanda.com; 37-8 Myeong-dong 8-gil; 11am-11pm; ; S Line 4 to Myeongdong, Exit 7) One of the most popular brands for affordable, young women's casual fashion, Stylenanda's flagship store is especially notable for its pink design. The 1st floor showcases its make-up brand, 3CE, with a full make-up bar. The 5th floor has a swimming-pool-themed cafe and, during the summer, there's a rooftop cafe with a great view of the neighbourhood.

PRIMERA COSMETICS

Map p238 (www.primera.co.kr; 22 Myeongdong 4-gil; 10am-10pm; S Line 4 to Myeong-dong, Exit 5) The flagship store of this Korean cosmetics brand specialises in organic skin products and essential oils using germinated sprouts.

MARKET M* HOMEWARES

Map p238 (Flask; www.market-m.co.kr; 13-1 Namsan-dong 2-ga; noon-9pm; S Line 4 to Myeong-dong, Exit 3) Enjoy a free cup of coffee in the guesthouse area of Myeong-dong while browsing this upmarket version of Ikea, selling well-designed, simple wooden furniture and other products such as bags, storage and stationery from Korea and Japan. Look for the delightful waxed-paper bags by Japanese brand Siwa.

ÅLAND FASHION & ACCESSORIES

Map p238 (02-1566 7477; www.a-land.co.kr; 30 Myeong-dong 6-gil; 11am-10pm; S Line 4 to Myeongdong, Exit 6) Spread over three levels, this multilabel boutique mixes up vintage with new designer men's and women's fashion and homewares.

JOONGANG BUILDING C AND D ARTS & CRAFTS

Map p238 (Gate 2, Namdaemun Market; ⌚7am-6pm Mon-Fri, to 2pm Sat; Ⓢ Line 4 to Hoehyeon, Exit 5) One of the best places in Seoul for traditional crafts is the wholesale handicrafts market in the upper floors of Building C and D at Namdaemun Market (p86), where you'll find discounted prices for the same souvenirs you find in Insa-dong. Also here are traditional Korean cookware and utensils, perfect for those dinner parties back home.

LOTTE DEPARTMENT STORE DEPARTMENT STORE

Map p238 (롯데백화점; ☎02-771 2500; http://store.lotteshopping.com; 81 Namdaemun-ro; ⌚10.30am-8pm Mon-Thu, to 8.30pm Fri-Sun; Ⓢ Line 2 to Euljiro 1-ga, Exit 8) Retail behemoth Lotte spreads its tentacles across four buildings: the main department store, Lotte Young Plaza, Lotte Avenue and a duty-free shop. Also here is a multiplex cinema, restaurants and a **hotel** (롯데호텔서울; Map p238; ☎02-771 1000; www.lottehotelseoul.com; 30 Eulji-ro; r from ₩319,000; ❄@📶🏊; Ⓢ Line 2 to Euljiro 1-ga, Exit 8).

SPORTS & ACTIVITIES

★SEOUL GLOBAL CULTURAL CENTER ART

Map p238 (☎02-3789 7961; www.seoulculturalcenter.com; 5th fl, M-Plaza Bldg, 27 Myeong-dong 8-gil; ⌚10am-7pm; Ⓢ Line 4 to Myeongdong, Exit 6) Set up to promote Korean culture to foreigners, this centre offers classes in anything from *hanji* (handmade paper) craft to painting and calligraphy, as well as Korean film screenings, photo ops wearing traditional clothing, or K-Pop dance lessons. Most activities are free; visit the website for schedules and events.

UNDERGROUND ARCADES

In addition to Myeong-dong's abundance of overground retailers, there are hundreds to be discovered in a series of underground arcades. The longest, stretching 4km beneath Eulji-ro from City Hall to Dongdaemun, is Eulji-ro Arcade; many of the stalls here stock fashions that are a throwback to yesteryear. More upmarket vendors selling handicrafts and antiques can be found in the Sogong Arcade beneath Sogong-ro.

SEOUL PLAZA ICE SKATING RINK SKATING

Map p238 (서울광장 스케이트장; www.seoulskate.or.kr; 110 Sejong-daero; per hour incl skate rental ₩1000; ⌚10am-9.30pm Sun-Thu, to 11pm Fri & Sat Dec-Feb; 👪; Ⓢ Line 1 or 2 to City Hall, Exit 5) This outdoor ice-skating rink opens in winter with a magical setting in front of the glimmering glass Seoul City Hall (p85) building and art deco Seoul Metropolitan Library (p84). Two rinks are available: a small one for beginners and a larger rink for regular skating. Gloves are required for all skaters and can be rented for ₩1000.

KOREA WHAL CULTURE ASSOCIATION ARCHERY

Map p238 (www.koreabow.or.kr; 20 arrows ₩2100; 1½hr lesson ₩5000; ⌚9am-6pm) Along the Northern Namsan circuit is the archery practice ground and hall for the Korea Whal Culture Association; *whal* means 'bow', and Koreans have trained expert archers for centuries. You can practice firing arrows too. Lessons for foreigners are held 10am Saturday.

Western Seoul

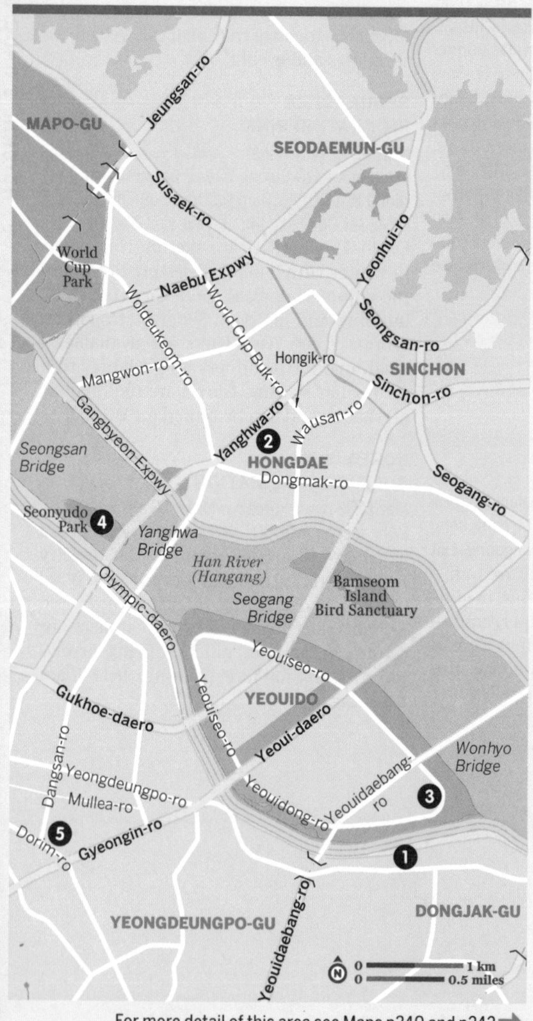

For more detail of this area see Maps p240 and p242

Neighbourhood Top Five

❶ **Noryangjin Fish Market** (p98) Shopping at Korea's largest seafood market, where you can buy everything from king crabs to sea cucumbers, and have it cooked up on the spot.

❷ **FF** (p101) Hitting Hongdae for its buzzing nightlife, where you can dance the night away, see the latest K-Indie band or pose over cocktails.

❸ **63 Sky Art Gallery** (p96) Enjoying the view and the contemporary Korean artworks from the 60th-floor observation deck.

❹ **Seonyudo Park** (p96) Cycling alongside the Han River to landscaped gardens cleverly blended in with old industrial buildings.

❺ **Mullae Arts Village** (p96) Exploring where artists rub shoulders with metalworking factories and closed weekend shutters reveal murals.

Explore Western Seoul

The areas of Hongdae, Edae and Sinchon are all packed with places for students to be diverted from their studies. Hongik is Korea's leading art and design institution, so this is a particularly fertile patch for chaotic creativity and unbridled hedonism; it's also the epicentre for the K-Indie scene, with scores of live-music clubs and dance spots. Up the road, French architect Dominique Perrault's stunning redesign of the Ewha campus centre has put that area on the archi-tour map.

Major retailers have moved into Hongdae, pushing up rents and pushing out smaller, independent boutiques, cafes and bars to nearby areas such as Sangsu-dong and Yeonnam-dong. The latter is Seoul's latest hip 'hood, benefiting from the 6.3km-long Gyeongui Line Forest Park on its southern flank. The park path was built on land formerly used for a railway line that has been buried underground.

Yeouido, a 3km-long and 2km-wide island on the southern side of the Han River, is home to skyscrapers housing media, finance and insurance companies, as well as the National Assembly and stock-exchange buildings. Attractions here include Yeouido Park and Yeouido Hangang Park, both lovely places to relax or go for a bike ride, and the observation deck of 63 Sky Art Gallery (p96) provides a bird's-eye view of the city. Nearby Noryangjin (p98), Seoul's premier fish market, has moved into a new modern building, while further southwest you can go on a street-art safari in Mullae Arts Village (p96).

Local Life

- **Partying** Join the students and other locals for an outdoor drink or picnic at the Gyeongui Line Forest Park (p94) or Hongdae Playground (p100).
- **Markets** Shop for handmade souvenirs and listen to local musicians at Hongdae's Free Market (p102) in the park opposite Hongik University or Yeonnam-dong's Dongjin Market (p103). In warmer months, eat, drink, be entertained and shop at the Oil Tank Culture Park Forest Picnic Market (p102).
- **Blossoms** Yeouido is gorgeous in mid-April when the island's many cherry trees blossom; at its peak they're lit up at night and seemingly the whole of Seoul decamps here.

Getting There & Away

- **Subway** The best way to get to all these areas; Hongik University is a stop on the A'REX (Airport Express) line from both Incheon and Gimpo International Airports on the way to Seoul Station.

Lonely Planet's Top Tip

For details on the latest gigs in Hongdae (and elsewhere) check out Do Indie (www.doindie.co.kr/en), then book tickets in person at **XIndie Ticket Lounge** (☎02-322 2218; http://xindieticket.kr; 41-1 Eoulmadang-ro; ⏲1-9pm Tue-Sun; Ⓢ Line 6 to Sangsu, Exit 1).

Best Places to Eat

- Hongik Sutbul Galbi (p98)
- Tuk Tuk Noodle Thai (p97)
- Menya Sandaime (p98)

For reviews, see p97.

Best Place to Drink

- Anthracite (p99)

For reviews, see p99.

Best Places for Live Music

- Mudaeruk (p101)
- Club Evans (p101)
- FF (p101)

For reviews, see p101.

SIGHTS

There are no palaces here: most of the sights in Hongdae are the streets themselves, as well as an arts centre and one decent museum. Other traditional sights are further south near or across the Han river.

★GYEONGUI LINE FOREST PARK PARK

Map p240 (경의선숲길, Yeontral Park; www.gyeonguiline.org; 27 Susaek-ro; ; Line 2 to Hongik University, Exit 3) This 6.3km park, named for the former Gyeongui Line (on which it was built), is a narrow, long green space that runs along the discarded railroad tracks above Gajwa Station to Hyochang Park station. Within are nooks for reading, grassy picnic areas, exercise equipment and more.

The Gyeongui Line was built by the Japanese in 1905 and abandoned in the early 1950s. Since the park opened in 2016, many restaurants, cafes and bars in its bordering regions have surfaced. Parts of the park are themed: for instance, Yeonnam-dong (next to Hongik University Station exit 3), nicknamed Yeontral Park because of its Central Park–like atmosphere, is popular for picnics (albeit on uncomfortable artificial grass) and is also a great place to grab a beer (available at several nearby craft-beer marts), people-watch and enjoy the warm weather on a nice day or night. The area between Hongik University station and Sinchon is known as Gyeongui Line Book Street.

GYEONGUI LINE BOOK STREET PARK

Map p240 (경의선책거리; www.gbookst.or.kr; 50-4 Wausan-ro 35-gil; bookshops 11am-8pm; Line 2 to Hongik University, Exit 6) FREE This extension of the Gyeongui Line Forest Park is a book-themed pathway of bookshops housed in train-carriage-like containers. The street commemorates the high concentration of publishing companies in the area – over 1000! Most use it as a leafy space to stroll between Sinchon and Hongik University station or as a peaceful refuge, where young lovers whisper sweet nothings in the evenings on the steps. Along the way there are creepily realistic statues, and signs telling the history of the train line.

OIL TANK CULTURE PARK CULTURAL CENTRE

(마포 문화비축기지, Mapo Culture Storage Station; 02-376 8410; http://parks.seoul.go.kr/template/sub/culturetank.do; 87 Jeungsan-ro; 9am-9pm; P; Line 6 to World Cup Stadium, Exit 3) FREE Originally built after Korea's first oil crisis in 1973 and reopened in 2017, this cultural centre is made up of five abandoned oil tanks. Planted in a remote corner of the city, there is an other-worldly feeling as you navigate the performance hall, exhibition hall, information exchange centre, cafe and amphitheatre. Seeing a concert in the amphitheatre, surrounded by trees, is a must-do, though the rusted structure itself is a favourite among photographers at any time.

WAR & WOMEN'S HUMAN RIGHTS MUSEUM MUSEUM

Map p240 (전쟁과여성인권박물관; 02-392 5252; www.womenandwar.net; 20 World Cup Buk-ro 11-gil; adult/teenager/child ₩3000/2000/1000; 1-6pm Tue-Sat; Mapo06, Mapo08, Mapo15, 7016 or 7737, Line 2 to Hongik University, Exit 1, then) In Korea the survivors of sexual slavery by the Japanese military during WWII (known euphemistically as 'comfort women') are respectfully called *halmoni* (grandmother). When you enter this well-designed and powerfully moving museum you'll be given a card printed with the story of a *halmoni,* helping you to connect with the tragic history of these women.

FOOTBALL FAENTASIUM MUSEUM

(풋볼 팬타지움; www.faentasium.com; 240 Woldeukeom-ro; ₩15,000; 9am-6pm; P; Line 6 to World Cup Stadium, Exit 1) This interactive museum at the World Cup Stadium & Mall (p102) is a must for football fans, despite the steep admission fee. Korean football history and its players in the K League are detailed through modern displays, with plenty of selfie opportunities, and memorabilia such as trophies and posters. Games to amuse children (and the young at heart) include VR headset football or shaking hands with famous players, and rooms for kicking a ball at digital goalkeepers.

JEOLDUSAN MARTYRS' SHRINE MUSEUM

(절두산 순교성지; 02-3142 4434; www.jeoldusan.or.kr; 6 Tojeong-ro; museum by donation; shrine 24hr, museum 9.30am-5pm Tue-Sun; Line 2 or 6 to Hapjeong, Exit 7) Jeoldusan means 'Beheading Hill' – this is where up to 2000 Korean Catholics were executed in 1866 following a royal decree, most thrown off the high cliff here into the Han River. Next to the chapel (where Mass is held daily at 10am and 3pm), the museum includes

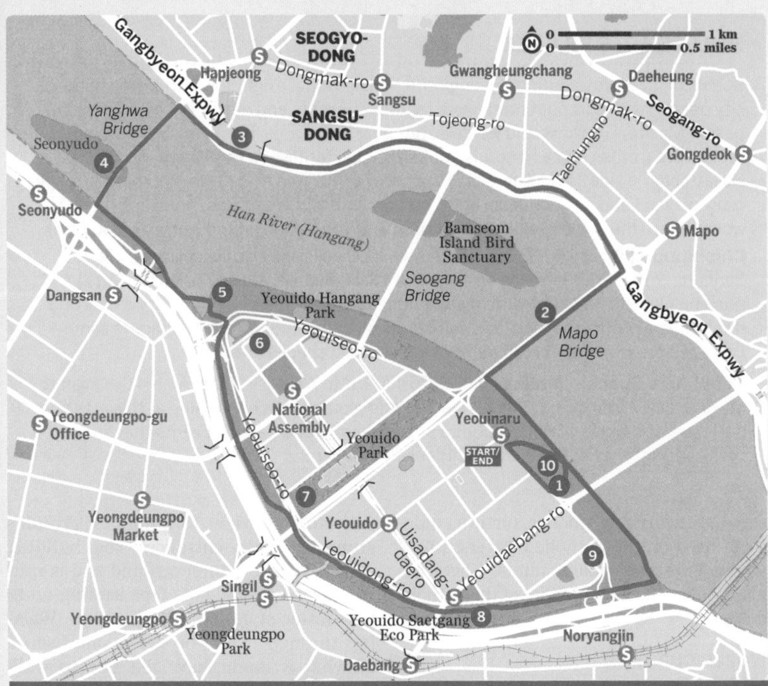

Neighbourhood Trail
Han River Cycle Ride

START SUBWAY LINE 5 TO YEOUINARU STATION, EXIT 3
END YEOUIDO HANGANG PARK
LENGTH 15KM; THREE HOURS

It's possible to walk this 15km route around Yeouido and across the river via the island park of Seonyudo, but it's quicker and more fun to use a bicycle, which you can rent at several outlets in Yeouido Hangang Park, the starting point for the ride.

Walk east from the subway exit towards the Hangang Cruise Terminal in Yeouido Hangang Park, where you'll find a 1 **bicycle rental stall** (first hour ₩3000, every extra 15 minutes ₩500; open 9am to 5pm); bring some form of photo ID for them to keep as a deposit.

Cycle west and out of the park across the 2 **Mapo Bridge**, taking the blue ramp down to the north bank of the river. Head west for about 4km until you reach a steep cliff, at the top of which is 3 **Jeoldusan Martyrs' Shrine** (p94). Continue west to the Yanghwa Bridge and carry your bike up the stairs to the pathway on the west side. On an island about halfway along the bridge is the beautifully landscaped 4 **Seonyudo Park** (p96). There are wonderful river views from the park (which used to be a water-filtration plant) as well as a cafe at which you can take a break.

Continue from the park back to the south bank of the Han River and pedal back towards Yeouido. At the western tip of the island you can pause to view the ritzy 5 **Seoul Marina** and the 6 **National Assembly** (p97). Also have a look around central 7 **Yeouido Park**, which includes a traditional Korean garden.

Continue along the bike paths on the southern side of the island; 8 **Yeouido Saetgang Eco Park** here is wilder and more natural. As you round the eastern tip of Yeouido look up to see clouds reflected in the gold-tinted glass of the 63 City sky-scraper and its 60th-floor 9 **63 Sky Art Gallery** (p96). After returning your bike to the rental stall look out for the quirky 10 **monster sculpture** based on the hit horror movie *The Host*.

MULLAE ARTS VILLAGE

Something very interesting is going on in Mullae-dong, a light-industrial area of the city packed with compact metalwork factories. Artists and designers have moved in beside the steel workers and welders, bringing to the area inventive street art, small restaurants, cafes and a handful of quirky shops. **Mullae Arts Village** (문래예술촌; Mullae-dong; S Line 2 to Mullae, Exit 7) is a photogenic area that rewards exploring, especially on weekends when (decorated) factory shutters are closed, revealing more artworks. From the subway exit head straight and you'll soon hit the warren of factories.

Chichipopo Library (☎02-2068 1667; www.facebook.com/chichipopolibrary; 428-1 Dorim-ro; ⏰10am-11.30pm Mon-Fri, 11am-11pm Sat & Sun; 📶; S Line 2 to Mullae, Exit 7) A relaxing place to hang out with mismatched furniture, cheap western-style eats and drinks and a rooftop garden, this self-serve cafe, library and gallery space is something of a creative hub for Mullae, with co-working spaces available.

Seoul Arts Space – Mullae (☎02-2676 4300; http://english.sfac.or.kr; 5-4 Gyeongin-ro 88-gil; S Line 2 to Mullae, Exit 7) It's worth finding out what's happening at this arts and performance space which includes a studio theatre and gallery. Events that are part of the springtime Festival Bom (p24) are staged here.

some of the grizzly wooden torture equipment used on the Catholic martyrs, 103 of whom have been made saints. There are also books, diaries and relics of the Catholic converts.

WORLD CUP PARK — PARK

(월드컵공원; http://parks.seoul.go.kr; 251 World Cup-ro; ⏰Pyeonghwa & Nanjicheon parks 24hr, other parks vary; P; S Line 6 to World Cup Stadium, Exit 1) FREE These five connected parks (Pyeonghwa, Nanjicheon, Nanji Hangang, Haneul Park and Noeul) were created for the 2002 FIFA World Cup out of former landfill and waste ground. Today it's one of Seoul's largest green spaces, threaded through with cycle and walking paths, sporting facilities, and leafy relaxation spots. Climb hilly Haneul Park for great views across the area.

63 SKY ART GALLERY — OBSERVATORY

Map p242 (www.63art.co.kr; 50, 63-ro; adult/teenager/child ₩13,000/12,000/11,000; ⏰10am-10pm; S Line 5 to Yeouinaru, Exit 4) The top-class, regularly changing art exhibitions at this 60th-floor gallery have the extra thrill of an observation deck. It's held within the gold-tinted glass skyscraper 63 City, which also features some ho-hum spaces, such as an aquarium.

EWHA WOMANS UNIVERSITY — ARCHITECTURE

(www.ewha.ac.kr; Ewhayeodae-gil; S Line 2 to Ewha Womans University, Exit 2) FREE Come to this venerable university, founded in 1886 by American Methodist missionary Mary Scranton, to view Dominique Perrault's stunning main entrance. The building dives six storeys underground and is split by a broad cascade of steps leading up to the Gothic-style 1935 Pfeiffer Hall. Walking through here, you get a small sense of what it might have felt like to walk through the parting of the Red Sea.

Inside, on the ground floor, you'll find cafes, shops and the **Arthouse Momo cinema** (☎02-363 5333; http://arthousemomo.co.kr; tickets ₩9000) .

MODERN DESIGN MUSEUM — MUSEUM

Map p240 (근현대디자인박물관; ☎070-7010 4346; www.designmuseum.or.kr; 36 Wausan-ro 30-gil; adult/child ₩5000/4000; ⏰10am-6pm Tue-Sun; S Line 2 to Hongik University, Exit 9) The items displayed on the two floors of this small museum trace the history of modern design in Korea from the 1880s to contemporary times. Not much is labelled in English, but it's still a fascinating collection that spans a wide range of products from 19th-century books and newspapers to 1960s toys and electronics and posters for the 1988 Olympics.

SEONYUDO PARK — PARK

(선유도공원; http://hangang.seoul.go.kr; 343, Seonyu-ro; ⏰6am-midnight; S Line 9 to Seonyudo, Exit 2) FREE A former water-filtration plant on an island in the Han River has been transformed into this award-winning park. The old industrial buildings have been cleverly adapted as part of the new landscaping and gardens, which include lily-covered ponds, plant nurseries and exhibitions halls. Either walk here from the subway station or cycle from Yeouido (p95).

NATIONAL ASSEMBLY NOTABLE BUILDING

Map p242 (국회의사당; ☎02-788 3656; http://korea.assembly.go.kr; 1 Uisadang-daero; ⏰9am-5pm Mon-Fri, to 4pm Sat & 1st Sun of month; Ⓢ Line 9 to National Assembly, Exit 1) FREE Home to South Korea's parliament since 1975, the pleasant grounds here with a fountain and an elaborate *hanok* (traditional wooden house; used for official functions) are worth a wander. The United Nations–like interior of the green domed building can be viewed only as part of a tour (except Sundays); apply three days in advance by email.

EATING

There's not much fine dining in these parts, but you'll find an abundance of places serving the kind of inexpensive dishes and drinks that students love – fried chicken, dumplings, ramen, bowl food, pasta, street snacks and burgers. The laneways of Yeonnam-dong are all about hip casual restaurants with Korean and international cuisine. The grid of streets between Hongik and Sinchon stations is lined with BBQ joints.

★TUK TUK NOODLE THAI THAI $

(☎070-4407 5130; http://blog.naver.com/tuktuknoodle; 161-8 Seongmisan-ro; mains ₩9000-15,000; ⏰noon-3.30pm & 5-10pm; Ⓢ Line 2 to Hongik University, Exit 3) Credited with kicking off a trend for more authentic Thai restaurants in Seoul, Tuk Tuk's Thai chefs whack out a broad menu of spicy dishes that don't compromise on flavour. Their success saw them move to this minimally decorated two-level space deep in a quiet area of Yeonnam-dong, which still requires queuing on weekends.

Their other popular venture nearby, Soi Yeonnam (p98), serves Thai street food.

DDOBAGI CHICKEN KOREAN $

Map p240 (또바기치킨; ☎02-3142 0991; 27 Wausan-ro, Sangsu-dong; dishes ₩9000; ⏰5pm-2am Mon-Sat, to 1am Sun; ❄ ; Ⓢ Line 6 to Sangsu, Exit 4) One of the most famous and best-value chicken joints in Seoul. Portions are smallish, but the fried exterior is crispy-perfect and the juiciness of the meat will have you dreaming about it for days. Half-and-half combinations are the most popular; choices include original, sweetly marinated, soy marinated or spicy.

AOITORI BAKERY BAKERY $

Map p240 (아오이토리베이커리; ☎02-333 0421; www.fb.me/aoitori.seoul; 8 Wausan-ro 29-gil; snacks from ₩3000; ⏰8am-10pm;) An excellent place to start your Hongdae day is at this tiny Japanese bakery-cafe, which combines sweet breads with savoury flavours. Try the excellent bacon croissants with dollops of mustard, or *yakisoba* (fried noodle) filled buns. Grab a matcha- or orange-zest roll for your travels.

HIMESIYA JAPANESE $

Map p240 (히메시야; ☎070-8245 4562; 3-18 Dongmak-ro 15-gil; mains ₩5000-12,000; ⏰11.30am-3pm & 4.30-9.30pm; ❄; Ⓢ Line 6 to Sangsu, Exit 1) One of the most loved Japanese restaurants in the Hongdae area, Himesiya's dishes are more fusion than they are authentically Japanese. Still, the meals are cheap and delicious and students line up to eat here at dinnertime. The menu offers sushi, curry and udon, but the *donburi* (rice bowls) are not to be missed.

GYEONGJU RESTAURANT KOREAN $

Map p240 (경주식당; ☎02-322 1674; 49-7 Wausan-ro 13-gil; meals from ₩9000; ⏰11.30am-3.30pm & 5.30-11pm; ❄ ; Ⓢ Line 6 to Sangsu, Exit 1) Located in a small house, Gyeongju Restaurant serves home-cooked Korean food. The Large Meat Set for four people comes with 300g of lamb, 450g of pork and several side dishes. Unlike most meat restaurants in Korea, which focus less on design, Gyeongju Restaurant is decorated in vintage brown accents and serves meals on beautiful china.

DONGMU BAPSANG KOREAN $

(동무밥상, Comrade's Table; ☎02-322 6632; 10 Yanghwajin-gil; noodles ₩10,000; ⏰11.30am-3pm & 5-9pm Tue-Sat; ❄ ; Ⓢ Line 2, 6 to Hapjeong, Exit 5) One of the most authentic North Korean restaurants in Seoul, using quality ingredients to produce simple flavours. Owner-chef Yu Jeong-chol worked at one of the most famous restaurants in Pyongyang before defecting. North Korean specialities from the short menu such as *naengmyun* (Pyongyang-style iced noodles) and *mandu-guk* (dumpling soup) are not to be missed.

MENYA SANDAIME JAPANESE $

Map p240 (☎02-332 4129; www.menyasandaime.com; 24 Hongik-ro 3-gil; mains ₩7500-9000; ⌚noon-10pm; Ⓢ Line 2 to Hongik University, Exit 9) On a street with several other Japanese restaurants, this atmospheric ramen shop is the real deal and proof that being part of a chain need not compromise food quality. It's a great place for single diners, who can sit at the counter watching hip chefs craft bowls, such as black ramen, with its smoky broth and charred pork.

SOI YEONNAM THAI $

(소이연남; ☎02-323 5130; 267 Donggyo-ro; mains ₩9000-13,000; ⌚11.30am-2.30pm & 5-9pm; Ⓢ Line 2 to Hongik University, Exit 3) An offshoot of Tuk Tuk Noodle Thai (p97). An Astroturf lawn and some outdoor furniture fronts this Thai street-food restaurant where you can dig into a short menu of spicy noodle soup, fried spring rolls and papaya salad.

FELL & COLE ICE CREAM $

Map p240 (☎070-4411 1434; www.fb.me/FELLnCOLE; 310-11 Sangsu-dong; 1 scoop ₩5000; ⌚noon-9pm; Ⓢ Line 6 to Sangsu, Exit 1) A sweet diversion in Hongdae, Fell & Cole's fabulous flavours of ice cream and sorbet are changing all the time but might include perilla leaf, parsley lemonade, burnt banana and *kalimotxo* (aka Jesus Juice).

★HONGIK SUTBUL GALBI BARBECUE $$

Map p240 (홍익숯불갈비; ☎02-334 3354; 146-1 Eoulmadang-ro; mains ₩12,000-16,000; ⌚3.30pm-4am; Ⓢ Line 2 to Hongik University, Exit 7 or 8) Real charcoal (rather than hotplates) brings out the flavours of the fine cuts of pork and beef at this *galbi* (beef ribs) joint; look for the stove on the street corner. Staff will do most of the cooking, then just wrap the smoky meat and sides in lettuce. It's open late, but expect to queue at dinner time.

ANH VIETNAMESE $$

(안; ☎070-4205 6266; www.facebook.com/eatanh; 262-13 Donggyo-ro; mains ₩11,000-13,000; ⌚noon-3pm & 5-10pm; ❄📶) Anh serves southern-Vietnamese-inspired dishes. While its *pho* is quite good, the standout meal is the *bun thit nuong cha gio* (grilled meat on noodles and topped with crispy spring rolls, tender meat and fresh vegetables). It's worth the hour-long wait outside.

TOP EXPERIENCE
FRESH CATCH AT NORYANGJIN MARKET

Even if you don't plan to buy any of the exotic fish and seafood that is supplied from Noryangjin Fish Market to Seoul's restaurants, local fishmongers and the public, a visit is an atmospheric and photogenic experience. In 2016 the fish market moved to a multistorey, modern (some vendors say sterilise and cramped) building to house the 700 stalls and many restaurants that form the complex.

It's worth staying up to 1am for the start of the seafood **auctions** to catch the market at its most exciting. If you just want a leisurely meal, wander to a stall at lunch or dinner, pick your produce – snapping crabs, fresh prawns, and the dark-orange-and-red *meongge* (Korean sea squirt, definitely an acquired taste) or prepared platters of *hoe* (raw fish slices) – then head to the **restaurant** area within the market and, for raw dishes such as live octopus, have it prepared (usually around ₩3000 person), or prepared and cooked (starting from an extra ₩5000 depending on what you have). Either way it comes fresh and served up with a variety of side dishes. A good restaurant is **Busan Ilbeonji** (p99).

DON'T MISS

- Eating at one of the restaurants
- Early-morning auctions

PRACTICALITIES

- 노량진수산시장
- Map p242, D4
- ☎02-2254 8003
- www.susansijang.co.kr
- 674 Nodeul-ro
- ⌚24hr
- Ⓟ
- Ⓢ Line 1 to Noryangjin, Exit 1

MUWOL TABLE KOREAN $$

Map p240 (무월식탁; ☎02-322 8648; 44 Eoulmadang-ro; meals from ₩10,000; ⏲11.30am-11pm; P ❄ 📶; S Line 6 to Sangsu, Exit 1) In an industrial-chic space adorned with a forest of plants, Muwol Table focuses on decent portion sizes. Each meal comes with a small bowl of rice, a single serving of meat, one soup of the day and three side dishes. The broiled pork (*bossam*) set, which comes with a sweet, fermented radish, is a popular option.

CIURI CIURI ITALIAN $$

Map p240 (☎02-749 9996; www.fb.me/ciuriciuri seoul; 2nd fl, 314-3 Sangsu-dong; mains ₩16,000-23,000; ⏲noon-3pm & 6-10pm Mon-Fri, noon-3pm & 5.30-10pm Sat & Sun; S Line 6 to Sangsu, Exit 1) Run by Italian couple Enrico and Fiore, the tasty and unusual – for Seoul – specialities here hail from Sicily, such as *arancine* (saffron-flavoured risotto balls), *anelletti* (small ring pasta) and a special type of sausage. The place is decorated as if you're on holiday in Sicily, with straw-hat lampshades and colourfully painted tiled tables.

BUSAN ILBEONJI SEAFOOD $$

Map p242 (부산일번지; ☎02-2254 7980; 2nd fl, Noryangjin Market; mains ₩15,000-30,000; ⏲10.30am-10.30pm; S Line 1 to Noryangjin, Exit 1) Generous fresh fish and crab meals at this stand in the Noryangjin Market are a bargain. Try *kkotge* (spicy blue-crab soup), which includes side dishes such as garnished tofu, sweet red beans, green salad and grilled fish.

63 BUFFET PAVILION BUFFET $$$

Map p242 (☎02-789 5731; www.63buffet.co.kr; 63 City, 50, 63-ro; lunch Mon-Fri ₩75,000, dinner ₩88,000; ⏲noon-3pm & 6-10pm Mon-Fri, 11am-3.30pm & 5-10pm Sat & Sun; ❄ ✍; S Line 5 to Yeouinaru, Exit 4) With too many temptations to count, this gourmet buffet is a good way to sample a range of Asian and other cuisines, with plenty of steak, seafood and vegetarian choices. Discounts for children up to 18.

DRINKING & NIGHTLIFE

Hongdae is saturated with bars and clubs, particularly between Sangsu subway and Hongik University. The bars in the laneways of Yeonnam-dong are good for a quiet romantic drink, craft beer or posing.

★ANTHRACITE CAFE

Map p240 (☎02-322 0009; www.anthracitecoffee.com; 10 Tojeong-ro 5-gil; ⏲11am-midnight Mon-Sat, to 11pm Sun; 📶; S Line 6 to Sangsu, Exit 4) An old shoe factory is the location for one of Seoul's top independent coffee-roaster and cafe operations. Drinks are made using the hand-drip method at a counter made out of an old conveyor belt. Upstairs is a spacious lounge and there's outdoor seating on the roof.

★SU NORAEBANG KARAOKE

Map p240 (수노래방; ☎02-322 3111; www.skysu.com; 67 Eoulmadang-ro; room per hr ₩2000-20,000; ⏲24hr; S Line 6 to Sangsu, Exit 1) Sing your heart out and be noticed at this luxe karaoke bar: some rooms resemble lounge bars, while others have floor-to-ceiling windows fronting onto the street so you can show off your K-Pop moves. Rates rise from noon to 6am, with the most expensive period from 8pm to the early hours.

GOPCHANG JEONGOL BAR

Map p240 (곱창전골; ☎02-3143 2284; 8 Wausan-ro 29ra-gil; beer ₩5000; ⏲7pm-4am; S Line 2 to Hongik University, Exit 5) Fans of this veteran music bar (opened 1999) in the heart of Hongdae love its old-school vibes, '70s interior and for solely playing Korean music. Hear Korean rock legends such as the Kim Sisters and admire the collection of rare Korean rock vinyl. There's standard *soju* (local vodka) and local beer; if it's crowded you might have to order food.

CHANNEL 1969 LOUNGE

(채널1969; ☎010 5581 1112; www.facebook.com/channel.1969.seoul; B1, 35 Yeonhui-ro; drinks from ₩6000; ⏲6pm-3am; 📶; S Line 2 to Hongik University, Exit 3) One of the last truly alternative spaces in the Hongdae-Yeonnam-dong area, this cultural space and bar turns itself into a club and lounge on weekends and is especially popular with the artsy crowd. Drinks are cheap and a lot of mingling happens outside where partygoers go for a smoke or a breath of fresh air.

BREAD BLUE CAFE

(☎070-4405 0723; 3 Sinchon-ro 12da-gil; coffee ₩3500; ⏲9.30am-10pm Mon-Fri, to 9pm Sat & Sun; 📶; S Line 2 to Hongik University, Exit 6) This vegan bakery-cafe is one of the few places to get an excellent soy latte in Seoul. Dairy-free temptations include dense matcha muffins, macaroons, filled panini, garlic bread, tofu pizza swirls and tiramisu.

SUZIE Q BAR

Map p240 (수지큐; ☎02-338 9929; 10 Wausan-ro 15-gil; ⏲5-11pm Sun-Thu, to 2am Fri & Sat; 📶; Ⓢ Line 2 to Hongik University, Exit 8) A dark and wonderful LP bar in Hongdae lined with over 15,000 records. Jot down your song requests and pass it to the cool older DJ who *might* play one on vinyl, if it pleases him. Tip: rock, Korean classics and even disco rule in this basement. Solo beer drinkers very welcome.

HONGDAE PLAYGROUND BEER GARDEN

Map p240 (홍익문화공원; 19-3 Wausan-ro 21-gil; ⏲24hr; Ⓢ Line 2 to Hongik University, Exit 8) An icon of Hongdae and known simply as 'Playground', small Hongik Munhwa park turns into an impromptu outdoor party most nights. Weekends are especially sociable when students and foreigners grab a *soju* (local vodka) or beer from stores nearby and hold rowdy dance-offs to music by 'DJs' and buskers.

NB2 CLUB

Map p240 (72 Wausan-ro; entry incl 2 drinks Sun-Thu ₩10,000, Fri & Sat ₩15,000; ⏲9pm-6am; Ⓢ Line 2 to Hongik University, Exit 8) Hip hop club owned by YG Entertainment (Big Bang, One, previously Psy), with '90s classics and modern EDM hits. Sociable, high-energy and open late. Cover charge gets you entry to smaller sibling NB1 (more top 40) across the road; expect long queues on Saturdays.

ARCADE BAR SEOUL BAR

(지능계발; ☎02-336 1945; www.instagram.com/arcadebarseoul; 82 Mangwon-ro 2-gil; beer from ₩6000; ⏲noon-11.30pm Tue-Thu, to midnight Fri-Sun; 📶; Ⓢ Line 6 to Mangwon, Exit 2) This two-storey bar and cafe is all about its dozen vintage video games on the basement level. Drinks include decent coffee and a few craft beers on tap; video games (from ₩500) range from Street Fighter to Pac-Man. Occasionally, the bar attempts a party vibe in the basement with a fog machine and loud EDM.

DUKES COFFEE SHOWROOM COFFEE

Map p240 (듁스커피쇼룸; ☎02-333 2121; www.instagram.com/gpo_dukes; 10 Eoulmadang-ro 2-gil; coffee ₩5000; ⏲8am-5pm Mon-Fri, from 11am Sat; Ⓢ Line 6 to Sangsu, Exit 4) The owners of this coffee 'showroom' studied the art of the bean for years in Melbourne to fine-tune their barista skills before opening up this venue in 2017. Instead of picking out a coffee from a menu, you consult with the baristas on your personal preferences and take a cup that they suggest for you.

MAN PYUNG COCKTAIL BAR

(만평; ☎010 4755 9997; 2F, 27 Tojeong-ro; cocktails ₩8000; ⏲6pm-2am; 📶; Ⓢ Line 2 or 6 to Hapjeong, Exit 4) A 2nd-floor vinyl bar, Man Pyung is often the only venue open past midnight on this Hapjeong-dong cafe street. Opened by two DJs, this bar is one for die-hard music fans and not necessarily for cocktail connoisseurs. Come for the cool factor and order a simple cocktail.

HELLO, STRANGER CAFE

Map p240 (안녕 낯선사람; ☎070-4115 5610; http://blog.naver.com/cafestranger; 40 Eoulmadang-ro 5-gil; ⏲8.30am-11pm Mon-Fri, noon-11pm Sat & Sun; 📶👪; Ⓢ Line 2 or 5 to Hapjeong, Exit 5) A cafe well known for its eye-catching storefront, Hello Stranger is a warm, cosy coffeeshop located on the outskirts of Hongdae. Filled with art magazines, novels and flowers, the cafe is a favourite of many artists in the neighbourhood.

CLUB MWG CLUB

Map p240 (www.facebook.com/clubmwg1; 6-5 Wausan-ro 19-gil; ⏲10pm-5am Fri & Sat; Ⓢ Line 2 to Hongik University, Exit 2) Myoung Wol Gwan (MWG) translates as 'bright moon house' but lunar sightings are not on the agenda from this dark, basement venue, one of Hongdae's longest-running. Come here for the LGBTIQ+-friendly Meet Market (www.facebook.com/meetmarketseoul) queer party events as well as indie bands and DJ nights.

YRI CAFE CAFE

Map p240 (이리카페; ☎02-323 7861; http://cafe.naver.com/yricafe; 27 Wausan-ro 3-gil; ⏲11am-1am Mon-Fri, to 2am Sat & Sun; Ⓢ Line 6 to Sangsu, Exit 4) Browse local and imported books and magazines on art and design at this convivial bohemian hang-out that works just as well as a daytime cafe and workspace as it does a night-time drinks venue.

FOX WINE BISTRO WINE BAR

Map p240 (포도먹는 여우; ☎02-3143 7191; www.fb.me/foxwinebar; 402-14, Seokyo-dong; ⏲6pm-2am Mon-Sat; Ⓢ Line 6 to Sangsu, Exit 1) This classy wine bar is a sign of Hongdae's ever-growing sophisticated side. There are over

400 different bottles on the menu; unfortunately, little is sold by the glass. The pasta and salads are also highly rated.

KEG B PUB

Map p240 (☎02-334 1979; www.fb.me/kegbpub; 19 Wausan-ro 13-gil; ⏲5.30pm-1am Mon-Thu, to 2am Fri, 3pm-2am Sat, 3pm-noon Sun; Ⓢ Line 6 to Sangsu, Exit 1) This cosy craft-beer pub on the top floor of a small backstreet block is a good place to savour a pint or two. Choose between four local beers on tap and scores of bottled ales from around the world, served alongside snacks such as pizza, fried chicken and nachos.

M2 CLUB

Map p240 (엠투; ☎02-3143 7573; 20-5 Jandari-ro; Sun-Thu ₩10,000, Fri & Sat ₩20,000; ⏲9.30pm-4.30am Sun-Thu, to 8am Fri & Sat; Ⓢ Line 6 to Sangsu, Exit 1) Deep underground is M2, the largest and first of Hongdae's EDM clubs. It may have lost some of its cool cred but it's still popular for its grand space (high ceiling, large stage, good lights and visuals) and top local and international DJs spinning progressive house and other dance music.

LABRIS LESBIAN

Map p240 (라브리스; ☎02-333 5276; 81 Wausan-ro; cover incl 1 drink ₩10,000; ⏲9pm-6am Fri & Sat; Ⓢ Line 6 to Sangsu, Exit 1) This 8th-floor, comfortable women-only space is lesbian-oriented but not exclusively so. A female DJ plays dance music, and there are cocktails and *anju* (bar snacks). Fridays can be very quiet.

☆ ENTERTAINMENT

Hongdae is one of the city's best areas to head for clubs, bars and live music. Students ensure that most parks are turned into hubs for predrinks. Yeonnam-dong is the best area for cool calm bars, some with live music. The most popular clubs and noisier live venues tend to be near Hongik University. It is quite common to bar- and club-hop on any of the party nights – generally Thursday to Saturday.

★MUDAERUK LIVE MUSIC

Map p240 (무대륙; ☎02-332 8333; www.mudaeruk.com; 12 Tojeong-ro 5-gil; admission from ₩15,000; 📶; Ⓢ Line 6 to Sangsu, Exit 4) The 'Lost Continent of Mu' has been hiding out in Sangsu-dong all these years? Join those in the know for live bands, piano, improv jazz or electronic music in the basement on weekends. Upstairs is a stylish cafe-bar with craft beer, sharing boards of food and great fish and chips.

★FF LIVE MUSIC

Map p240 (☎010 9025 3407; 407-8 Seogyo-dong; admission ₩10,000; ⏲8-11pm Sun & Tue-Thu, 7pm-6am Fri & Sat; Ⓢ Line 6 to Sangsu, Exit 1) A top live venue with up to eight local indie bands playing at the weekend until midnight. Afterwards it becomes a dance club with DJs.

★CLUB EVANS JAZZ

Map p240 (☎02-337 8361; www.clubevans.com; 63 Wausan-ro; admission ₩10,000; ⏲7.30pm-midnight Sun-Thu, to 2am Fri & Sat; Ⓢ Line 6 to Sangsu, Exit 1) Appealing across the generations, Evans offers top-grade jazz and a great atmosphere. If you want a seat, get here early or book ahead – live music usually happens 9pm to 11pm. It releases its own label CDs, too. Monday is jam night.

OWL'S ROOFTOP LIVE MUSIC

Map p240 (옥탑방 부엉이; ☎02-332 6603; http://fb.me/owlsrooftop; 2nd fl, 43 Dongmak-ro 9-gil; ⏲6pm-1am Sun-Thu, to 3am Fri & Sat, live music from 8pm; Ⓢ Line 2 to Hongik University, Exit 8) FREE With live jazz, bands and acoustic music, great Korean food (clam and tofu stew; apple bbq pork) and beer (or bottles of berry *makgeolli*), this place, with views

LOCAL ART SCENE

The visually striking **KT&G Sangsang-Madang** (KT&G 상상마당; Map p240; ☎02-330 6200; www.sangsangmadang.com/main/HD; 65 Eoulmadang-ro; ⏲shop noon-11pm, gallery 1-10pm; Ⓢ Line 2 to Hongik University, Exit 5) is home to an art-house cinema, a concert space (hosting top indie bands) and galleries that focus on experimental, fringe exhibitions. There's also a great design shop for gifts on the ground floor. The architect, Bae Dae-yong, called his design the 'Why Butter Building' as the pattern of concrete across its glazed facade is said to resemble both butterfly wings and butter spread on toast.

over a buzzing corner of Hongdae, makes for a good night, or at least a great start.

POST TERRITORY UJJEONGUK ARTS CENTRE

Map p240 (탈영역 우정국; Ujjeonguk; 02-336 8553; www.ujeongguk.com; 42 Dongmak-ro 20-gil, Mapo-gu; S Line 6 to Sangsu, Exit 3) FREE This former post office turned art centre focuses on the theme of sharing and communication. With many exhibitions, concerts and seminars put on by and for young Korean artists, the experimental space is a must-visit for insight into Seoul's up-and-coming arts scene. Some events are in Korean, such as seminars and lectures, but most are nonverbal.

NANTA THEATRE HONGDAE PERFORMING ARTS

Map p240 (02-739 8288; www.nanta.co.kr; 357-4 Seogyo-dong; tickets ₩40,000-60,000; shows 5pm & 8pm; S Line 2 to Hongik University, Exit 9) Set in a kitchen, this long-running, high-octane show mixes varied ingredients – magic tricks, circus acts, drumming with kitchen utensils, comedy, dance, martial arts and audience participation – to produce a clever and entertaining musical pantomime that has broken box office records. There's an additional venue in Myeong-dong (p88).

CINEMATEQUE KOFA CINEMA

(한국영상자료원; 02-3153 2001; https://eng.koreafilm.or.kr; 400 World Cup buk-ro; S Line 6 to Susaek, Exit 2) FREE Free classic and contemporary Korean films are on the bill at one of the three cinemas in this home of the Korean Film Archive. See the website for directions from the subway exit.

DGBD LIVE MUSIC

Map p240 (디지비디; 02-322 3792; http://cafe.daum.net/dgbd; 23 Jandari-ro; admission ₩10,000; 8-11pm; S Line 2 or 6 to Hapjeong, Exit 3) First-generation K-Indie bands such as Crying Nut came into the spotlight at this legendary live-music venue. It's standing-room-only and there's a balcony.

INDIE ART-HALL GONG PERFORMING ARTS

(02-2632 8848; www.gongcraft.net; 30 Seonyuseo-ro 30-gil; S Line 5 to Yangpyeong, Exit 2) Marked by a huge brick chimney, this still-operating steel product factory has a large space on its 2nd floor devoted to a wide range of arts. Expect everything from visual- and performance-art shows to live gigs by K-Indie rockers. There's a shop selling some art and a cafe too. It's a short taxi hop from Mullae.

WORLD CUP STADIUM SPECTATOR SPORT

(월드컵주경기장; 02-2128 2002; www.seoulworldcupst.or.kr; 240, World Cup-ro; S Line 6 to World Cup Stadium, Exit 1) Built for the 2002 Football World Cup, this 66,000-seat venue is still used as a sports and events stadium. Die-hard football fans may want to visit the pricey but fun interactive museum (p94) here that focuses on K League history.

Also in the stadium is multiplex cinema, shopping store Homeplus, a gym, a swimming pool and 24-hour sauna World Cup Spaland.

CAFÉ BBANG LIVE MUSIC

Map p240 (카페 빵; http://cafe.daum.net/cafebbang; 12 Wausan-ro 29-gil; 7pm-6am; S Line 2 to Hongik University, Exit 8) You're sure to catch something interesting here. Apart from gigs by indie artists and bands, it also hosts film screenings, art exhibitions and parties.

SHOPPING

Markets and small boutiques are the best places to get a flavour of this area's creative vibe. In summer the Oil Tank Culture Park Forest Picnic Market (www.bamdokkaebi.org; 87 Jeungsan-ro; 4-9pm Sat & Sun Apr-Oct; S Line 6 to World Cup Stadium, Exit 2) is a good place for designer accessories.

★FREE MARKET GIFTS & SOUVENIRS

Map p240 (www.freemarket.or.kr; Hongdae Playground, 19-3 Wausan-ro 21-gil; 1-6pm Sat Mar-Nov; S Line 2 to Hongik University, Exit 9) Going strong since 2002, this lively weekly market helps to propel talented young creatives on to big-time retail. It's a great opportunity to meet the crafters and buy a unique souvenir, be it a hand-painted baseball cap, a colourful piece of jewellery or a leather bag. A good line-up of singers and bands play all afternoon, too.

★GENTLE MONSTER FASHION & ACCESSORIES

Map p240 (www.gentlemonster.com; 48 Dongmak-ro 7-gil; noon-9pm; S Line 2 or 6 to Hapjeong, Exit 3) Sunglasses at night is *the* Hongdae look and this hip place is where to pick up the edgiest of shades and frames as worn by K-Popsters and TV stars. Imaginative and fun art installations change roughly every 25 days on the ground floor.

★D-CUBE CITY MALL

(www.dcubecity.com; Kyungin-ro; ⏲stores 11am-9.30pm Mon-Fri, to 10pm Sat & Sun; Ⓢ Line 1 or 2 to Sindorim, Exit 1) Seoul's shopping malls hardly come any more stylish than this one in the previously industrial hub of Guro. The interior spaces surround a waterfall that cascades down seven floors, and plenty of terraces allow relaxing in fine weather. There are good restaurants and a superbly designed Korean food court in the basement.

★KEY ARTS & CRAFTS

Map p240 (☎02-325 9955; 48-5 Wausan-ro 29-gil; ⏲1-9pm Wed-Mon, to 8pm Tue; Ⓢ Line 2 to Hongik University, Exit 8) Representing scores of artists and craftspeople, several of whom also sell their goods at the Free Market on Saturday, this small gallery and showroom offers affordable, exclusive items, from jewellery and soft toys to fabric art and paintings.

MECENATPOLIS MALL MALL

(www.mecenatpolismall.co.kr; 45 Yanghwa-ro; ⏲10am-10pm; Ⓢ Line 2 or 6 to Hapjeong, Exit 9 or 10) Local and international brands, including Uniqlo and Muji, are arranged on several levels around open plazas at one of Seoul's best-designed malls with a distinctive canopy of umbrellas. Stars from K-Pop groups such as Big Bang live in the ritzy apartments that tower above the complex.

DONGJIN MARKET MARKET

(동진시장; ☎02-325 9559; www.facebook.com/makedongjin; 198 Seongmisan-ro; ⏲5-9pm Fri, 1-7pm Sat & Sun; Ⓢ Line 2 to Hongik University, Exit 3) An old market arcade has become a Friday-night and weekend hot spot for browsers in hip Yeonnam-dong. Secondhand clothing, homemade cookies, an overload of jewellery, various crafts and more can be picked up here.

OBJECT RECYCLE FASHION & ACCESSORIES

Map p240 (☎02-3144 7778; www.insideobject.com; 31 Yeonnam-ro 1-gil; ⏲10am-noon & 2-5pm Mon-Fri; Ⓢ Line 2 to Hongik University, Exit 9) Although there's a bigger branch of Object in Hongdae, this one is notable for specialising in products that involve some element of re- or up-cycling, such as jeans and shirts made into bags, clocks from vinyl records and side tables from cardboard boxes.

SPORTS & ACTIVITIES

YONSEI UNIVERSITY LANGUAGE

(☎02-2123 3465; www.yskli.com; 50 Yonsei-ro; courses from ₩947,000; Ⓢ Line 2 to Sinchon, Exit 6) The university runs part- and full-time Korean-language and culture classes for serious students.

WORLD CUP SPALAND SPA

(월드컵 스파랜드; ☎02-308 3094; www.sponspa.co.kr; 240, World Cup-ro; ₩9000-10,000; ⏲24hr; Ⓢ Line 6 to World Cup Stadium, Exit 1) A 24-hour sauna at World Cup Stadium.

YEOUIDO HANGANG SWIMMING POOL SWIMMING

Map p242 (☎02-785 0478; Yeouido Hangang Park; adult/youth/child ₩5000/4000/3000; ⏲9am-7pm Jul-Aug; Ⓢ Line 5 to Yeouinaru, Exit 2) Don't expect to get much swimming done at this summertime-only outdoor-pool complex which is typically flooded with locals just wanting to splash around and keep cool.

INTERNATIONAL SEON CENTER HEALTH & WELLBEING

(국제선센터; ☎02-2650 2242; http://seoncenter.com; 167 Mokdongdong-ro; Ⓢ Line 5 to Omokygo, Exit 8) Come here for free meditation classes in English, including thoughts on Buddhist teaching, every Saturday from 7pm to 9pm. A Templestay program is available from Wednesday to Saturday, check www.en.templestay.com for details.

The center is a 650m walk from the subway.

DAVIDNNP/SHUTTERSTOCK ©

1. National Folk Museum of Korea (p59)
Excellent museum of the Korean people and their way of life.

2. N Seoul Tower & Namsan (p81)
Watch the lights of Seoul from the iconic tower (designed by Jangjongryul) on the city's guardian mountain.

3. Banpo Bridge Rainbow Fountain (p125)
Floodlit fountains on display at night.

4. Gyeongui Line Forest Park (p94)
Picnic in this long green space along the old Gyeongui railway line.

NAMI CHWANG/SHUTTERSTOCK ©

KEITMA/SHUTTERSTOCK ©

3

MEZAIRI/SHUTTERSTOCK ©

Itaewon & Yongsan-gu

Neighbourhood Top Five

❶ **National Museum of Korea** (p108) Surveying centuries of Korean culture and art, and taking time to explore the attached gardens.

❷ **Leeum Samsung Museum of Art** (p110) Exploring contemporary masterpieces alongside traditional Korean crafts at Seoul's premier gallery.

❸ **War Memorial of Korea** (p109) Paying homage to those who gave their lives and learning more about a conflict that remains unresolved.

❹ **Linus' BBQ** (p112) Indulging in some of Seoul's most varied cuisine with an impressive array of world food, like this hip local take on Alabama BBQ.

❺ **Magpie Brewing Co** (p116) Heading out for a hedonistic night on the tiles, kicking off with a brew where the Seoul craft-beer scene began.

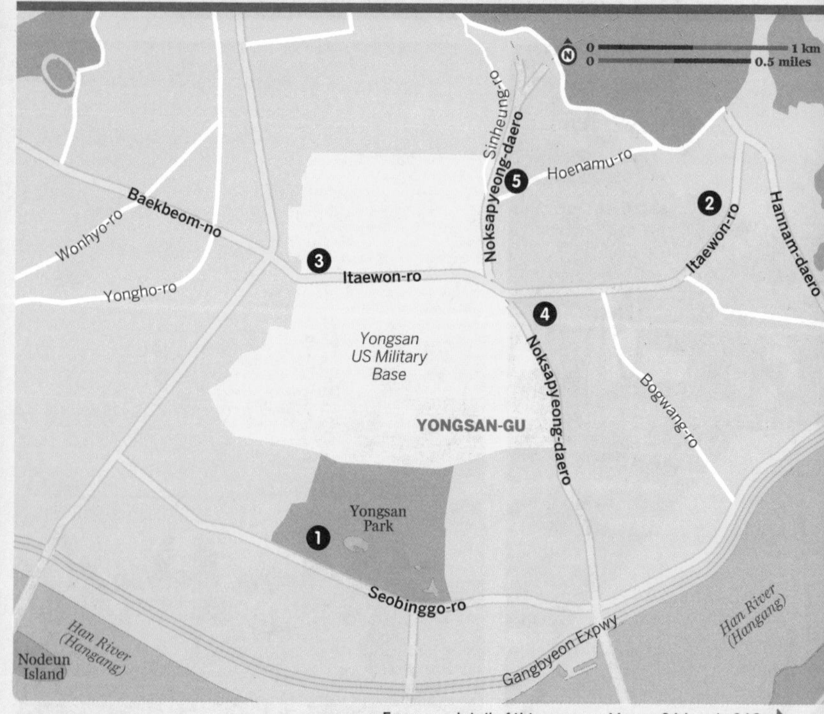

For more detail of this area see Maps p244 and p246

Explore Itaewon & Yongsan-gu

Yongsan-gu has long been defined by Yongsan Garrison, the US army base hidden behind concrete and barbed wire. Next door is Itaewon, where army personnel and expats shop and relax in an international mix of restaurants, bars and, umm, other places. For this reason, it has had a dodgy rep. While it retains its gritty edge, and the hostess and transvestite bars of 'Hooker Hill' (not to mention the cluster of Seoul's most foreigner-friendly gay hang-outs on 'Homo Hill'), it's now one of Seoul's trendiest dining and shopping districts.

The vibe has spilled over into adjacent areas. Head down Itaewon-ro, the main drag, in one direction and you'll hit classy Hannam-dong, home to celebrity Seoulites, the Leeum Samsung Museum of Art, designer boutiques and a bijou cafe scene. In the other direction, Haebangchon (aka HBC) and Gyeongridan have a laid-back mix of restaurants, cafes and craft-beer bars. In these areas, English is as widely spoken as Korean.

The third in a trio of affectionately nicknamed hills is 'Halal Hill' near the mosque, home to Seoul's Islamic community and a large Arabic-speaking population. Also along Usadan-ro is an emerging hip 'hood, which came about with the arrival of artists relocating here to set up studio spaces.

Two major cultural institutions, the National Museum and the War Memorial of Korea, are area highlights, and there are fine opportunities to de-stress, either in one of Seoul's most elaborate *jjimjil-bang* (sauna) complexes or by strolling or cycling along the Han River Park, around a 15-minute downhill walk from Itaewon.

Local Life

- **Shopping** Itaewon is the best place to find clothes and shoes in foreigner-friendly large sizes as well as to have something tailor-made. The lanes around Hannam-dong are increasingly home to small fashion boutiques, a counterpoint to the fashion flagships like Comme des Garcons (p117) on the main drag.
- **Religion** The beautiful Seoul Central Mosque (p110), Korea's largest such house of worship, sits atop a hill in Itaewon, surrounded by halal restaurants and shops with imported items from Islamic countries.

Getting There & Away

- **Subway** Line 6 is best for Itaewon and around, with Samgakji the closest station to the War Memorial of Korea; transfer here to Line 4 for the National Museum.
- **Tour bus** The War Memorial of Korea and National Museum are both stops on the City Tour Bus route.

Lonely Planet's Top Tip

To uncover the area's local life and its best dining, nightlife and shopping gems, veer south off the brash, commercial main drag, Itaewon-ro, and explore the network of winding alleyways roughly bookended by Noksapyeong and Hangangjin subway stations.

Best Places to Eat

- Linus' BBQ (p112)
- Casablanca Sandwicherie (p111)
- Plant Cafe & Kitchen (p111)
- Passion 5 (p111)
- Coreanos Kitchen (p111)

For reviews, see p111.

Best Places to Drink

- Southside Parlor (p114)
- Cakeshop (p113)
- Magpie Brewing Co. (p116)
- Soap (p114)
- Sunset Beach (p114)
- Grand Ole Opry (p114)

For reviews, see p113.

Best Places to Shop

- Yongsan Crafts Museum (p117)
- Comme des Garcons (p117)
- Millimetre Milligram (p117)
- Ando (p117)
- Eelskin Shop (p117)

For reviews, see p117.

TOP EXPERIENCE

FIND TREASURES AT THE NATIONAL MUSEUM

Korea's National Museum (designed by Chang-Il Kim) occupies an imposing, marble-lined, modernist complex, set in landscaped parklands. The massive Great Hall displays a fraction of the museum's 270,000 cultural treasures, which date from prehistoric times to the Joseon dynasty.

Hour-long, English-language tours leave from the **Great Hall** lobby at 11am and 2pm; alternatively, access the free museum wi-fi and download the museum's own app, which also serves as an audioguide.

The size of the museum is overwhelming, but among the must-see exhibits in the ground-floor galleries are the **Baekje Incense Burner**, a decorative metal piece that's an extraordinary example of the artistry of the 6th- to 7th-century Baekje dynasty; and the **Golden Treasures from the Great Tomb of Hwangham**, a delicate 5th-century gold belt and crown dripping with jade gems.

In the 3rd-floor sculpture and craft galleries, search out the **Pensive Bodhisattva** from the 7th century and beautiful examples of pottery. Also look down on the top of the Goryeo-dynasty **Ten Storey Pagoda** carved from marble. The surrounding park is best appreciated in good weather, when the Great Hall is perfectly reflected in the large **Reflecting Pond**. The original **Bosingak Bell** is in the grounds near the picturesque **Dragon Falls**.

Outside is the **Special Exhibition Hall**, which hosts blockbuster shows on anything from Renaissance painting to the Silk Road, with tickets costing around ₩10,000. Those interested in Korean language can visit the National Hanguel Museum (p110), which provides an overview of its relatively recent history.

Kids don't miss out either with the **Children's Museum** offering a snapshot of Korean culture with plenty of hands-on features and play spaces.

For picnic snacks in the park, there's a convenience store near the main entrance, as well as several cafes and restaurants in the complex.

DON'T MISS

- The Great Hall
- Reflecting Pond
- Dragon Falls

PRACTICALITIES

- 국립중앙박물관
- Map p246, C4
- www.museum.go.kr
- 137 Seobinggo-ro
- admission free
- ⌚10am-6pm, to 9pm Sat, to 7pm Sun
- S Line 1 or 4 to Ichon, Exit 2

TOP EXPERIENCE

SEE HISTORY AT THE WAR MEMORIAL OF KOREA

This huge, three-floor museum documents the history of warfare in Korea. Its main focus is the Korean War Room, where photos, maps and artefacts give a fascinating insight into what the Korean War (1950–53) was like.

Indoor Exhibits

Exhibits cover the surprise 4am attack from the North (spearheaded by 240 Russian-made tanks), the build-up of UN (mainly US) forces in Busan, the daring amphibious landing at Incheon, and the sweep north followed by the surprise Chinese attack – all of which took place in 1950.

On the 1st floor are paintings and panoramic displays illustrating many fierce battles fought against invading Mongol, Japanese and Chinese armies. Many items are only vaguely dated, but there is a replica of one of Admiral Sunsin's famous iron-clad turtle warships (called *geobukseon*), which he used to defeat the Japanese navy in the 1590s.

Other displays cover Korea's involvement in the Vietnam War (4700 Koreans died), North Korean attacks on the South since 1953, and Korea's UN peacekeeping roles.

Outdoor Exhibits

Outside, a sombre memorial walkway is inscribed with the names of every casualty from the Allied forces. Surrounding the museum are tanks, helicopters, missiles and planes galore, including a huge B-52 bomber. Several stirring monuments include the 11m-high **Statue of Brothers** depicting reconciliation between North and South Korea.

There's also a children's museum outside, presenting the history of war in Korea with an introduction to national war heroes of old and a 'training ground' play area.

DON'T MISS

- Korean War Room
- Statue of Brothers
- Outdoor Exhibit Areas

PRACTICALITIES

- 전쟁기념관
- Map p246, C2
- www.warmemo.or.kr
- 29 Itaewon-ro
- admission free
- 9.30am-6pm Tue-Sun
- S Line 4 or 6 to Samgakji, Exit 12

SIGHTS

NATIONAL MUSEUM OF KOREA — MUSEUM

See p108.

WAR MEMORIAL OF KOREA — MUSEUM

See p109.

STAIRWAY FLEA MARKET — MARKET

Map p244 (Usadan-ro) Held on the last Saturday of each month, this market attracts hundreds of shoppers to Usadan-ro on top of Itaewon Hill, where local artists sell their works on the stairs, and set up stalls along the street, which is lined with artist studios, galleries, pop-up shops and cool hole-in-the-wall bars and eateries.

SEOUL CENTRAL MOSQUE — MOSQUE

Map p244 (서울 중앙성원; 732-21 Hannam-dong; S Line 6 to Itaewon, Exit 3) FREE Its twin minarets rising tall and resplendent over 'Halal Hill', Seoul's impressive mosque, which opened in 1976, caters primarily to the Arabic, Asian and African immigrant worshippers who are settled in the Itaewon area.

NATIONAL HANGEUL MUSEUM — MUSEUM

Map p246 (www.hangeul.go.kr; 139 Seobinggo-ro; ⏲10am-6pm, to 9pm Sat; S Line 1 or 4 to Ichon, Exit 2) FREE Give your Korean-language skills a brush up with this museum dedicated to *hangeul*, the much-lauded Korean alphabet and writing system created in the 15th century. There's a weekly guided tour in English on Wednesdays at 2pm; call ahead to book.

ITAEWON BUGUNDANG HISTORY PARK — PARK

Map p244 (이태원부군당역사공원; 33 Noksapyeong-daero 40da-gil, Yongsan-gu; S Line 6 to Noksapyeong, Exit 2) FREE Even longtime residents of Itaewon might be surprised if you tell them that it is indeed possible to find historical relics in the heart of the neighbourhood. Located atop a hill directly facing N Seoul Tower (p81) is the **Bugundang Shrine**, which dates back to 1619 but was moved here from Namsan in 1917.

Although the shrine building itself is only open twice a year, the park offers stunning views of the Yongsan area, Namsan Mountain and N Seoul Tower, making

TOP EXPERIENCE

DISCOVER THE WORLD OF ART AT LEEUM

A masterful combination of contemporary architecture and exquisite art, Leeum Samsung Museum of Art is made up of three contrasting buildings designed by leading international architects. It's fronted by a **sculpture garden**, containing Anish Kapoor's tower of mirrored-orbs, *Tall Tree and Eye*, and satellite-like dish *Sky Mirror*.

The gallery is divided into three main buildings, covering a mix of modern and traditional art. Contemporary-art lovers will want to focus on **Museum 2**, featuring early- and mid-century paintings, sculptures and installations by esteemed Korean and international artists. Here you'll find three floors of works by the likes of Lee Joong-seop, Nam Jun Paik, Damien Hirst, Andy Warhol, Francis Bacon, Jean-Michel Basquiat and Jeff Koons. Getting an audioguide is highly recommended, or you can visit at 3pm weekends for the free 1½-hour tours in English.

For traditional Korean art, **Museum 1** is a must, though there's a lot to cover with four floors separated into fine art and calligraphy, ceramics and celadon, metalwork and Buddhist art.

The museum's third element, the **Samsung Child Education & Culture Center** is used for special exhibitions of Korean and international shows.

DON'T MISS

- Museums 1 & 2
- Samsung Child Education & Culture Center
- Outdoor art installations

PRACTICALITIES

- Map p244, G3
- www.leeum.org
- 60-16 Itaewon-ro 55-gil
- adult/child ₩10,000/5000
- ⏲10.30am-6pm Tue-Sun
- S Line 6 to Hangangjin, Exit 1

it a great spot for sunset-viewing. There's also a monument dedicated to Ryu Gwan-sun, a female Christian freedom fighter who died while imprisoned by the Japanese aged just 17.

EATING

Itaewon offers foodies a smorgasbord of obsessively authentic eats, from Turkish kebabs to Thai curries, with many multicultural eateries run either by immigrants or Koreans who've spent time overseas. Inbound Korean-Americans have popularised regional US fare in the 'hood, whether that's Detroit pizza, Alabama barbecue or KoMex (a creative fusion of Korean and Tex-Mex). Up the hill near the mosque are halal restaurants and ethnic supermarkets selling items you won't find elsewhere in Seoul.

★PLANT CAFE & KITCHEN — VEGAN $

Map p244 (플랜트; ☎02-749 1981; www.plantcafeseoul.com; 2nd fl, 117 Bogwang-ro, Yongsan-gu; meals from ₩12,000; ⏲11am-9pm Mon-Thu, to 10pm Fri & Sat; ; SLine 6 to Itaewon, Exit 4) Vegan wraps, avocado burgers, chickpea tagines and peanut stews are just some of the virtuously delicious highlights at this popular vegan hang-out started by a local food blogger. The plant-filled space is also a tranquil spot to nurse a cup of homemade *yuja* (citrus fruit) tea or on-tap kombucha.

★PASSION 5 — BAKERY, DESSERTS $

Map p244 (272 Itaewon-ro, Hannam-dong; sandwiches from ₩5000; ⏲7.30am-10pm; SLine 6 to Hangangjin, Exit 2) A luxe spin-off of the Paris Baguette chain, Passion 5 is the Rolls-Royce of Korean bakeries, offering a mouthwatering experience as you wander the gleaming arcade past a sea of perfect pastries, cakes, handmade chocolates, house-baked breads, bulgogi sandwiches and much more. It has a cafe, too, and seating throughout the complex.

★CASABLANCA SANDWICHERIE — SANDWICHES $

Map p246 (☎02-797 8367; 33 Sinheung-ro, Haebangchon; sandwiches ₩7000-8000; ⏲noon-10.45pm Tue-Sun; ; SLine 6 to Noksapyeong, exit 2) These mouth-watering, deep-filled sandwiches served on wide, half-loaves of pillowy bread are beloved by locals and expats. Try the wickedly seasoned (and messy) Moroccan chicken. Also does North African–style *shakshuka* (poached eggs; ₩10,000) and a thick lentil soup (₩3000). There's a long fridge of craft beer in the cosy dining room.

MOROCOCO CAFE — MOROCCAN $

Map p246 (모로코코 카페; ☎010 4228 8367; www.facebook.com/morococofe; 34 Sinheung-ro, Yongsan-gu; mains from ₩9000; ⏲noon-10pm Tue-Sun; ; SLine 6 to Noksapyeong, Exit 2) Cute North African–themed spot offering a chalkboard of half a dozen halal dishes like carrot salad, claypot lamb and the popular 'Morocco Over Rice' (₩9000) – shrimp, chicken, lamb or vegan with rice and vegies. Libations include spiced Moroccan tea and *'nas nas'* coffee (espresso dripped over foamed milk), bottled craft beer and wine.

It's from the same crew as Casablanca Sandwicherie (p111) across the street.

COREANOS KITCHEN — MEXICAN $

Map p244 (www.coreanoskitchen.com; 46 Noksapyeong-daero 40-gil; tacos for 2 ₩8000; ⏲noon-11pm, last order 10.15pm; SLine 6 to Itaewon, Exit 2) Lively KoMex restaurant specialising in 'skizzles' (essentially fusion fajitas) served on tabletop skillets in epic sharing portions. Tacos come in pairs; the corn tortillas are made in-house. Try to snag a terrace table for views over Itaewon.

HBC GOGITJIB — KOREAN, BARBECUE $

Map p244 (HBC 고깃집; 118-9 Itaewon-dong; barbecue ₩16,900; ⏲5pm-1am Mon-Fri, to 2am Sat & Sun; ; SLine 6 to Itaewon, Exit 1) Hungry revellers flock here for the nightly all-you-can-eat barbecue deal (₩16,900 per person), which includes beef ribeye and all the pork cuts on the menu for 90 minutes of protein guzzling. Sides are self-serve, and it has local beers and *soju* (local vodka).

It's up a side alley off the western end of the main bar strip north of Itaewon-ro.

TARTINE — CAFE $

Map p244 (☎02-3785 3400; www.tartine.co.kr; 4 Itaewon-ro 23-gil; small pecan pie ₩7800; ⏲10am-10.30pm; SLine 6 to Itaewon, Exit 1) This humble bakery-cafe just off Itaewon's main party strip bakes the best pecan pie this side of the Pacific, along with cranberry cheesecake, butter tart, apple crumble and lots more sweet-pie variations. Max out your sugar high with a cement-thick hot chocolate.

PIPIT BURGER BURGERS $

Map p244 (☎02-6497 0080; 8 Itaewon-ro 54-gil; burger with fries ₩12,000; ⏰11am-9.30pm, to 10pm Fri & Sat; ❄📶👶; Ⓢ Line 6 to Hangangjin, Exit 3) Harking back to the original San Bernardino McDonald's, this '50s-themed diner only grills one type of burger, but it's a beast. You can add bacon, double-up on the perfectly charred patties and go large with 'bottomless' (ie unlimited) crunchy fries. Don't fret: the craft-beer selection is anything but narrow.

PHO FOR YOU VIETNAMESE $

Map p244 (☎02-749 8947; 246-1 Noksapyeong-daero, Yongsan-gu; pho ₩11,000; ⏰10.30am-10pm Mon-Sun; Ⓢ Line 6 to Noksapyeong, Exit 2) This stripped-back canteen space ladles up huge plastic bowlfuls of *pho* dense with tender beef brisket and ribbons of rice noodles. The dark, deeply flavoured soup broth – a recipe from San Francisco, apparently – is the product of seriously slow cooking and good ingredients. Also does Vietnamese classics like *bánh mì,* beef *bun bo* and deep-fried appetiser sets. Local beers also available.

DOWNTOWNER BURGERS $

Map p244 (다운타우너; ☎070-8820 3696; www.instagram.com/downtownerseoul; 28-4 Itaewon-ro 42-gil, Yongsan-gu; burgers from ₩6800; ⏰11.30am-9.30pm Tue-Sun; 📶; Ⓢ Line 6 to Hangangjin, Exit 3) Foodies queue daily for the much lauded burgers here, painstakingly assembled (with Instagram in mind) and wrapped in cute zebra-striped paper. Pimp up your patty with cheese and bacon or the more popular avocado, and don't miss out on the guac fries. Oh, and the chicken strips.

MADDUX PIZZA PIZZA $

Map p244 (매덕스피자; ☎02-792 2420; 2nd fl, 26 Itaewon-ro 26-gil; slice from ₩4500, pizzas from ₩32,000; ⏰noon-10pm Tue-Sun; Ⓢ Line 6 to Itaewon, Exit 4) Keep your eyes peeled for those 'za-loving Ninja Turtles at this hip alleyway pizzeria serving jumbo-sized New York slices on paper plates. Choose from toppings like mac and cheese or spinach and artichoke, then raid the fridge for bottled craft beers and sodas.

PLANT BAKERY VEGAN $

Map p244 (☎070 4115 8388; www.plantcafeseoul.com; 20 Itaewon-ro 16-gil; baked goods from ₩3000; ⏰11am-8pm Mon-Sat; 🌿; Ⓢ Line 6 to Itaewon, Exit 4) This low-key vegan cafe on a quiet backstreet specialises in delicious dairy-free cakes, muffins, brownies, scones and cookies (some *sans* gluten too). The selection rotates regularly, but the chocolate peanut butter cake is a moreish mainstay. For vegan meals, seek out sister venue Plant Cafe & Kitchen (p111) a couple of streets away.

VATOS MEXICAN $

Map p244 (☎02-797 8226; www.vatoskorea.com; 2nd fl, 1 Itaewon-ro 15-gil; 2 tacos from ₩6900; ⏰11.30am-11pm Sun-Thu, from noon Fri & Sat; 📶; Ⓢ Line 6 to Itaewon, Exit 4) Itaewon's original KoMex eatery still does a roaring trade in soft corn tacos filled with *galbi* short rib and sides of *kimchi* carnitas fries, along with more standard Mexican fare. People come for the booze as much as the food; the monstrous margaritas, with upturned beer bottles sticking out the top, are quite something.

★LINUS' BBQ BARBECUE $$

Map p244 (☎02-790 2930; www.facebook.com/linusbbq; 136-13 Itaewon-ro; sandwich plus sides from ₩12,000; ⏰11.30am-3.30pm & 5.30-10pm; Ⓢ Line 6 to Noksapyeong, Exit 3) The portions are more modest than your typical Southern smokehouse, but the pulled pork and beef-brisket rolls with 'skinny ass' fries are some of the tastiest (and prettiest) plates of western food in Seoul. Count on a friendly, laid-back vibe in the industrial-styled dining space, with a good choice of craft beers and cocktails.

OLDE KNIVES STEAK $$

Map p246 (올드 나이브즈; 4 Sinheung-ro 11-gil; 200g steak ₩22,000; ⏰6pm-1am Tue-Sun) There's no menu at this hidden-gem HBC hang-out – just a grill behind a hardwood bar where striploin steaks are sizzled to perfection (₩22,000). If butter-soft beef with grilled vegies doesn't do it for you, it also makes carbonara-style pasta (₩18,000). The cocktails (from ₩16,000) are excellent.

NEKKID WINGS AMERICAN $$

Map p244 (네키드윙즈; ☎010 5891 7411; www.nekkidwings.com; 174-11 Noksapyeong-daero, Yongsan-gu; 10 wings & sides ₩15,000; ⏰5-11pm Mon-Thu, 11.30am-11pm Fri-Sun; ❄📶; Ⓜ Line 6 to

LOCAL KNOWLEDGE

USADAN-RO'S ART COMMUNITY

If the top of the hill near Seoul Central Mosque (p110) wasn't intriguing enough (its extraordinary diversity mixes Seoul's Islamic community, LGBTIQ+ community and red-light district), the enclave of artists who've relocated to Usadan-ro adds another layer of interest. Since rent prices in Hongdae have skyrocketed, this art community has moved in and set up studios, galleries, pop-up shops and hip hole-in-the-wall bars and eateries.

Aim to visit on the last Saturday of each month for the Stairway Flea Market (p110) with its street-party atmosphere as local artists sell their works on the stairs and stalls set up along the strip.

Noksapyeong, Exit 1) Get your hot wings basted a dozen different ways at this alleyway eatery, from classic buffalo to Korean-inspired 'Amazinger' (spicy ginger), soy wasabi and mandarin orange. The open kitchen also turns out shoestring fries, onion croquettes and pickles, and there are plenty of craft beers on offer, naturally.

ROOT HEALTH FOOD **$$**

Map p244 (루트; ☎02-797 9505; 2nd fl, 26-4 Itaewon-ro 55ga-gil; dishes ₩12,000; ⌚11am-9pm; 📶; ⓈLine 6 to Hangangjin, Exit 1) It didn't take Itaewon long to get on the food-bowl trend. Step up Root, serving zesty salad and poke bowls with a Korean twist from its sunny 2nd-floor dining room, along with things on toast, soups and 'salad sushi' – veggies, avo and rice rolled and served in *gimbap* (Korean sesame-oil flavoured rice wrapped in seaweed) form.

GINO'S NY PIZZA PIZZA **$$**

Map p244 (지노스 뉴욕 피자; ☎02-792 2234; www.facebook.com/ginoskorea; 46 Noksapyeong-daero 40-gil, Yongsan-gu; pizzas for 2 from ₩17,000; ⌚noon-10pm Tue-Sun; ⓈLine 6 to Noksapyeong, Exit 2) This wildly popular upstairs kitchen bakes an authentic range of New York–style pies along with appetisers like garlic knots, wings and messy fries. The queues got so big it opened another, more casual, venue opposite that sells pizza by the slice (closed Tuesdays). Craft beers and cocktails available.

LA FERME HEALTH FOOD **$$**

Map p244 (라페름; ☎02-790 6685; 32 Itaewon-ro 54-gil, Yongsan-gu; salads from ₩12,500; ⌚11.30am-9pm Tue-Sun, closed 3-4pm Tue-Fri; 📶; ⓈLine 6 to Hangangjin, Exit 3) Le Ferme (French for 'the farm') packs them in for superfood-rich detox dining with a French twist. Quinoa, tofu, avocado and mango feature in the substantial salads, while mains include chicken couscous and seafood risotto.

BAKER'S TABLE BAKERY, CAFE **$$**

Map p244 (☎070 7717 3501; 244-1 Noksapyeong-daero, Gyeongridan; mains from ₩10,000; ⌚8am-9pm, to 8pm Sun; ⓈLine 6 to Noksapyeong, Exit 2) German-run brunch hot spot serving stacked sandwiches and a mighty range of sweet and savoury pastries (it's generous with the free nibbles, so pop in and try before you buy). You'll also find mains like *Jaeger* schnitzel and bratwurst, soups, and hearty breakfast options. German beer on tap is another draw. Expect a wait on weekends.

DRINKING & NIGHTLIFE

Many a memorable night out starts or ends in the bars and clubs around Itaewon-ro. Craft-beer aficionados will certainly want to mosey on down to Gyeongridan, while those after a more mature vibe should check out the expat-oriented pubs and lounge bars of HBC. 'Homo Hill', south of Itaewon-ro, is the high point of Seoul's LGBTIQ+ scene, and clubbers have decent dancing options all over the neighbourhood.

★CAKESHOP CLUB

Map p244 (www.cakeshopseoul.com; 134 Itaewon-ro; admission incl 1 drink ₩20,000; ⌚10pm-5am Thu-Sat; ⓈLine 6 to Noksapyeong, Exit 2) Head underground to Itaewon's hippest club for electronic beats spun by international and top local DJs. Check their Facebook page to see who's playing.

★SOUTHSIDE PARLOR COCKTAIL BAR

Map p244 (☎02-749 9522; www.facebook.com/SouthsideParlor; 218 Noksapyeong-daero, Gyeongridan; cocktails from ₩14,000; ⏰6pm-midnight Sun-Thu, to 2am Fri & Sat; 📶; Ⓢ Line 6 to Noksapyeong, Exit 2) Having outgrown their Texas-taco-truck roots, these artisanal cocktail makers set up shop in Itaewon. Behind a copper bar, a crew of amiable bartenders concoct creative originals like their award-winning Chiquita Pepita with cucumber-infused tequila. A quality food menu includes Texas staples like fried chicken tacos and smoked *queso*. Weekday food specials help the medicine go down.

★GRAND OLE OPRY BAR

Map p244 (16 Usadan-ro 14-gil; beer ₩3000; ⏰6pm-1am, to 3am Fri & Sat; Ⓢ Line 6 to Itaewon, Exit 3) Bang in the middle of Itaewon's red-light district, this honky-tonk dive bar is a throwback GI hang-out and something straight out of a movie. The original owner, Mama Kim, still works the bar; she bought the club in 1975. Grab a ₩3000 drink, have a chinwag about Itaewon's colourful history, then do-si-do over to the wooden dance floor.

'The Star Spangled Banner' is played at the stroke of midnight on Friday and Saturday, as it has been here for over 40 years.

★VENUE/ CLUB

Map p244 (www.facebook.com/venuerok; 165-6 Itaewon-ro; ⏰10pm-5am Fri & Sat, to 3am Thu; Ⓢ Line 6 to Itaewon, Exit 1) This dive-y basement club attracts a fun-loving, unpretentious crowd for DJs spinning old-school hip-hop and R&B, house, disco and electronica. There's no cover charge, but there's a queue after midnight.

SUNSET BEACH BAR

Map p244 (165-6 Itaewon-ro; cocktail pouches ₩9000; ⏰7pm-3am; Ⓢ Line 6 to Itaewon, Exit 1) Some nights this shoebox of a bar is the most happening hang-out on the Itaewon strip. Maybe it's the Long Island Ice Teas served in plastic pouches (two is too many); maybe it's the zany local crowd; or maybe it's Junior, the hardman Korean bar manager with a heart of gold. We're going with all of the above.

SOAP CLUB

Map p244 (소프, Club Soap, Soap Seoul; ☎070-4457 6860; www.soapseoul.com; 14-9 Bogwang-ro 60-gil, Yongsan-gu; admission incl 1 free drink ₩20,000; ⏰10pm-5am Thu-Sat; Ⓢ Line 6 to Itaewon, Exit 3) Tucked away in the back alleys of Itaewon, this blue-hued basement club burst onto the scene in 2017, pulling in international DJs spinning to a young, up-for-it crowd.

BLACKLIST COCKTAIL BAR

Map p244 (3rd fl, 66-2 Itaewon-dong; cocktails from ₩12,000; ⏰7pm-2am Tue-Sun; 📶; Ⓢ Line 6 to Itaewon, Exit 4) You'll find a friendly welcome and a well-mixed selection of house and top-shelf cocktails in this intimate 3rd-floor bar run by Americans.

STANDING COFFEE ROASTERS CAFE

Map p244 (☎02-3785 1019; www.standingcoffee.co.kr; 210-8 Itaewon-dong; ⏰10am-6pm; 📶; Ⓢ Line 6 to Noksapyeong, Exit 2) For top-quality third-wave coffee at a great price, Standing Coffee Roasters can't be beat. This is its roastery, with a tiny shop and cafe attached. Buy a bag of beans (₩12,000 for 200g) and staff will brew you a free cup of joe. It also has a stand down the hill.

LIVING ROOM LOUNGE

Map p246 (☎010 3105 5256; 30-1 Sinheung-ro; beer from ₩5000; ⏰9pm-1am Wed, Thu & Sun, to 3am Fri & Sat) For a vibe somewhere between a club and a bar, duck in to Living Room, a cosy basement lounge attracting a friendly Haebangchon crowd for well-priced drinks, comfy sofas and DJs spinning funk, soul, classic hip hop and '80s at just the right volume.

Y.POT COFFEE CAFE

Map p244 (☎02-792 8162; 455-36 Itaewon-dong; coffee ₩5000; ⏰noon-11pm Tue-Sun; 📶; Ⓢ Line 6 to Itaewon, Exit 1) Run by a mild-mannered coffee nerd who roasts his own beans onsite, this is one of the least pretentious independent cafes in the area, and a handy pit stop when moving between Itaewon and Gyeongridan. Takeaway coffee is ₩2000 cheaper.

NAMSAN WINERY WINE BAR

Map p244 (☎02-792 5849; 5 Hoenamu-ro 10-gil; glass of wine ₩8000; ⏰6pm-2am, from noon Sat & Sun; Ⓢ Line 6 to Noksapyeong, Exit 2) If you're seeking refuge from all the craft beer and KoMex, this low-key wine bar is just the ticket. Serving Iberian wines with *petiscos* (Portuguese tapas), it's a pleasant place for an intimate soiree, and the owner couldn't be friendlier.

PET SOUNDS BAR

Map p244 (www.facebook.com/petsoundsbar; 3rd fl, 278-8 Itaewon 2-dong; beers from ₩4000; ⏲6pm-late; ⓈLine 6 to Noksapyeong, Exit 2) Named after Korean owner Jay's love affair with the Beach Boys' *Pet Sounds* album, this friendly upstairs rock bar provides a paper and pen to put in your song requests. Drinks are plentiful and reasonably priced. Jay also owns neon-clad jazz bar Boogie Woogie (p116) on the floor below.

AGAINST THE MACHINE BAR

Map p244 (어게슨트더머신; 48 Itaewon-ro 54-gil, Hannam-dong; drinks from ₩12,000; ⏲6pm-3am; ⓈLine 6 to Itaewon, Exit 3) This tiny backstreet bar, an ubercool beacon for local bohos, feels almost Parisian with its artsy vibe, low-fi beats and bartop candles buried under a mountain of wax. Drinks are limited to spirits and a single craft beer on tap.

FLOWER GIN BAR

Map p244 (250 Noksapyeong-daero, Gyeongridan; gin & tonic ₩9500; ⏲2pm-midnight Mon, Wed & Thu, from noon Fri-Sun; 📶; ⓈLine 6 to Noksapyeong, Exit 2) An inspired mix of florist-meets-gin-bar, the perfumed scents here match the drinks superbly. Run by a young female owner, this tiny bar only does gin-based drinks using Hendricks, infused with a slice of cucumber and a freshly plucked flower.

MOWMOW BAR

Map p244 (모우모우; 54-3 Itaewon-ro 27ga-gil; makgeolli from ₩12,000; ⏲5pm-3am Mon-Thu, 3pm-5am Sat, to 1am Sun; ⓈLine 6 to Itaewon, Exit 1) Order your *makgeolli* (milky rice wine)

ON THE HILL

Squished between 'Hooker Hill', 'Tranny Hill' and 'Halal Hill' (aka Little Arabia, the strip by the Seoul Mosque), 'Homo Hill' is a 50m alley so-called because of its cluster of gay-friendly bars and clubs. Most hardly have room to swing a handbag, so on warm weekends the crowds often spill into the street. All genders and sexual persuasions will feel welcome here, though foreigners (ie non-Koreans) have noted in the past that some venues didn't make them feel welcome.

Always Homme (올웨이즈옴므; Map p244; Usadan-ro 12-gil; ⏲9pm-4am Sun-Thu, to 5am Fri & Sat; ⓈLine 6 to Itaewon, Exit 3) The most welcoming gay bar on the strip, this place has flirty-friendly staff, low-playing music and a cosy open-air lounge set-up.

Trance (Map p244; Usadan-ro; admission incl 1 drink ₩10,000; ⏲11pm-5am Wed-Sun; ⓈLine 6 to Itaewon, Exit 3) Pouting drag princesses entertain in their own utterly unique style at this small gay club with a DJ and a stage. Drag performances usually kick off around 2.30am.

Queen (Map p244; www.facebook.com/queenbar; 7 Usadan-ro 12-gil; ⏲10pm-3am Thu, to 5am Sat & Sun; ⓈLine 6 to Itaewon, Exit 3) The undisputed queen of Homo Hill, this eternally popular gay bar is still the place to party in Itaewon.

Miracle (Map p244; Usadan-ro; ⏲8pm-5am Thu-Sat; ⓈLine 6 to Itaewon, Exit 3) One of Korea's few exclusively lesbian bars, this queer-only joint sits atop Homo Hill and gets going around midnight.

Almaz (Map p244; 4 Usadan-ro 12-gil; drinks from ₩8000; ⏲7pm-2am Wed-Thu, to 5am Fri & Sat; ⓈLine 6 to Itaewon, Exit 3) Gay-friendly Almaz is more chilled than other Homo Hill hot spots, drawing a mature crowd to its scarlet-hued lounge hung with glitter balls. Previously a private house, the garden serves as a patio for revellers.

Eat Me (Map p244; ☎07-4267 3270; www.facebook.com/eatmeitaewon; 137-5 Itaewon-dong 1; ⏲6.30pm-4am Wed-Sun; ⓈLine 6 to Itaewon, Exit 3) This Itaewon gay bar by the same folks behind Queen (p115) opposite is a good place to kick off the night with a cocktail before moving to more danceable spots on Homo Hill.

Soho (Map p244; Usadan-ro; ⏲10pm-5am Fri & Sat; ⓈLine 6 to Itaewon, Exit 3) A smart gay bar opposite Queen (p115) with a laid-back vibe and a club area for later in the evening.

Why Not (Map p244; Usadan-ro; ⏲7.30pm-3am Sun-Thu, to 5am Fri & Sat; ⓈLine 6 to Itaewon, Exit 3) This small but smartly turned-out gay bar has good cocktails and plenty of K-Pop.

CRAFT BEER VALLEY

At the epicentre of the craft-beer revolution in Seoul, the area north of Noksapyeong subway station has come to be known as Craft Beer Valley thanks to the string of brewers who set up shop in the vicinity. In a short time, this localised scene has paved the way for a greater diversity and quality of beer in Seoul, resulting in a shift in tastes that's seen locals gain a thirst for India pale ales (IPAs), amber ales, German-style wheat beers and smoky stouts.

Previously, government restrictions meant the industry was dominated by a handful of major brewers churning out industrial lagers like Hite, Cass and OB. It was this lack of diversity that led to an article in the *Economist* claiming that North Korean beer tasted infinitely better than its southern counterpart. Ouch. This proved to be the spark that lit the fuse, leading to a loosening of restrictions that enabled small-scale breweries to produce commercially. The rest is history, and now every second bar and restaurant in Itaewon sells craft beer, both local and imported.

Magpie Brewing Co (Map p244; www.magpiebrewing.com; 244-1 Noksapyeong-daero; beer from ₩7000; ⏲3pm-1am; S Line 6 to Noksapyeong, Exit 2) Seoul craft-beer pioneers Magpie pour some of the finest brews in Seoul from this rough-and-tumble alleyway venue, opened in 2011. Pull up a stool at the tiny bar or duck into the bunker-styled basement for low-hanging lighting and excellent pizza.

Booth (Map p244; www.theboothpub.com; Itaewon-dong 705, Gyeongridan; ⏲noon-1am; S Line 6 to Noksapyeong, Exit 2) The original Booth brewpub (there are now eight in Seoul) looks the part with its pop-art murals and warehouse-chic interior, but beer aficionados have more love for the suds at Magpie Brewing Co (p116) next door. A case of too much success being a curse, maybe? Grab a Bill's Pale Ale (its original brew) and a slice of pizza and make your own mind up.

White Rabbit (Map p244; 242 Noksapyeong-daero, Gyeongridan; beer from ₩8000; ⏲6pm-1am; S Line 6 to Noksapyeong, Exit 2) A one-man operation run by a local surfer, this cramped bar has an extensive selection of Korean and international craft beers chalked up on the board above the bar, and serves a small menu of pizza and sides.

by the half-litre or litre at this homey bar and restaurant up the hill from the main Itaewon dining alley. Or pair a *makgeolli* cocktail with a *pajeon* (Korean savoury pancake) crammed with creative and filling combos like pork belly, *kimchi* and cheese.

BURN BAR

Map p244 (☎02-794 8077; www.burninhal.com; 305-7 Itaewon-dong; cigars around ₩20,000, cocktails from ₩18,000; ⏲6pm-2am, to 3am Sat & Sun; S Line 6 to Noksapyeong, Exit 2) Blaze up a top-class Cuban, swirl your aged single malt and kick back in a leather club chair as you savor the sophisticated (and smoky) ambience at this throwback cigar bar. Live jazz plays nightly between 9pm and 11pm (cover charge ₩5000). Also has quality rums and classic cocktails.

ROSE & CROWN PUB

Map p244 (6 Itaewon-ro 19-gil; pint of lager ₩7900; ⏲3pm-2am Mon-Fri, to 3am Sat & Sun; wi-fi; S Line 6 to Itaewon, Exit 1) Foreigner-friendly Itaewon wouldn't be complete without a British pub, and this atmospheric two-storey boozer delivers with its pints of ale, fish and chips, cottage pie and live Premier League on the telly.

ENTERTAINMENT

BOOGIE WOOGIE JAZZ

Map p244 (☎010 2396 3050; www.facebook.com/boogiewoogieseoul; 2nd fl, 278-8 Itaewon 2-dong; cocktails from ₩8000; ⏲6pm-5am, to 3am Sun; S Line 6 to Noksapyeong, Exit 2) Shake your stuff to two shows nightly (7pm and 9pm) at this neon-clad live-music den featuring local jazz acts and a smattering of blues, funk and hip hop. It's run by the same musos behind Pet Sounds (p115) one floor up. When the bands finish, DJs spin until the early hours. Check the Facebook page to see what's on.

ALL THAT JAZZ JAZZ

Map p244 (☎02-795 5701; www.allthatjazz.kr; 3rd fl, 12 Itaewon-ro 27ga-gil; ₩5000; ⏰6pm-1am Sun-Thu, to 2.30am Fri & Sat; Ⓢ Line 6 to Itaewon, Exit 2) A fixture on the Seoul jazz scene since 1976, this place regularly features top local musicians; table reservations are recommended for the weekend. There are usually four sessions of live music per night with the first starting around 6.30pm. Showtimes are posted at the venue entrance and on the website.

SHOPPING

Oversized and tailored clothing are popular buys in Itaewon, while exclusive Hannam-dong is home to fashion flagships and back-alley boutiques. The street running south from Itaewon subway, Bogwang-ro, has been lined with antiques shops ever since the first departing US soldiers sold off their belongings. Secondhand mobile phones are among the best buys at Yongsan Electronics Market and neighbouring I'Park Mall.

YONGSAN CRAFTS MUSEUM ARTS & CRAFTS

Map p244 (☎02-2199 6180; 274 Itaewon-ro; ⏰10am-7pm Tue-Sun; Ⓢ Line 6 to Hangangjin, Exit 3) A fantastic place to buy top-quality traditional Korean handicrafts like *hanji* (Korean paper) ornaments and baskets, *najeon* (inlaid lacquerware), porcelain tea sets, *tal* (masks) and *bangjja* (bronzeware). Even if you're not buying, the museum-like shop floor makes it well worth a browse. You can find craft workshops on the 2nd floor.

COMME DES GARCONS FASHION & ACCESSORIES

Map p244 (261 Itaewon-ro; ⏰11am-8pm; Ⓢ Line 6 to Hangangjin, Exit 1) Uberstylish flagship boutique of the Japanese label. Take the elevator to the 4th floor then work your way down through the maze-like corridors.

MILLIMETRE MILLIGRAM STATIONERY, BAGS

Map p244 (☎02-549 1520; www.mmmg.net; 240 Itaewon-ro; ⏰11.30am-8pm; Ⓢ Line 6 to Itaewon, Exit 3) Usually shortened to MMMG, this stylish emporium tells a story on every storey, from Swiss brand Freitag on ground level up through to Japanese homewares, posh stationary and more.

EELSKIN SHOP FASHION & ACCESSORIES

Map p244 (All Seasons Eel Skin Co; ☎02-796 9628; 60-4 Itaewon-dong; purses from ₩50,000; ⏰9.30am-8pm; Ⓢ Line 6 to Itaewon, Exit 4) Back in the 1980s there were around 50 eel-leather shops in Itaewon. Now there's just Mr Choe's, which has sold his luxuriously supple handbags, belts, wallets and purses here for four decades. Handmade wallets go for ₩25,000 to ₩35,000, and purses ₩50,000 to ₩180,000. Prices depend on the quality and number of conger eels used (longer and wider skins are more expensive).

ANDO ANTIQUES

Map p244 (www.ando.or.kr; 99 Bogwang-ro; ⏰10am-7pm Mon-Sat; Ⓢ Line 6 to Itaewon, Exit 4) In a street famous for its antique stores (which originated when departing US soldiers sold their belongings), Ando is one of the most well known. The three-storey industrial space is done out like a beautifully curated museum of early-20th-century Americana. It ain't cheap, though.

VINYL & PLASTIC MUSIC

Map p244 (☎02-2014 7800; 248 Itaewon-ro; ⏰noon-9pm, to 6pm Sun; 📶; Ⓢ Line 6 to Itaewon, Exit 3) Vinyl is alive and kicking at this warehouse-sized music store that invites you to listen to the latest releases on a dozen or so turntables before buying. Opened by Hyundai Card, a Korean credit-card company, it also sells headphones and Bluetooth speakers. An upstairs cafe has digital jukeboxes on the tables and outdoor balcony seating.

I'PARK MALL MALL

Map p246 (www.iparkmall.co.kr; Yongsan; ⏰10.30am-9pm; Ⓢ Line 1 to Yongsan, Exit 2) With brand-name shopping and three floors of eateries, this giant department store sprawls around the major overground Yongsan station. Check out the wedding concourse in the heart of the mall, with multiple ceremonies taking place at once. The 8th floor is a great place to buy cheap secondhand phones and prepaid SIM cards.

YONGSAN ELECTRONICS MARKET ELECTRONICS

Map p246 (용산전자랜드; 125 Cheongpa-ro; ⏰10am-7.30pm; Ⓢ Line 1 to Yongsan, Exit 3) Korea isn't a particularly cheap country in which to pick up electronics (even for home-grown brands like Samsung), but this humongous collection of purveyors of technology might still appeal if you're on the hunt for a high-end gaming laptop or secondhand camera. For secondhand phones, the 8th floor of I'Park Mall (p117) is better.

WHAT THE BOOK BOOKS

Map p244 (☎02-797 2342; www.whatthebook.com; 86 Bogwang-ro, Yongsan-gu; ⏰10am-9pm; Ⓢ Line 6 to Itaewon, Exit 3) Itaewon's best bookshop sells a wide range of English-language fiction and nonfiction with an interesting section on Korean culture. Also stocks current editions of US magazines like *The New Yorker* and *Rolling Stone*.

SPORTS & ACTIVITIES

★DRAGON HILL SPA & RESORT SPA

Map p246 (드래곤힐스파; ☎010 4223 0001; www.dragonhillspa.co.kr; 40-713 Hangangno 3-ga; Mon-Fri day/night ₩10,000/12,000, Sat & Sun all day ₩12,000; ⏰24hr; Ⓢ Line 1 to Yongsan, Exit 1) Think of this foreigner-friendly *jjimjilbang* (upmarket sauna) as a wellness theme park with a dash of Las Vegas bling and Asian chic thrown in. One of Seoul's largest bathhouses, it has a unisex outdoor pool as well as traditional kiln saunas, ginseng and sauna baths, jacuzzis, an ice room, a 'fire-sweating' room and much more.

KORIDOOR TOURS BUS

Map p246 (☎02-6383 2570; www.koridoor.co.kr; 251 Hangangdae-ro, Yongsan-gu; Ⓢ Line 1 to Namyeong, Exit 1) Apart from running the very popular Demilitarized Zone (DMZ)/Joint Security Area (JSA) tour for the United Service Organizations (USO), this company also offers city tours and overnight trips to destinations like Jeju and Busan.

Gangnam & Southern Seoul

Neighbourhood Top Five

❶ **Olympic Park** (p121)
Strolling around 1700-year-old fortifications, museums and 200 quirky sculptures in a green space.

❷ **Bongeun-sa** (p123)
Making a lotus lantern and sipping tea with monks at the venerable temple juxtaposed against skyscrapers.

❸ **Lotte World** (p122) Getting high on an amusement-park thrill ride and in a fairy-tale carousel and castle in the tallest building in South Korea.

❹ **SMTown coexartium** (p124) Electric-kissing K-Pop holograms at a five-level museum to some of Korea's biggest idols.

❺ **Apgujeong** (p130)
Checking out eye-boggling price tags then dining and partying at world-class restaurants and clubs.

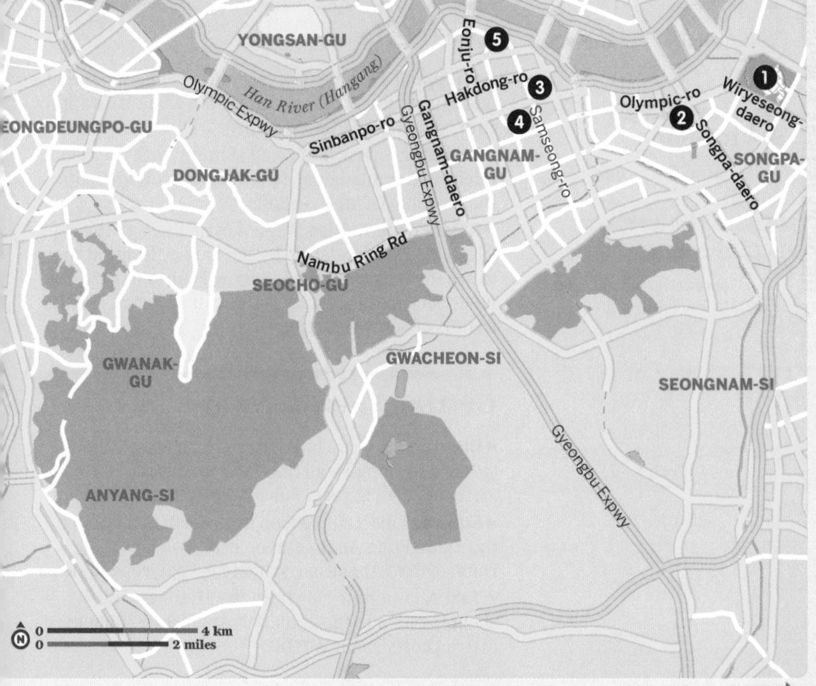

For more detail of this area see Maps p248, p250 and p252

Lonely Planet's Top Tip

Get a taste of world-class eating at a more budget-friendly price by visiting in the day. Plenty of top restaurants do set-lunch specials that are very similar to their night offerings, with the added bonus of including an entree and drink.

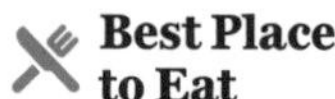

Best Places to Eat

- Jungsik (p127)
- Samwon Garden (p128)
- Normal by Ryunique (p127)

For reviews, see p126.

Best Places to Drink

- Neurin Maeul (p129)
- Mikkeller Bar (p128)
- Club Octagon (p128)

For reviews, see p128.

Best Places to Shop

- 10 Corso Como Seoul (p130)
- COEX Mall (p130)
- Galleria (p130)

For reviews, see p130.

Explore Gangnam & Southern Seoul

Gangnam refers to an administrative area, Gangnam-gu, and the parts of Seoul that lie south of the Han. Interesting sights are spread out and can feel suburban (though ritzy) after Itaewon and Myeongdong. Ranks of tower blocks bisected by highways can be intimidating to traverse on foot between areas, but it's interesting to see how wealthy Koreans live. Planning what you see by metro station helps to organise your time. Otherwise, the Gangnam City Tour Bus (p132) is worth considering.

If you are into theme parks and nature parks plan a day around Sports Complex and Jamsil stations. The Olympic Park (p121) area, the legacy of the 1988 Olympics, is a main sight with its green space, museums and galleries. Gangnam's wide open spaces allowed Lotte to create its giant theme park (p122), plus Seoul's tallest building nearby, filled with tourists.

For a taste of the high life 'Gangnam Style', the area between Apgujeong Rodeo, Cheongdam and Hak-dong stations will have you in designer heaven. Boutique shopping (p130), galleries, restaurants and K-Pop studios (p126) gather at Seoul's Fifth Ave. A Saturday lingering over brunch can turn into a night of world-class clubbing.

Nearby, tree-lined Garosu-gil has more-affordable shopping, and buzzes with students at night eating at interesting, budget-friendly restaurants near Sinsa station.

Local Life

- **Shopping** Taxi-hop between the designer boutiques of Apgujeong and Cheongdam – you wouldn't want to ruin your Jimmy Choo stilettos!
- **Clubbing** Sip cocktails and shimmy with the rich, celebs and wannabes at Seoul's flashiest nightspots such as Club Octagon (p128).
- **Riverside activities** Walk or cycle through the Han Riverside Park; and drop by the Banpo Bridge at night to see the Banpo Bridge Rainbow Fountain (p125), its food-truck market (p126) and the illuminated floating islands of Some Sevit (p124).

Getting There & Away

- **Bus** There are two intercity bus terminals: Nambu (p208) and Dong-Seoul (p207). Long-distance buses arrive at Seoul Express Bus Station (p207).
- **Subway** Line 2 runs a loop from north of the Han to the south. From Anguk station near Insadong, Line 3 runs south to Apgujeong station for Apgujeong Rodeo.
- **Taxi** A 13-minute ride from the Myeong-dong shopping area to the upmarket Apgujeong shopping district costs about ₩7200.

TOP EXPERIENCE

STROLL THE GROUNDS OF OLYMPIC PARK

You might not be into sports, but this expansive green space is more like an interesting open-air gallery converted from the legacy of the 1988 Olympics. There are relaxing walks between the interactive Olympics museum and sights to outdoor sculptures, ponds and the modern-art museum. The earthen fortification of the Mongchon-toseong (Mongchon Fortress), ringed by a moat, contains 3rd-century artefacts.

DON'T MISS

- World Peace Gate
- Seoul Baekje Museum
- SOMA

PRACTICALITIES

- 올림픽공원
- Map p252, F2
- 02-410 1114
- www.olympicpark.co.kr
- 424 Olympic-ro
- admission free
- 5am-10pm, car access from 6am
- P
- S Line 8 to Mongchon-toseong, Exit 1, or Line 5 to Olympic Park, Exit 3

History Museums

Olympic Park's **SOMA** (소마미술관; Seoul Olympic Museum of Art; 02-425 1077; http://soma.kspo.or.kr; adult/youth/child ₩13,000/9000/6000; 10am-7pm Tue-Sun) is a gigantic eco-designed space divided into five exhibition halls and a video hall over two levels, plus over 200 playful sculptures dotted in its park. Most of the exhibitions are paid and cover modern and contemporary local and big-ticket international artists such as Diego Rivera and Frida Kahlo – even her clothes are displayed. The video hall has provocative video-art installations by Nam June Paik – South Korea's best-known artist abroad and considered the inventor of video art – which include laser sculptures and studies of how technology interfaces with humanity.

Seoul Baekje Museum (http://baekjemuseum.seoul.go.kr; Wiryeseong-daero; 9am-9pm Tue-Fri, to 7pm Sat & Sun) FREE is dedicated to the history and culture of ancient Seoul. This part of the city was once the capital of the Baekje kingdom when Seoul was known as Hanseong (18 BCE–CE 475). This history is told through interesting and informative displays over three floors, with a full-scale model of workers constructing an earth rampart at the museum's centre. You can follow the other Baekje sites in the area on foot by yourself with a provided walking-tour map.

Less interesting is the smaller **Mongchon Museum** (몽촌역사관; 02-424 5138; 9am-6pm Tue-Sun) FREE, which exhibits some precious golden relics of the Baekje kings and the usual ceramic pots.

Olympic Memorials

Vistiors are greeted at the main entrance with the imposing **World Peace Gate**, with its mural-adorned winged arches. The huge monument was designed by Kim Jung-up and intended to impress visitors to the large Peace Plaza for the 1988 Olympics.

The **Seoul Olympic Museum** (https://88olympic.kspo.or.kr; 10am-6pm Tue-Sun;) FREE is an excellent way to learn about the games in a short space of time. What was once a homage to the 1988 Olympics with memorabilia and video highlights was given a modern makeover for the the Pyeongchang 2018 Winter Olympics with virtual reality headset experiences. You can learn about each sport by participating in games such as archery and football. Medals and character figurines of Olympics around the world adds to educational, family-friendly fun.

Also here are many **stadiums** used during the 1988 games, including the swimming pool, gymnastics hall and velodrome, among others.

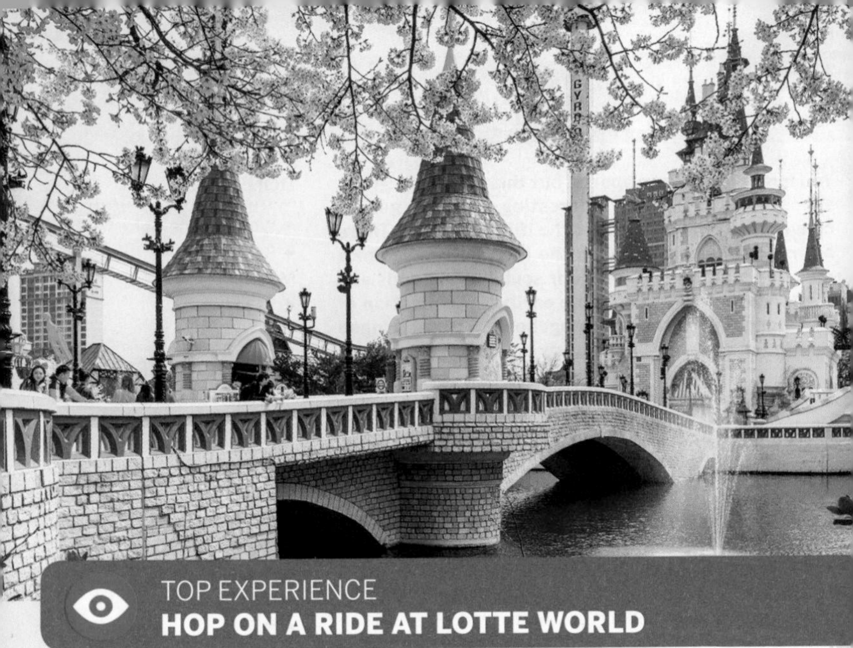

TOP EXPERIENCE

HOP ON A RIDE AT LOTTE WORLD

Kids *and* adults love the massive entertainment hub of Lotte World. It's a Korean version of Disneyland with the chipmunk-like Lotty and Lorry standing in for the iconic mouse couple.

One of the world's largest indoor theme parks, **Lotte World Adventure** has spinning rides and bumper cars, as well as an old-world charm with its ice-skating rink (p132), a monorail, 'flying' hot-air balloons, regular parades and a beautifully decorated carousel with 64 horses. The outdoor **Magic Island**, in the middle of Seokchon Lake, is the place for the more thrilling rides. Centred on a Magic Castle, here you'll hear the screams of excitement from people on roller-coaster rides, gyro swings and free-fall drops, as well as more child-friendly rides such as a Ferris wheel. Note that it's closed in bad weather.

On the 3rd floor the **Folk Museum** (museum only adult/youth/child ₩5000/3000/2000; ⏲9.30am-8pm Mon-Fri, to 9pm Sat & Sun) reenacts scenes from Korean prehistory to modern life. Dioramas and extremely detailed scale models give a peek into everyday living in ancient times, peering into courtyards, temples, markets and building cutouts. Some whizzbang mechanised wax models are brought to life, making this an absorbing worthwhile visit. Entrance is included in the day-passport ticket. Other attractions include a theatre, a multiplex cinema, a department store, a shopping mall, a hotel and restaurants.

DON'T MISS

- Lotte World Adventure
- Magic Island
- Folk Museum
- Ice-skating rink

PRACTICALITIES

- 롯데월드
- Map p252, E3
- ☎02-1661 2000
- www.lotteworld.com
- 240 Olympic-ro
- adult/youth/child ₩36,000/32,000/29,000, passport incl most rides ₩52,000/45,000/41,000
- ⏲9.30am-10pm
- 👪
- S Line 2 or 8 to Jamsil, Exit 3

TOP EXPERIENCE

EXPLORE BONGEUN-SA

This Buddhist temple is the most emblematic of Seoul. An easy climb meandering up the hill reveals beautiful shrines and halls among the trees, which are framed by the silvery skyscrapers of upmarket Gangnam. Founded in AD 794, the buildings of Bongeun-sa have been rebuilt multiple times over the centuries. Enter the temple through **Jinyeomun** (Gate of Truth), protected by its guardians, the four celestial kings. On the left is a small office where an English-speaking volunteer guide is usually available. A small pond with floating carp sculptures and a laughing Buddha usher you up the stairs to the main shrine, **Daewungjeon**. It is easy to identify by its lattice doors and distinctive adornments. A small 14th-century bell is hidden in one corner. To the right is the **funeral hall**, while behind are smaller **shrine halls** and a towering 23m-high outdoor statue of the Maitreya (Future) Buddha, who is believed will one day return to relieve people of suffering. Head nearby to see the oldest hall, **Panjeon**, constructed in 1856.

It's highly recommended to take part in a Thursday **templelife program** (http://temple.bongeunsa.org; ₩20,000), which include lotus-lantern making, *dado* (tea ceremony), a temple tour and Seon (Zen) meditation. Staying overnight in the two-day templestay program (₩70,000) is a worthwhile and unique experience. The overnight stay is held every fourth Saturday and needs to be booked three weeks in advance.

DON'T MISS

- Jinyeomun
- Daewungjeon
- Panjeon
- Templelife program

PRACTICALITIES

- 봉은사
- Map p252, B3
- ☎02-3218 4895
- www.bongeunsa.org
- 531 Bongeunsa-ro
- admission free
- ⏲3am-10pm
- Ⓢ Line 2 to Samseong, Exit 6

SIGHTS

Modern architecture, K-Pop landmarks, glitzy galleries and seeing how the rich and famous shop and live feature heavily in Apgujeong. In the east are concentrated sights within Lotte Tower and Olympic Park. Elsewhere, calmer highlights include the temple of Bongeun-sa, royal tombs, a museum specialising in traditional Korean music, and the floating islands of Some Sevit. Walking between areas can involve long empty roads: easier options are the subway, buses, taxis or Gangnam City Tour Bus.

OLYMPIC PARK — PARK

See p121.

LOTTE WORLD — AMUSEMENT PARK

See p122.

★TANGENT — ARCHITECTURE

Map p252 (Yeongdong-daero; S Line 2 to Samseong, Exit 6) Hyundai Development Company commissioned Daniel Libeskind to work with Seoul-based firm Himma on its headquarters opposite COEX Mall. The result, Tangent, is one of Seoul's boldest architectural statements, an enormous sculpture in glass, concrete and steel, reminiscent of a painting by Kandinsky, or an embroidery hoop.

SOME SEVIT — ARCHITECTURE

Map p250 (세빛섬, Sebitseom; www.somesevit.com; Hanggan Riverside Park; most cafes & restaurants 11.30am-10pm; P; S Line 3, 7 or 9 to Express Bus Terminal, Exit 8-1) FREE At the south end of Banpo Bridge are these three artificial floating islands interconnected by walkways. Each features futuristic buildings in a complex that comprises restaurants, an exhibition hall and an outdoor stage. Definitely aim to visit at night when its buildings are lit up spectacularly by LED lights, as is the Banpo Bridge Rainbow Fountain.

SMTOWN COEXARTIUM — ARTS CENTRE

Map p252 (www.smtownland.com; 513 Yeongdong-daero; 11am-10pm) FREE This five-level interactive shrine to K-Pop in the COEX Mall (p130) has already become a pilgrimage hot spot for fans since opening in 2018. The photo hall is selfie heaven and includes the albums, props, miniatures and memorabilia of all of SM Entertainment's stars, the most famous being Girls' Generation, Super Junior, Shinee, Exo, Taemin and BoA. Get closer to the shiny outfits and trophies won by the idols in the ticketed SM Museum (₩18,000), and interact with their holograms at the SM Theatre while watching augmented reality concerts.

SEOUL ARTS CENTER — ARTS CENTRE

Map p250 (서울 예술의전당, SAC; www.sac.or.kr; 2406 Nambusunhwan-ro; 11am-8pm; S Line 3 to Nambu Bus Terminal, Exit 5) FREE As well as being home to Seoul's premier concert halls (p130), this art centre also has three art galleries. **Seoul Calligraphy Museum** is devoted to hand-drawn *hangeul* (Korean phonetic alphabet) and Chinese characters, showcasing both traditional and contemporary examples of this art form. The **Hangaram Art Museum** is spread over four levels featuring rotating art shows, while **Hangaram Design Museum** has exhibits which focus on contemporary art and design.

LOTTE WORLD TOWER — NOTABLE BUILDING

Map p252 (롯데월드타워, Seoul Sky; 02-3213 5000; www.lwt.co.kr; 300 Olympic-ro; adult/child ₩27,000/24,000; 9.30am-11pm; P; S Line 2, 8 to Jamsil, Exit 1) Completed in early 2017, Seoul's latest landmark is the 555m-high Lotte World Tower – the tallest skyscraper in Korea (and sixth highest in the world). Its sleek contemporary design is loosely inspired by traditional Korean ceramics and features the world's highest observation deck, **Seoul Sky**, with a glass-floored skywalk, art gallery, cafes, six-star hotel and the mega Lotte World Mall (p131) complex.

SAMSUNG D'LIGHT — SHOWROOM

Map p250 (www.samsungdlight.com; Samsung Electronics Bldg, 11 Seocho-daero 74-gil; 10am-7pm Mon-Sat; S Line 2 to Gangnam, Exit 8) FREE Spread over three floors, one of which is devoted to selling the latest lines of gadgets, this showroom showcases the technology of the Korean electronics giant Samsung, the headquarters of which are in the same building. Whether you're a techno geek or not, it's fun to play around with the interactive displays and digital gizmos.

MUSEUM OF GUGAK — MUSEUM

Map p250 (02-580 3300; www.gugak.go.kr; National Gugak Center, 2364 Nambusunhwan-ro; 9am-6pm Tue-Sun; S Line 3 to Nambu

Bus Terminal, Exit 5) FREE A part of the National Gugak Center (p130), this engaging museum covers *gugak* (traditional Korean music) with displays of Korean stringed instruments and unique drums among others that are rarely heard today. Some you're able to play, such as the Jeongak *gayaguem* (12-stringed zither dating from Joseon dynasty). It's a five-minute walk from Seoul Arts Center.

GANGNAM STYLE SCULPTURE SCULPTURE

Map p252 (513 Yeongdong-daero; ⏲24hr; SLine 2 to Samseong, Exit 6) FREE The horse dance in Psy's music video for 'Gangnam Style' has been iconified as a giant pair of bronze hands on a stage on the east side outside COEX Mall. The song plays as you approach it, and it's lit up at night.

BANPO BRIDGE RAINBOW FOUNTAIN FOUNTAIN

Map p250 (반포대교 달빛무지개분수; Banpo Bridge, Banpo-dong; 22-404, 22-405, 405 or 740, SLine 3, 7 or 9 to Express Bus Terminal, Exit 8-1) FREE Covered with 10,000 lights, the Banpo Bridge Rainbow Fountain's coloured water rains down in messy arcs from the double-decker Banpo Bridge. More spectacle than spectacular, spanning 1140m, it's the world's longest fountain, and is best viewed from **Banpo Hangang Park**. The 20-minute show usually happens between late April and the end of August at noon, 8pm, 8.30pm and 9pm Monday to Friday; and noon, 6pm, 7.30pm, 8pm, 8.30pm and 9pm on Saturday and Sunday. Shows are cancelled if it's raining.

K-WAVE EXPERIENCE CULTURAL CENTRE

Map p248 (2nd fl, Gangnam Tourist Information Center, 161 Apgujeong-ro; ⏲10am-7pm; SLine 3 to Apgujeong, Exit 6) FREE Upstairs from the Gangnam Tourist Center, this is the place to live out all your K-Pop fantasies, with a full makeover to transform you into a K-Pop star. Choose from a wardrobe of clothing, wigs and bling, as well as makeup, for that cheesy photo op. Also here is a bunch of CDs, DVDs and kitschy K-Wave souvenirs.

313 ART PROJECT GALLERY

Map p248 (www.313artproject.com; 313 Dosan-daero; ⏲11am-6pm Mon-Fri; SLine 3 to Apgujeong, Exit 3) In the middle of Apgujeong's chic art hub, this slick gallery shows contemporary works by emerging and established artists, both local and from abroad.

GANGNAM STYLE 'HORSE DANCE' STAGE LANDMARK

Map p250 (Gangnam-daero; ⏲24hr; SLine 2 to Gangnam, Exit 11) FREE Outside Gangnam subway is the multimedia Gangnam Style stage, a shrine to Psy – somewhat ironic given the song was a parody of the neighbourhood. While you're here head down Gangnam-daero (redubbed U-Street) to see 12m-high, 1.4m-wide media poles displaying video art. Visit early evening to soak up the electric atmosphere.

GANGNAM ARCHI-TOUR

Given the generally blank historical canvas and wide-open spaces of Gangnam, architects have been able to push the envelope a bit more with their designs south of the river. Here are a few to look out for.

Some Sevit (p124) On three islands on the Han River, these futuristic buildings have glass, undulating facades covered in LEDs that glow colourfully each evening.

Tangent (p124) An enormous sculpture in glass, concrete and steel, reminiscent of a painting by Kandinsky.

Starfield Library (Map p252; 02-6002 3031; www.starfield.co.kr; Central Plaza, COEX Mall; ⏲10.30am-10pm; SLine 2 to Samseong, COEX Exit) A 13m-tall, neon-lit, designer shrine to books inside the COEX Mall.

GT Tower East (Map p250; 411 Seocho-daero, Seocho-gu; SLine 2 to Gangnam, Exit 9) The slinky-like curvaceous stylings rise like a giant sculpture.

Urban Hive (Map p250; 476 Gangnam-daero; SLine 9 to Sinnonhyeon, Exit 3) Above Sinnonhyeon station, this building looks like an enormous concrete beehive.

Galleria (p130) A sequin-like surface with glass discs that turn psychedelic at night.

K-STAR ROAD STREET

Map p248 (Hallyu Star Ave; Apgujeong Rodeo St; ⌚24hr; Ⓢ Bundang Line to Apgujeongrodeo, Exit 7) FREE Gangnam's 'Hallyuwood Walk of Fame' pays homage to K-Pop stars in the form of cutesy bear sculptures dedicated to K-Wave singers and actors.

MOONLIGHT RAINBOW FOUNTAIN VIEWPOINT VIEWPOINT

Map p250 (🚌22-404, 22-405, 405 or 740, Ⓢ Line 3, 7 or 9 to Express Bus Terminal, Exit 8-1) This park offers a good vantage point of the nightly fountain show coming off Banpo Bridge.

SEONJEONGNEUNG TOMB

Map p252 (선정릉; ☎02-568 1291; http://royal tombs.cha.go.kr; Seonjeongneung Park, 1 Seolleung-ro 100-gil; adult/teenager/child ₩1000/500/free; ⌚6am-8pm Tue-Sun; Ⓢ Line 2 or Bundang Line to Seolleung, Exit 8) Seonjeongneung Park contains two main burial areas for kings and queens from the Joseon dynasty. The first tomb is for **King Seongjong** (r 1469–94), who was a prolific author and father. Nearby is the tomb of King Seongjong's second wife, **Queen Jeonghyeon Wanghu**.

A 10-minute walk further on through the thickly wooded park is the tomb of King Seongjong and Queen Jeonghyeon's second son, **King Jeongjong**, who reigned from 1506 to 1544. Although he ruled for 38 years he was a weak king and court factions held the real power, as they often did during the Joseon period. At this tomb you can see the full layout – the gateway and the double pathway to the pavilion where memorial rites were carried out – but you can't go near the tomb.

There is another Joseon-dynasty tomb complex at **Donggureung** (동구릉; 197 Donggureung-ro; adult/child ₩1000/500; ⌚6am-6pm Tue-Sun; 🚌88, Ⓢ Jungang Line 1 to Guri, Exit 1), about 20km northeast of Seoul.

EATING

Upmarket restaurants are common, especially in Apgujeong, where you will find modern takes on Korean cuisine, with many ranking as top spots in Asia. Head to Garosu-gil for an especially high concentration of casual restaurants offering fancy versions of international fast food, such as Mexican fusion, vegan bowl food, kebabs, burgers and pasta as well as Korean *galbi* (beef ribs).

HARU JAPANESE $

Map p248 (하루; ☎02-514 5557; 56 Eonju-ro 172-gil, Gangnam-gu; mains ₩6000-9000; ⌚11.40am-4pm & 5-9.40pm; Ⓢ Bundang Line to Apgujeongrodeo, Exit 5) Haru's decades-long run alone could be considered a feat in Seoul – not to mention the constant (fast-moving) lines out the door and topping local 'best cheap eats' lists. The pan-soba is particularly queue-worthy – two fistfuls of freshly made cold buckwheat noodles with icy broth on the side. Or point to the photo menu's hot and juicy *donkatsu* (fried pork cutlet) cooked to perfection.

BANPO ROMANTIC MOONLIGHT MARKET INTERNATIONAL $

Map p250 (서울 밤도깨비 야시장, Seoul Bamdokkaebi Night Market; www.bamdokkaebi.org; Banpo Hangang Park, Sinbanpo-ro 11-gil; snacks ₩1000-12,000; ⌚6-11pm Fri & Sat Apr-Oct; Ⓟ; 🚌22-404, 22-405, 405 or 740, Ⓢ Line 3, 7 or 9 to Express Bus Terminal, Exit 8-1 or 2) In warmer weather, the Banpo Bridge Park area becomes a festive night market with food trucks serving international cuisine – Indian, Vietnamese, pasta, burgers and even alcohol from trucks decked out in laser lights. There are music and cultural events, and plentiful craft stalls. Eat in the park while watching the Banpo Bridge Rainbow Fountain or stroll over to Some Sevit.

BROOKLYN THE BURGER JOINT BURGERS $

Map p248 (브루클린 더 버거 조인트; ☎02-545 0718; 12 Dosan-daero 15-gil; burgers from ₩9000; ⌚24hr; Ⓢ Line 3 to Sinsa, Exit 8) Open all day, everyday, this diner-like burger joint takes its interior-design cues from 1950s America, soundtracked by the likes of 2010s Wu-Tang Clan. More creative choices include C.R.E.A.M (Cheese Rules Everything Around Meat). Sets are served on a plate of steak fries. Save room for dessert – there are 43 milkshakes on the menu, including some boozy ones.

JILHAL BROS KEBAB $

Map p252 (질할브로스; ☎02-542 1422; www.fb.me/JilhalBros; 32 Apgujeong-ro 79-gil; bowls from ₩6500; ⌚11am-10pm; Ⓢ Line 7 to Cheongdam, Exit 10) Nestled in K-Pop paradise (between entertainment companies JYP and SMTown), Jilhal Bros has managed to capture the hearts of sunglasses-adorned celebrities ordering takeaway. Imitating the famous Halal Guys cart in midtown

Manhattan, Jilhal Bros serves up chicken or lamb over rice with a simple salad as well as wraps and *gyros*.

GANGNAM GYOJA DUMPLINGS $

Map p250 (강남교자; ☎02-536 4133; www.gangnamgyoja.com; 1308-1 Seocho-dong; dumplings or noodles ₩8000; ⏰10.30am-10pm; Ⓢ Line 2 to Gangnam, Exit 7) Specialising in big bowls of *kalguksu* (handmade knife-cut noodles in spicy soup) and steamed pork dumplings, this simple restaurant focuses on the great food that made it famous. There are other seasonal noodle dishes on the English picture menu.

COREANOS KITCHEN MEXICAN $

Map p248 (☎02-547 4427; www.coreanoskitchen.com; Basement, 25 Seolleung-ro 157-gil; tacos from ₩3800, burritos from ₩10,000; ⏰noon-11pm; Ⓢ Bundang Line to Apgujeongrodeo, Exit 5) What was originally a hipster food truck in Austin, Texas, Coreanos (which is Spanish for 'Korean') brings its winning formula of kimchi tacos to Seoul. Tastes here are a fusion of authentic Mexican street food with Korean flavours: think hand-pressed soft-corn tortilla tacos filled with anything from *galbi* (beef ribs) to kimchi pork belly.

It also does *tortas*, burritos and craft beer. There's another branch in Itaewon (p111).

GILBERT'S BURGERS & FRIES BURGERS $

Map p248 (☎02-546 5453; www.fb.me/gilbertsburger; 47 Dosan-daero 15-gil; burgers from ₩10,000; ⏰11am-3pm & 4.30-10pm Mon-Thu, to 11pm Fri-Sun; Ⓢ Line 3 to Sinsa, Exit 8) From the moment those salivating aromas of sizzling burgers hit you, there's no return from this underground diner which is a homage to American food. Its signature burger is the well-stacked Mr President, which comes with a 7oz beef patty. Wash it down with a good choice of American craft beers and sodas.

LAY BRICKS CAFE $

Map p248 (☎02-545 5513; 46 Nonhyeon-ro 153-gil; snacks from ₩12,000; ⏰11am-1am Mon-Sat, noon-midnight Sun; Ⓢ Line 3 to Sinsa, Exit 8) A popular hang-out with a passing array of characters – artists, models and fashionistas – this industrial brick coffee house does a delicious *patbingsu* (red bean and fruit on milky shaved ice), particularly popular in summer, as well as sandwiches. It roasts its own coffee and has a decent selection of craft beer too.

MIN'S KITCHEN FUSION $$

Map p248 (민스키친; ☎02-544 1007; www.minskitchen.kr; 10-4 Dosan-daero 45-gil; mains ₩10,000-60,000, set lunch/dinner from ₩28,000/98,000; ⏰11.30am-3pm & 5.30-10pm Mon-Sat; Ⓢ Bundang Line to Apgujeongrodeo, Exit 5) Korean cuisine, while delicious, can overwhelm with punchiness. Min's Kitchen opts for fresh, delicate flavours in dishes such as shrimp bibimbap. The long menu is not radical but is done well, with its best modern touches shining through artful tasting menus including bulgogi 'taco' and acorn jelly.

SEASONS TABLE KOREAN, BUFFET $$

Map p252 (☎02-419 5561; www.seasonstable.co.kr; Olympic Park, 424 Olympic-ro; lunch weekday/weekend ₩13,900/22,900, dinner ₩22,900; ⏰11am-10pm; 🖉; Ⓢ Line 5 to Olympic Park, Exit 3) Located within the main Olympic Park gate, this buffet buzzes with diners here for excellent-value, all-you-can-eat Korean and fusion dishes. There's an excellent spread of traditional and seasonal-based dishes of grilled meats, stews, savoury pancakes and good vegetarian options.

CINE DE CHEF ITALIAN $$

Map p248 (☎02-3446 0541; www.cinedechef.com; Sinsa-dong; mains ₩12,000-24,000, set menu ₩42,000-50,000; ⏰10.30am-9pm; Ⓢ Line 3 to Apgujeong, Exit 3) This classy Italian restaurant combines a two- or three-course meal with a movie afterwards in one of two super-comfy screening rooms (the double movie ticket is ₩40,000 extra).

★JUNGSIK KOREAN $$$

Map p248 (정식당; ☎02-517 4654; www.jungsik.kr; 11 Seolleung-ro, 158-gil; 5-course lunch/dinner from ₩88,000/130,000; ⏰noon-3pm & 5.30-10.30pm; Ⓢ Bundang Line to Apgujeongrodeo, Exit 4) This place was voted number 25 in *Asia's 50 Best Restaurants* in 2018; neo-Korean cuisine hardly gets better than this. At the Apgujeong outpost of the New York restaurant named after creative chef-owner Yim Jungsik, you can expect inspired and superbly presented contemporary mixes of traditional and seasonal ingredients over multiple courses. Book at least one month in advance.

★NORMAL BY RYUNIQUE FUSION $$$

Map p248 (노멀바이류니끄; ☎02-546 9279; 42 Apgujeong-ro 10-gil; mains from ₩27,000, Quick Ryunique ₩60,000; ⏰noon-3pm & 5-10.30pm

Mon-Fri, noon-10.30pm Sat & Sun; P ❄; S Line 3 to Sinsa, Exit 8) 'Normal' is the casual counterpart to restaurant Ryunique. A contemporary bistro that makes fine dining affordable, the menu consists of American- and French-inspired dishes à la carte or one of two set meals. The excellent seven-course Quick Ryunique can include a shrimp rice-paper wrap, langoustine ramen, and berry mousse dessert.

★GATI ITALIAN $$$

Map p248 (가티; ☎02-517 3366; www.instagr.am/restaurant_gati; 24 Dosan-daero 1-gil; mains ₩25,000-38,000, set menu ₩49,000; ⏰11.30am-3pm & 5.15-9.45pm Mon-Fri, from noon Sat & Sun; S Line 3 to Sinsa, Exit 8) This fine Italian restaurant is as casually cool as its all-black-wearing diners, but the food is seriously top-notch. Homemade squid-ink linguine with scallops in roe cream is a standout. Opt for the praiseworthy four-course set menu and you'll notice fusion touches in the *galbi* (beef ribs) salad or sashimi. Nearby artsy Garosu-gil is good for a post-dinner stroll.

★SAMWON GARDEN KOREAN $$$

Map p248 (삼원가든; ☎02-548 3030; www.samwongarden.com; 835 Eonju-ro; mains ₩39,000-81,000, set menu galbi ₩41,000-65,000; ⏰11.40am-10pm; S Line 3 to Apgujeong, Exit 2) Serving top-class *galbi* (beef ribs) for over 30 years, Samwon is a Korean idyll, surrounded by beautiful traditional gardens including several waterfalls. It's one of the best places in the city for this kind of barbecued-beef meal. There are also more inexpensive dishes such as *galbitang* (beef short rib soup) for ₩15,000.

RYUNIQUE FUSION $$$

Map p248 (류니끄; ☎02-546 9279; www.ryunique.co.kr; 40 Gangnam-daero 162-gil; set lunch/dinner ₩120,000/230,000; ⏰noon-3pm & 6-10.30pm; P ❄; S Line 3 to Sinsa, Exit 8) Chef Ryu Tae-hwan brings French, Japanese and Korean dishes to fine dining at Ryunique. Often described as avant-garde and adventurous, the courses at Ryunique are recognised for beautiful plating in addition to their flavours. Every meal is a journey – hay is burnt to create a countryside ambience, 'seashells' are edible, the barbecue quail is a knockout, and cotton candy imitates snow.

DRINKING & NIGHTLIFE

Garosu-gil is fuelled by the young and hip in shabby-chic bars. There are plenty of places to get slightly dressed up, offering fancy cocktails, artisanal *makgeolli* (milky rice wine) and craft beer, the fanciest being around Gangnam-daero and Apgujeong. This area is home to megaclubs, some ranked best in the world, but they don't get going till late, have picky dress codes, and sometimes don't let in foreigners on a whim.

★CLUB OCTAGON CLUB

Map p250 (www.octagonseoul.com; 645 Nonhyeon-ro; admission before 11pm & after 4am ₩10,000, 11pm-4am ₩30,000; ⏰10pm-6am Thu-Sat; S Line 7 to Hak-dong, Exit 4) Voted number seven in the world's top clubs by *DJ Mag* in 2018, Octagon is one of Gangnam's best for serious clubbers. High-profile resident and guest DJs spin house, trap, hip-hop and techno in a warehouse-sized space over its powerful Funktion 1 sound system to an appreciative crowd here to party till dawn.

MIKKELLER BAR CRAFT BEER

Map p248 (미켈러; ☎070-4231 4723; www.mikkeller.dk/mikkeller-seoul; 33 Dosan-daero 17-gil; beers from ₩4500; ⏰5pm-midnight Mon-Thu, 5pm-1am Fri, 2pm-1am Sat, 2-10pm Sun; S Line 3 to Sinsa, Exit 8) Danish brand famous for 'phantom' brewing (pop-up type service with locals), Mikkeller has its first Korean location in this small, one-room bar with colourful wall paintings. The beer menu, which changes seasonally, features international beers and Mikkeller's own brews, plus local brewers like Galmegi from Busan as guest taps – check the calendar on its website.

CAFE MORE CAFE

(카페모아; ☎02-880 0888; 1717 Nambusunhwan-ro; coffee from ₩2000; ⏰8am-10.30pm; 📶 ♿; S Line 2 to Bongchon, Exit 4) Part coffee shop and part Braille library, this bright and spacious cafe caters to the sight-impaired community. The library consists of hundreds of Braille books and two computers, and the cafe often donates a part of its profits to charities for the sight-impaired, in addition to making a decent cup of coffee.

ART C COMPANY BAR, CAFE

Map p248 (아트씨컴퍼니; ☎02-549 0110; www.artc-company.com; 33 Apgujeong-ro; coffee/cocktails from ₩4000/16,000; ⏰9am-3am; Ⓢ Line 3 to Sinsa, Exit 8) A three-storey design and music-themed cafe located in an alley adjacent to Garosu-gil. Each floor brings a slightly different atmosphere, from cafe decorated with vinyl records and turntables, to kitsch basement bar and lounge decorated with towering contemporary artworks and pumping out retro music and hip-hop until 3am. The rose-petal-topped 'Rose Garden' cocktail is delicious and not too strong.

NEURIN MAEUL BAR

Map p250 (느린마을, Slow Brew Pub; ☎02-587 7720; http://slowbrewpub.com; 7 Seochodae-ro 73-gil; ⏰11am-11pm; Ⓢ Line 2 to Gangnam, Exit 9) The Gangnam branch of this Baesangmyeon Brewery bar is a bit snazzier than others, but remains a good place to sample quality traditional Korean alcohol. Its signature Neurin Maeul *makgeolli* (milky rice wine) is the standout – it's divided into the four 'seasons', which refers to the differing production stages; you can sample each before ordering. Look for the rusty shipping container.

GREENMILE COFFEE CAFE

Map p248 (☎02-517 2404; www.facebook.com/greenmilecoffee; 11 Seolleung-ro 127-gil; coffee from ₩4000; ⏰8am-7pm Mon-Fri; 📶; Ⓢ Line 7 to Gangnam-gu Office, Exit 2) Fitted out in designer furniture and caffeine-related paraphernalia, this cool little cafe is a great spot for coffee. It roasts all its single-origin beans onsite, sourced from Africa to Latin America. As well as the usual espresso, pour-overs and cold drip, it's also the proud owner of laboratory-like, halogen-powered equipment that does sensational siphon brews.

COFFEE BAR K COCKTAIL BAR

(☎02-516 1970; 517 Eonju-ro; ⏰7pm-3am Mon-Sat; Ⓢ Line 2 to Seolleung, Exit 5) If you're into whisky, this swank Japanese bar is for you, as it sports one of the largest selections of drams in the city. It's also famed for its cocktails, all of which come at a price; expect to pay at least ₩20,000 a drink.

MOON JAR BAR

Map p248 (달빛술담; ☎02-541 6118; https://dbsuldam.modoo.at; 38 Apgujeong-ro 46-gil; 750mL makgeolli from ₩7000; ⏰11.30am-2.30pm & 5.30pm-1am; 📶; Ⓢ Line 3 to Apgujeong, Exit 3) Rustic charm meets Apgujeong chic at this convivial *makgeolli* (milky rice wine) bar and cafe spread over two floors. The menu has several different types of quality *makgeolli* served in kettles with dishes such as *pajeon* (seafood pancakes) and spicy crab fried rice.

PONGDANG MICROBREWERY

Map p248 (☎02-6204 5513; www.pongdangsplash.com; 49 Apgujeong-ro 2-gil; ⏰5pm-1am Mon-Thu, to 2am Fri, 4pm-2am Sat, 4pm-midnight Sun; Ⓢ Line 3 to Sinsa, Exit 6) The original bar for this Korean microbrewery does a good selection of pale ales, and Belgian and wheat beers, enjoyed at Pongdang's bar or tables surrounded by arcade machines.

STEAMERS COFFEE FACTORY CAFE

Map p248 (☎02-518 4697; 10 Apgujeong-ro 4-gil, Gangnam-gu; coffee ₩4000-6000; ⏰8.30am-9.30pm Mon-Fri, noon-10pm Sat; 📶; Ⓢ Line 3 to Sinsa, Exit 6) Bringing third-wave coffee to Sinsa-dong, Steamers does Ethiopian and Colombian single-origin brews in its shabby-chic industrial brick cafe.

BOOTH BAR

Map p250 (☎02-714 4335; www.thebooth.co.kr; 2nd fl, 11 Gangnam-daero 53-gil; beer from ₩5000; ⏰5pm-1am Mon-Fri, from noon Sat, noon-11pm Sun; Ⓢ Line 2 to Gangnam, Exit 5) A popular brew pub with its roots in Noksapyeong's Craft Beer Valley (p116), this Gangnam branch has several of its beers on tap, including its signature Bill's Pale Ale. It has a casual set-up of camping chairs, oil-drum tables and murals on the walls, and does pizza by the slice (₩4000).

☆ ENTERTAINMENT

★SEOUL RACECOURSE HORSE RACING

(서울경마장, Let's Run Park; ☎02-509 2309; www.kra.co.kr; Gyeongmagongwon-daero, Gwacheon-si; ₩2000, Champions Suite ₩15,000; ⏰Fri-Sun, races from 10.45am; 📶; Ⓢ Line 4 to Seoul Racecourse Park, Exit 2) Enjoy a day at the races at Seoul's impressive and hugely popular horse-racing track. A 40,000-capacity grandstand faces the sandy track and its backdrop of verdant hills, where giant screens show the odds, the races and close-ups of the horses. You'll need a subway card to get through the turnstiles; once inside, make a beeline for the ground-floor **Foreigner Information Desk** to collect the day's form guide in English and a handy leaflet explaining how the betting system works.

A great tip is to head to the foreigner-only **Champions Suite** on the 5th floor (you'll need your passport). For ₩15,000 you get comfy seats, a panoramic view, free tea and coffee, and cheap beer all day. There are only 45 seats, so turn up early, or you can book in advance. High-rollers be warned – the largest bets permitted at the racecourse are ₩100,000.

★NATIONAL GUGAK CENTER TRADITIONAL MUSIC

Map p250 (국립국악원 예악당; ☎02-580 3300; www.gugak.go.kr; 2364 Nambusunhwan-ro; tickets from ₩10,000; ⏲9am-6pm Tue-Sun; Ⓢ Line 3 to Nambu Bus Terminal, Exit 5) Traditional Korean classical and folk music and dance are performed, preserved and taught at this centre, which is home to the Court Music Orchestra, the Folk Music Group, Dance Theater and Contemporary Gugak Orchestra. The main theatre, Yeakdang, puts on an ever-changing program by leading performers every Saturday, usually at 3pm.

MEGABOX COEX CINEMA

Map p252 (www.megabox.co.kr; 524 Bongeunsa-ro; tickets ₩9000; ⏲7am-2am; Ⓢ Line 2 to Samseong, COEX Exit) Cineplex with 17 screens and 4000 comfortable seats, showing films in original language. Sometimes screens live ballet and opera performances.

LG ARTS CENTER PERFORMING ARTS

Map p250 (☎02-2005 0114; www.lgart.com; 508 Nonhyeon-ro; Ⓢ Line 2 to Yeoksam, Exit 7) Major local and international artists and companies perform at this multi-hall, state-of-the-art venue.

SEOUL ARTS CENTER PERFORMING ARTS

Map p250 (서울 예술의전당, SAC; ☎02-580 1300; www.sac.or.kr; 2406 Nambusunhwan-ro; tickets from ₩10,000; Ⓢ Line 3 to Nambu Bus Terminal, Exit 5) The national ballet and opera companies are based at this sprawling arts complex, which includes a circular opera house with a roof shaped like a Korean nobleman's hat. It also houses a concert hall and a smaller recital hall in which the national choir, the Korea and Seoul symphony orchestras and drama companies stage shows.

There are regular free shows, which are held at weekends on the outdoor stage. Check the website for the extensive program.

SHOPPING

Even if you can't afford to buy the designer threads or artworks in the many boutiques and galleries of Apgujeong, it can still be fun to browse. Garosu-gil, one of Gangnam's most famous strips, is worth a stroll for brand-name stores, cute fashion boutiques and budget accessories aimed at students, plus art galleries, restaurants and cafes. Head to Lotte World Mall if you want to shop in the country's tallest building; and to COEX Mall if you want to get lost in the maze of stores in the largest underground shopping complex in the world.

★10 CORSO COMO SEOUL FASHION & ACCESSORIES

Map p248 (www.10corsocomo.co.kr; 416 Apgujeong-ro; ⏲11am-8pm, cafe to 11pm; Ⓢ Bundang Line to Apgujeongrodeo, Exit 3) Inspired by its shopping complex in Milan, this outpost of the fashion and lifestyle boutique is about as interesting as Gangnam retail can get. The blend of fashion, art and design includes several local designers and big-ticket global labels. There's also a brilliant selection of international books and CDs to browse, and a chic cafe for an espresso or glass of wine.

GALLERIA DEPARTMENT STORE

Map p248 (☎02-344 9414; http://dept.galleria.co.kr; Apgujeong-ro; ⏲10.30am-8pm Mon-Thu, to 8.30pm Fri-Sun; Ⓢ Bundang Line to Apgujeongrodeo, Exit 7) One of Seoul's most luxurious department stores. If you want to play Audrey Hepburn staring wistfully into Tiffany's, don a Helen Kaminski hat, try on a Stella McCartney dress or slip into a pair of Jimmy Choos, the east wing of fashion icon Galleria is the place to be.

COEX MALL MALL

Map p252 (☎02-6002 5300; www.starfield.co.kr; 513 Yeongdong-daero; ⏲10am-10pm; Ⓢ Line 2 to Samseong, COEX Exit) One of Seoul's premier malls and the world's largest underground mall, the shiny COEX is a vast maze of department stores loaded with shops selling fashion, lifestyle, accessories and electronics, as well as the Starfield Library (p125), SMTown coexartium (p124) shrine to K-Pop and a multiplex cinema. It's also a launching point to the airport (p207), and has several hotels.

PLEASURE LAB — ADULT

Map p248 (플레저랩; ☎02-516 0610; www.pleasurelab.net; 3F, 10 Dosan-daero 13-gil; ⏲noon-9pm Mon-Sat, to 6pm Sun; Ⓢ Line 3 to Sinsa, Exit 8) The second location of the first sex shop in South Korea designed for women, Pleasure Lab does its best to make sure that women feel safe to ask any questions. Run by two ladies willing to brave the industry, the shop sells a wide variety of dildos and vibrators, condoms, lingerie and books.

Unlike its Hapjeong location, the Garosu-gil location also has a section for men. Brightly lit and friendly, this sex shop is certainly a gem among the others. Stop by to have a look around, pick up an adult gift for yourself or just to ask questions about sex culture in Korea. Private consultations available by reservation.

HYUNDAI DEPARTMENT STORE — DEPARTMENT STORE

Map p248 (http://ehyundai.com; 65 Apgujeong-ro; ⏲10.30am-8pm; Ⓢ Line 3 to Apgujeong, Exit 6) Hyundai's flagship branch is a classy department store in Apgujeong, where you're greeted by uniformed doormen that exude old-fashioned elegance circa 1920s New York. It's mostly about high-end fashion and accessories, including Korean designers on the 3rd floor.

LOTTE WORLD MALL — MALL

Map p252 (www.lwt.co.kr; 300 Olympic-ro; ⏲10.30am-10pm; Ⓢ Line 2 or 8 to Jamsil, Exit 1) At the base of Korea's tallest building (p124) lies its largest shopping mall, comprising six floors of luxury and duty-free department stores, a mega cinema complex and a concert hall. There's also a department store at the nearby amusement park (p122).

STEVE J & YONI P — FASHION & ACCESSORIES

(☎070-7730 5467; www.stevejandyonip.com; 45 Gangnam-daero; ⏲11am-10pm; Ⓢ Line 3 to Sinsa, Exit 8) Collaborating on the super-fashionable women's streetwear in this boutique are local designers Steve J and Yoni P. Their T-shirts, sweatshirts and colourful printed clobber are stocked by high-class boutiques around the world, but their flagship store is down this happening little street in Hannam-dong.

LAB 5 — FASHION & ACCESSORIES

(☎02-551 5000; http://lfive.co.kr/lab5; COEX Mall, 513 Yeongdong-daero; ⏲10am-10pm; Ⓢ Line 2 to Samseong, COEX Exit) No need to root around Dongdaemun Market for the latest hot K-designers, with this store in the COEX Mall showcasing the designs of 100 rising stars including participants of *Project Runway Korea*.

MEDICAL TOURISM IN GANGNAM

In a city that has one of the highest rates per capita in the world for cosmetic surgery, nowhere is this industry more visible than downtown Gangnam. As you stroll along Apgujeong-ro and Dosan-daero in Sinsa-dong, you'll find the streets lined with hundreds of boutique clinics, surgeries and high-rise medical centres that all specialise in plastic surgery. The sight of postoperative patients walking around in sunglasses with bruised, busted-up faces is not uncommon.

While estimates from the BBC have reported around 50% of Korean women in their 20s have had work done, it's an industry that also caters to an international clientele. Around one-third of patients are from abroad, mainly Chinese, Japanese and Russian. It's an industry not lost on the tourism department, which has set up the Gangnam Medical Tour Center. Sharing space with the main tourist office in Gangnam, it produces shelfloads of leaflets listing medical centres, as well as interactive features where you can get a range of 'before' and 'after' photos, as well as have your skin analysed, which will give you a rundown on your flaws and the work you need to have done.

The Korean Wave pop phenomenon has had much influence in shaping the public consciousness about what defines beauty. This has seen not only the standard nip, tucks and implants, but more extreme trends such as double eyelid surgery, which creates a more 'Westernised' appearance.

BOON THE SHOP

CLOTHING

Map p248 (☎02-2056 1234; www.boontheshop.com; 21 Apgujeong-ro 60-gil; Ⓢ Bundang Line to Apgujeongrodeo, Exit 4) There are two close-by branches of this multibrand boutique that's a byword for chic, high-end fashion. The original, worth a look if only for its gorgeous sculpture of a giant string of pearls hanging in the midst of an atrium, is the women's store. it mainly stocks exclusive niche designer brands from overseas; if you need to ask the price you can't afford to shop here.

The men's **store** (Map p248; ☎02-3444 3300; 35 Seonreung-ro 162-gil; Ⓢ Bundang Line to Apgujeongrodeo, Exit 3) is a two-minute walk around the corner.

SPORTS & ACTIVITIES

SPA LEI

SPA

Map p248 (스파레이; ☎02-545 4002; Cresyn Bldg, 5 Gangnam-daero 107-gil; admission ₩14,000, massage 30min ₩30,000; ⏲2pm-midnight; Ⓢ Line 3 to Sinsa, Exit 5) Luxurious women-only spa providing excellent services in an immaculate, stylish environment. Staff are helpful and used to dealing with foreigners. There are also basic 24-hour sleeping facilities.

GANGNAM CITY TOUR BUS

BUS

Map p250 (☎010-7444 6090; www.seoulcitybus.com; 422 Gangnam-daero; adult/child ₩12,000/10,000; ⏲10.20am-5.20pm Tue-Sun; Ⓢ Line 2 to Gangnam, Exit 11) A hop-on, hop-off, trolley-bus-like tour that covers Gangnam district's main sights including Seonjeongneung, Bongeunsa Temple, COEX Mall, Lotte World, Olympic Park, Apgujeong Rodeo Street and Samsung D'light. Tickets on board or from in front of Megabox City cinema (Gangnam station, Exit 11).

KUKKIWON

MARTIAL ARTS

Map p250 (국기원세계태권도본부; ☎02-567 1058; www.kukkiwon.or.kr; 32 Teheran-ro 7-gil; ⏲office 9am-6.30pm Mon-Thu, to 4pm Fri; Ⓢ Line 2 to Gangnam, Exit 12) There's no better place to spectate Korea's very own home-grown martial arts than here at the world headquarters for taekwondo. It hosts a regular schedule of taekwondo displays, training courses and tournaments. Call ahead to check when you might be able to see a weekday training session. Also visit its **museum** while you're here.

SEOUL SPORTS COMPLEX

SPORTS

Map p252 (서울종합운동장; Jamsil Sports Complex; ☎02-2240 8800; http://stadium.seoul.go.kr; 10 Jamsil-dong; tickets from ₩7000; Ⓢ Lines 2 or 8 to Sports Complex, Exit 6) Even if you're not a baseball fan it's worth coming along to **Jamsil Baseball Stadium** (₩15,000-25,000; ⏲games usually 6.30pm) for a game for its raucous atmosphere and off-field entertainment such as K-Pop cheerleaders. Also here is **Olympic Stadium**, which is used for major concerts.

LOTTE WORLD ICE SKATING RINK

ICE SKATING

Map p252 (롯데월드 아이스링크; www.lotteworld.com/icerink; B3 fl, Lotte World Adventure, 240, Olympic-ro; per session incl rental adult/child ₩15,000/14,000; ⏲11am-9.30pm Mon-Fri, 10am-10.30pm Sat & Sun; 👪; Ⓢ Line 2 or 8 to Jamsil, Exit 1) The indoor ice-skating rink at Lotte World is in a fairyland setting, under a beautiful glass dome surrounded by the sounds of the theme park one floor above. Watch out for tiny speedsters training to become future Winter Olympic champions.

Dongdaemun & Eastern Seoul

Neighbourhood Top Five

1 Dongdaemun Design Plaza & Park (p135) Uncovering layers of Seoul's history, from its foundation as the capital of the Joseon dynasty to its 21st-century architectural wonders.

2 Daelim Changgo (p138) Cruising the streets of Seongsu-dong, Seoul's answer to Brooklyn, before finishing with a drink in the 'hood's hippest cafe.

3 Gwangjang Market (p137) Gorging on a sea of Seoul food in the city's busiest snack alleys.

4 Dongdaemun Market (p139) Shopping your way through high-rise malls and sprawling markets into the early hours of the morning.

5 Seoul K-Medi Center (p136) Learning about the traditional Korean approach to medicine, then shopping for curative herbs in the surrounding market.

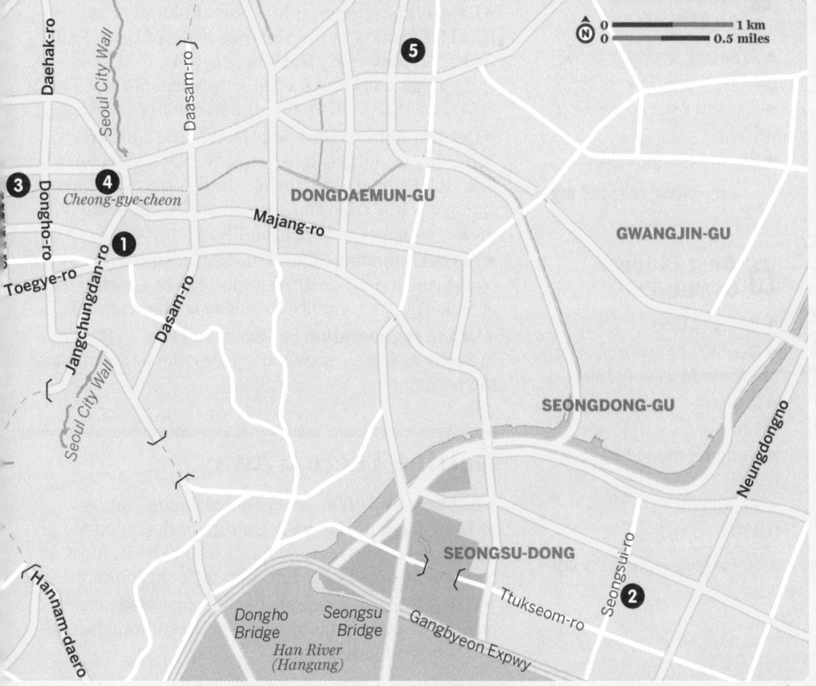

For more detail of this area see Maps p238 and p247

Lonely Planet's Top Tip

Some of the most fun and authentic places to eat in Gwangjang Market are the little restaurants hidden in the side arcades or along the edges of the main alleyways. Look for venues packed with locals; the more bottles of *soju* (local vodka) on the tables the better!

Best Places to Eat

- Gwangjang Market (p137)
- I Love Sindangdong (p137)
- Onion (p137)
- Pyeongando Jokbal Jip (p138)
- Samarkand (p138)

For reviews, see p137.

Best Places to Drink

- Amazing Brewing Co (p139)
- Baesan Warehouse Cafe (p138)
- Dalim Changgo (p138)

For reviews, see p138.

Best Places to Shop

- Su;py (p139)
- Seoul Yangnyeongsi Herb Medicine Market (p139)
- Dapsimni Antiques Market (p139)
- Dongdaemun Market (p139)
- Seoul Folk Flea Market (p140)

For reviews, see p139.

Explore Dongdaemun & Eastern Seoul

Taking its name from the Great East Gate (Heunginjimun) to the city, Dongdaemun – an area for centuries synonymous with shopping in Seoul – is famous for its architectural showpiece, the Zaha Hadid–designed Dongdaemun Design Plaza & Park (DDP), home also to layers of archaeological history uncovered during its construction.

It's fascinating to explore the ribbon of indoor markets that stretch around it and along either side of the Cheong-gye-cheon, spilling out into side streets where you can find anything and everything from succulents and sewing-machine parts to every hue of zipper and variety of kimchi. Much of the action is wholesale, with traders haggling over deals until the break of dawn, but there's also plenty of retail, particularly in fashion goods. Further east there are more quirky markets to discover, including ones devoted to herbal medicines, antiques and secondhand goods.

Across the Han River, the old shoemaking district of Seongsu-dong has undergone a style renaissance, its former factories and workshops repurposed into gorgeously hip cafes. Dubbed 'Seoul's Brooklyn', it's an off-the-beaten-track highlight for street photographers and cool-seekers.

Local Life

- **Late-night shopping** Join bargain-hunters as they trawl for fashion in the high-rise malls of Lotte Fitin (p140), **Hyundai City Outlets** (Map p247; 17-2 Eulji-ro 6-ga; ⏲11am-11pm; Ⓢ Lines 2, 4 & 5 to Dongdaemun Stadium, Exit 13 or 14) and Doota (p140) into the wee hours.
- **Central Asian delicacies** Head to the backstreets behind Lotte Fitin (p140) to uncover Dongdaemun's Silk Road, home to a Central Asian population where signage is in Cyrllic and specialty delis sell smoked meats, homebaked breads and Russian vodka.
- **Herbal remedies** Natural medicines, such as arrowroot by the cup and invigorating tonics, can be knocked back at Seoul Yangnyeongsi Herb Medicine Market (p139).
- **Urban regeneration** See Seoul's answer to Brooklyn in Seongsu-dong – warehouse-chic cafes, street art and hip boutiques.

Getting There & Away

- **Subway** Hop off at either Dongdaemun station or Dongdaemun History & Culture Park station for the Dongdaemun area. Seongsu station is the most convenient stop for the hip cafes of Seongsu-dong.
- **Walk** The paths alongside the Cheong-gye-cheon provide pleasant strolling access between Dongdaemun and Seoul Yangnyeongsi.

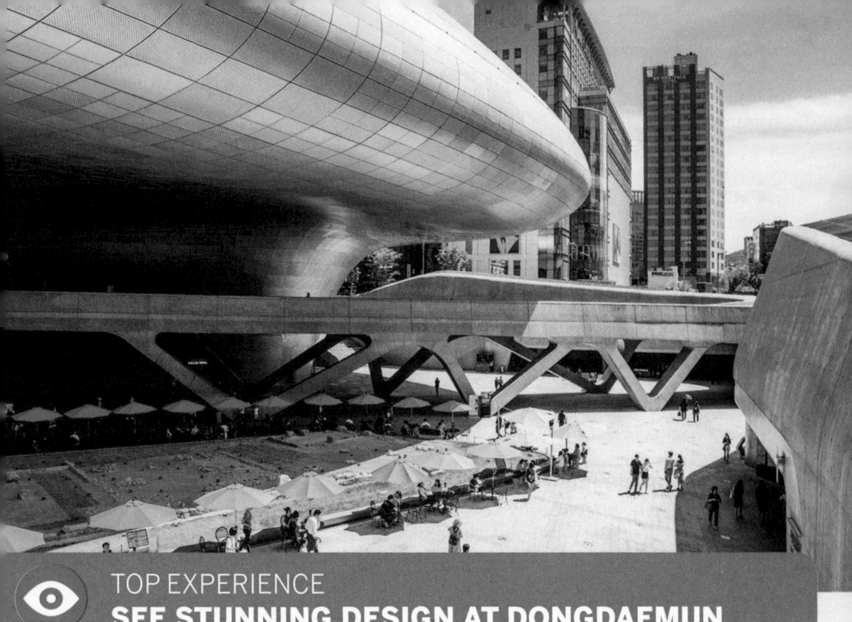

TOP EXPERIENCE
SEE STUNNING DESIGN AT DONGDAEMUN

Seoul's contemporary architectural masterpiece, Dongdaemun Design Plaza & Park (DDP) is a cultural space home to galleries, event spaces and design shops. Dubbed the 'largest three-dimensional atypical structure in the world', the aluminium and concrete landmark was designed by the late Zaha Hadid to replace the crumbling old sports stadium here.

Architecture & Exhibitions

Covered in 45,000 aluminium panels and fitted with LED lights that pulsate meditatively at night, Dongdaemun Design Plaza comprises public spaces, convention centres and an underground plaza as well as lawns that rise up on to its roof.

The interior of this cultural complex looks equally impressive, filled with floors of galleries, exhibition spaces, design shops and studios interconnected by flowing pathways and sculpted staircases. Ticket prices for exhibitions range from free to ₩10,000.

Dongdaemun History & Culture Park

During the site's excavation, major archaeological remains from the Joseon dynasty were uncovered, including original sections of the Seoul City Wall. The remains have been incorporated into the park and include the arched floodgate **Yigansumun**. The **Dongdaemun History Museum** provides the historical background to the ancient foundations preserved outside, while the **Dongdaemun Stadium Memorial** relives key moments from the history of the stadium built by the Japanese in 1925 and demolished in 2007. Two of the floodlight towers are still standing.

DON'T MISS

- Dongdaemun Design Plaza
- Dongdaemun History Museum
- Dongdaemun Stadium Memorial
- Dongdaemun History & Culture Park

PRACTICALITIES

- 동대문디자인플라자; DDP
- Map p247, B3
- 02-2153 0408
- www.ddp.or.kr
- 28 Eulji-ro, Jung-gu
- admission free
- 10am-7pm Tue, Thu, Sat & Sun, to 9pm Wed & Fri
- Lines 2, 4 or 5 to Dongdaemun History & Culture Park, Exit 1

SIGHTS

DONGDAEMUN DESIGN PLAZA & PARK — CULTURAL CENTRE

See p135.

★SEOUL K-MEDI CENTER — MUSEUM

(서울한방진흥센터, Seoul Yangnyeongsi Herb Medicine Museum; http://kmedi.ddm.go.kr; 26 Yangnyeongjungang-ro; museum entry ₩1000, foot bath or machine massage ₩5000; ⏲10am-6pm Tue-Sun; ⓈLine 1 to Jegi-dong, Exit 2) Learn about the history and practice of traditional Korean medicine at this impressive facility styled to resemble Bojewon, a clinic from the early Joseon dynasty strategically located here outside the City Walls to prevent the spread of infection. There's a vast array of natural ingredients on show (the Korean word for medicine is *boncho,* literally 'roots and grasses'), and afterwards you can treat your feet with a herbal bath on the upstairs terrace.

SAJIN CHANGGO — GALLERY

(사진창고; ☎02-461 3070; 26 Seongsuiro 7-gil, Seongdong-gu; ⏲9.30am-10pm; ⓈLine 2 to Seongsu, Exit 4) Literally meaning 'photo warehouse', Sajin Changgo is a rough-and-tumble gallery space showcasing edgy film photography from Korean artists. The works are arranged around tables where the artists themselves often hang out, making use of the cafe inside the entrance (coffee from ₩3900), from where you can also buy prints, postcards and books.

SEOUL CITY WALL MUSEUM — MUSEUM

Map p247 (한양도성박물관; ☎02-724 0243; 283 Yulgok-ro, Jongno-gu; ⏲9am-7pm Tue-Sun; ⓈLine 1 or 4 to Dongdaemun, Exit 1) FREE With interactive displays and historical artefacts, this modern museum offers an engaging history of the 18.6km-long barrier that has girdled Seoul since the late 14th century. Overlooking Heunginjimun beside a stretch of the City Wall, it also makes a logical embarkation point for a wall hike.

HEUNGINJIMUN — GATE

Map p247 (Dongdaemun; ⓈLine 1 or 4 to Dongdaemun, Exit 6) The Great East Gate to Seoul's City Wall has been rebuilt several times in its 700-year history and, after recent renovations, it's looking majestic. It's stranded in a traffic island, so it's not possible to enter inside the gate, but there are good photo ops from **Dongdaemun Seonggwak Park** to the north, which is also where you'll find the City Wall Museum and a trail following the City Wall up to Naksan Park (p146) and Ihwa Mural Village (p144).

CHEONG-GYE-CHEON MUSEUM — MUSEUM

(청계천문화관; ☎02-2286 3434; www.cgcm.go.kr; 530 Cheonggyecheon-ro, Seongdong-gu; ⏲9am-7pm Tue-Sun; ⓈLine 2 to Yongdu, Exit 5) FREE To fully comprehend what a mammoth and expensive effort it was to resurrect Cheong-gye-cheon, Seoul's long buried east–west stream, pay a visit to this excellent museum. It's also a good starting point for a walk along the revitalised waterway – 2.5km west to Dongdaemun Market (p139). Don't miss the **Cheong-gye-cheon Cardboard House** (⏲10am-8pm Tue-Sun) FREE museum opposite, a wooden shack typical of the slum housing that sprawled along the stream after the Korean War.

SEOUL FOREST — PARK

(서울숲; 685 Seongsu 1-ga 1-dong, Seongdong-gu; ⏲24hr; 👪; ⓈBundang Line 2 to Seoul Forest, Exit 2) FREE A hunting ground in Joseon times, this large park offers a number of family-friendly attractions, including a sika deer enclosure, adventure playgrounds, butterfly and insect gardens, wetlands and a skate park. Beside the east gate you'll find **Under Stand Avenue**, a row of shipping containers repurposed into cafes, shops and social enterprises.

EUNGBONGSAN PARK — VIEWPOINT

(응봉산공원; 271 Eungbong-dong, Seongdong-gu; ⓈJungang Line to Eungbong, Exit 1) FREE For panoramic vistas of the Han River and Eastern Seoul, take a short hike up the steps to the pavilion atop Eungbongsan, the verdant hill that makes up little-visited Eungbongsan Park. In spring masses of forsythia blossoms paint the park yellow.

HONGNEUNG ARBORETUM — NATURE CENTRE

(홍릉수목원; www.kfri.go.kr; 57 Hoegi-ro; ⏲10am-5pm Sat & Sun; ⓈLine 6 to Korea University, Exit 3) FREE A hidden gem, the National Institute of Forest Science opens its idyllic grounds to the public on weekends. A forest pathway winds for a few kilometres between rare trees and herb gardens. A mound at the rear was once a royal tomb like **Yeonghwiwon and Sunginwon** (서울 영휘원과 숭인원; 205 Cheongnyangri-dong; ₩1000; ⏲9am-

WORTH A DETOUR

SEONGSU-DONG

About 8km east of the city centre, the nondescript neighbourhood of Seongsu-dong never had much going for it beyond low-rise industrial units and factories manufacturing shoes. In just a few short years, however, the area has stepped up its game (pun intended), undergoing a style rebirth that has earned it the moniker 'Seoul's Brooklyn'. Still well off the tourist trail, Seongsu-dong has become the darling of hip young Seoulites chasing the latest cafe and shopping trends. Street art has injected colour and cool into the streets, while semi-derelict warehouses and factories have been appropriated into stunning venues worked over by graphic artists and designers, while still retaining their worn, post-industrial character.

Onion (p137), formerly a metal factory, hawks artisanal baked goods and fabulous coffee in a tumbledown space with cosy seating areas hewn from exposed-brick workshops. It makes a a strong case for Seoul's must gorgeous cafe space, but even it gets upstaged by Daelim Changgo (p138) the other side of the overground subway line ('*changgo*' means warehouse in Korean), a cafe-bar carved out of a pair of cavernous factory buildings and strewn with funky wall art, bizarre sculptures, and an interior garden complete with real trees and neon flowers. Across the street, fashion store Su;py (p139) sells designer streetwear, gifts, bags and couture in a wistfully retro space with an attached cafe-bar, while around the corner, Sajin Changgo (p136) showcases edgy film photography by local artists, who also hang out in the attached cafe, mixing with the area's hipsters.

And no newly cool neighbourhood would be complete without its own craft-beer brand. Step up Amazing Brewing Co (p139), a Korean-run microbrewery and bar making delicious, locally inspired beers like Seoul Forest, named after the famous park next door.

5.30pm; 🚌201, 1226, ⓢLine 6 to Korea University, Exit 4) nearby, but it was moved in 1919.

CHILDREN'S GRAND PARK PARK
(서울 어린이대공원; ☎02-450 9311; www.childrenpark.or.kr; 216 Neungdong-ro, Gwangjin-gu; amusement park rides ₩4000; ⏲5am-10pm, amusement park 10am-6.30pm, zoo 9.30am-5.30pm; 👪; ⓢLine 5 or 7 to Children's Grand Park, Exit 1) FREE Let your little ones run wild in this enormous playground, which includes amusement rides, a zoo, a botanical garden, a wetland eco area and a giant musical fountain. The latest addition is a smart **Children's Museum** with plenty of hands-on edutainment.

EATING

★ONION BAKERY $
(어니언; ☎070-7816 2710; www.instagram.com/cafe.onion; 8 Achasan-ro 9(gu)-gil; coffee from ₩4500; ⏲8am-10pm Mon-Fri, 10am-10pm Sat & Sun; ❄📶; ⓢLine 2 to Seongsu, Exit 2) Seoul's hippest cafe-bakery, Onion is the epitome of industrial-chic cool, set within a semiderelict concrete building that just begs to be photographed. Scenesters queue out the door to take their turn loading trays with artisanal baked goods, sandwiches and frankly fabulous coffee, before finding a little perch of exposed brick to call their own.

★GWANGJANG MARKET KOREAN $
Map p238 (광장시장, Kwangjang; www.kwangjangmarket.co.kr; 88 Changgyeonggung-ro, Jongno-gu; dishes ₩4000-15,000; ⏲8.30am-10pm; ⓢLine 1 to Jongno-5ga, Exit 8, or Line 2 or 5 to Eulji-ro 4-ga, Exit 4) This sprawling fabric market is now best known as Seoul's busiest *meokjagolmok* (food alley), thanks to the 200 or so food stalls, kimchi and fresh-seafood vendors that have set up shop amid the silk, satin and linen wholesalers. It's a hive of delicious sights and smells. Foodies flock here for the golden fried *nokdu bindaetteok* (mung-bean pancake; ₩4000 to ₩5000) – paired beautifully with *makgeolli* (milky rice wine).

★I LOVE SINDANGDONG KOREAN $
Map p247 (아이러브 신당동; ☎02-2232 7872; www.ilovesindangdong.com; 302-4 Sindang-dong; tteokbokki for 2 from ₩11,000; ⏲24hr, closed 1st & 3rd Mon of month) The *tteokbokki* at this raucous restaurant comes in bubbling

saucepans as part of a witches brew of rice cakes, fish cake, instant ramen, vegies, egg and tofu in a volcanic sauce. It's pure, junky comfort food and great fun; you can pay extra to pimp it up with seafood and cheese. Also on offer are *gimbap* (Korean sesame-oil flavoured rice wrapped in seaweed), cheap draught beer and occasional live music.

Open since 2001, it's hands down the most popular eatery at Sindang-dong Tteobokki Town.

PYEONGANDO JOKBAL JIP NORTH KOREAN $

Map p247 (평안도 족발집; ☎02-2279 9759; 174-6 Jangchungdan-ro; jokbal for 2 from ₩30,000; ⏰11.30am-11pm; Ⓢ Line 3 to Dongguk University, Exit 3) Out of sight in an alleyway, this is one of the best spots in town to try *jokbal* (braised pigs' trotters). Staff maintain a continuous cleaving of pig forelegs to keep up with diners gorging on collagen-rich pork slices wrapped in leaves with garlic and other condiments. *Jokbal* is said to pair perfectly with *soju* (local vodka), so don't hold back.

SAMARKAND CENTRAL ASIAN $$

Map p247 (사마르칸트, Samarikant; 12 Eulji-ro 42-gil; beef or lamb skewers ₩5000, mains from ₩10,000; ⏰10am-11pm; 📶; Ⓢ Line 2, 4 or 5 to Dongdaemun, Exit 12) This family-run Uzbekistan restaurant is a part of Dongdaemun's 'Little Silk Road', an intriguing district behind Lotte Fitin (p140) that's home to a community of Russian-speaking traders from the 'stans, Mongolia and Russia. The matriarch dishes up tasty halal fare with a bling smile (note the double row of gold teeth), including lamb *shashlik* that goes beautifully with fresh *lepeshka* bread and Russian beer.

OR:ER CAFE $

(오르에르, orer; ☎02-462 0018; 18 Yeonmujang-gil; cake from ₩7000; ⏰11am-10pm, shop 1-8pm Tue-Sun; ❄📶👪; Ⓜ Line 2 to Seongsu, Exit 4) Centred on a cafe that serves dainty cakes, coffee and Fortnum and Mason teas, vintage-styled OR:ER feels throughout like an elegant old home. The 3rd floor is a delightful vintage shop (closed Mondays), and there's a charming garden out back.

SINDANG-DONG TTEOBOKKI TOWN KOREAN $

Map p247 (신당동 떡볶이 타운; Sindang-dong, Jung-gu; ⏰11am-10pm Mon-Sat; Ⓢ Line 2 or 6 to Sindang, Exit 7 or 8) Historic street lined with vendors and restaurants selling all manner of *tteobokki* (rice cake) dishes.

DONGDAEMUN MARKET MARKET $

Map p247 (동대문시장; dishes from ₩6000; ⏰10am-10pm; Ⓢ Lines 1 & 4 to Dongdaemun, Exit 8) Within the Dongdaemun Shopping Complex of the main market, there's an excellent choice of street food ranging from vendors to small restaurants, including several that specialise in charcoal BBQ *samchi* (Spanish mackerel).

WOORAEOAK NORTH KOREAN $$

Map p238 (우래옥; ☎02-2265 0151; 62-29 Changgyeonggung-ro, Jung-gu; noodles ₩13,000; ⏰11.30am-10pm; Ⓢ Line 2 or 4 to Eulji-ro 4ga, Exit 4) Tucked away in the sewing-machine parts section of Dongdaemun's sprawling market streets is this elegant old-timer specialising in bulgogi and *galbi* (barbecued beef; from ₩33,000). For a more affordable lunch try the much-lauded, Pyongyang-style *naengmyeon* (buckwheat cold noodles, ₩13,000), paired with delicious kimchi.

DRINKING & NIGHTLIFE

★DAELIM CHANGGO CAFE

(대림창고; ☎02-498 7474; 78 Seongsui-ro, Seongdong-gu; pizzas from ₩25,000; ⏰10am-11pm; 📶; Ⓢ Line 2 to Seongsu Station, Exit 3) Hands down the most stunning converted *changgo* (warehouse) venue in 'Seoul's Brooklyn', Daelim Changgo is the ultimate synthesis of Seoul's obsessions for cafes, design, art and selfies. Choose from single-origin coffee, draught beers and wood-fired pizza and find a spot in either of two cavernous former workshops to sit and marvel at the funky wall art, sculptures, and interior garden complete with buzzing neon flowers.

BAESAN WAREHOUSE CAFE CAFE

(바이산 대림창고; ☎02-6238 8130; 78 Seongsui-ro; coffee from ₩6000; ⏰11am-11pm; Ⓢ Line 2 to Seongsu, Exit 3) Anywhere else in Seoul (except maybe Hongdae), this vast, industrial-chic hang-out would be cream of the crop with its street-art styling, quality baked goods and teas made to look like craft beer (they do sell real beer too). It's just that Daelim Changgo next door is possibly the most spectacular cafe in Asia. What you gonna do?

AMAZING BREWING CO BREWERY
(☎02-465 5208; www.amazingbrewing.co.kr; 4 Seongsuil-ro 4-gil; 250mL pours from ₩5000; ⊙6pm-1am Mon-Fri, from 4pm Sat & Sun; 📶; Ⓢ Line 2 to Ttukseom, Exit 5) Amazing serves around 20 of its own beers at this hip brewing facility and bar. Seoul Forest, a New England pale ale, is named after the park next door. Another beer named Cosmos Hawking Radiation...well, that's anyone's guess. There are international guest beers too, and you can order hot dogs, wings and pizza.

ENTERTAINMENT

YES 24 LIVE HALL LIVE PERFORMANCE
(www.yes24livehall.com; 20 Gucheonmyeon-ro; Ⓢ Line 5 to Gwangnaru, Exit 2) Formerly AX-Korea, this pop-concert venue holds around 4000 people.

JANGCHUNG ARENA STADIUM
Map p247 (장충체육관; ☎02-2236 4197; www.sisul.or.kr/global/main/en/sub/gymnasium.jsp; 241 Dongho-ro, Jung-gu; Ⓢ Line 3 to Dongguk University, Exit 5) Volleyball matches, *ssireum* (traditional Korean wrestling) competitions and pop concerts are held at this 4500-seat indoor arena, which looks like a huge cooking pot.

SHOPPING

★**SU;PY** CLOTHING
(☎02-6406 3388; www.supyrocks.com; 71 Seongsui-ro, Seongdong-gu; ⊙11am-10pm Tue-Sun; Ⓢ Line 2 to Seongsu, Exit 3) See what's coming next in Korean fashion at this fabulously well-designed boutique, which offers streetwear, gifts and bags on the ground floor and more formal styles upstairs. Even if you're not buying, the shop design, especially upstairs, deserves your attention. There's also su;py cafe next door.

DONGDAEMUN MARKET MARKET
Map p247 (동대문시장; Dongdaemun; ⊙24hr Mon-Sat; Ⓢ Line 1 or 4 to Dongdaemun, Exit 8) The bargaining never stops at this colossal retail and wholesale cluster, best visited at night when local buyers come clamouring for deals. The labyrinthine market buildings comprise some 30,000 retailers; only serious shopaholics need apply. Head to the multilevel Pyounghwa Clothing Market for fashion and accessories (though don't expect haute couture), and the **Dongdaemun Shopping Complex** (⊙8am-7pm Mon-Sat) for a broader range of goods.

SEOUL YANGNYEONGSI HERB MEDICINE MARKET HEALTH & WELLNESS
(www.seoulya.com; Jegi-dong; ⊙9am-7pm; Ⓢ Line 1 to Jegidong, Exit 2) Also known as Gyeongdong Market, Korea's biggest Asian medicine market runs back for several blocks from the traditional gate on the main road and includes thousands of clinics, retailers, wholesalers and medicine makers. If you're looking for a leaf, herb, bark, root, flower or mushroom to ease your ailment, it's bound to be here.

Be sure to visit the Seoul K-Medi Center (p136) within the market to brush up on your pharmacy smarts, or simply to chill over a cleansing cuppa or maybe a herbal foot bath.

DAPSIMNI ANTIQUES MARKET ANTIQUES
(⊙10am-6pm Mon-Sat; Ⓢ Line 5 to Dapsimni, Exit 2) One for serious collectors, this sprawling collection of antique shops is spread over three separate precincts. Here you can browse through old dusty treasures – from *yangban* (aristocrat) pipes and horsehair hats to wooden shoes, fish-shaped locks and embroidered status insignia – which are anywhere from 100 to 600 years old.

S-FACTORY MALL
(☎02-6388 8316; www.sfactory.kr; 11 Yeonmujang 15-gil; ⊙11am-9pm; Ⓢ Line 2 to Seongsu, Exit 3) Just opened at time of research is this postindustrial shopping mall, art centre and office complex housed in an old factory unit. The open-air roof has a variety of restaurants and cafes.

PYOUNGHWA CLOTHING MARKET CLOTHING
Map p247 (평화시장; Dongdaemun Market; ⊙7-10pm; Ⓢ Line 1 or 4 to Dongdaemun, Exit 8) Part of Dongdaemun Market, the Pyounghwa Clothing Market is a mind-bending warren of identical stalls selling clothes, fabric and accessories. You've got to wonder how the vendors find their individual booths among the many thousands here! Much of the action is wholesale, and liveliest after dark. Weekends are quiet.

LOTTE FITIN DEPARTMENT STORE

Map p247 (www.lottefitin.com; 264 Eulji-ro, Jung-gu; ⏲11am-midnight; 📶; Ⓢ Line 2, 4 or 5 to Dongdaemun History & Culture Park, Exit 11) In the same mould as Doota, if slightly more focused on global brands, this high-rise department store has multiple levels of clothing, cosmetics, accessories and other goods.

DOOTA DEPARTMENT STORE

Map p247 (☎02-3398 3114; www.doota.com; 275 Jangchungdan-ro, Jung-gu; ⏲10.30am-5am, to midnight Sun, Doota Duty Free until 11pm; Ⓢ Line 2, 4 or 5 to Dongdaemun History & Culture Park, Exit 14) Cut through Dongdaemun's commercial frenzy by heading to its leading fashion department store, which is full to the brim with domestic and foreign brands. Fifteen floors, above and below ground, are dedicated to clothing, accessories and cosmetics. When you start flagging, there are plenty of cafes and a food court on the 6th floor.

SEOUL FOLK FLEA MARKET MARKET

(서울풍물시장; 19-3 Cheonho-daero 4-gil, Dongdaemun-gu; ⏲10am-7pm, closed 2nd & 4th Tue of month; Ⓢ Line 1 or 2 to Sinseol-dong, Exit 6 or 10) You could kit out half the world's hipster cafes from the teetering stacks of dusty ornaments, table lamps, musical instruments and valve radios crammed inside this two-storey, canvas-tented market. You might also dig up some traditional Korean bric-a-brac like wooden masks and ink drawings. A cheap food court ladles up *sundubu jjigae* (tofu and kimchi stew) for ₩4000.

Northern Seoul

Neighbourhood Top Five

1 Ihwa Mural Village (p144) Heading up the slopes of Naksan to these 'moon villages' and being rewarded with wonderful views of the city.

2 Korea Furniture Museum (p143) Admiring traditional buildings and Joseon-period furnishings in a splendid hillside setting.

3 Seodaemun Prison History Hall (p145) Touring the old cell blocks and learning about the horrors of the Japanese colonial period.

4 Korean Stone Art Museum (p144) Discovering scores of stone sentinels alfresco at this excellent museum.

5 Inwangsan Guksadang (p144) Witnessing ancient shamanistic ceremonies and hike up Inwangsan to the city's finest views.

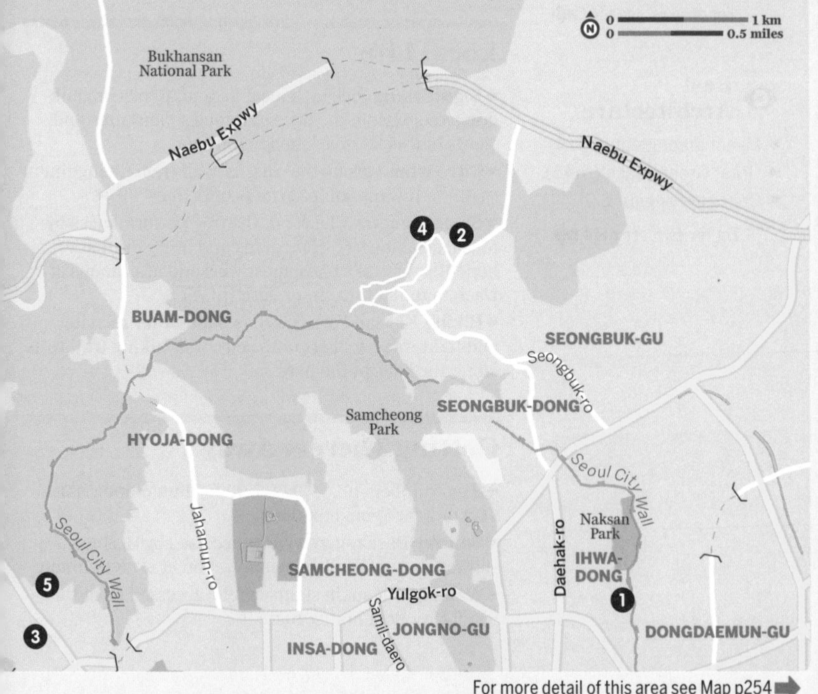

For more detail of this area see Map p254

Lonely Planet's Top Tip

For info on what's showing at the scores of venues in Daehangno, and for discounts of up to 50% on tickets, go to the **Daehangno Information Center** (p149) or the **Seoul Theater Center** (p149).

Best Places to Eat

- Gyeyeolsa Chicken (p146)
- Jaha Sonmandoo (p147)
- Scoff (p147)
- Deongjang Yesool (p147)

For reviews, see p146.

Best Places to Drink

- Club Espresso (p149)
- Sanmotoonge (p147)
- Suyeon Sanbang (p147)

For reviews, see p147.

Best Architecture

- Myeongjeongjeon (p144)
- Great Greenhouse (p145)
- Changgyeonggung (p144)

For reviews, see p144.

Explore Northern Seoul

The city's northern districts seldom figure prominently on international-tourist itineraries, which is a pity as they're home to some of Seoul's most charming neighbourhoods and fascinating sights, including the best sections of the old City Walls. Start exploring in the university district of Daehangno, a performing-arts hub with some 150 theatres ranging from intimate fringe-style venues to major auditoriums such as the Arko Art Theater (p149).

Hike to Naksan Park (p146) and follow the wall northwest over to Seongbuk-dong, a leafy mountainside community known as the Beverly Hills of Seoul because of its grand mansions, many of them home to ambassadors and CEOs. Here you'll find the outstanding Korea Furniture Museum (p143), the Korean Stone Art Museum (p144) and serene Buddhist temple Gilsang-sa (p146).

Continue following the walls to the summit of Inwangsan with its weirdly eroded rocks, temples and Guksadang (p144) shrine. The area has a special atmosphere because of the outdoor shamanist ceremonies that invoke the spirits of the departed. At the foot of the mountain is the large Seodaemun Independence Park (p146), with monuments that celebrate Korea's march towards nationhood, free from the interference and colonisation of China and Japan. The haunting displays at the Seodaemun Prison History Hall (p145) provide a sobering end to this tour, which can occupy several days.

Local Life

- **Sightseeing** Pick up a local area map to Seongbuk-dong and explore the myriad temples, museums and sights of this laid-back neighbourhood.
- **City vistas** Trek up the old City Wall from Changuimun (p145) to Inwangsan (p34) for Seoul's finest views.
- **Street theatre** Check out the free performances by musicians, dancers, comedians and other dramatic hopefuls that take place most weekend afternoons at Daehangno's Marronnier Park (p146).
- **Hiking** Naksan Park (p146) is popular for relaxing and light exercise. Part of the city-wall hiking trail runs along the back of the park.

Getting There & Away

- **Bus** Numbers 1020, 7022, 7212 for Buam-dong, 1111, 2112 or 2 for Seongbuk-dong.
- **Subway** Daehangno is easily accessed by Hyehwa subway station. For Seodaemun get off at Dongnimmun.
- **Walking** The main sights can be accessed from the Seoul City Wall hiking route.

TOP EXPERIENCE

EXPLORE THE KOREA FURNITURE MUSEUM

Almost as exclusive as its hillside location in leafy Seongbuk-dong, this architecture and traditional furniture museum is a gem. Reservations are required to visit the compound in which 10 beautiful buildings serve as the appetiser to the main course: a collection of furniture, including chests, bookcases, chairs and dining tables made from varieties of wood, such as persimmon, maple and paulownia. Some are decorated with lacquer, mother-of-pearl or tortoiseshell.

Buildings & Gardens

The museum is the personal project of a former Yonsei University professor who has amassed some 2500 pieces, of which around 500 are on show at any one time. Equally impressive are the compound's collection of wooden buildings, such as the **kitchen house** with its seemingly contemporary design of windows, as well as a **villa** that was once part of Changdeokgung. The **panoramic views** from the gardens and inside the buildings are also lovely.

Visiting the Museum

You need to apply several days in advance via a reservation page on the website to visit this museum. From the subway, take bus 2, which stops a few minutes away from the museum entrance, but if you don't fancy walking up a narrow, busy road then take a taxi.

DON'T MISS

- Furniture collection
- Kitchen House
- Villa from Changdeokgung

PRACTICALITIES

- 한국가구박물관
- Map p254, E1
- ☎02-745 0181
- www.kofum.com
- 121 Daesagwan-ro, Seongbuk-dong
- ₩20,000
- ⏲11am-5pm Tue-Sat
- Ⓢ Line 4 to Hansung University, Exit 6

SIGHTS

Some of the area's best sights are clustered in Seongbuk-dong, on the east slope of Bukaksan just beyond the Seoul City Wall. This wealthy neighbourhood has poured huge sums of money into tourism in recent years, opening several excellent museums and galleries. To the south, Ihwa Mural Village makes for a pleasant half-day sightseeing, together with several galleries and museums nearby, and the 15th-century palace of Changgyeonggung.

KOREA FURNITURE MUSEUM — MUSEUM

See p143.

★KOREAN STONE ART MUSEUM — MUSEUM

(우리옛돌박물관; www.koreanstonemuseum.com; 66 Daesagwan-ro 13-gil; adult/youth/child ₩7000/5000/3000; ⏲10am-6pm Tue-Sun; Ⓢ Line 4 to Hansung University, Exit 6) A score of centuries-old stone sentinels stand guard on the hillside at this wonderful museum overlooking Seongbuk-dong. A road winds through sculpted gardens revealing collections of various stone figures as you go. You'll learn to tell your *muninseok* from your *dongjaseok* (the former wear the hats of government officials while the latter have double-knot hairdos); there's also more crudely carved *beoksu* – totems placed at the entrance to Korean villages to protect against evil spirits and illnesses.

Start by working your way up through the interior galleries before heading out to the gardens via the roof. To get here, take bus 2 from outside Hansung University station. Korean Stone Art Museum is the last stop.

There's also a Buddhist temple, **Jeongbeopsa**, next door, and the start of a marked hiking trail up the back of Bukaksan (p34).

★IHWA MURAL VILLAGE — AREA

Map p254 (이화 벽화 마을; Ihwa-dong, Jongno-gu; Ⓢ Line 4 to Hyehwa, Exit 2) High on the slopes of Naksan is one of the city's old *daldongnae* (literally 'moon villages') where refugees lived in shacks after the Korean War. Sixty years later it has morphed into a tourism hot spot thanks to a collection of quirky sculptures and imaginative murals on walls along the village's steep stairways and alleys.

The euphemistic name *daldongnae* alludes to the fact that residents had a great view of the moon from their hovels high on the hillside. It's a fair old slog up the steps to reach the top, but you'll be rewarded with wonderful views of the city (and epic sunsets) from a row of lookout cafes.

★INWANGSAN GUKSADANG — SHRINE

(인왕산 국사당; Inwangsan, Seodaemun-gu; Ⓢ Line 3 to Dongnimmun, Exit 2) This ornate shrine atop Inwangsan is one of Seoul's most important sites for shamanism, Korea's ancient, highly ritualised and somewhat taboo folk religion. If you're lucky, you might witness a *gut* (service) performed by female *mudang* (shamans), invoking the spirits to bless a marriage, bring good fortune or cure illness. The Japanese demolished the original shrine on Namsan in 1925, and it was rebuilt here.

With its turquoise-painted doors, the shrine is just past **Seonamjeong** (선암정사), a temple with bell pavilion and gates painted with a pair of traditional door guardians.

WHANKI MUSEUM — MUSEUM

(환기미술관; ☎02-391 7701; www.whankimuseum.org; 63 Jahamun-ro 40-gil; ₩8000-10,000; ⏲10am-6pm Tue-Sun; Ⓢ Line 3 to Gyeongbokgung, Exit 3) Surrounded by sculptures, this attractive museum showcases a rotating display of works by Kim Whan-ki (1913–74), a local pioneer of modern abstract art who is known as the 'Picasso of Korea'. From the subway, catch bus 1020, 7212, 7016 or 1711.

CHANGGYEONGGUNG — PALACE

Map p254 (창경궁, Palace of Flourishing Gladness; ☎02-762 4868; http://english.cha.go.kr; 185 Changgyeonggung-ro, Jongno-gu; adult/child ₩1000/500; ⏲9am-6pm Tue-Sun; Ⓢ Line 4 to Hyehwa, Exit 4) Originally built in the 15th century by King Sejong for his father, this is one of Seoul's 'five grand palaces'. It backs onto the more impressive Changdeokgung (p60) – the two palaces shared the secret garden. The throne hall, **Myeongjeongjeon**, is the oldest surviving hall of all Seoul's palaces. It was rebuilt in 1616, making it a rare example of intact 17th-century Joseon architecture. The oldest surviving structure here is the **Okcheongyo** stone bridge (1483), which crosses the stream ahead of the front gate.

The smaller buildings beyond the main hall were where the kings and queens lived in their separate households. From here, paths wind past a European-style garden and ornamental pond to the **Great Greenhouse**, a splendid Victorian-esque glass structure built by the Japanese in 1909.

Like Seoul's other palaces, Changgyeonggung was destroyed twice by the Japanese – first in the 1590s and again during the colonial period from 1910 until 1945, when the palace suffered the indignity of being turned into a zoo. Only a fifth of the palace buildings survived or have been rebuilt.

Look out for dates (usually in early May) when the palace is open for night viewing and illuminated, making it a romantic spot – if you can ignore the crowds. There are free English guided tours at 11am and 4pm daily.

ARKO ART CENTER GALLERY

Map p254 (아르코미술관; ☎02-760 4850; www.arkoartcenter.or.kr; 3 Dongsung-gil; ⏲11am-6pm; Ⓢ Line 4 to Hyehwa, Exit 2) FREE A great place to see contemporary art, this impressive red-brick complex has a trio of interlinking galleries that house regularly changing, often avant-garde exhibitions. Opened in 1979, it was designed by Kim Swoo Geun, one of Korea's most famous postwar architects.

LOCK MUSEUM MUSEUM

Map p254 (쇳대박물관; ☎02-766 6494; 100 Ihwajang-gil; adult/child ₩4000/3000; ⏲9am-6pm Tue-Sun; Ⓢ Line 4 to Hyehwa, Exit 2) One of Seoul's quirkier private collections makes for a surprisingly absorbing exhibition. It focuses on the artistry of locks, latches and keys of all kinds, mainly from Korea but also with some international examples, including a gruesome-looking chastity belt. Clad in Corten steel, the building contrasts nicely with a colourful wall mural nearby.

Come here also to pick up an English-language map to the mural art and small house museums of Ihwa Maeul.

CHANGUIMUN GATE

(창의문; 118 Changuimun-ro; ⏲9am-4pm; 🚌1020, 7022, 7212, Ⓢ Line 3 to Gyeongbokgung, Exit 3) FREE One of the 'four small gates' in Seoul's City Wall, this is also the start point for the City Wall hike up Bukaksan (p34). If you plan on doing the hike, you'll need to show your passport at the booth by the gate in exchange for a pass, which must be worn at all times.

TOP EXPERIENCE
LEARN HISTORY AT SEODAEMUN PRISON

Now a museum, Seodaemun Prison History Hall was built by the colonial Japanese in 1908. Though it was only designed to house 500 prisoners, up to 3500 were packed inside during the height of the 1919 anti-Japanese protests. The factories where prisoners were forced to make bricks and military uniforms have gone, but some of the prison-made bricks with Chinese characters on them have been used to make pavements, and the whole complex has been expertly restored.

In the **main exhibition hall** chilling tableaux display the various torture techniques employed on Korean patriots. Photographs of the prison are on view along with video footage, and you can go into cells in the **central prison building**. The most famous victim was Ryu Gwan-sun, an 18-year-old Ewha high-school student, who was tortured to death in 1920. You can see the **underground cell** where this happened, as well as a separate **execution building** where other prisoners were killed and the tunnel via which their bodies were secretly removed. The prison continued to be used by Korea's various dictatorships in the postwar years right up until its closure in 1987.

DON'T MISS

- Exhibition hall
- Central prison building
- Ryu Gwan-sun's cell

PRACTICALITIES

- 서대문형무소역사관
- https://sphh.sscmc.or.kr/_eng/
- 251 Tongil-ro
- adult/youth/child ₩3000/1500/1000
- ⏲9.30am-6pm Tue-Sun Mar-Oct, to 5pm Tue-Sun Nov-Feb
- Ⓢ Line 3 to Dongnimmun, Exit 5

The current gatehouse structure dates back to 1741, making it the oldest of the four small gates in Seoul's City Wall.

SEONJAM MUSEUM MUSEUM

Map p254 (성북선잠박물관; ☎02-744 0027; http://museum.sb.go.kr; 96 Seongbuk-ro; adult/child ₩1000/500; ⏲10am-6pm Tue-Sun; Ⓢ Line 4 to Hansung University, Exit 6) FREE An engaging little museum about Seongbuk-dong's long vanished Seonjam altar, which was where royal sericulture (silk production) rites were held during the Joseon dynasty. Locals restarted the annual ceremony in 1993, and the museum's ongoing mission is to also recreate the altar, the original location of which is thought to be 100m or so east along the main road. From the subway, take Bus 1111 or 2112.

HANYANGDOSEONG EXHIBITION HALL MUSEUM

Map p254 (☎02-766 8520; 63 Changgyeonggung-ro 35-gil; ⏲10am-5pm; Ⓢ Line 4 to Hansung University, Exit 5) FREE Adjacent to Hyehwamun, this former home of various mayors of Seoul was built in 1941 directly on top of the Seoul City Wall. It's now a Wall museum with a small cafe and garden, and a popular rest spot for walkers. The foundations of the house have been exposed on one side to reveal parts of the Wall.

SEODAEMUN INDEPENDENCE PARK PARK

(서대문독립공원; 101 Hyeonjeo-dong; ⏲24hr; Ⓢ Line 3 to Dongnimmun, Exit 4) Apart from the former prison, this park, dedicated to those who fought for Korean independence, also features **Dongnimmun**, an impressive granite archway modelled after the Arc de Triomphe. Built by the Independence Club in 1898, it stands where envoys from Chinese emperors used to be officially welcomed to Seoul.

SAMCHEONG PARK PARK

(41 Waryonggongwon-gil; 🚌2, 11) On the lower slopes of Bukaksan (p34), this park is busiest in April when locals come to admire the cherry blossoms. Hiking trails here connect up with the Seoul City Wall.

NAKSAN PARK PARK

Map p254 (낙산공원; http://parks.seoul.go.kr; 54 Naksan-gil; ⏲24hr; Ⓢ Line 4 to Hyehwa, Exit 2) FREE The lofty slopes above Daehangno offer fantastic city views and contain an impressive section of the Seoul City Wall, which you can follow in either direction (and often on both sides) between Dongdaemun and Seongbuk-dong. The park gets its name from the Korean word *'nakta'*, meaning 'camel', for its hump-like appearance.

HYEHWAMUN GATE

Map p254 (혜화문; 307 Changgyeonggung-ro; Ⓢ Line 4 to Hyehwa, Exit 4) One of the 'four small gates' of the Seoul City Wall, Hyehwamun is also known as Dongsomun (literally 'small east gate'). Originally built in 1396, it was reconstructed in 1994 on this spot slightly to the north of its original location.

GILSANG-SA TEMPLE

Map p254 (길상사; ☎02-3672 5945; www.kilsangsa.info; 68 Seonjam-ro 5-gil, Seongbuk-gu; ⏲10am-6pm Mon-Sat; Ⓢ Line 4 to Hansung University, Exit 6) FREE This modern hillside temple is a pleasure to visit at any time of the year, but particularly in May when the grounds are festooned with lanterns for Buddha's birthday. The buildings once housed the elite restaurant Daewongak, where *gisaeng* (female entertainers accomplished in traditional arts) performed. In 1997 the property was donated by its owner, a former *gisaeng*, to a Buddhist monk to be turned into a temple. From the subway take bus 2; it stops right outside the temple entrance.

MARRONNIER PARK PLAZA

Map p254 (마로니에공원; 104 Daehak-ro; Ⓢ Line 4 to Hyehwa, Exit 2) More plaza than park, Marronnier Park usually has something happening on afternoons and evenings at the outdoor stage, as well as pockets of sculpture to admire. Named after the chestnut trees planted here, it once formed part of Seoul National University before the institution was moved south to the Gwanak Campus in the mid-1970s.

EATING

Charming Buam-dong has a couple of must-try eateries perfectly placed for a post-hike meal: Gyeyeolsa Chicken for traditional fried chicken and Jaha Sonmandoo for *mandu* (dumplings).

★GYEYEOLSA CHICKEN FAST FOOD $

(계열사; ☎02-391 3566; 7 Baekseokdong-gil; chicken ₩20,000; ⏲noon-11.30pm Tue-Sun; 📶; Ⓢ Line 3 to Gyeongbokgung, Exit 3) The fried-chicken purists here say cluck-off to chilli and other gimmicks, simply serving delicious, golden-fried chicken pieces heaped together with crisp potato wedges. One basket serves two nicely. It's a popular spot, and it packs you in tight. From the subway, take bus 1020, 7022, or 7212.

★JAHA SONMANDOO KOREAN $
(자하손만두; ☎02-379 2648; 12 Baekseokdong-gil; dumplings from ₩6500; ⏰11am-9.30pm; Ⓢ Line 3 to Gyeongbokgung, Exit 3) Around lunchtime and on weekends Seoulites queue up at this posh mountainside *mandu* (dumpling) house for elegantly wrapped dough parcels stuffed with veggies, beef and pork, served either boiled or in soup. A couple of orders is enough of these whoppers; the sweet cinnamon tea to finish is free. From the subway, take bus 1020, 7022 or 7212.

SCOFF BAKERY $
(☎070-8801 1739; 149 Changuimun-ro; baked goods ₩2000-5000; ⏰11am-6pm Wed-Sun; Ⓢ Line 3 to Gyeongbokgung, Exit 3) British baker Jonathan exhibits admirable bake-off skills in his selection of sweet treats ranging from scones and ginger cake to coconut macaroons – but the lemon sponge gets our vote. Ideal for a takeaway nibble while wandering Buam-dong. From the subway, take bus 1020, 1711, 7016, 7018, 7022 or 7212.

DEONGJANG YESOOL KOREAN $
Map p254 (된장예술, Bean Art and Wine; ☎02-741 4516; 9-2 Daehak-ro 11-gil; set meal ₩11,000; ⏰11am-10pm; 🅥; Ⓢ Line 4 to Hyehwa, Exit 3) Serves a tasty fermented-bean-paste-and-tofu stew that comes with a big variety of nearly all vegetarian side dishes at a bargain price – no wonder it's well patronised by the area's student population. Look for the stone carved lions flanking the door.

GEUMWANG DONGASEU INTERNATIONAL $
Map p254 (금왕돈까스, Geumwang Tonkatsu; ☎02-763 9366; 138 Seongbuk-ro; mains ₩10,000; ⏰9.30am-10pm Tue-Sun; Ⓢ Line 4 to Hansung University, Exit 6) For a Korean interpretation of Western food circa 1987, try the breaded pork, fish or beef cutlets (something approaching a schnitzel) at this retro Seongbuk-dong eatery. Bathed in a rather sweet tomato sauce, they come on enormous plates with a heap of rice, salad, pasta and mushy peas. From the subway, catch bus 1111 or 3.

HYEHWA KALGUKSU NOODLES $
Map p254 (혜화 칼국수; ☎02-743 8212; 13 Changgyeonggung-ro 35-gil; noodles ₩9000; ⏰11am-10pm; Ⓢ Line 4 to Hyehwa, Exit 4) This throwback Korean eatery, painted duck-egg blue, serves simple bowls of *guksi* noodles in a milky-white, beef-bone broth with leeks and zucchini. Homey and simple, it also does delicious cod fritters that look like giant fish fingers.

WOOD AND BRICK BAKERY $$
Map p254 (120 Seongbuk-ro, Seongbuk-dong; pastries from ₩3300; ⏰8am-10pm; 📶; Ⓢ Line 4 to Hansung University, Exit 6) Refuel with sandwiches, pastries and coffee at this pleasant bakery-cafe, part of a small chain known for its baked goods and macarons. It also stocks beer, wine, cheese and deli meats – all the fixings for a posh picnic. From the subway, take bus 1111 or 2112.

DRINKING & NIGHTLIFE

What Northern Seoul lacks in nightlife, it makes up for in atmospheric cafes and teahouses, many with gardens and gorgeous views.

★SUYEON SANBANG TEAHOUSE
Map p254 (수연산방; 8 Seongbuk-ru 26-gil; tea from ₩8500; ⏰11.30am-10pm; Ⓢ Line 4 to Hansung University, Exit 6) Seoul's most charming teahouse is housed in a 1930s *hanok* and surrounding garden that once belonged to famous writer Lee Tae-jun, who settled in the North after the Korean War to an unknown fate. Apart from a range of medicinal teas and premium-quality, wild green tea, it also serves traditional sweets; the salty-sweet pumpkin soup with red-bean paste is a taste sensation.

Find it around the corner from the Seongbuk Museum of Art, and avoid weekend afternoons when it gets busy. From the subway, catch bus 1111 or 2112.

★SANMOTOONGE CAFE
(산모퉁이; ☎02-391 4737; www.sanmotoonge.co.kr; 153 Baekseokdong-gil; ⏰11am-10pm; Ⓢ Line 3 to Gyeongbokgung, Exit 3) Being featured in a Korean TV drama can do wonders for your business, but punters would still flock to this mountainside hot spot regardless for the wonderful views and hilarious clutter

Neighbourhood Walk
Inwangsan Shamanist Walk

START DONGNIMMUN STATION, EXIT 2
END SEODAEMUN PRISON HISTORY HALL
LENGTH 4KM, THREE HOURS

On this hillside walk you can see Seoul's most famous shamanist shrine, small Buddhist/shamanist temples and part of Seoul's medieval City Walls, as well as enjoy a bird's-eye view from Inwangsan's summit. Treat the area and people with consideration, and remember that taking a photograph could interfere with an important ceremony.

To get here, take subway Line 3 to Dongnimmun station. From 1 **exit 2** of the subway turn down the first small alley on your left. At the five-alley crossroads, fork right up the steps and you'll soon reach the colourful 2 **entrance gate** to the shamanist village.

Turn left where the houses and small temples are terraced up the rocky hillside. Most are decorated with colourful murals of birds and blossom on their outside walls, and wind chimes clink in the breeze.

On the main path is a temple, 3 **Seonamjeong**, and, up the steps, the shamanistic shrine 4 **Inwangsan Guksadang** (p144). Walk left and up some steps to the extraordinary 5 **Seonbawi** (Zen Rocks), so-called because they are thought to look like a pair of giant monks in prayer. A path continues up around the Dali-esque rocks and you can climb to higher 6 **giant boulders** for expansive views across the city.

To reach Inwangsan's peak, head back to Guksadang and follow the paths up the gully to where they meet the path along the mountain ridge and the lower side of the Seoul City Wall. At a set of 7 **wooden steps** you can climb over to the other side of the wall. From here it's around a 15-minute hike to the summit of 8 **Inwangsan** (p34).

Retrace your steps down the wall to where it ends, and turn right along the road for 10 minutes until you reach 9 **Dongnimmun** (p146), and Seodaemun Independence Park across the road. Finish your walk by having a look around the 10 **Seodaemun Prison History Hall** (p145).

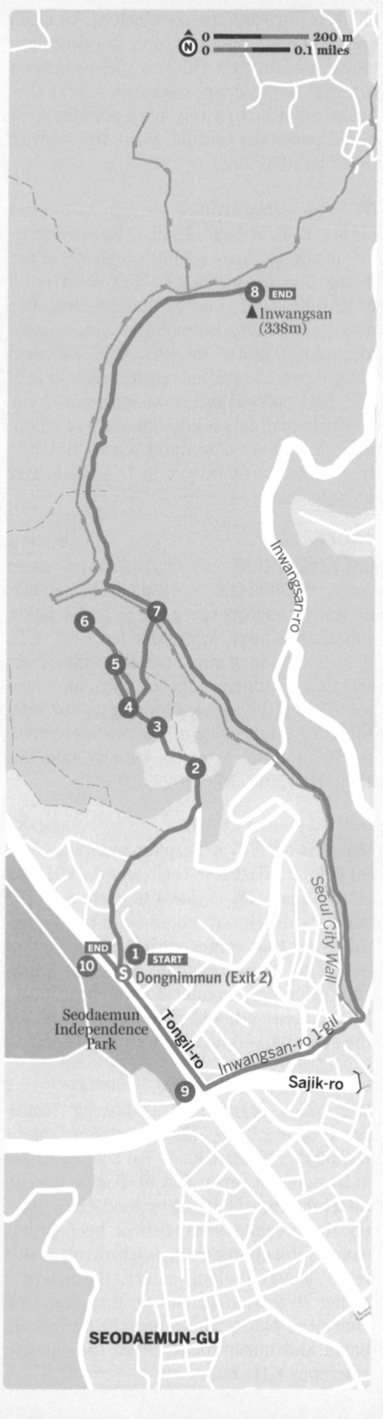

of *objets d'art* and bric-and-brac both inside and on the terraces. Order drinks and snacks at the counter then snag the perfect sunset perch.

From the subway, catch bus 1020, 7022 or 7212 up to Changuimun (p145), from where it's a further 15-minute walk up the hill.

★CLUB ESPRESSO COFFEE

(www.clubespresso.co.kr; 132 Changuimun-ro; ⏲9am-10pm; Ⓢ Line 3 to Gyeongbokgung, Exit 3) Pouring some of Seoul's best coffee since 1990, this elegant roaster, cafe and shop imports its beans from all corners of the globe; there are usually a couple of free samples on the go. The caffeine kick should give you the energy to climb nearby Bukaksan. From the subway, catch bus 1020, 7022 or 7212.

APE SEOUL CAFE

Map p254 (아베 서울; ☎010 7390 8742; https://apeseoul.kr; 1 Changgyeonggung-ro 35na-gil; honey latte ₩7000; ⏲Tue-Sun 11am-10pm; 📶; Ⓢ Line 4 to Hansung University, Exit 6) 🍃 Referring not to large simians but bees (*ape* meaning 'bee' in Italian), Ape Seoul is a honey-themed cafe run by beekeeper-barista Park Jin. Get your latte topped with organic honey from bees raised in the vicinity and pair it with one of several honey-based pastries. Park also runs Urban Bees Seoul, a beekeeping cooperative.

HAKRIM CAFE

Map p254 (학림다방; www.hakrim.pe.kr; 119 Daehak-ro; coffee ₩5000; ⏲10am-11pm; 📶; Ⓢ Line 4 to Hyehwa, Exit 3) Little has changed in this retro Seoul classic since the place opened in 1956, save for the price of the coffee. Worn wooden booths and dark, creaking corners make it popular with couples. As well as teas, lattes and the like, it has a few beers, cocktails and wine.

MIX & MALT BAR

Map p254 (☎02-765 5945; www.facebook.com/mixmalt; 3 Changgyeonggung-ro 29-gil; ⏲7.30pm-2am Sun-Thu, to 3am Fri & Sat; 📶; Ⓢ Line 4 to Hyehwa, Exit 4) Order your cocktails from an iPad at this two-tiered, open-fronted bar that also specialises in malt whisky. A menu of US-inspired comfort food, fireplaces in winter and an outdoor deck for summer completes a classy package.

GAEPUL CAFE

Map p254 (☎02-517 2525; 26 Naksanseonggwakseo 1-gil; coffee ₩5000; ⏲11am-10pm; 📶; Ⓢ Line 4 to Hyehwa, Exit 2) One of a row of cutesy cafes at the very top of Ihwa Mural Village (p144) and parallel to the Seoul City Wall, Gaepul boasts an L-shaped outdoor deck for dreamy sunset vistas.

SLOW GARDEN CAFE

Map p254 (111 Seongbuk-ro; brunch ₩14,000; ⏲9am-11.30pm; 📶; Ⓢ Line 4 to Hansung University, Exit 6) Chandeliers and recycled wood make up the shack-chic decor of this greenhouse-like cafe-restaurant that serves pizza, pasta, risotto and brunch dishes like eggs benny and French toast. From the subway, catch bus 1111 or 2112.

☆ ENTERTAINMENT

ARKOPAC THEATRE

Map p254 (☎02-3668 0007; www.koreapac.kr; 17 Daehak-ro 10-gil; Ⓢ Line 4 to Hyehwa, Exit 2) In this large, red-brick complex designed by Kim Swoo-geun are the main and small halls of both the Arko Art Theater and Daehangno Arts Theater. Come here for a varied dance-oriented program of events and shows.

JAZZ STORY LIVE MUSIC

Map p254 (☎02-725 6537; www.jazzstory.kr; 88 Hyehwa-ro; ₩5000; ⏲6pm-2am; Ⓢ Line 4 to Hyehwa, Exit 2) Lined with shelves of old LPs and with a baby grand piano on the stage, this neighbourhood venue is serious about live jazz, soul and pop. Expect three sessions of music nightly, beginning around 7pm until past midnight. Drinks start from ₩10,000. From the subway, catch bus 1111 or 2112.

There's another, smaller venue, Jazz Story 2, tucked against the Seoul City Wall up by Naksan Park.

SEOUL THEATER CENTER THEATRE

Map p254 (3 Daemyeong-gil; ⏲1-8pm Tue-Fri, 11am-8pm Sat, to 7pm Sun; Ⓢ Line 4 to Hyehwa, Exit 4) At this creative hub, cultural space and lending library, thespians will want to pick up the bilingual Daehangno Culture Map, which marks the staggering number of performance spaces spread over the neighbourhood.

DAEHANGNO INFORMATION CENTER THEATRE

Map p254 (Marronnier Park, 104 Daehak-ro; ⏲11am-8pm Tue-Sat, to 7pm Sun; Ⓢ Line 4 to Hyehwa, Exit 2) Buy tickets here for the theatres around Daehangno. The staff can tell which (if any) shows are performed in English or have English subtitles.

SHOPPING

FILIPINO SUNDAY MARKET MARKET

Map p254 (288 Changgyeonggung-ro; ⏱9am-6pm Sun; Ⓢ Line 4 to Hyehwa, Exit 1) Seoul's Filipino community gathers every Sunday to shop, meet, chat and eat Filipino food. Join the throng for authentic eats like goat stew, barbecued meats and grilled banana, or stock up on imported coconut drinks, tinned goods and cassava cakes.

10X10 FASHION & ACCESSORIES

Map p254 (www.10x10.co.kr; 31 Daehak-ro 12-gil; ⏱11am-10pm; Ⓢ Line 4 to Hyehwa, Exit 1) Korean-designed youthful clothing and accessories are just a few of the types of colourful goods sold here alongside stationery, kitchenware, candles and the like. It's typical of the kind of cheap, student-focused retail that's abundant in this area.

SPORTS & ACTIVITIES

Hike up Bukaksan, the tallest of Seoul's four guardian mountains, following an intact and heavily guarded section of the city's original fortress walls. It's a stiff climb, but views of the city from the summit of the mountain repay the effort of getting there. Other popular hikes in Northern Seoul include Inwangsan and Ansan. See Hiking (p33) for details.

Day Trips from Seoul

Demilitarized Zone & Joint Security Area p152
For history buffs and collectors of weird and unsettling experiences, a visit to the Demilitarized Zone (DMZ) buffer between North and South Korea is not to be missed; in the Joint Security Area (JSA) you can straddle the line between the two countries.

Suwon p154
Stride around the World Heritage–listed, 18th-century fortress walls, drop by the restored Joseon-dynasty temporary palace and enjoy the charms of the Korean Folk Village.

Incheon p158
Korea opened up to the world at the end of the 19th century in this port city where you'll find a colourful Chinatown, creative Art Platform and pleasant beaches on nearby islands.

Ganghwado p161
Connected to the mainland by bridge, this island has a rich history that briefly saw it as the capital of Korea in the 13th century. Today, it's all about peaceful surrounds, temples and delicious seafood.

TOP EXPERIENCE

SEE LIVING HISTORY AT THE DMZ

The 4km-wide, 240km-long buffer known as the Demilitarized Zone (DMZ) slashes across the peninsula, separating North and South Korea. Lined on both sides by tank traps, electric fences, landmines and armies in full battle readiness, it's a sinister place where the tension is palpable. Surreally, it's also a major tourist attraction, with several observation points allowing you to peek into the Democratic People's Republic of Korea (DPRK; North Korea).

DON'T MISS

- Joint Security Area (JSA)
- Dora Observatory
- Third Infiltration Tunnel

PRACTICALITIES

- **Location** 55km north of Seoul
- **Tours** Koridoor Tours and Panmunjom Travel Centre are the two main tour operators.

Joint Security Area

Unquestionably the highlight of any trip to the DMZ is the **Joint Security Area** (JSA, Panmunjeom) at Panmunjeom. An improbable tourist destination, it's here where the infamous Military Demarcation Line separates South and North Korea. Soldiers from both sides often stand metres apart eyeballing one another from their respective sides of the blue-painted UN buildings. You'll be taken inside the meeting room where the 1953 truce was signed – the only place where you can safely walk into North Korea.

Tours kick off with a briefing by US or Republic of Korea (ROK, South Korea) soldier guides at Camp Bonifas, the joint US-ROK army camp just outside the DMZ, before being transferred to another bus to the JSA.

Within the blue conference room at the JSA, where official meetings are still sometimes held, microphones on the tables constantly record everything said, while ROK soldiers stand guard inside and out in a modified taekwondo stance – an essential photo op. Their North Korean counterparts keep a steady watch, usually, but not always, from a distance.

Though your tour will be a quiet one, the soldier guide will remind you that this frontier is no stranger to violent incidents. One of the most notorious was in 1976 when two US soldiers were hacked to death with axes by North Korean soldiers after the former tried to chop down a tree obstructing the view from a watchtower. Camp Bonifas is named after one of the slain soldiers.

Back on the bus you'll be taken to one of Panmunjeom's lookout posts from where you can see the two villages within the DMZ: Daeseong-dong in the South and Gijeong-dong in the North. You'll also see the **Bridge of No Return** where POW exchange took place following the signing of the Korean Armistice Agreement in 1953.

Ironically, the forested surrounds here, long since abandoned, are some of the most ecologically pristine in Korea, even thought to be home to the Siberian tiger.

Living Inside the DMZ

The 1953 *Korean Armistice Agreement* created two villages in the DMZ. On the south side, less than 1km from Panmunjeom, is **Daeseong-dong** (대성동 or 'Freedom Village'), where around 200 people live in modern houses with high-speed internet connections and earn a tax-free annual income of more than US$80,000 from their 7-hectare farms. There's an 11pm curfew and headcount, and soldiers stand guard while the villagers work in the rice fields or tend their ginseng plants.

On the North Korean side of the line is **Gijeong-dong** (기정동). The North translates this as 'Peace Village' but the South calls it Propaganda Village because virtually all the buildings are believed to be empty or just facades – the lights all come on and go off here at the same time at night. The village's primary feature is a 160m-high tower flying a flag that weighs nearly 300kg, markedly larger than the one on the South Korean side.

It's believed that some workers from the Kaesong Industrial Complex (defunct at time of research) were living in Gijeong-dong.

Both villages occasionally blast the other with propaganda from loudspeakers, but these were silenced in April 2018 days before the two sides held their historic summit at the DMZ.

Visiting the DMZ by Train

A fun and cheap way to tour the DMZ (minus the JSA) is to ride the frankly bizarre DMZ train operated by Korail, which trundles out of Seoul Station at 10.15am Wednesday to Sunday on its way to **Dorasan** (도라산역; ₩500), the last station before North Korea. With its carriages emblazoned with pink flowers and love hearts, you could almost be going to Pyongyang Disneyland, not one of the most fiercely guarded frontiers on the planet.

It takes a leisurely 1½ hours to reach the DMZ, during which time you can buy beer and crisps from the train kiosk and look at a display of Korean war photographs. Crossing the heavily fortified Imjin River, you'll pass the remains of a bridge destroyed in the Korean War before arriving at Imjingang station for a passport check. Then it's the final leg to Dorasan, where you transfer to coaches to begin a tour which includes **Dora Observatory** (binoculars ₩500; ⏲10am-5pm Tue-Sun), **Dorasan Peace Park** and the **Third Infiltration Tunnel** (제3땅굴; ⏲9am-5pm Tue-Sun).

The DMZ train tour (₩31,000) should be booked at least one day in advance from the **Seoul Travel Guide Centre** inside Seoul station. It's also possible to book just the train on the Korail website (www.letskorail.com), but you'll still need to pay for the tour and a return ticket on board the train if you want to get further than Imjingang station. Passports are a must.

Getting There & Away

The only way into this heavily restricted area is on an organised tour, either by coach or on the DMZ train from Seoul station.

Run by the USO, the US army's social and entertainment organisation, **Koridoor Tours** (☎02-795 3028; www.koridoor.co.kr; ₩96,600; ⏲office 8am-5pm Mon-Sat; Ⓢ Line 1 to Namyeong, Exit 2) has long been regarded as one of the best. Try to book at least a month in advance. Lunch isn't included.

A reputable company with knowledgable guides, **Panmunjom Travel Centre** (Map p238; ☎02-771 5593; http://panmunjomtour.com; Koreana Hotel, 9th fl, Office B/D; tours ₩77,000-130,000) is notable for having a North Korean defector who sometimes (but not always) comes along to answer your questions. Prices include lunch.

TAKE A BREAK

➡ Most DMZ tours eat at the same appropriately utilitarian canteen, **Paju Restaurant**, serving a basic Korean buffet for ₩7000.

➡ Souvenir shops sell North Korean rice and other food products from across the border.

To visit the JSA or ride the DMZ train you'll need to bring your passport. Note citizens of certain countries are not permitted to enter the JSA. There are also strict dress and behavioural codes; usually collared shirts for men, and no ripped jeans, revealing clothing or open-toed shoes. Alcohol consumption is also prohibited. Only children over 10 years are permitted.

Suwon

Explore

A popular day trip out of Seoul, sprawling Suwon (수원) is the largest city in Gyeonggi-do province, with World Heritage–listed fortifications still looping around its heart. Suwon almost became the country's capital in the 18th century, when Joseon dynasty ruler King Jeongjo built the 5.7km-long walls in 1794–96 ahead of moving the royal court south. However, the king died, power remained in Seoul, and Suwon ended up with one hell of a tourist sight. The city is located around 30km south of Seoul.

The Best...

- **Sight** Hwaseong (p154)
- **Place to Eat** Yeonpo Galbi (p157)
- **Place to Stay** Hotel Dono (p158)

Top Tip

Suwon's hotels and hostels close to or inside Hwaseong are good enough for a night or two if you plan to stick around and see all the city has to offer.

Getting There & Away

Long-distance buses depart from **Suwon bus terminal** (www.suwonterminal.co.kr), heading to major cities including Incheon (₩4800, 1½ hours, every 15 minutes), Busan (₩24,900, five hours, 10 daily), Daegu (₩19,900, 3½ hours, six daily) and Gwangju (from ₩16,000, three hours, every 30 minutes).

There's also an airport bus (from ₩12,000, 70 minutes) leaving every 30 minutes opposite the Suwon tourist information centre.

From Seoul, the Budang Line and Line 1 run to Suwon (₩1850, one hour). KTX trains from Seoul are speedier (from ₩4600, 30 minutes) but not as frequent.

From Suwon train station, high- and regular-speed trains depart frequently to cities all over Korea, including Busan (from ₩26,900, 5½ hours), Daegu (from ₩18,200, three hours), Daejeon (₩8100, 70 minutes) and Jeonju (from ₩15,100, three hours). High-speed trains take about half the time, but are double the cost.

Need to Know

- **Area Code** 031
- **Location** 48km south of Seoul
- **Suwon Tourist Information Centre** (031-228 4673; www.swcf.or.kr/english; 9am-6pm; S Suwon, Exit 4)
- **Tourist Information Booth** (031-228 4672; 9am-6pm)

SIGHTS

★HWASEONG FORTRESS

(화성; www.swcf.or.kr/english; adult/child ₩1000/500; 24hr) The World Heritage–listed fortress wall that encloses the original town of Suwon is what brings most travellers to the city. Snaking up and down Paldal-san (143m), the fortification wall stretches a scenic 5.7km past four majestic gates, command posts, pavilions, observation towers and fire-beacon platforms. Built by King Jeongjo and completed in 1796, it was constructed of earth and faced with large stone blocks and grey bricks, nearly all of which have been restored.

It takes around two hours to complete the circuit. Try to go outside the wall for at least part of the way, as the fortress looks much more impressive the way an enemy would see it.

Start at **Paldalmun** (팔달문), also known as Nammun (South Gate); the most iconic of Hwaseong's four main gates, it stands at the heart of the city on a busy roundabout. From here follow the steep steps off to the left up to the **Seonam Gangu** (서남각루, South-west Pavilion), an observation point near the peak of Paldal-san.

At the top of Paldal-san, near **Seojang-dae** (서장대, Western Command Post), is the large **Hyowon Bell** which you can can pay to ring (three tolls for ₩1000) and **Seono-dae** (서노대, West Crossbow Platform), an octagonal tower on the summit that was used by crossbow archers, and offers spectacular panoramic views of the city.

On the north edge of the fortress wall is **Hwahongmun** (화홍문), a water gate that bridges the Suwon-cheon gurgling beneath it. Nearby **Dongbukgongsimdon** (동북공심돈), the northeast observation tower, has a unique rounded, oval shape and stands three storeys tall (8m), with a spiral staircase threading the centre of the structure.

WORTH A DETOUR

EVERLAND RESORT

Opened in 1976, **Everland** (에버랜드; ☎031-320 5000; www.everland.com; adult/teenager/child ₩54,000/46,000/43,000; ⏲9.30am-10pm Sep-Jun, to 11pm Jul & Aug; 🚌5002) is Korea's largest theme park, with five zones of rides, fantasy buildings and impressive seasonal gardens. The lush hillside setting, 40km south of Seoul, is part of the appeal. Thrill-seekers will want to head straight to T Express, a gargantuan wooden roller coaster added in 2008 that boasts a 45m near-vertical drop. But its the littler kids who'll find the most fun here, with gentle rides, animal attractions, shows and two parades daily. At night, the illuminated park takes on a magical atmosphere, and if you can last until 9.30pm you'll catch the fireworks. Appealingly retro in places, some of Everland's rides, like the big wheel, are actually decommissioned relics left just for show.

Next door is **Caribbean Bay** (캐리비안 베이; www.everland.com; adult/child ₩50,000/39,000; ⏲9am-7pm Sep & Jun, 8am-10pm Jul & Aug), an impressive indoor and outdoor water park with white-knuckle luges, flumes, tubes, a lazy river and a not-so-lazy wave pool. It's best avoided on summer weekends, when you'll even be queuing for the Jacuzzi tub. Caribbean Bay is part of Everland theme park but requires a separate ticket.

Good luck trying to persuade the kids to exit Everland to visit the **Hoam Art Museum** (호암미술관; ☎031-320 1801; http://hoam.samsungfoundation.org; adult/child ₩4000/3000, free with Everland ticket; ⏲10am-6pm Tue-Sun), but if you manage it you'll be richly rewarded with the personal collection of Lee Byung-chull, the founder of Samsung Group, which also runs the theme park. Korean modern art, together with wooden furniture, silk paintings, ceramics and calligraphy from earlier dynasties, are displayed in a traditional-styled building adjacent to the serenely beautiful Hee Won Korean gardens.

To get here from Seoul take bus 5002 (₩2000, 50 minutes, every 15 minutes) from the **Everland bus stop** (Map p250) in Gangnam. From outside Suwon's train station, hop on bus 66 or 66-4 (₩1700, one hour, every 30 minutes).

Further on, the **Bongdon Beacon Towers** (봉돈), a row of brick chimneys, were used to send messages and alerts around the country using a system of fire and smoke signals. They would have had a clear line of sight to Hwaseong Haenggung (p156) in order to alert the king of various threats.

If you don't fancy the walk, head up the hill at the rear of the palace to the find the **Hwaseong Trolley** (adult/teenager/child ₩3000/2000/1000; ⏲10am-5.20pm) that winds in and out of the fortress wall to the **archery field** (10 arrows ₩2000; ⏲9.30am-5.30pm; 👪) at **Dongjangdae** (동장대, East Command Post), also nicknamed Yeonmudae, a reference to its second function as a training camp. The grassy area was used as a sword and archery training ground for 200 years after the fortress opened.

Other notable structures in the fortress complex include **Janganmun** (장안문), the main north gate of Hwaseong and the largest gate of its kind in Korea. Visitors coming from Seoul would have entered the city here. It was reconstructed in the 1970s. The northwest watchtower **Seobuk Gongsimdon** (서북공심돈) stands guard next to **Hwaseomun** (화서문), the west gate, surrounded by its own fortress walls in miniature.

If you want to find out more about the fortress, including how detailed court records aided the 1970s reconstruction process, check out the Suwon Hwaseong Museum.

In August the fortress is illuminated with light shows at night.

HWASEONG HAENGGUNG PALACE

(화성행궁; adult/child ₩1500/700; ⏲9am-6pm Tue-Sun) Sitting at the base of Paldalsan (143m), King Jeongjo's palace was built in the late 18th century as a residence for when he visited to worship at his father's tomb. The palace was mostly destroyed during the Japanese colonial period and has been meticulously reconstructed. From March to November, various traditional performances are held at the plaza in front of the palace, including a changing-of-the-guard ceremony (2pm Sunday) and martial-arts display (11am Tuesday to Sunday).

Hwaseong & Haenggung

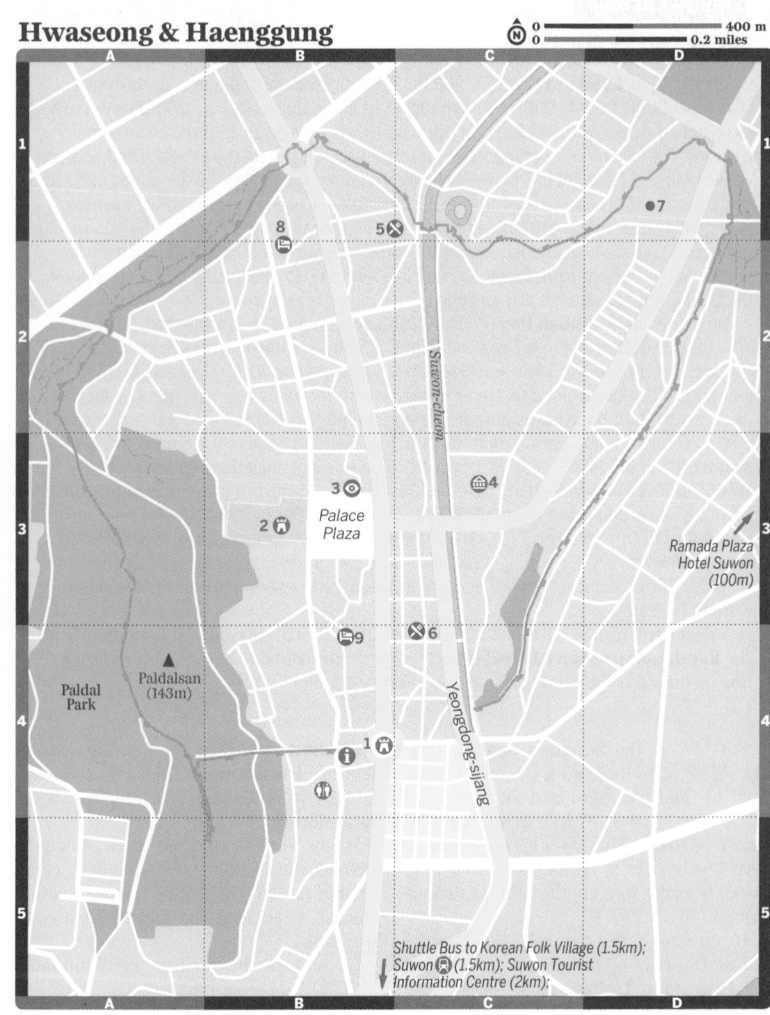

Every October a grand royal procession is re-enacted here as part of Suwon's annual festival.

KOREAN FOLK VILLAGE CULTURAL CENTRE
(한국민속촌; ☎031-288 0000; www.koreanfolk.co.kr; 90 Minsokchon-ro, Yongin-si; adult/teenager/child ₩18,000/13,000/11,000; ⏰9.30am-6.30pm May-Sep, to 6pm Oct-Apr; 👪; 🚌10-5, 37) This 245-acre themed experience is designed to transport you back to the Joseon dynasty as you wander through picturesque grounds filled with thatched and tiled buildings relocated here from around Korea. Performers wearing *hanbok* (traditional clothing) craft pots and handmake paper, while others tend to vegetable plots and livestock. Throughout the day there are shows by traditional musicians, dancers, acrobats and tightrope walkers, and you can watch a staged wedding ceremony.

The **Folk Museum** offers a fascinating snapshot of 19th-century Korean life, and there are many hands-on activities for kids, as well as a child-oriented amusement park, which costs extra, plus several traditional restaurants.

From Suwon station, take bus 37 or 10-5 to Korean Folk Village, or there's a free shuttle bus that leaves from outside the

Hwaseong & Haenggung

station at 10.30am, 12.30pm and 2.30pm. The last shuttle bus leaves the folk village at 4.30pm (5pm on weekends). After that time, walk to the far end of the car park and catch city bus 37 (₩1300, one hour, every 20 minutes) back to Suwon station.

NAM JUNE PAIK ART CENTRE GALLERY

(백남준아트센터; 031-201 8500; http://njpac-en.ggcf.kr; 10 Paiknamjune-ro, Giheung-gu, Yongin-si; 10am-6pm Tue-Sun; 10, 66, S Bundang Line to Sanggal, Exit 4) FREE This gallery features the pioneering new-media work of internationally acclaimed avant-garde artist Nam June Paik (1932–2006). It's not far from Korean Folk Village .

From Suwon station take bus 10 or 66 or the Budang Line subway to Sanggal station (from where it's a 10-minute walk). En route you'll pass **Gyeonggi Provincial Museum** (6 Sanggal-ro, Giheung-gu, Yongin-si; 10am-8pm Mon-Fri, to 10pm Sat & Sun) FREE, worth a stop for its fine collection of cultural artefacts.

MR TOILET HOUSE MUSEUM

(해우재, Haewoojae; 031-271 9777; www.haewoojae.com; 458-9 Jangan-ro, Jangan-gu; 10am-6pm Tue-Sun, to 5pm winter; 65, 301) FREE A contender for Korea's wackiest museum, Mr Toilet House is the former residence of Suwon's mayor, the late Sim Jae-duck. Designed like a toilet, it houses hilarious poo-related exhibits and a **sculpture garden**, as well as covering more serious sanitation issues – the museum is also an NGO established to improve public sanitation worldwide. Kids especially will love it, and there's a **children's museum** across the road with an observatory deck for viewing the toilet house.

Jae-duck was famous for his efforts in beautifying Suwon's public toilets during the lead-up to the FIFA World Cup (2002), decorating them in art, flowers and classical music – many of which remain around the city today.

To get here take bus 65 or 301 from Hwaseong Haenggung (25 minutes) and get off at Dongwon High School, from where it's a 10-minute walk. A taxi from Suwon station should cost about ₩10,000.

IPARK MUSEUM OF ART ARTS CENTRE

(SIMA, 수원시립아이파크미술관; http://sima.suwon.go.kr; adult/child ₩4000/1000; 10am-6pm Tue-Sun) This contemporary-styled museum on the plaza in front of Hwaseong Haenggung hosts a variety of art-related exhibitions across its five galleries.

SUWON HWASEONG MUSEUM MUSEUM

(수원화성박물관; adult/child ₩2000/free; 9am-6pm, closed 1st Mon of month) Head to this modern museum to find out how detailed court records from 1801 were vital to ensure authenticity in the 1970s reconstruction process of Suwon Hwaseong (p154).

EATING & DRINKING

Suwon is renowned for its *galbi* (beef ribs), usually eaten at long-standing city-centre restaurants like Yeonpo Galbi.

Suwon doesn't party like Seoul, but you'll find a few bars, *hof* (local pubs) and karaoke rooms east of the station.

YEONPO GALBI KOREAN $$

(연포갈비; 56-1 Jeongjo-ro 906beon-gil; ribs from ₩20,000; 11.30am-10pm) This famous restaurant grills up all manner of mouth-watering *galbi* (beef ribs). At lunch, go for the special Suwon version of *galbitang* (₩12,000) – ribs in a seasoned broth with noodles and leeks. Find it down the steps from Hwahongmun, the water gate on the north edge of the fortress wall.

YONGSUNG FRIED CHICKEN FAST FOOD $$

(용성통닭, Yongseong Tongdak; 031-242 8226; 800-7 Jeongjo-ro; chicken ₩15,000; 11.30am-1am Wed-Mon;) This is a popular *chimaek* (chicken and beer) spot, with golden-fried, juicy chicken pieces and cheap jugs of cold brew.

SLEEPING

HWASEONG GUESTHOUSE GUESTHOUSE $
(☎010-5316 3419; www.hsguesthouse.com; 11 Jeongjo-ro 801beon-gil, Jeongju-ro; dm/s/d ₩18,000/30,000/35,000; ❄@📶) It ain't the Ritz, but these spacious dorms and doubles are the cheapest in town, sharing bathrooms and a communal kitchen with cooking facilities.

HOTEL DONO HOTEL $$
(☎031-258 8881; www.hoteldono.com; 68 Sinpung-ro, Paldal-gu; d ₩100,000; ❄📶) High-quality digs offering spacious, modern rooms within easy access of Hwaseong (p154). Rates include pick-up from Suwon station, and iced coffee on arrival.

The **Suwon Centre for Traditional Culture**, a open-air folk-arts complex, is next door.

RAMADA PLAZA HOTEL SUWON HOTEL $$$
(라마다프라자 수원호텔; ☎031-230 0031; www.ramadaplazasuwon.com; 150 Jungbu-daero; r from ₩172,000; ❄@📶) The Ramada is a modern affair with decent rooms and facilities, including a gym, deli and restaurants. It's about five minutes by taxi east of Suwon's fortress (p154).

Book online for sizeable discounts.

Incheon

Explore

South Korea's third-largest city, Incheon (인천) is an expanding metropolis and industrial port. Its colourful Chinatown and Open Port areas are the most tourist-friendly parts of the city to explore, and easily accessible via subway from Seoul. Come here to eat Chinese food, discover pockets of concession-era architecture, stroll the seafront boardwalk at Wolmido and visit the fish market at Yeonan, where you can catch ferries to the West Sea islands or beyond to China.

Located 36km west of Seoul, Incheon is where Korea opened up to the world in 1883, ending centuries of self-imposed isolation. In 1950, during the Korean War, the American General Douglas MacArthur led UN forces in a daring landing behind enemy lines here.

The Best...

- **Sight** Incheon Art Platform (p158)
- **Place to Eat** Samchi St (p161)
- **Place to Drink** Caligari Brewing (p161)

Top Tip

Visit midweek to avoid massive queues for restaurants on weekends in Chinatown.

Getting There & Away

- **Incheon International Airport** (p206) Not located in Incheon itself, but rather on Yeongjongdo, over one hour away by bus.
- **Subway** Subway Line 1 from Seoul station (₩1850) takes around 70 minutes; the line branches at Guro so make sure you're on an Incheon-bound train.

Need to Know

- **Area Code** 032
- **Location** 36km west of Seoul
- **Tourist Information** Booths at **Incheon station** (☎032-777 1330; http://english.incheon.go.kr; ⏰9am-6pm), **Wolmido promenade** (☎032-765 4169; ⏰6am-9pm), the **bus terminal** (☎032-430 7257; ⏰10am-6pm) and outside the **subway station** (http://english.incheon.go.kr; ⏰9am-6pm) have very helpful staff, and lots of excellent maps, brochures (in English) and suggestions for Incheon, Songdo and the islands.

SIGHTS

INCHEON ART PLATFORM ARTS CENTRE
(www.inartplatform.kr; Open Port; ⏰9am-6pm Tue-Sun) FREE This attractive complex of 1930s and '40s brick warehouses was turned over to the Incheon Foundation for Arts and Culture, which has created gallery spaces and artist residency studios. Performances and events are also held here, and there is a light-filled cafe with plenty of art books.

The platform offers residency programs and studio space for artists; visit the website for more info.

INCHEON FISH MARKET MARKET
(인천종합어시장, Grand Fishery Market; www.asijang.com; Yeonan; ⏰5am-9pm; 🐾) This large fish and seafood market has row upon

Incheon

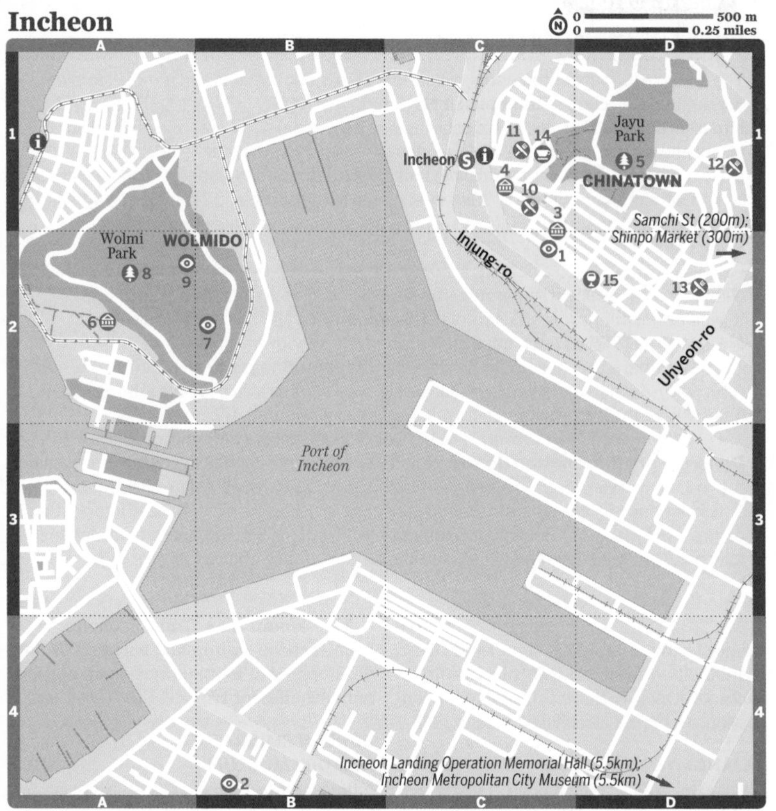

row of vendors hawking every kind of edible sea beast, which can be consumed right here at several small restaurants and cafes. Bus 12 or 24 will get you here from Dong-incheon subway station.

INCHEON METROPOLITAN CITY MUSEUM MUSEUM

(인천광역시립박물관; http://museum.incheon.go.kr; Songdo; ⏲9am-6pm Tue-Sun; 🚌8, 16, 521, Ⓢ Suin Line to Songdo, Exit 1) FREE The city's main museum offers an excellent collection of celadon pottery and some interesting historical displays dating from the Three Kingdoms. It's located next to the **Incheon Landing Operation Memorial Hall** (인천상륙작전기념관; www.landing915.com; Songdo; ⏲9am-6pm Tue-Sun; 🚌8, 16, 521, Ⓢ Suin Line to Songdo, Exit 1) FREE.

INCHEON OPEN PORT MUSEUM MUSEUM

(인천개항박물관; www.icjgss.or.kr/open_port; Open Port; adult/teenager/child ₩500/300/200;

Incheon

WORTH A DETOUR

BUKHANSAN NATIONAL PARK

The sweeping mountaintop vistas, maple leaves, rushing streams and remote temples of granite-peak-studded **Bukhansan National Park** (북한산 국립공원; ☎031-873 2791; http://english.knps.or.kr; Ⓢ Line 1 to Dobongsan or Mangwolsa) FREE draw over five million hikers and rock climbers annually. Even though the park covers nearly 80 sq km, it's so close to Seoul (45 minutes by subway) that it does get crowded, especially on weekends.

The park is divided into the Bukhan-san area in the south and Dobong-san area in the north, each featuring multiple scenic – but strenuous – hikes to mountain peaks. Bring plenty of water.

In the northern area a popular excursion is the hike up **Dobong-san** (740m), which climaxes with the spectacular ridgetop peak climb. Be sure to take signed detours to visit atmospheric forested temples **Cheonchuk-sa** (천축사) on the way up and **Mangwol-sa** (망월사) upon descent – around a four-hour trek in total.

The southern part has South Korea's highest peak, **Baegundae** (836m), a 3½-hour return trip via the Bukhansanseong trail. For rock climbers, nearby **Insu-bong** (810m) has some of the best multipitch climbing in Asia and routes of all grades.

For Dobong-san, take subway Line 1 to Dobongsan station, a 15-minute walk from **Dobong Park Information Centre**, which has a basic hiking map in English. If you take the route down via Wondol-bong (recommended) you'll finish at Mangwolsa station.

Baegundae is accessed from Bukhansanseong or Jeongneung; both have information centres with maps. For Bukhansanseong take subway Line 3 to Gupabal station and then take bus 704. For Jeongneung take Line 4 to Gireum station and bus 110B or 143.

⏲9am-6pm) Built in 1897, this is one of three former Japanese banks along the same street. Exhibitions within present the history of Incheon's Open Port area since foreign concessions were first established here in 1883.

JAJANGMYEON MUSEUM — MUSEUM

(Chinatown; ₩1000; ⏲9am-6pm) Housed in a building dating to 1907, this imaginative museum celebrates the origins of the much-loved noodle dish *jajangmyeon*, thought to be adapted from the snacks of Chinese labourers who came over from Shandong Province to work in Incheon's Open Port area at the turn of the 20th century.

There's not much in English here, so pick up the leaflet.

WOLMIDO — AREA

(월미도; http://wolmi.incheon.go.kr; 🚌2, 23, 45) Historically notable as the site of the Incheon Landing Operations during the Korean War, today the former island of Wolmi (it was joined to the mainland in 1989), is a leisure area offering a Coney Island–style waterfront boardwalk and small amusement park. It also has the forested Wolmi Park with tranquil walking trails leading to traditional gardens, the **Wolmi Observatory** (월미산 유리전망대; Wolmi Park; ⏲6am-10pm) FREE with its panoramic views and the Korean Emigration History Museum.

The **Wolmi Sea Train** monorail runs from Incheon station and encircles Wolmido, stopping at four stations, in an approximately half-hour trip.

KOREAN EMIGRATION HISTORY MUSEUM — MUSEUM

(http://mkeh.incheon.go.kr; ⏲9am-6pm Tue-Sun) FREE This museum offers interesting insights into the outbound journeys of Korean migrants, with a focus on those settling throughout the Americas. It's located at the base of Wolmi Park (p161).

JAYU PARK — PARK

(자유공원; Open Port) You can explore this picturesque hilltop park, designed by a Russian civil engineer in 1888, while walking between Chinatown and the Open Port area. It contains the monument for the centenary of Korea–USA relations and a statue of General MacArthur, who led the Allied amphibious landings at Incheon, turning the tide of the Korean War.

WOLMI PARK — PARK

(월미공원; http://wolmi.incheon.go.kr/index.do; Wolmido; ⏲6am-10pm, garden 9am-8pm) FREE This large, forested park has walking trails, a replica of a traditional Korean garden, and the hilltop Wolmi Observatory, offering views across the port and to Yeongjongdo.

EATING & DRINKING

In Chinatown you can sample local takes on Chinese cuisine including *jajangmyeon* (noodles in black bean sauce), *jjampong* (noodles in a spicy seafood soup) and *onggibyeong* (dumplings baked inside clay jars).

Incheon's well-known seafood can be enjoyed at source at the city's fish market (p159), or along Samchi St.

DADABOK CHINESE $

(다다복; ☎032-765 9888; 24 Chinatown-ro 55beon-gil, Gaho-dong, Jung-gu; dumplings from ₩5000; ⏲11am-7.30pm) Set back from the bedlam of Chinatown, this unassuming restaurant is the local pick for the tastiest *mandu* (filled dumplings), with a choice of pork or shrimp with veg, either pan-fried, steamed or boiled. Note the early closing time.

SINPO MARKET KOREAN $

(신포시장, Sinpo-sijang; Sinpo-dong; street-food items ₩1000-10,000; ⏲10am-8pm; Ⓢ Dongincheon) Several stalls along this pair of covered arcades specialise in *dakgangjeong* (fried chicken in a sweet, spicy sauce). The best vendors usually have a line of locals patiently queuing for their takeaway box. Another popular snack here is *hotteok* (fried, syrup-filled pancakes).

SAMCHI ST SEAFOOD $$

(동인천 삼치거리; Uhyeon-ro 67beon-gil, Dongincheon-dong, Jung-gu; samchi around ₩13,000; Ⓢ Dongincheon, Exit 8) Lined with nautically themed lights, this strip of restaurants specialises in delicious and affordable grilled *samchi* (Spanish mackerel). Paired with a few bottles of *makgeolli* (milky rice wine), it makes for a fun evening out. The eatery at No 53 has an English menu. It's a short walk from Dongincheon station.

MANDABOK CHINESE $$

(만다복; ☎032-773 3838; www.mandabok.com; Chinatown; mains ₩7000-30,000; ⏲11am-10pm) Guarded by a pair of terracotta warriors, and boasting a saloon-style interior balcony, this is one of Chinatown's fanciest restaurants. The banquet dishes here are best suited to group dining, but there's also noodle-type fare towards the back of the menu.

★CALIGARI BREWING BREWERY

(칼리가리 브루윙; www.caligaribrewing.com; 2-1 Haeandong 3(sam)-ga; beers from ₩5900; ⏲5pm-1am; 📶) One of the best spots for a beer in the Old Port area, this brewery with attached taproom slots perfectly into its old warehouse setting. A row of towering tanks faces a small bar pouring a range of craft beers, and you can order snacks and pizza if you're feeling peckish.

CAFE CASTLE CAFE

(Cafe 성; ☎032-773 2116; Chinatown; coffees ₩5000; ⏲noon-10am; 📶) FREE Enjoy coffee, tea, cocktails and snacks at this homely cafe with a fantastic harbour view from its rooftop garden. Tricky to find, it's at the top of the steps that go up from the centre of Chinatown, next to the red arch.

Ganghwado

Explore

South Korea's fifth-largest island, Ganghwado (강화도) is worth a side trip for its hilltop temples and other low-key attractions, as well as its fascinating history. For a brief period in the mid-13th century, when the Mongols were rampaging through the mainland, the island became the location of Korea's capital. Situated at the mouth of the Han River, Ganghwado continued to have strategic importance – it was the scene of bloody skirmishes with French and US forces in the 19th century as colonial powers tried to muscle in on the 'hermit kingdom'.

Ganghwado's main town and base for visiting is Ganghwa-eup.

The Best...

- **Sight** Goryeogungji Palace (p162)
- **Place to Eat** Wangjajeong (p163)
- **Place to Stay** Hotel Everrich (p164)

Top Tip

If time is tight, consider taking a tour. Several leave from Seoul - check with the KTO Tourist Information Centre (p214). There's also one that starts from Geonam station on Sundays (₩10,000; book four days in advance by calling 032-772 4000).

Getting There & Away

- **Bus** Frequent buses run from near Seoul's Sinchon station to Ganghwa-eup's

bus terminal (강화터미널; Ganghwa-eup) (₩2900, one hour 50 minutes, every 10 minutes 4am to 10pm). From Incheon, you can jump on bus 800 from Jemulpo station (₩2100, 1 hour 40 minutes).

Need to Know

- **Area Code** 032
- **Location** 56km from Seoul
- **Tourist Information Centre** (☎032-930 3515; www.ganghwa.incheon.kr; Ganghwa-eup bus terminal; ⏰9am-6pm)

SIGHTS

★GORYEOGUNGJI PALACE PALACE
(고려궁지; Ganghwa-eup; adult/child ₩900/600; ⏰9am-6pm) The partially restored remains of a small palace, dating back to the Goryeo dynasty (918–1392), sit on a hillside in Ganghwa-eup. The palace was completed around 1234, a few years after King Gojong moved his capital to Ganghwado to better resist Mongol invasion.

Directly downhill from the palace is the **Ganghwa Anglican Church** (c 1900), notable in that it is designed like a traditional Korean temple. Follow the alleyways down to the **Yongheunggung Royal Residence**, where King Cheoljong lived in the 19th century.

The palace and town were once encircled by a **7km fortress wall**, snaking over the surrounding hilltops much like the one in Seoul. Destroyed in 1866 by French troops who invaded Korea in response to the execution of nine French Catholic missionaries, it has since been partially rebuilt, and three major gates have been renovated.

The palace is a 15-minute walk from the bus terminal.

BOMUN-SA TEMPLE
(보문사; ☎032-933 8271; Seongmodo; adult/youth/child ₩2500/1700/1000; ⏰9am-6pm; 🚌31, 35) Situated high in the pine-forested hills of the west-coast island of Seongmodo, this temple has some superbly ornate painting on the eaves of its buildings. The grotto and 10m-tall Buddha rock carving are standouts. The walk to reach Bomun-sa is steep and has many stairs – catch your breath at the top.

To get here, take bus 31 or 35 from Ganghwa bus terminal, which crosses a road bridge over to Seongmodo (one hour).

GANGHWA DOLMEN PARK ARCHAEOLOGICAL SITE
(강화 고인돌 유적; ⏰24hr) FREE In a grassy field beside Ganghwa History Museum, marvel at **Bugeun-ri Dolmen** (부근리 고인돌), a trio of giant stones hefted into a megalithic tomb (the two 'door' stones are missing). Dating to the Bronze Age, the top stone is estimated to weigh 75 tonnes. It's a scenic spot with expansive valley views; no wonder the site was chosen for its auspicious purpose.

There are close to 150 dolmen scattered throughout Ganghwa, 70 of which are World Heritage–listed.

GANGHWA HISTORY MUSEUM MUSEUM
(http://museum.ganghwa.go.kr; adult//child ₩3000/2000; ⏰9am-6pm Tue-Sun; 🚌1, 3, 23, 25) Covering 5000 years of the island's history, the exhibits at this imaginative museum start with Ganghwa's ancient (and Unesco-listed) dolmen sites and continue up to the US Navy attack on the island in 1871.

Your ticket also gets you into the **Ganghwa Natural History Museum** next door, an ambitious little place containing a sperm-whale skeleton and some competent taxidermy. Both are a 20-minute bus ride from Ganghwa bus terminal.

GANGHWA PEACE OBSERVATORY OBSERVATORY
(강화평화전망대; adult/child ₩2500/1700; ⏰9am-6pm; 🚌1, 2) This multiplex observatory just 2km from North Korea offers prime views into the 'hermit kingdom'. Through binoculars (₩500 for two minutes) you can spy villages, workers in rice fields, military towers and distant mountain ranges. There's a short, introductory video in English, but you'll need to request it to be played.

Bus 26 will get you here, with bus 27 returning to Ganghwa-eup terminal (35 minutes).

GAPGOT DONDAE FORTRESS
(갑곶돈대; ₩2700; ⏰9am-6pm Tue-Sun; 🚌5) This fortress and observation post was one of several built along the coast to guard the Ganghwa strait here during the 13th century at the time of the Mongol invasions. An attached museum has rusting cannons among other artefacts.

WORTH A DETOUR

MUUIDO

If you're looking for a beachside escape within easy reach of Seoul, the tiny island of Muuido (무의도) fits the bill. Broad stretches of golden sand and forested walking trails are just a short ferry hop away from more developed Yeongjongdo (home to Incheon airport). A road bridge was under construction at time of research, however, so you might want to get there before the developers do.

Note also that swimming is only possible during high tide; at low tide the water recedes substantially, turning it into mudflats.

Hanagae Beach (하나개 해수욕장; www.hanagae.co.kr; adult/child ₩2000/1000) is Muuido's best, with plenty of golden sand, a handful of seafood restaurants and basic beach huts under the pine trees or on the beach. Walking trails loop around the headland to the south. Kids will enjoy the giant zip-wire ride over the sand (summer only).

The best budget choice on the island is **Hanagae Beach Huts** (Hanagae Beach; huts ₩30,000), a row of stilted beach boxes plonked directly on Hanagae Beach. Huts are basic heated *ondol* (traditional, sleep-on-a-floor-mattress) rooms, with very thin bedding, and shared bathrooms. There's a ₩10,000 key deposit, and showers costs ₩1000. There are also private pension rooms for ₩50,000 to ₩100,000 which offer value for groups. Otherwise, **Island Garden** (섬뜰아래; 010 3056 2709; www.islandgarden.kr; r ₩70,000-150,000, camping ₩50,000;) offers apartment-style rooms, plenty of sea-facing decking and its own grassy plot for camping; Island Garden also has a tiny private beach. The friendly owners speak some English.

To get here, head to Incheon International Airport Terminal 1 where you catch bus 222 or 2-1 (₩1200, 20 minutes, hourly) to the islet of Jamjindo (잠진도), connected by causeway to Yeongjongdo. From there, take the ferry for the five-minute crossing to Muuido (₩3800 return, half-hourly until 7pm, 6pm in winter). Bus 306 is also an option from Incheon, but involves a 15-minute walk to the jetty. You can also ride the **Maglev** (7.30am-8.15pm) FREE train from the airport's Terminal 1 to Yongyu station, then walk to the jetty.

WEST GATE — GATE

A reconstruction of the old Joseon dynasty-era gate to Goryeogungji Palace just beside the modern road. A water gate crosses the stream just to the south. From here you can hike up the fortress wall in a southerly direction to a pavilion above the other side of the valley.

JEONDEUNG-SA — BUDDHIST TEMPLE

(전등사; 032-937 0125; www.jeondeungsa.org; adult/youth/child ₩3000/2000/1000; 7am-sunset) This temple in Ganghwado's southeast sits on a forested hilltop within the walls of **Samrangseong Fortress**. A free vegetarian lunch is served from around noon; wash your own dishes afterwards. You can also spend the night as part of the Templestay (p164) program (₩80,000) .

EATING & DRINKING

Ganghwado is known for its eel dishes. A couple of good eel-barbecue joints styled like log cabins can be found just beyond Ganghwa-eup's reconstructed West Gate.

Bomun-sa is known for plates of *twigim* (tempura) seafood accompanied by local ginseng-infused *makgeolli* (milky rice wine).

WANGJAJEONG — KOREAN $$

(왕자정; Ganghwa-eup; meals ₩8000-25,000; 10am-9.30pm;) Enjoy healthy, delicious vegetarian dishes such as *mukbap* (acorn jelly rice) and *kongbiji* (bean soup) while overlooking the walls of Goryeogungji Palace (p162).

JUNGNIM DAWON — TEAHOUSE

(죽림다원; Jeongeungsa-sa; tea ₩5000; 9am-5.30pm) This atmospheric teahouse and garden within Jeondeung-sa (p163) is frequented by resident monks sipping on traditional Korean teas, while presumably contemplating the meaning of life, the universe and everything.

Take a taxi here from the bus terminal (p162), otherwise it's a long walk.

SLEEPING

Apart from the options here, there are several chilled out *minbak* (private homes with rooms for rent) on Seongmodo, the tiny island just west of Ganghwado that houses Bomun-sa (p162).

HOTEL EVERRICH HOTEL **$$**
(호텔에버리치; ☎032-934 1688; www.hoteleverrich.com; d ₩110,000;) Perched on the side of a mountain and offering expansive views towards the mainland, this 70-room hotel has a nature-lodge vibe, with minimalist white rooms, a pool and a pleasant Italian restaurant. Trails above the hotel connect up with the fortress wall hike.

JEONDEUNG-SA TEMPLE TEMPLESTAY **$$**
(☎032-937 0152; http://eng.templestay.com; dm incl food & activities from ₩80,000) Part of the Templestay program, the hilltop temple of Jeondeung-sa (p163) encourages visitors to check in and then tune in to their inner Buddha. Prices include vegetarian meals, cultural activities and dawn wake-up calls.

NAMCHIDANG GUESTHOUSE **$$**
(남취당; ☎032-937 0119; http://kyl3850.com/pension/index.php?uid=3; r from ₩100,000;) This purpose-built *hanok* (traditional wooden home) pension has wood-fired *ondol* (traditional, sleep-on-a-floor-mattress) rooms and free bicycle hire. It's located a couple of kilometres from Jeondeung-sa (p163); buses 3, 7 and 41 run here from Ganghwa bus terminal. (p162)

Sleeping

Seoul offers the lot, from no-frills guesthouses to hanok *(traditional wooden homes) homestays to five-star palaces, but reserve well in advance, especially if visiting during busy travel periods such as Chinese New Year and Japan's Golden Week holidays (usually the end of April or early May). Many hotels raise rates at weekends, and some quote without the 10% tax added.*

Backpacker Guesthouses

Backpacker-style guesthouses are mostly concentrated around Myeong-dong, Itaewon and Hongdae, but you'll find them in other districts too. Rooms – dorms, singles, twins and doubles – tend to be tiny, but nearly always have a bathroom. Staff usually speak English. Communal kitchens are common, as are terraces; lounges less so. All have free internet and most have laundry.

Hanok Guesthouses

Traditional *hanok* (single-storey wooden courtyard houses) are increasingly being turned into guesthouses or homestays – you'll find most in Bukchon and Ikseon-dong. Staying in one can be a unique and memorable experience; some offer cultural programs such as dressing in *hanbok* (traditional Korean clothing) or cooking classes. At homestays, the owners may also offer pick-ups and meals.

Rooms are small and you'll usually sleep on *yo* (padded quilts and mattresses) on the floor, but *ondol* (underfloor heating systems) keep them snug in winter. At cheaper *hanok* you'll share the bathroom, while some offer en suite rooms. Rates usually include breakfast.

Hanok are largely shunned by contemporary Seoulites as places to live, and in the city there remain only a few hundred *hanok*, which the tourist market has helped preserve, so it's an experience worth partaking in while you still can.

Hotels & Love Motels

Budget hotels are scattered throughout Seoul. The rooms are always on the small size but have bathrooms and come with plenty of facilities. However, staff rarely speak English.

Usually clustered around nightlife areas, love motels cater for couples seeking by-the-hour intimacy, which, when understood within the cultural context of Korean families often living in close quarters, is less seedy than it sounds. Moreover, you don't generally need to book, and some of the extravagantly decorated rooms are a bargain compared with what you'd pay for similar facilities at a top-end hotel.

Serviced Apartments & Longer-Term Rentals

Even for short stays, serviced apartments can be a great option, offering conveniences such as proper kitchen and laundry facilities. Renting an apartment long-term can be tricky because of the traditional payment system that involves paying a huge deposit to the landlord and/or having to pay all your rent up front.

NEED TO KNOW

Price Ranges

The following price ranges refer to a double room with bathroom. Prices include tax and service charges.

$ less than ₩60,000

$$ ₩60,000–250,000

$$$ over ₩250,000

Taxes & Service Charges

Budget and midrange places usually include a value-added tax (VAT) of 10% in their rates; rates listed here include all taxes. Be aware that top-end hotels might slap a service charge of 10% on the bill on top of VAT (so a total of 21% over the quoted rate).

Tipping

Not expected.

Transport

High-end hotels typically offer pricey airport transfers, but most fall within range of Seoul's excellent public-transport system. KAL (p206) buses connect both airports with several major hotels.

Wi-Fi

Usually offered for free, but some hotels may charge by the day for internet access.

Weekend Rates

Rates at many places can be up to 20% higher on Friday and Saturday nights.

Lonely Planet's Top Choices

Park Hyatt Seoul (p173) Sophisticated contemporary design hotel overlooking COEX.

Small House Big Door (p170) Art hotel in downtown Seoul full of designer touches.

Itaewon G Guest House (p172) Cool backpacker with a sensational rooftop hang-out.

K-Grand Hostel Dongdaemun (p173) Spotless twins and doubles, free breakfast and a great rooftop terrace.

Best By Budget

₩

Urbanwood Guesthouse (p171) Cool, colourful apartment in the heart of Hongdae.

Zaza Backpackers (p169) Pick of the hostels in Myeongdong's backpacker enclave.

Itaewon G Guest House (p172) Grungy apartment block converted to great backpacker spot.

Nagwonjang Hotel (p168) Designer touches in the heart of Ikseon-dong.

₩₩

Hotel 28 (p170) Hip, Korean-film-themed boutique hotel.

Lee Kang Ga (p171) Attractive Korean design features in the rooms here.

Metro Hotel (p169) Splashes of style abound at this Myeongdong base.

₩₩₩

Grand Hyatt Seoul (p172) Oozing class on the hillside of Namsan, overlooking Itaewon.

Plaza (p170) Large rooms look down upon grassy Seoul Plaza and the historic-meets-contemporary facade of City Hall.

Hotel Shilla (p174) Seoul's very own luxury pile with a three-star Michelin restaurant.

Park Hyatt Seoul (p173) Uber-stylish Gangnam pad.

Best Serviced Apartments

Fraser Suites (p169) Top-class serviced apartments in Insa-dong.

Oriens Hotel & Residences (p170) Great location and professional service for a reasonable price.

Uljiro Co-Op Residence (p174) Tiny, affordable apartment-style rooms in Seoul's market mecca.

Best Hanok Guesthouses

Rak-Ko-Jae (p169) Beautifully restored *hanok*, with an enchanting garden and traditional sauna.

Chi-Woon-Jung (p169) *Hanok* guesthouses don't come any more luxurious than this beauty.

Uhbu's Guesthouse (p173) Brightly painted, budget *hanok* with tiny dorms and cute social areas.

Best Homestays

Kims (p174) Stylish family home with bountiful breakfasts and beautiful Bukaksan views.

Eugene's House (p174) Traditional *hanok* home shared with an English-speaking Seoul family.

Bukchon Maru (p169) *Hanok* homestay with family recipe breakfasts.

Where to Stay

NEIGHBOURHOOD	FOR	AGAINST
Gwanghwamun & Jongno-gu	Characterful *hanok* guesthouses; Insa-dong and Bukchon are on your doorstep.	Light on top-end options, and some of the most touristy parts of town.
Myeong-dong & Jung-gu	Good selection of places at all levels. Central location and direct access to Mt Namsan and shopping in Myeong-dong and Namdaemun.	Myeong-dong perpetually busy – not for those seeking peace and tranquillity.
Western Seoul	Good for budget travellers who want to party. Yeouido is recommended only if you have business on the island.	You will spend a fair amount of time on the subway to get to the major sights.
Itaewon & Yongsan-gu	Reasonably central location close to some major sights. Several budget choices, and perfect for Itaewon's plentiful dining and nightlife.	Limited choice of accommodation, and the most 'western' area of Seoul.
Dongdaemun & Eastern Seoul	Close to major malls and markets. Some good cheap options.	Hotels tend to fill up with wholesale shoppers from other Asian countries.
Gangnam & Southern Seoul	For those who will settle for nothing less than top-end brands. Buzzing nightlife.	Very light on budget options. Barrelling highways and dearth of historical sights.
Northern Seoul	*Hanok* homestays offer a peaceful escape in the hills above the city.	Not all areas accessible by subway.

Gwanghwamun & Jongno-gu

The neighbourhoods in walking distance to palaces lean towards boutique- and business-style hotels with fewer bargains or places with a social atmosphere. Three- and four-star hotels are clustered south of Changdeokgung between Insadong and Ikseon-dong. There are opportunities to stay in a *hanok* in Bukchon and Ikseon-dong, though expect charm more than comfort at lower budgets.

AN HOSTEL HOSTEL $

Map p234 (☎02-1577 0988; www.theankorea.co.kr; 141 Myo-dong; d incl breakfast ₩60,000; ; Line 1, 3 or 5 to Jongno 3-ga, Exit 6) If clean neutral tones are your thing, the An will appeal. White and slate grey abound in the small rooms, modern bathrooms and shared spaces – living room, kitchen and laundry. English is spoken and it's a good, clean, private option to explore the villagey laneways of Ikseon-dong nearby.

NAGWONJANG HOTEL BOUTIQUE HOTEL $

Map p234 (낙원장 호텔; ☎070-4467 1408; www.nagwonjang.com; 25 Supyo-ro 28-gil, Ikseon-dong; d ₩55,000-70,000; @; Line 5 to Jongno 3-ga, Exit 6) A boutique hotel located in the heart of Ikseon-dong, Nagwonjang Hotel is the result of a collaboration between several artists. Originally a love motel built in the '80s, the smallish double rooms feature vintage decor and prices remain affordable. An outdoor cafe space and rooftop views further the value for money.

The hotel opened its doors in 2017, modelled after American chain, Ace Hotel. At six storeys, it stands proudly as the tallest building around. Guests of the hotel also receive 10% off at nearby restaurants.

★DOO GUESTHOUSE GUESTHOUSE $$

Map p230 (☎02-3672 1977; www.dooguesthouse.com; 103-7 Gyedong-gil; s/d without bathroom incl breakfast ₩50,000/80,000; @; Line 3 to Anguk, Exit 3) Mixing old and new is this enchanting *hanok* in a garden setting with a traditional-style room where breakfast is served. The shared bathrooms are high quality, with bidets and walk-in showers. The rooms have TVs and DVD players.

★HOTEL THE DESIGNERS BOUTIQUE HOTEL $$

Map p234 (☎02-2267 7474; www.hotelthedesigners.com; 89-8 Supyo-ro; r/ste from ₩132,000/168,000; ; Line 1 or 3 to Jongno 3-ga, Exit 15) Eighteen designers were given free rein to decorate the suites at this sophisticated love motel, tucked off the main road. Check the website for the different themes: our favourite is Camp Ruka-baik, with a tent, deck chairs, tree-bark-covered poles and guitar for a camping-in-the-city experience. Large discounts when booked online.

If you just want a taste of these fantasy rooms then short stays (four hours Sunday to Thursday, three hours Friday and Saturday) are also available for ₩40,000.

HIDE & SEEK GUESTHOUSE GUESTHOUSE $$

Map p232 (☎02-6925 5916; www.hidenseek.co.kr; 14 Jahamun-ro 6-gil; s/tw incl breakfast from ₩65,000/75,000; ; Line 3 to Gyeongbokgung, Exit 5) Stylish design marks out this appealing five-room guesthouse, tucked away in Tongui-dong, beside the remains of an ancient pine tree, and occupying a modern, two-storey house with a broad outdoor terrace. Breakfast is served in the cute Stella's Kitchen cafe.

WWOOF KOREA GUESTHOUSE GUESTHOUSE $$

Map p230 (☎070-8288 1289; www.wwoofkoreaguesthouse.com; 52-11 Gyedong-gil; s/d incl breakfast from ₩70,000/100,000, without bathroom from ₩60,000/90,000; ; Line 3 to Anguk, Exit 1) This rustic *hanok*, its three *ondol* rooms arranged around a courtyard with pickle jars and a *sansuyu* tree, is run by Helen, the director of the Korea branch of World Wide Opportunities on Organic Farms (WWOOF). Hence breakfast items and tea in the teahouse are all organic and you can buy the organic plum juice as a souvenir.

HOSTEL KOREA 11TH HOSTEL $$

Map p234 (☎070-4705 1900; www.cdg.hostelkorea.com; 85 Donhwamun-ro; dm/s/d from ₩22,000/53,900/108,900; @; Line 3 to Anguk, Exit 4) The best of the larger hostels popping up in this area occupying old office or apartment buildings. This one has a colourful, fun design, great location, roomy capsule-style dorm beds and a fabulous rooftop chill-out area with panoramic views.

BIBIMBAP GUESTHOUSE GUESTHOUSE **$$**
Map p234 (비빔밥 게스트하우스; ☎070-8153 4040; www.bibimbapguesthouse.com; 21-10 Supyo-ro 28-gil; s/tw incl breakfast ₩70,000/140,000; ❄📶; Ⓢ Line 1, 3 or 5 to Jongno 3ga, Exit 4) One of several guesthouses that are springing up in centuries-old *hanok* in Ikseon-dong, this one is run by a young crowd. The spartan rooms are all *ondol* with *yo* mattresses and have attached bathrooms. Significant discounts when booked online.

BUKCHON MARU GUESTHOUSE **$$**
Map p230 (☎010 3253 8751; www.bukchonmaru.com; 152 Changdeokgung-gil; d/q incl breakfast from ₩80,000/140,000; ❄📶; Ⓢ Line 3 to Anguk, Exit 3) The family that runs this *hanok* in the Bukchon Hanok village have lived here for over 30 years and cook traditional breakfasts using family recipes, and speak some English. The three *ondol* rooms are basic, authentic and comfortable, though only the family room has its own bathroom. There is a free *hanbok* experience.

★**CHI-WOON-JUNG** GUESTHOUSE **$$$**
Map p230 (취운정; ☎02-742 3410; www.rkj.co.kr; 31-53 Gahoe-dong; s/d incl breakfast from ₩500,000/1,100,000; ❄📶; Ⓢ Line 3 to Anguk, Exit 2) The *hanok* as an exclusive luxury experience doesn't get much finer than this stunning property that has just four elegant guest rooms, all with beautifully tiled bathrooms and pine-wood tubs. Completely remodelled since Korean president Lee Myung Bak once lived there, it is decorated with beautiful crafts and has a Zen-calm garden wrapped around it with views of Bukchon Hanok Village.

★**RAK-KO-JAE** GUESTHOUSE **$$$**
Map p230 (락고재; ☎02-742 3410; www.rkj.co.kr; 98 Gyeo-dong; s/d incl breakfast ₩198,000/275,000; ❄@; Ⓢ Line 3 to Anguk, Exit 2) This beautifully restored *hanok*, with an enchanting garden, is modelled after Japan's ryokan. The guesthouse's mud-walled sauna is included in the prices, as is breakfast, but dinner (₩30,000 to ₩50,000) must be booked in advance. The en suite bathrooms are tiny.

FRASER SUITES APARTMENT **$$$**
Map p234 (☎02-6262 8888; www.frasershospitality.com; 18 Insa-dong 4-gil, Jongno-gu; 1-/2-/3-bedroom apt incl breakfast ₩330,000/440,000/550,000; ❄@📶🏊; Ⓢ Line 1, 3 or 5 to Jongno 3-ga, Exit 5) These fully equipped serviced apartments are modern, light and spacious, great for a long-term stay, for which discounts are available. Staff try hard to make this a home away from home and its location, steps away from Insadong-gil, is ideal for sightseeing.

🛏 Myeong-dong & Jung-gu

ZAZA BACKPACKERS HOSTEL **$**
Map p238 (자자 백팩커스; ☎02-3672 1976; www.zazabackpackers.com; 18-6 Namsandong-2ga; s/d ₩50,000/60,000; ❄@📶; Ⓢ Line 4 to Myeondong, Exit 3) In the guesthouse enclave that's sprung up along the hill to Namsan, Zaza is one of the best with its contemporary building full of design touches and friendly young staff who speak English. Neutrally decorated rooms have their own private washing machine and kitchenette, attracting longer-term guests.

HOTEL 8 HOURS DESIGN HOTEL **$**
Map p238 (☎02-3789 8882; www.hotel8hours.com; 26-10 Namdaemun-ro 1-gil; tw ₩40,000; 🚭❄@📶; Ⓢ Line 1 or 2 to City Hall, Exit 8) This hotel is the perfect option for travellers looking for a clean, budget space right in downtown. The rooms are quite small, ranging from 13 to 20 sq metres, but each has been designed to fit two to four guests. It gets plus points for free wi-fi and coffee, but minus points for the lack of windows.

NAMSAN GUESTHOUSE GUESTHOUSE **$**
Map p238 (남산게스트하우스; ☎02-752 6363; www.namsanguesthouse.com; 79-3 Toegye-ro 18-gil; dm/tw incl breakfast ₩30,000/65,000; ❄@📶; Ⓢ Line 4 to Myeongdong, Exit 2) Taking over the neighbourhood on the slopes of Namsan, this long-running backpackers' favourite now has three locations in the immediate area. Each varies from the other – pod-style dorms for females here; a rooftop terrace at the popular **Namsan Guesthouse 2** (Map p238; ☎02-778 7800; www.namsanguesthouse.com; 33-3 Namsan-dong; d/tr ₩65,000/85,000; ❄📶; Ⓢ Line 4 to Myeongdong, Exit 3) – but all make for good budget choices.

★**METRO HOTEL** HOTEL **$$**
Map p238 (메트로호텔; ☎02-2176 3199; www.metrohotel.co.kr; 14 Myeong-dong 9ga-gil; s/d/tw incl breakfast from ₩83,000/143,000/198,000; ❄@📶; Ⓢ Line 2 to Euljiro 1-ga, Exit 6) An excellent midrange, small, professionally run

hotel with boutique aspirations. Splashes of style abound, from the flashy, metallic lobby to its laptops. Room size and design vary – ask for one of the larger ones with big windows (room numbers that end in 07).

★SMALL HOUSE BIG DOOR BOUTIQUE HOTEL **$$**

Map p238 (스몰 하우스 빅 도어; ☎02-2038 8191; www.smallhousebigdoor.com; 6 Namdaemun-ro 9-gil; r incl breakfast ₩115,000-250,000; ❄📶; ⓈLine 2 to Euljiro 1-ga, Exit 1 or 2) Down a narrow street in central Seoul, this suave little art hotel is quite the find. Its white-toned rooms all feature locally designed, handmade furniture and beds, and maximise the use of space with ingenious slide-out desks and TVs. Pricier rooms have outdoor sitting areas and sky windows.

Head up to its rooftop lounge to hang out, or downstairs to the lively cafe with gallery and performance space.

★SPLAISIR BOUTIQUE HOTEL **$$**

Map p238 (☎02-772 0900; www.splaisir.com; 15 Namdaemun-ro 5-gil; d & tw incl breakfast ₩131,000-327,000; ❄📶; ⓈLine 1 or 2 to City Hall, Exit 8) This hotel has rooms dedicated to Line Friends – cartoon characters from popular Japanese-Korean social-media app Line – so fans of cuteness overload and giant stuffed chickens staring at them while sleeping will be in four-star paradise here near Namdaemun Market. Otherwise, immaculate, minimalist rooms – dressed in bamboo browns and whites holding hinoki-wood soaking tubs and soft beds – are much calmer.

HOTEL 28 BOUTIQUE HOTEL **$$**

Map p238 (호텔28; ☎02-774 2828; www.hotel28.co.kr/; 13 Myeongdong 7-gil; d from ₩110,000; ❄@📶; ⓈLine 2 to Euljiro, Exit 6) Opened in 2016, this boutique hotel was founded by veteran actor Shin Young-kyun and takes on a Korean cinema theme. Each room has stills of films that Shin starred in and the lobby and the hallways are decorated with film reels. The hotel also collaborates with entertainment company YG for its hotel restaurant called YG Republique, located on the 1st floor.

CRIB49 GUESTHOUSE **$$**

Map p238 (크립 49 게스트하우스; ☎070-8128 5981; www.crib49.com; 49 Toegye-ro 20na-gil; d/tr incl breakfast from ₩80,000/120,000; ❄@📶; ⓈLine 4 to Myeongdong, Exit 3) Up the hill near Namsan's cable car, the *ondol* rooms at this smart guesthouse have mattresses on the floor, and minimalist decor with Scandinavian-style shelving and plasma TVs. Its rooftop deck has Namsan views and there's a small kitchen.

NINE TREE HOTEL MYEONG-DONG HOTEL **$$**

Map p238 (나인 트리 호텔 명동; ☎02-750 0999; www.ninetreehotel.com; 51 Myeong-dong 10-gil; s/d incl breakfast ₩162,000/200,000; ❄📶; ⓈLine 4 to Myeong-dong, Exit 8) There's plenty to like about this snazzy hotel well placed in the heart of Myeong-dong's shopping district. The smart boutique-y rooms have city views, a pillow menu of nine different types, Japanese-style electronic toilets, clothes press, foot-massage machines, minibar and a coffee-maker. Plus there are substantial discounts if you book online.

ORIENS HOTEL & RESIDENCES APARTMENT **$$**

Map p238 (오리엔스 호텔 & 레지던스; ☎02-2280 8000; www.orienshotel.com; 50 Samil-daero 2-gil; studio/2-bedroom apt from ₩144,000/188,000; ❄@📶; ⓈLine 3 or 4 to Chungmuro, Exit 4) A great location, friendly and professional service and reasonable rates make this one of the best serviced-apartment options for short or long stays. Rooms are plainly furnished but have everything you need. Note that many of the cheaper studios have windows onto an internal light well, so can be rather gloomy.

★PLAZA HOTEL **$$$**

Map p238 (더 플라자; ☎02-771 2200; www.hoteltheplaza.com; 23 Taepyeong-ro 2-ga; r from ₩290,000; ❄@📶🏊; ⓈLine 1 or 2 to City Hall, Exit 6) You can't get more central than the Plaza, opposite the striking rising glass edifice of City Hall. Rooms sport a smart design with giant angle-poise lamps, circular mirrors and crisp white linens contrasting with dark carpets. It also has some chic restaurants and a good fitness club with a swimming pool.

BANYAN TREE CLUB & SPA HOTEL **$$$**

Map p238 (☎02-2250 8074; www.banyantreeclub.net; 60 Jang Chang Dan-ro; r from ₩448,000; ❄@📶🏊; ⓈLine 3 to Beotigogae, Exit 1) Billing itself a 'sanctuary for the senses', the Banyan Tree occupies a hilltop tower designed by feted local architect Kim Swoon Guen, and offers just four rooms per floor. Calmly decorated and coolly sophisticated, each has a giant relaxation pool and amazing views. Guests have access to the darkly luxurious club with its leisure facilities.

In summer there's big outdoor pool surrounded by private cabanas; in winter it becomes a skating rink.

WESTIN CHOSUN SEOUL HOTEL $$$

Map p238 (웨스틴 조선호텔 서울; ☎02-771 0500; www.westin.com/seoul; 106 Sogong-ro; r from ₩436,000; ; Line 2 to Euljiro 1-ga, Exit 4) Dating from the late 1970s, this is not Seoul's most spectacular hotel, but the relaxing atmosphere and the conscientious staff keep it a cut above the rest. Each stylish room decorated in soft caramel tones comes with a coffee-maker, shaving mirrors, bathroom scales and a choice of 10 types of pillows. Keep an eye out for the Henry Moore sculpture in the lobby.

Western Seoul

★URBANWOOD GUESTHOUSE HOSTEL $

Map p240 (☎070-8613 0062; www.urbanwood.co.kr; 3rd fl, 48-20 Wausan-ro 29-gil; s/d incl breakfast from ₩60,000/80,000; ; Line 2 to Hongik University, Exit 8) Creatively decorated in bright colours and modern furnishings, this cosy guesthouse feels more like a cool arty apartment. Martin, the convivial English-speaking host, knows the area well and will whisk you up a mean coffee on the professional barista machine in the well-appointed kitchen.

Also has apartments to rent in the area.

★KPOPSTAY HOSTEL $

Map p240 (☎010 9955 1969; http://kpopstay.com; 6-153 Changjeon-dong; dm ₩23,000-29,000, q ₩150,000; ; Line 2 to Hongik University, Exit 8) There is a stream of K-Pop on the TVs at this memorabilia-adorned hostel in the heart of Hongdae's bar area next to Hongik University. But even if you aren't a K-Pop fan, designer-like dorms make Kpopstay an excellent choice – soft beds in pod-style bunks with total-privacy curtains and especially large individual lockers.

ROI HOUSE GUESTHOUSE $

(☎070-811 2626; www.roihouse.wix.com/english; 14 Donggyo-ro 41-gil; dm/tw incl breakfast from ₩25,000/80,000; ; Line 2 to Hongik University, Exit 3) Modern, with larger rooms than most guesthouses and a quiet location on a tree-lined street in Yeonnam-dong, this is a very pleasant place to stay that's within walking distance of Hongdae. Owner Park Simon speaks English well.

COME INN HOSTEL $

Map p240 (☎070-8958 7279; www.comeinnkorea.com; 20-10 Wausan-ro 21-gil; dm/s/tw without bathroom, incl breakfast ₩15,000/33,000/45,000; ; Line 2 to Hongik University, Exit 9) Bang in the centre of Hongdae is this compact, 3rd-floor guesthouse offering private rooms and female-only dorms, all of which share common bathrooms. There's a comfy lounge and a broad outdoor terrace with views across the area.

★WOWFACTOR STAY GUESTHOUSE $$

Map p240 (☎010 9615 2789; www.wowfactorstay.com; 28 World Cup buk-ro 5ga-gil; d/q incl breakfast from ₩80,000/120,000; ; Line 2 to Hongik University, Exit 1) The husband-and-wife team who converted this house have keen design sensibilities. K-Pop-fanatic Jacqueline chooses photogenic, homey decor and cooks delightful Korean breakfasts designed to wow on social media. Colour-themed studios are chic, with premium bedding, and all have their own modern bathroom. It's a few blocks from Hongdae's epicentre of shopping and bars, but within a quiet garden.

★LEE KANG GA GUESTHOUSE $$

Map p240 (☎02-323 5484; www.leekanghouse.com; 4th fl, 12 World Cup buk-ro 11-gil; d incl breakfast from ₩85,000; ; 15, 7711, 7737 or 7016, Line 2 to Hongik University, Exit 1) Near the War & Women's Human Rights Museum (p94), this appealing guesthouse is worth the trek from Hongdae. Rooms are attractively decorated with *hanji* (traditional paper) wallpaper, silky pillows and pine-wood furniture and a few have balconies and washing machines. There are great views from the rooftop kitchen and garden.

MARIGOLD HOTEL HOTEL $$

Map p240 (☎02-332 5656; www.hotelmarigold.co.kr; 112 Yanghwa-ro; s/tw from ₩160,000/180,000; ; Line 2 to Hongik University, Exit 9) Part of the reliable business-hotel chain Benikea, the Marigold's rooms are spacious and aim for contemporary chic with amber onyx tiles and fake animal-skin headboards on the beds. The deluxe rooms even stretch to copies of Eames recliner chairs.

A buffet breakfast is ₩15,400 extra and guests get a discount at the Happy Day Spa in the basement.

CONRAD SEOUL HOTEL **$$$**

Map p242 (02-6137 7000; www.conradseoul.co.kr; 23-1 Yeouido-dong; r from ₩343,000; ; Line 5 or 9 to Yeouido, Exit 3) Superior service, luxe rooms decorated in natural tones, and sweeping views of the Han River and city are what you'd expect here – and it absolutely delivers. The natural choice for business travel on the island.

MARRIOTT EXECUTIVE APARTMENTS APARTMENT **$$$**

Map p242 (02-2090 8000; www.measeoul.com; 8 Yeoui-daero; apt from ₩235,000; ; Line 5 or 9 to Yeouido, Exit 1) If you're going to stay on Yeouido then these top-grade, beautifully decorated serviced apartments are one way to go. The complex, which faces onto a park on the south of the island, also has a gym, a pool and the fancy bakery-cafe Paul.

Itaewon & Yongsan-gu

★ITAEWON G GUEST HOUSE HOSTEL **$**

Map p244 (이태원 G 게스트하우스; 010 2082 8377; www.gguest.com; 14-38 Bogwang-ro 60-gil; dm/s/d incl breakfast ₩17,000/40,000/72,000; ; Line 6 to Itaewon, Exit 3) Run by the welcoming and convivial Shrek Lee, this hostel is easily the best budget digs in Itaewon. Fourteen dorms and four twins are stacked in a converted block at the end of the lane that houses trendy nightclub Soap (p114). It's a good place to meet other travellers, either in the downstairs kitchen or chilling on the rooftop.

Other perks include free laundry, filter coffee and bikes for the nearby Han River cycling path. Also offers halal kitchen utensils and a prayer room for Muslim guests – a nod to the mosque (p110) down the road. Book directly with the hostel and it promises a 10% to 15% discount.

ITAEWON HOSTEL & INN HOSTEL **$**

Map p244 (이태원 인; 02-6221 0880; www.itaewoninn.com; 103-2 Bogwang-ro; dm/s/d ₩16,000/35,000/70,000; ; Line 6 to Itaewon, Exit 4) A short stumble down the hill from the bars, this well-run hostel offers a mix of dorms and private rooms (including affordable en suite singles with TVs and towels). Rooms are plain but bathrooms are decent, and the rooftop terrace is vast. The location, on a street of characterful antique shops yet close to the action, is excellent.

PHILSTAY HOSTEL B&B GUESTHOUSE **$**

Map p244 (02-749 8855; www.philstay.co.kr; 120-4 Itaewon-dong; dm/d & tw/tr/f ₩20,000/60,000/75,000/130,000; ; Line 6 to Itaewon, Exit 1) Offering clean, modern rooms kitted out with mini-fridges, TVs and Japanese toilets, this hostel is one of the better choices on the hill overlooking Itaewon's nightlife. It has a communal kitchen and roof terrace but no bar or restaurant.

IP BOUTIQUE HOTEL HOTEL **$$**

Map p244 (IP 부티크 호텔; 02-3702 8000; www.ipboutiquehotel.com; 737-32 Hannam-dong; d weekdays/weekends ₩157,000/181,500; ; Line 6 to Itaewon, Exit 2) Looking a little dated despite giant images of fruit on the white walls, this not-quite-boutique hotel (it has 128 rooms) is nevertheless in a good location and offers plenty of comforts like coffee-pod machines, in-room smartphones and rain showers.

★GRAND HYATT SEOUL HOTEL **$$$**

Map p244 (그랜드 하얏트 서울; 02-797 1234; www.seoul.grand.hyatt.com; 322 Sowol-ro; r from ₩375,000; ; Line 6 to Hangangjin, Exit 1) Making the most of its hilltop aspect, the Grand Hyatt is lord of all it surveys. On a clear day, the views from the lobby lounge, through a soaring wall of glass, are magnificent. Service is flawless, and although the contemporary-styled rooms are a bit smaller than at rivals, they don't lack for luxurious accoutrements. The outdoor pool becomes an ice rink in winter.

Choose between sensational views of the city or Namsan. A free shuttle runs to Itaewon and Myeongdong till 9pm.

Gangnam & Southern Seoul

SEOUL OLYMPIC PARKTEL HOTEL **$**

Map p252 (서울올림픽파크텔; 02-421 2114; www.parktel.co.kr; Olympic Park, 88-8 Bangdong; dm ₩22,000; ; Line 8 to Mongchontoseong, Exit 1) If you're a youth-hostel member you can stay in this functional business hotel in the 'bunk room' at a youth-hostel rate. Inside Olympic Park, it's a long way from most sights, but the dorms – actually hotel rooms with two double bunks and two pull-out beds – have big windows with park views.

You can sign up for YH membership on the spot.

★TRIA HOTEL HOTEL **$$**

Map p250 (호텔 트리아; ☎02-553 2471; www.triahotel.co.kr; 16 Teheran-ro 33-gil; r/ste from ₩86,000/113,000; ❄@📶; Ⓢ Line 2 to Yeoksam, Exit 8) An excellent-value, midrange option that's very affordable for this end of town, the 50-room boutiquey Tria has lots going for it. Opt for any room above standard and you'll get a whirlpool bath. The hotel is tucked away in the streets behind the Renaissance Hotel, a five-minute walk from the subway exit.

LA CASA GAROSUGIL HOTEL **$$**

Map p248 (라까사 호텔 서울; ☎02-546 0088; www.hotellacasa.kr; 83 Dosan-daero 1-gil; s/d incl breakfast from ₩178,000/224,000; ❄@📶; Ⓢ Line 3 to Sinsa, Exit 6) The first venture into the hospitality business by classy Korean furniture and interior-design store Casamia packs plenty of chic style. The rooms are attractive and spacious with quirky details such as the travel-themed pillowcases, while the lobby also has plenty of design features and art books. It's handy for Garosu-gil.

H AVENUE HOTEL MOTEL **$$**

Map p250 (에이치 에비뉴 호텔; ☎02-508 6247; 12 Teheran-ro 29-gil; r from ₩85,000; ❄@📶🏊; Ⓢ Line 2 to Yeoksam, Exit 8) Fantastic value, this love motel is most notable for its roof-terrace rooms which come with their own roof-deck swimming pools and views over Namsan and the nearby cathedral; stay midweek for the best deals. While essentially a love motel, it comes without all the usual, weird trappings.

★PARK HYATT SEOUL HOTEL **$$$**

Map p252 (파크 하얏트 서울; ☎02-2016 1234; www.seoul.park.hyatt.com; 606 Teheran-ro; r from ₩355,000; ❄@📶🏊; Ⓢ Line 2 to Samseong, Exit 1) A discreet entrance – look for the rock sticking out of the wall – sets the Zen-minimalist tone for this gorgeous property. Each floor only has 10 rooms with spot-lit antiquities lining the hallways. Spacious open-plan rooms have floor-to-ceiling windows that boast city views and come with luxurious bathrooms classed among the best in Asia.

IMPERIAL PALACE HOTEL HOTEL **$$$**

Map p250 (☎02-3440 8000; www.imperialpalace.co.kr; 248-7 Nonhyun-dong; r from ₩193,000; ❄@📶🏊; Ⓢ Line 7 to Hak-dong, Exit 1) A name like this raises expectations, and they are all met at Seoul's most luxurious hotel. The antiques and wood panelling create a stately, genuinely European ambience, and from the magnificent lobby to the well-appointed rooms and immaculate spa, opulence and no-expense-spared are the twin themes. A buffet of delights is doled out at several onsite restaurants; there's also an onsite gym.

🛏 Dongdaemun & Eastern Seoul

★K-GRAND HOSTEL DONGDAEMUN HOSTEL **$**

(케이 그랜드 호스텔; ☎02-2233 9155; 339-1 Wangsimni-ro; tw & d/tr/f incl breakfast from ₩40,000/60,000/70,000; ❄📶; Ⓢ Line 2 to Wangsimni, Exit 4) A spotlessly clean, superbly run western-style hostel, the K-Grand occupies the top half of a 10-storey building, with great views as standard from its spacious en suite rooms. Sealing the deal is a sociable kitchen with free tea and coffee, English-speaking staff, cheap laundry, two subway stations close by and a wonderful rooftop terrace.

UHBU'S GUESTHOUSE GUESTHOUSE **$**

(☎070-8125 4858; 19-5 Gosanja-ro 33-gil; incl breakfast dm/d ₩22,000/63,000, d without bathroom ₩52,000; ❄📶; Ⓢ Line 1 to Jegi-dong, Exit 3) There are mixed and female dorms and three tiny doubles in this brightly painted *hanok,* one of many time-worn nuggets in a shabby city block that somehow escaped redevelopment. You also get a communal kitchen and covered courtyard, plus free brekkie and Korean-style pyjamas courtesy of the English-speaking owner.

TOYOKO INN SEOUL DONGDAEMUN HOTEL **$$**

Map p247 (토요코인 서울 동대문; ☎02-2267 1045; www.toyoko-inn.com; 337 Toegye-ro, Jung-gu; s/d incl breakfast from ₩66,000/77,000; ❄@📶; Ⓢ Lines 2, 4 or 5 to Dongdaemun History & Culture Park, Exit 4) The small, clean and well-equipped rooms at this Japanese business hotel are great value, and well located for Dongdaemun's shopping.

ULJIRO CO-OP RESIDENCE APARTMENT $$

Map p247 (02-2269 4600; http://rent.co-op.co.kr; 32 Eulji-ro 6-ga, Jung-gu; studios from ₩77,000; ; Line 2, 4 or 5 to Dongdaemun History & Culture Park, Exit 12) These tiny, all-white studio apartments with attached kitchenette provide a little nest high above the 24-hour hurly-burly of Dongdaemun Market. Everything is bright, modern and mini-sized – not much elbow room. Rates vary and apartments tend to book out early; you can also try the same company's Western Co-Op Residence a few doors down.

★**HOTEL SHILLA** HOTEL $$$

Map p247 (신라호텔; 02-2233 3131; www.shillahotels.com; 249 Dongho-ro, Jung-gu; r from ₩250,000; ; Line 3 to Dongguk University, Exit 5) The luxurious flagship of Korea's homegrown Shilla hotel group, Hotel Shilla is one of Seoul's best, with a VIP location on 9 acres of private hillside near Namsan (there's a regular shuttle bus up from the subway exit). Highlights include an all-season outdoor pool and La Yeon, the hotel's modern Korean haute cuisine restaurant, with three Michelin stars.

JW MARRIOTT DONGDAEMUN SQUARE HOTEL $$$

Map p247 (JW 메리어트 동대문 스퀘어 서울; 02-2276 3000; www.jwmarriottdongdaemun.com; 279 Cheonggyecheon-ro, Jongno-gu; r from ₩300,000; ; Line 1 or 4 to Dongdaemun, Exit 9) Tacked on to the end of Dongdaemun Market (p139), the five-star JW is a swish pad to come home to after a busy day (or night) shopping at the wholesale malls next door. Rooms are fabulously well equipped, but it's worth upgrading to one with views of Heunginjimun and retractable blinds that open to the stars.

VISTA WALKERHILL SEOUL HOTEL $$$

(비스타 워커힐 서울; 02-465 2222; www.whotels.com/seoul; 177 Walkerhill-ro, Gwangjin-gu; r from ₩250,000; ; Line 5 to Gwangnaru, Exit 2) Formerly the W Seoul, the trademark pinks have given way to more restrained whites and greys at this elegantly rebranded, high-tech hotel perched on a hillside in the far east of the city. It's a good place to get away from it all, especially at Skyard, a terrace with sun loungers, spa pools and gorgeous views of the Han River.

There's a free shuttle bus to Gwangnaru station.

Northern Seoul

INSIDE BACKPACKERS HOSTEL $

Map p254 (02-3672 1120; 5 Sungkwunkwan-ro 4-gil; dm/s/tw without bathroom ₩15,000/30,000/40,000; ; Line 4 to Hyehwa, Exit 4) A friendly if scruffy budget choice with plenty of character and room options – although note that most are very tiny with thin walls. Rates are a few thousand won higher for stays on Friday and Saturday nights.

MOGGOJI HOUSE GUESTHOUSE $

Map p254 (모꼬지 한옥 게스트하우스; 010 5328 2837, 010 9389 2837; www.moggoji-house.com; 13-6 Hyehwa-ro 16-gil; dm/d without bathroom incl breakfast ₩30,000/60,000; ; Line 4 to Hyehwa, Exit 1) There are only three rooms, two of them small dorms with western-style beds, at this lodging in a modernised *hanok* midway between Daehangno and Seongbuk-dong. It's comfortable but less traditional than some *hanoks*. The owner speaks some English.

EUGENE'S HOUSE HOMESTAY $$

Map p254 (02-741 3338; www.eugenehouse.co.kr; 36 Hyehwa-ro 12-gil; s without bathroom ₩55,000, d/q ₩110,000/200,000; ; Line 4 to Hyehwa, Exit 1) This traditional *hanok* homestay has rooms ranging from a tiny single to a four-futon set-up, with the owner and his family (he speaks a bit of English) living in one corner of the quadrangle. Cosy, quiet and with a lived-in feel, it has a good location just below Seongbuk-dong.

★**KIMS** HOMESTAY $$

(그김가네 게스트하우스; 010 9073 4457; ghbuamthekims@naver.com; 13, Baekseokdong 1-gil; s & dm/tw & d ₩55,000/90,000; ; 1020, 7017, 7212 to Changuimun) A more relaxed alternative to central digs is this beautifully designed, modern homestay in the hills above the city. The swish family home of a retired Korean couple, it has several room configurations available, including one with a balcony offering glorious views of Bukaksan (p34). Mrs Kim knocks up a gourmet breakfast.

Understand Seoul

History

The mighty walls of Korea's modern capital rose in 1394, when King Taejo, founder of the Joseon dynasty, settled the government seat in the valley of Hanyang (later to become Seoul) and ordered the building of Gyeongbokgung, the Palace of Shining Happiness, at the foot of Bukaksan. But the city's roots stretch back many centuries before that, while its development in recent times into an economic powerhouse and the second-largest metropolitan area in the world has been breathtaking.

Japanese Colonisation

Since recorded time, external forces have had designs upon Korea – Japan to the east, China and Mongolia to the west. Brutal invasions – many lasting and painful – comprise the fabric of Korean history. Japanese armies rampaged through the peninsula in 1592, burning temples and palaces to the ground, but were forced out five years later by Koreans aided by the Chinese.

Seoul, meaning 'capital' in Korean, has only been the official name of the city since 1945. Before the Joseon dynasty it was known as Hanyang, afterwards Hanseong. During Japanese rule, it was called Keijo in Japanese, Gyeongseong in Korean.

However, three centuries later, Japan returned with a vengeance. When a large-scale peasant rebellion raged uncontrollably in Korea in 1894, Japan stepped in to 'help'. One year later, Japanese assassins fatally stabbed Queen Min, King Gojong abdicated in 1907, and in 1910 the cession was complete.

This period marked the subjugation, and attempted eradication, of Korean identity. Locals were made to take Japanese names and were forbidden to speak their national tongue. As Japan exploited Korea's resources, only 20% of Koreans were able to even start elementary school. Though some Koreans collaborated with their colonial rulers and reaped great profit, most were unable to rise above second-class citizenship in their own land.

Korean Versus Korean

Down the ages there has been no shortage of internal conflict, either, on the Korean peninsula. The Three Kingdoms period, preceding the Goryeo dynasty (from which comes the name 'Korea'), was marked by

TIMELINE

c 18 BCE

Hanseong, capital of the kingdom of Baekje (Paekche), is established in the Seoul area. For four centuries Baekje rules the peninsula until falling to the Goguryeo kingdom.

10th century

After conquering the Silla dynasty, the Goryeo dynasty change the name of Hanseong to Namgyeong, meaning 'southern capital', and make it one of their three capital cities.

1392

Having overthrown the Goryeo dynasty, General Yi Seong-gye ascends the throne, naming himself King Taejo and establishing the Joseon dynasty that will go on to rule Korea for 500 years.

continual feuds. Korea was unified in 918 CE, but peasant rebellions remained commonplace throughout the Joseon era.

The Korean War (1950–53) represents another such conflict along internally riven lines – the more agrarian south had always resented the wealthier north, and vice versa. When the nation was at last returned to Korea with the Allied victory in 1945, the decision to divide the country into protectorates – with the north to be overseen by the USSR and the south by the US – soon led to rival republics. On 25 June 1950, under the cover of night, the North Korean army marched over the mountains that rim Seoul, marking the start of the brutal civil war.

Seoul's sudden fall to the North caught the populace by surprise; the government of President Syngman Rhee fled southward, destroying the only Han River highway bridge and abandoning the remaining population to face the communists. During its 90-day occupation of the city, North Korea's army arrested and shot many who had supported the Rhee government.

End of the Korean War

In September 1950 UN forces led by US and South Korean troops mounted a counter-attack. After an amphibious landing at Incheon, they fought their way back into Seoul. During a series of bloody battles, whole districts of the capital were bombed and burned in the effort to dislodge Kim Il Sung's Korean People's Army. When at last UN forces succeeded in reclaiming the city, much of it lay in smouldering ruins.

Later that year, as UN forces pushed northward, the Chinese Army entered the war on the North Korean side and pushed back down into Seoul. This time the invaders found a nearly empty city. Even after the UN regained control in March 1951, only a fraction of Seoul's population returned during the two years of war that raged along the battlefront until the armistice in July 1953. Instead, they holed up in rural villages and miserable camps, slowly trickling back into the shattered capital that was once their home.

Widespread hunger, disease, crime and misery comprised daily life for hundreds of thousands. On the slopes of Namsan a wretched village called Haebang-chon (Liberation Town) housed tens of thousands of war refugees, widows and beggars. Sex workers lined up at the gates of the US military bases in Yongsan in a desperate effort to earn a few dollars. Even a decade after the war, average male life expectancy hovered barely above 50.

History Books

The Dawn of Modern Korea (Andrei Lankov, 2007)

Korea's Place in the Sun (Bruce Cumings, 1997)

The Korean War (Max Hastings, 1987)

1394

King Taejo decrees that Hanyang (Seoul) is the capital of the Joseon kingdom, mobilising some 200,000 labourers to surround the city with a great wall, remnants of which still remain.

1446

Sejong the Great oversees the invention of *hangeul*, Korea's famed script, which was presented to citizens in the document known as the Hunminjeongeum.

1796

King Jeongjo moves the royal court to Suwon to be closer to his father's grave, and builds the Hwaseong fortress (now a World Heritage site) to protect the new palace.

1897

As an independence movement grows in Korea, King Gojong declares the founding of the Korean Empire, formalising the end of the Joseon Dynasty's longstanding ties to China.

Military Rule

Historically, Seoul was never an egalitarian society. A registry from the mid-1600s suggests that perhaps three quarters of the city's population were slaves. Social inequality continued through the Japanese colonial period, and after the Korean War ended in 1953 dictatorships sprang up in the South.

In 1968 North Korean agents launched an assassination attempt on then-president Park Chung-hee by climbing over Bukaksan in an attempt to infiltrate the presidential compound Cheongwadae.

The Syngman Rhee regime (1948–60) rigged its own re-election (by mass arrests of opposition leaders and changes to the constitution) several times until 19 April 1960, when a popular rebellion led by unarmed students sought to overthrow the president. Police opened fire on the group, which had gathered in downtown Seoul; by dusk, nearly 200 people lay dead. Rhee's right-hand man, Gibung Lee, committed suicide, as did his family. Rhee resigned a few days later and was spirited away to exile in Hawaii by the US Air Force.

What came to be known as the April Revolution resulted in eight months of democracy under a cabinet system of government led by Prime Minister Chang Myon. However, on 16 May 1961, the civilian government was replaced by a military junta led by Major General Park Chung-hee. In 1963 Park was narrowly elected South Korea's president. He would retain an iron grip on power for 16 years, during which scores of political dissidents were executed or disappeared.

Miracle on the Han

After forcibly taking the reins of the government, Park quickly went to work defining national economic goals. He often followed patterns set by Imperial Japan, such as fostering big businesses (*zaibatsu* in Japanese, *jaebeol* in Korean) as engines of growth. Conglomerates such as Hyundai and Samsung achieved – and still retain – incredible economic influence.

In 1969 the completion of the Hannam Bridge kicked off Seoul's major expansion south of the Han River, and Namsan Tower (now N Seoul Tower) was erected.

Under Park, fear and brutal efficiency combined to deliver results. Wages were kept artificially low to drive exports, and by the mid-1970s Seoul was well on its way to becoming a major world city. Slums were bulldozed, and the city spread in all directions. Expressways, ring roads and a subway network connected these new districts.

Seoul was undoubtedly at the heart of a Korean economic miracle, but the city was also the scene of increasingly strident protests and demonstrations for an end to effective military rule. Park was assassinated in 1979 by his own chief of central intelligence. He was succeeded by another general – Chun Doo-hwan – who crushed pro-democracy uprisings all over the country (most notoriously in the southwestern city of Gwangju). However, by 1987, as over a million citizens participat-

1900

Modernisation continues as a railroad between the port of Incheon and Seoul opens and an electricity company provides public lighting and a streetcar system.

1910

Having gradually increased its power and forced King Gojong to abdicate, Japan annexes Korea, beginning 35 years of colonial rule.

1948

Following WW2, the Republic of Korea is founded in the southern part of the peninsula, while Kim Il Sung sets up the Democratic People's Republic of Korea in the north.

1950–53

North Korean forces occupy Seoul for 90 days before UN forces led by US and South Korean troops mount a counterattack. An armistice ends the Korean War three years later.

ed in the nationwide anti-government protests, Chun had little choice but to step down to allow democratic elections.

Democracy – At Long Last

The result of the first direct presidential election for 16 years in 1988 was that Roh Tae-woo, a former military man and supporter of Chun, won out over a divided opposition. The country's first civilian president in 30 years, Kim Young-sam, was elected in 1992, and replaced in 1998 by former dissident Kim Dae-jung, a 'radical' who had survived several assassination attempts during the Park Chung-hee reign.

Once in power, Kim worked to achieve détente with North Korea under what was known as a 'Sunshine Policy'. His presidency was followed by that of equally liberal Roh Moo-hyun (who committed suicide in May 2009 following his involvement in a bribery scandal).

In 2012 many government ministries were shifted to a 'mini capital' at Sejong City, 120km south of Seoul. The aim is decentralisation and moving part of the nation's administration away from the northern border.

Economic Powerhouse

South Korea's 17th president (and former Seoul mayor), Lee Myung-bak, was a fascinating change from the two previous administrations. Formerly the hard-nosed CEO of the Hyundai construction *jaebeol* (huge, often family-run, corporation), Lee was nicknamed 'the bulldozer' – derisively by those who loathed him, glowingly by his supporters – for his penchant for ramming through his policies. It was under Lee's tenure as mayor that the Cheong-gye-cheon stream project was begun.

Under Lee's administration, Seoul consolidated its grip on the nation's economy and was ranked as one of the most competitive cities in the world. In 2010 it was appointed a Unesco City of Design in recognition of its cultural heritage and promotion of strong design policies, and hosted the G-20 Economic Summit.

Geomancy (feng shui, or *pungsu-jiri* in Korean) decreed Seoul's location: the Han River supplied yin force and access to the sea, and the Bukhan mountain range supplied yang energy and protection from the north.

King Sejong's Gift

As the seat of government, Seoul has borne the brunt of bad policies during periods of lacklustre rule, but has reaped the fruits of its wisest leaders' thinking. The greatest of these leaders was King Sejong (r 1418–50) who sponsored many cultural projects, consolidated border defences and served as a model of Confucian probity. At his direction, court scholars devised the phonetic *hangeul* alphabet, a simple system of writing the Korean language that made it possible for anyone to learn to read. King Sejong's alphabet is one reason why Korea enjoys universal literacy today.

1960–61

Popular protests oust President Syngman Rhee. Attempts at democratic rule fail, a military coup topples the unstable elected government and installs General Park Chung-hee into power.

1979

After surviving a couple of assassination attempts (one of which kills his wife), Park is finally shot dead by the trusted head of his own Central Intelligence Agency.

1987

Following sustained national protests, with the strongest concentration in Seoul, Korea's last military dictatorship, under Chun Doo-hwan, steps down to allow democratic elections.

1988

Seoul hosts the Summer Olympics, building a huge Olympic Park and major expressway. The international showcase leads to increased trade and diplomatic relations.

Seoul and Pyongyang Olympics?

When Oh Se-hoon won the by-election to become the mayor of Seoul in 2021, it was one of the shortest terms in office, pending an election – but it was action packed with the lifting of a decades-old ban on abortion (in certain circumstances) in the country, as well as the resurgence of a pandemic that the city had initially nipped in the bud. Yet he still had his sights set well on the future with an eyebrow-raising (and ultimately unsuccessful) proposal for Seoul to jointly host the Olympics with North Korea's Pyongyang in 2032.

2002

Seoul serves as one of the host cities for the World Cup, with the opening game of the soccer tournament held at the new World Cup Stadium.

2010

Seoul hosts the G-20 Economic Summit and becomes World Design Capital, but its centrepiece – Dongdaemun Design Plaza & Park, by architect Zaha Hadid – remains uncompleted.

2018

North Korean leader Kim Jong-un meets with South Korean President Moon Jae-in at the DMZ for a historic summit between the two nations.

2021

The mayor of Seoul, Park Won-Soon, is found dead, apparently from suicide, amid sexual-harassment allegations by a former secretary.

Flavours of Seoul Cuisine

So you thought Korean cuisine was mainly about kimchi and barbecued beef? A few days in Seoul will swiftly bring you up to speed. Prepare to be blown away by the diversity and spicy deliciousness of the nation's food scene, ranging from rustic stews and tasty street snacks to glorious royal banquets involving elaborate preparation and presentation. Savouring soothing traditional teas and herbal infusions is also one of Seoul's great pleasures, as is sampling the local alcoholic beverages.

Food

A traditional Korean meal (either breakfast, lunch or dinner) typically consists of meat, seafood or fish served at the same time as soup, rice and a collection of dipping sauces and *banchan,* the ubiquitous cold side dishes. The fermented kimchi cabbage or radish is the most popular side

Above *Samgyeopsal* (barbecued pork belly).

dish, but there are many others, such as bean sprouts, black beans, dried anchovy, spinach, quail eggs, shellfish, lettuce, acorn jelly and tofu. It's a healthy and balanced approach to eating – no wonder Korean cooks refer to food as 'medicine'.

The pinnacle of Korean dining is *jeongsik* or *hanjeongsik*. These banquets cover the table with food and include fish, meat, soup, *dubu jjigae* (spicy tofu stew), *doenjang jjigae* (soybean-paste stew), rice, noodles, steamed egg, shellfish and lots of cold vegetable side dishes, followed by a cup of tea. It's invariably too much to eat, and it's meant to be – don't feel obliged to gobble up everything put in front of you.

Joseon kings and queens used to scoff specially prepared *juk* (rice porridge) with abalone, pine nuts and sesame seeds as a pre-breakfast meal.

Specialities

Barbecue

Seoul's many barbecue restaurants have a grill set into the tables on which to cook slices of beef *(bulgogi),* beef ribs *(galbi),* pork belly *(samgyeopsal),* chicken *(dak),* seafood or vegetables. The server often helps out with the cooking.These meals are usually only available for two diners or more.

Bulgogi, galbi and *samgyeopsal* are served with a dish of *ssam,* typically lettuce and perilla leaves. Take a leaf in one hand (or combine two leaves for different flavours) and use your chopsticks to load it with meat, side-dish flavourings, garlic and sauces. Then fold it into a little package and eat it in one go.

Japchae is a Chinese-style dry dish of transparent noodles stir-fried in sesame oil with strips of egg, meat and vegetables. It's sometimes served as a side dish or by royal-cuisine restaurants.

Rice Dishes

Bibimbap (literally 'mixed rice') is a hearty one-bowl dish of rice, vegetables and minced beef, often with a fried egg on top. Add *gochujang* (fermented chilli paste) to taste and thoroughly mix it all together before digging in. *Sanchae bibimbap* is made with wild greens; *dolsot bibimbap* is served in a heated stone pot, which crisps the underside of the rice and keeps the dish piping hot. *Boribap* is rice with barley mixed in.

Akin to simplified sushi rolls are *gimbap* – rice rolled in dried seaweed with strips of carrot, radish, egg and ham threading the centre. 'Nude' *gimbap* has no dried seaweed wrap. Sold mainly in convenience stores, *samgak gimbap,* triangular-shaped rice parcels filled with beef, chicken, tuna or *kimchi* and wrapped in *gim* (dried seaweed), are a cheap and tasty snack once you've mastered the art of taking them out of the plastic wrapping.

Traditional, slow-cooked rice porridge *(juk)* is mixed with a wide choice of ingredients and is popular as a healthy, non-spicy comfort food.

RULES OF KOREAN DINING

- Take off your shoes in traditional restaurants where diners sit on floor cushions.
- Pour drinks for others if you notice that their glasses are empty. It's polite to use both hands when pouring or receiving a drink. Don't pour drinks for yourself (unless you're alone).
- Ask for *gawi* (scissors) if you're trying to cut meat and your utensils won't do it.
- Don't touch food with your fingers, except when handling *ssam* (salad leaves used as edible wrapping for other foods).
- Use a spoon rather than chopsticks to eat rice.
- Don't leave your chopsticks or spoon sticking up from your rice bowl. This is taboo, only done with food that is offered to deceased ancestors.
- Don't blow your nose at the table.

Barbecued meat is often eaten wrapped in lettuce with rice, flavourings and sauces

Chicken

Samgyetang is a small whole chicken stuffed with glutinous rice, red dates, garlic and ginseng root, and boiled in broth. *Dakgalbi* is pieces of spicy chicken, cabbage, other vegetables and finger-sized pressed rice cakes, all grilled at your table. *Jjimdak* is a spiced-up mixture of chicken pieces, glass noodles, potatoes and other vegetables. Many informal *hof* (pubs) serve inexpensive barbecued or fried chicken to accompany the beer.

Fish & Seafood

Fish *(saengseon)* and other seafood *(haemul)* is generally served broiled, grilled or in a soup, while *hoe* is raw fish like *sashimi*. Fish is usually served whole. Visit Noryangjin Fish Market to indulge in raw fish, steamed crab, grilled prawns and barbecued shellfish feasts. *Nakji* (octopus) is usually served in a spicy sauce; if you're brave, try the raw version of *sannakji* (baby octopus) – the chopped-up tentacles still wriggle on the plate. *Haemultang* is a seafood soup containing so much chilli that even locals have to mop their brows.

Vegetarian

Although rice and vegetables make up a considerable part of their diet, few Koreans are fully vegetarian. It can be a struggle for vegetarians in ordinary restaurants, because even seemingly vegetarian dishes may contain small amounts of meat, seafood or fish sauce added for flavour. The same is true of kimchi, which may contain anchovies. As a general guide, dishes to order include *bibimbap* (you'll need to request it without meat, or egg), *beoseotjeongol* (mushroom hotpot), *doenjang jjigae* (soybean paste stew), *dubu jjigae* (spicy tofu soup), *jajangmyeon* (noodles and sauce), vegetable *pajeon* (pancakes), and pumpkin *juk* (rice porridge).

Food Books

Eumsik dimibang (Lady Jang; 1670)

Traditional Food: A Taste of Korean Life (Korean Foundation; 2011)

A Korean Mother's Cooking Notes (Chang Sun-young; 1997)

Korean Cuisine: A Cultural Journey (Chung Haekyung; 2009)

Growing Up in a Korean Kitchen (Hi Soo Shin Hepinstall; 2001)

Yakisoba (fried noodles)

Soups & Stews

Soups (*tang* or *guk*) are a highlight of Korean cuisine. 'A meal without soup is like a face without eyes', goes a traditional saying. They vary from spicy seafood and tofu soups to austere broths such as *galbitang* and *seolleongtang,* made from beef bones; the latter is a Seoul speciality. *Gamjatang* is a spicy peasant soup with meaty bones and potato. Tip: if a soup is too spicy, mix in some rice. *Mul kimchi* is a cold, gazpacho-type minimalist soup, and is not spicy.

Stews *(jjigae)* are usually served spiced and sizzling in a heated stone pot. Popular versions are made with tofu *(dubu jjigae),* soybean paste *(doenjang jjigae)* and kimchi. *Beoseotjeongol* is a less spicy but highly recommended mushroom hotpot.

Dating from 1670, the Joseon-era cookbook *Eumsik dimibang* was written by Lady Jang (1598–1680), a member of the *yangban* ruling class. It's regarded as Korea's first cookbook written in *hangeul* (the Korean phonetic alphabet), and made a comeback in 2015 when it was re-published.

Kimchi

Traditionally, kimchi was made to preserve vegetables and ensure proper nutrition during the harsh winters, but it's now eaten year-round and adds zest, zip and a long list of health benefits to any meal. A cold side dish of the spicy national food is served at nearly every Korean meal, whether it's breakfast, lunch or dinner.

Kimchi is generally made with pickled and fermented cabbage seasoned with garlic and red chilli, but it can also be made from cucumbers, white radish and other vegetables. Note, kimchi is not always vegetarian as it can have anchovies added.

Dumplings, Noodles & Pancakes

Mandu (dumplings) and *wangmandu* (literally 'king-sized dumplings') can be filled with minced meat, seafood, vegetables and herbs. Fried, boiled or steamed, they make a tasty snack or addition to a meal. *Manduguk* is *mandu* in soup with seaweed and makes a perfect light lunch.

There's a whole range of *guksu* (noodles) to sample. A much-loved Pyongyang speciality is *naengmyeon,* chewy buckwheat noodles in an icy, sweetish broth, garnished with shredded vegetables and topped with hard-boiled egg – add red-chilli paste or *gyeoja* (mustard) to taste. Popular in summer, it is often eaten after a meat dish like *galbi.* Use the scissors provided to cut up the noodles so they're easier to eat.

Kalguksu is thick, hand-cut noodles usually served in a bland clam-and-vegetable broth. *Ramyeon* is instant noodles often served in a hot chilli soup. Seoulites believe in fighting fire with fire and claim it's a good cure for hangovers.

Pajeon are thick, savoury pancakes the size of pizzas, often filled with spring onions and seafood. *Bindaetteok* are just as big and even more filling, made from ground mung beans with various fillings and fried until a crispy, golden brown – they're best eaten at Gwangjang Market.

Street Food

Some of the best food you'll eat in Seoul is off the street – from snack stalls set up in market alleyways, street carts on the roadside or late-night *pojenchmacha* (tent bars) outside subway stations. Food is always freshly cooked and can range from inexpensive staples such as *bindaetteok* (mungbean pancakes) and *sundae* (blood sausage), to *bibimbap* or ready-made snacks to chow down on the run.

Tteokbokki (hot rice cakes slathered in a bright-red spicy sauce) is a quintessential Korean favourite, along with skewered snacks ranging from spicy grilled meats and *odeng* (boiled fish cakes) to an assortment of sausages on a stick. *Twigim* is also ubiquitous: deep-fried battered prawns, squid or vegetables similar to Japanese tempura.

Freshly baked sweet snacks are abundant. Steaming *gyeran ppang* (egg cooked in puck-shaped bread) are popular in winter, while *bungeoppang* (fish-shaped pastries filled with sweet red-bean paste) and *hotteok* (deep-fried dough pancakes made with brown sugar, nuts, honey and cinnamon) are all delicious comfort foods.

Pressed fish and dried squid are both old-school snacks, and a popular accompaniment to beer. Those feeling more adventurous can munch on *beondegi* (silkworm larvae), which are sold by the cup from street vendors.

For something more Westernised, 'toast' is a trusty favourite – sandwiches cooked on a hot plate and filled with egg, ham, cheese and often sweetened with kiwi jam. They're equally good for breakfast or a late-night tipsy snack.

Royal palace cuisine, a style of cooking now replicated in fancy restaurants for the general public, requires elaborate preparation and presentation. It includes dishes such as *gujeolpan* (snacks wrapped in small pancakes) and *sinseollo* (hotpot).

MAKGEOLLI APPRECIATION

In line with the recent revival of traditional Korean culture among the younger generation, old-time drinks such as *makgeolli* have become revered. It's a trend worth exploring, akin to the craft beer movement, where local brewers strive for chemical-free, top-quality, handcrafted products. However, it's very much a local scene, and one that's hard to crack. So thankfully several groups have emerged, on a mission to spread the word about the wonder that is *makgeolli*.

Sool Company (p31) offers lessons on how to brew your own *makgeolli* based on recipes from the 340-year-old cookbook *Eumsik dimibang*, and runs traditional liquor brewery tours and tastings, among other events.

TAKASHI IMAGES/SHUTTERSTOCK ©

Above Tea ceremony

Left Namdaemun Market (p86) stall

Odeng (boiled fish cakes)

Dining Etiquette

If you're invited out by Korean colleagues or friends, you'll find it difficult if not downright impossible to pay the bill, or even contribute towards it. Arguing about who should have the honour of picking up the cheque is a common scene at the cashier's desk.

Meals are usually eaten communally, so dishes are placed in the centre of the table and diners put a little from each common dish in their own dish or bowl.

At some traditional restaurants, customers sit on cushions at low tables on raised sections of the floor (the *ondol,* an underfloor heating system, is beneath). Before stepping up, always remove your shoes.

Budae jjigae (or *Johnsontang*) is a unique Seoul dish that originated in the hungry years after the Korean War. At this time tins of ham, sausages and baked beans from American army bases (such as Yongsan) were bought on the black market and mixed with noodles and vegetable scraps to make a meal.

Drinks

Bottled and canned soft drinks are everywhere. Some uniquely Korean choices are grape juice with whole grapes inside and *sikhye,* rice punch with rice grains inside. Health tonics, fortified with vitamins, fibre, ginseng and other medicinal herbs, are available in shops and pharmacies; many claim to boost your virility.

Tea

Tea *(cha)* is a staple, with the term also used to describe drinks brewed without tea leaves. The most common leaf tea is *nokcha* (green tea); *hongcha* (black tea) is harder to find. Non-leaf teas include the ubiquitous *boricha* (barley tea), *daechucha* (red-date tea), *omijacha* (five-flavour berry tea), *yujacha* (citron tea) and *insamcha* (ginseng tea). They may be served hot or cold.

Soju (local vodka)

Alcoholic Beverages

Koreans drink so much *soju* – a highly potent mix of ethanol mixed with water and flavouring – that the Jinro-brand *soju* (you'll see the green bottles everywhere) is the top-selling brand of spirits *worldwide*. The size of the *soju* bottle is calculated to fill only seven shot glasses. It might go down easily, but *soju* can induce a monstrous hangover the next day. Go for the higher-quality stuff distilled from grain (try Andong Soju or Jeonju Leegangju); it offers a far more delicate flavour, but can have an alcohol content of up to 45%.

Makgeolli is a traditional farmers brew made from unrefined, fermented rice wine. Generally around 5% to 8% alcohol, it has a cloudy appearance and a sweetish flavour. It is traditionally served in a brass kettle and poured into shallow brass bowls, although Seoul has several bars now where higher-quality styles of *makgeolli* (as opposed to hangover-inducing convenience-store brands), akin to a range of Japanese sake, are served and savoured.

A host of other sweetish traditional spirits are brewed or distilled from grains, fruits and roots. Many are regional or seasonal. *Bokbunjaju* is made from wild raspberries, *meoruju* from wild fruit, *maesilju* from green plums and *insamju* from ginseng.

Beer is also a popular choice of beverage. The big local brands are Cass, Hite and OB, all widely available from convenience stores and *hof*. Craft beer is now firmly established in Seoul, too, with microbreweries and brew pubs all over the city producing a range of locally inspired ales.

Belief Systems & Cultural Traditions

Seoul was once divided strictly along nearly inescapable class lines and hierarchical distinctions, but its sensibility is now much like any modern city. People often hold loyalties to school, company and church, but egalitarianism has given way to greater individualism. Still, strong traces of Korea's particular identity linger. Remnants of its Confucian past coexist alongside 'imported' spiritual beliefs, denting the myth that modernisation necessitates secularisation.

The Main Belief Systems

Of the four streams of spiritual influence in Korea, Confucianism and Buddhism are the most important. Christianity, which first made inroads into Korea in the 18th century, also plays a major role in the lives of many, while the ancient superstitions of shamanism endure as well.

Above: Traditional temple ceremony

Confucianism

The state religion of the Joseon dynasty, Confucianism still lives on as a kind of ethical bedrock (at least subconsciously) in the minds of most Koreans, especially the elderly.

The Chinese philosopher Confucius (552–479 BCE) devised a system of ethics that emphasised devotion to parents and family, loyalty to friends, justice, peace, education, reform and humanitarianism. He also urged that respect and deference should be given to those in positions of authority – a philosophy exploited by Korea's Joseon-dynasty ruling elite. Confucius firmly believed that men were superior to women and that a woman's place was in the home.

Visit the spirit shrines of Joseon royalty at the splendid Jongmyo. A grand Confucian ceremony honouring the deceased is held there every May.

These ideas led to the system of civil-service examinations *(gwageo),* where one could gain position through ability and merit, rather than from noble birth and connections (though it was, in fact, still an uphill battle for the common-born). Confucius preached against corruption, war, torture and excessive taxation. He was the first teacher to open his school to all students solely on the basis of their willingness to learn.

As Confucianism trickled into Korea, it evolved into neo-Confucianism, which combined the sage's original ethical and political ideas with the quasi-religious practice of ancestor worship and the notion of the eldest male as spiritual head of the family.

Buddhism

When first introduced during the Koguryo dynasty in 370 CE, Buddhism coexisted with shamanism. Many Buddhist temples have a *samseong-gak* (three-spirit hall) on their grounds, which houses shamanist deities such as the Mountain God.

THE CONFUCIAN MINDSET

Confucianism is a social philosophy, a prescription for achieving a harmonious society. Not everyone follows the rules, but Confucianism does continue to shape the Korean paradigm. These are some of the key principles and practices.

➡ Obedience and respect towards seniors – parents, teachers, the boss, older brothers and sisters – is crucial. Heavy penalties (including physical punishment) are incurred for stepping out of line.

➡ Seniors get obedience, but they also have obligations. Older siblings help out younger siblings with tuition fees, and the boss always pays for lunch.

➡ Education defines a civilised person. Despite having built a successful business, a high-school graduate would still feel shame at their lack of scholastic credentials.

➡ Men and women have separate roles. A woman's role is service, obedience and management of household affairs. Men don't do housework or look after children.

➡ Status and dignity are critical. Every action reflects on the family, company and country.

➡ Everything on and beyond the earth is in a hierarchy. People never forget who is senior and who is junior to them.

➡ Families are more important than individuals. Everyone's purpose in life is to improve the family's reputation and wealth. No one should choose a career or marry someone against their parents' wishes – a bad choice could bring ruin to a family. Everyone must marry and have a son to continue the family line. For these reasons homosexuality is considered a grossly unnatural act.

➡ Loyalty is important. A loyal liar is a virtuous person.

➡ Be modest and don't be extravagant. Only immoral women wear revealing clothes. Be frugal with praise.

Confucian ceremony

About 90% of Korean Buddhist temples belong to the Jogye order (www.koreanbuddhism.net). Buddha's birthday in May is a national holiday, which includes an extravagant lantern parade in Seoul.

The religion was persecuted during the Joseon period, when its temples were tolerated only in the remote mountains. Buddhism suffered another sharp decline after WWII as Koreans pursued more worldly goals. But South Korea's success in achieving developed-nation status, coupled with a growing interest in spiritual values, is encouraging a Buddhist revival. Temple visits have increased and large sums of money are flowing into temple reconstruction.

Korean Buddhism is also gaining international attention by operating templestay programs for travellers. Many Koreans take part in these templestays, regardless of whether they are Buddhist or not, as a chance to escape societal pressures and clear their minds.

Christianity

Korea's first exposure to Christianity was in the late 18th century. It came via the Jesuits from the Chinese imperial court when a Korean aristocrat was baptised in Beijing in 1784. The Catholic faith took hold and spread so quickly that it was perceived as a threat by the Korean government and was vigorously suppressed, creating the country's first Christian martyrs.

Christianity got a second chance in the 1880s, with the arrival of American Protestant missionaries who founded schools and hospitals, and gained many followers – so many, in fact, that today Christianity is reckoned to have more followers than Buddhism.

Shamanism

Historically, shamanism influenced Korean spirituality. While not a religion per se, it does involve communication with spirits through intermediaries known as *mudang* (female shamans). Although not widely

Girls in *hanbok* (traditional clothing)

practised today, shamanist ceremonies are sometimes held to cure illness, ward off financial problems or guide a deceased family member safely into the spirit world.

Ceremonies involve contacting spirits who are attracted by lavish offerings of food and drink. Drums beat and the *mudang* dances herself into a frenzied state that allows her to communicate with the spirits and be possessed by them. Resentments felt by the dead can plague the living and cause all sorts of misfortune, so their spirits need placating. For shamanists, death does not end relationships. It simply takes another form.

On Inwangsan in northwestern Seoul, ceremonies take place in or near the historic Inwangsan Guksadang shrine.

Koreans give their family name first, followed by their birth name, which is typically two syllables, ie Lee Myung-bak. There are less than 300 Korean family names, with Kim, Lee (or Yi) and Park accounting for 45% of the total.

Competitive Lives

The country's rise from the ashes of the Korean War, construction workers on the job seven days a week, computer-game addicts: they're all strands cut from the same cloth, namely the country's tenacious, pit-bull spirit. Once Seoulites lock onto something, it's difficult for them to break away. Life is competitive and everything is taken seriously, be it tenpin bowling, hiking or overseas corporate expansion.

'A person without education is like a beast wearing clothes' is a proverb that nails Korea's obsession with education. To get into one of the top Seoul universities, high-school students go through a gruelling examination process, studying 14 hours a day, often in private cram schools at night, for their one annual shot at the college entrance test.

Seoulites are also fanatical about health. The millions of hikers who stream into the mountains on weekends are not only enjoying nature

MINDING YOUR KOREAN MANNERS

Most locals understand that visitors do not mean any disrespect when they commit a minor social faux pas. But you'll be even more warmly received when it is obvious that you've gone out of your way to burnish your graces, Korean style.

Shoes off In any residence, temple, guesthouse or Korean-style restaurant, leave your shoes at the door. And socks are better than bare feet.

Artful bow Though you may see members of the royal court drop to the ground to greet the king on Korean TV dramas, a quick, short bow – essentially a nod of the head – is most respectful for meetings and departures.

All hands on deck Give and receive any object using both hands – especially name cards (essential for any formal and many informal meetings), money and gifts.

Giving gifts When you visit someone at their home, bring along a little token of your appreciation. The gift can be almost anything – flowers, fruit, a bottle of liquor, tea or something from your home country. Your host may at first strongly refuse your gift. This is a gesture of graciousness. Keep insisting, and they will accept it 'reluctantly'. For the same reason, your host will not open the package immediately.

Paying the bill Fighting to pay the bill is a common phenomenon, though the quid pro quo is that one person pays this time and the other fights a little harder to pick up the cheque next time. If a Korean takes you under his or her wing, it's difficult to pay for anything.

Get over here Don't beckon someone using your forefinger. Place your hand out, palm down and flutter all your fingers at once.

Loss of face In interpersonal relations, the least desirable outcome is to somehow 'lower the harmony *(gibun)*'. A mishandled remark or potentially awkward scene should be smoothed over as soon as possible, and if you sense someone actively trying to change the subject, go with the flow. An argument or any situation that could lead to embarrassment should be avoided at all costs.

Smile, you're embarrassed Often, potential loss of face – say, when someone realises they are clearly in the wrong – will result in an unlikely reaction: a wide smile. No, you're not being mocked; you've just been told 'I'm sorry'. So if a taxi almost mows you down, only to roll down his window and flash you a big grin, he's not off his rocker – he's showing his embarrassment, which is both a form of apology and a gesture of sympathy.

but also keeping fit. Thousands of health foods and drinks are sold in markets and pharmacies, which stock traditional as well as Western medicines. Nearly every food claims to be a 'wellbeing' product or an aphrodisiac – 'good for stamina' is the local phrase.

Contemporary & Traditional Culture

Driven by the latest technology and fast-evolving trends, Seoul can sometimes seem like one of the most connected cities on the planet. On subway trains and in the streets, passengers tune into their favourite TV shows via their smartphones and tablet computers. In PC *bang* (computer-game rooms), millions of diehard fans battle at online games, while in *noraebang* (karaoke rooms), wannabe K-Popsters belt out the latest hit tunes.

General fashions in Seoul tend to be international and up to the moment, too. However, it's not uncommon to see some people wearing *hanbok,* the traditional clothing that follows the Confucian principle of unadorned modesty. Women wear a loose-fitting short blouse with long sleeves and a voluminous long skirt, while men wear a

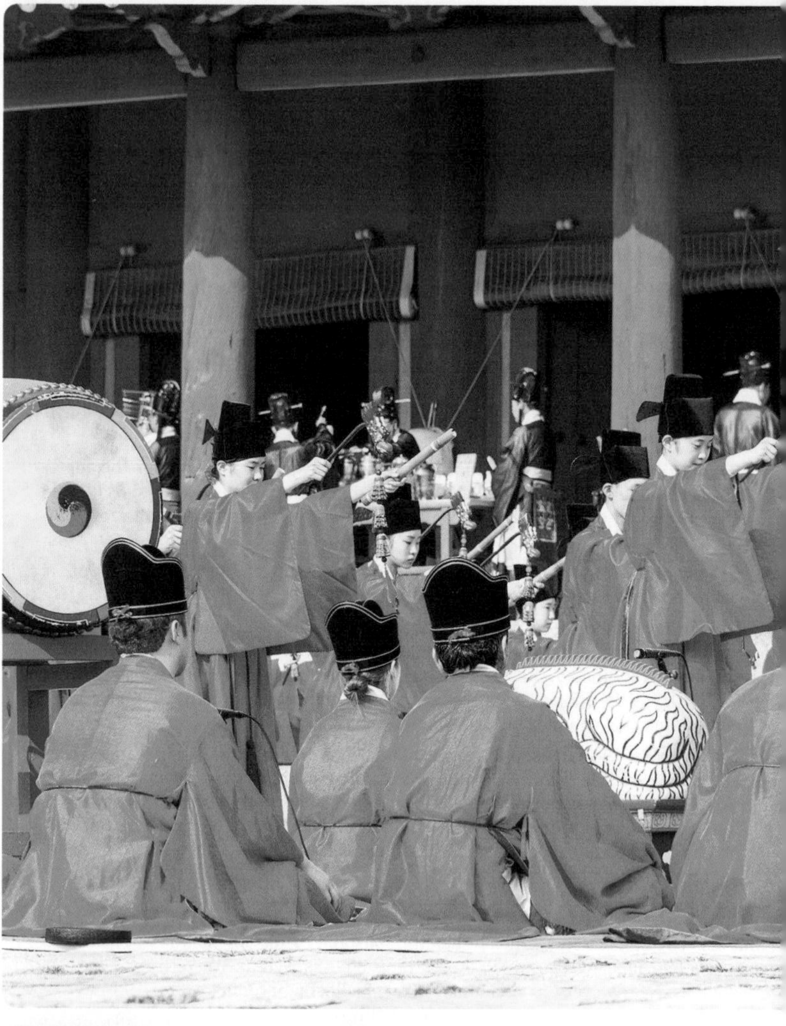

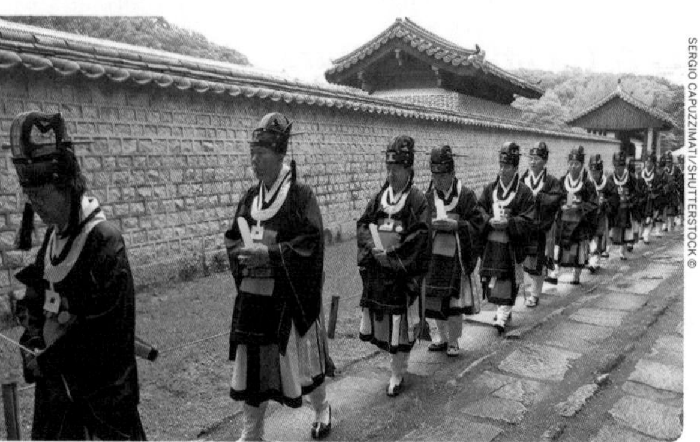

Above: Ceremony at Jongmyo (p62)
Left: Jongmyo Daeje (p24) procession

SERGIO CAPUZZIMATI/SHUTTERSTOCK ©

Bongeun-sa (p123)

jacket and baggy trousers. Today *hanbok* is worn mostly at weddings or special events, and even then it may be a more comfortable 'updated' version.

Fortune-Telling

These days most people visit one of the city's street-tent fortune-tellers for a bit of fun, but no doubt some still take it seriously. For a *saju* (reading of your future), inform the fortune-teller of the date, including the hour, of your birth; another option is *gunhap* (a love-life reading), where a couple gives their birth details and the fortune-teller pronounces their compatibility. Expect to pay ₩10,000 for *saju* and double that for *gunhap*. If you don't speak the language, you'll need someone to translate.

Culture Books

- *Notes on Things Korean (Suzanne Crowder Han; 1995)*
- *Understanding Koreans and Their Culture (Choi Joon-sik; 2007)*
- *Korea Bug (J Scott Burgeson; 2005)*
- *48 Keywords that Describe Korea (Kim Jin-woo & Lee Nam-hoon; 2006)*

Seoul's Architectural Treasures

Seoul's skyline – dominated by skyscrapers and endless high-rise apartments – at first suggests no building has survived the war and economic modernisation. But examples of architecture from all periods of Seoul's history do remain, resulting in a juxtaposed hotchpotch that at times finds a quirky harmony. Explore the city and you'll discover not only fortress walls, grand palaces and decorative temples, but also charming early-20th-century *hanok* (traditional wooden homes) and dramatic contemporary structures, such as the new City Hall and Dongdaemun Design Plaza.

Above: Korean *hanok* (traditional wooden home)

Traditional Architecture

There are three main types of traditional architecture found in Seoul: palaces, temples and homes. They are all primarily made of wood, with no nails used – a system of braces and brackets holds the elements together.

They were (and often still are) heated using an ingenious system of circulating underfloor smoke tunnels called *ondol*.

Palaces

During the Joseon era (1392–1897), five main palaces were constructed in the royal capital. These were cities unto themselves, massive complexes with administrative offices, residences, pleasure pavilions and royal gardens, all hemmed in by imposing walls. A prominent feature is the roof of these structures, which is made from heavy clay tiles with dragons or other mythical beasts embossed on the end tile. The strikingly bold, predominantly green-and-orange paintwork under the eaves is called *dancheong*. Ceilings are often intricately carved and coloured.

After centuries of invasion and war, Seoul's palaces have been painstakingly rebuilt multiple times, sometimes changing their shape altogether.

Constructed around the 1st century CE, the Mongchon-toseong (Mongchon Clay Fortress) was built on the southern banks of the Han River during the kingdom of Baekje (18 BCE–475 CE). It's still there in Olympic Park.

Temples, Shrines & Royal Tombs

Korean temples, like palaces, are painted in natural colours. On the outside, murals depict the life of Buddha or parables of self liberation; inside are paintings of Buddhist heavens – and occasionally hells. Look for intricately carved lattice in the Buddhist shrines, and for a *sansingak*, or Mountain God Hall, which contains an image of the deity in question and represents the accommodation of Korean Buddhism to Korea's pre-existing shamanist beliefs.

Also visually striking in their command of space and use of natural materials are the royal shrines and burial tombs of the Joseon dynasty, 40-odd of which are on the Unesco World Heritage list. In these tombs, each similarly arranged on hillsides according to the rules of Confucianism and feng shui, are buried every Joseon ruler right up to the last, Emperor Sunjong (r 1907–10).

Top Traditional Buildings

Gyeongbokgung (p58)

Bosingak (p70)

Jongmyo (p62)

Sajikdan (p66)

Sungnyemun (p84)

Deoksugung (p82)

Hanok

Traditional houses, or *hanok*, are complex in design yet masterfully understated. These one-storey homes are crafted entirely from wood, save for the clay tiled roofs, and insulated with mud and straw. They're heated by the underfloor system called *ondol*. Traditionally, windows were made of a thin, translucent paper that allows daylight to stream in.

Unlike the ostentatious manor homes of Europe, even an aristocrat's lavish *hanok* was designed to blend with nature; they are typically left unpainted, their brown-and-tan earth tones giving off a warm, intimate feel. All of the rooms face inwards onto a courtyard (or *madang*), which usually includes a simple garden. Life was lived on the floor, so all the furniture was low-slung, and people sat and slept on mats rather than chairs and beds.

Social rank dictated the decorations, beam size, roof pitch and number of rooms – these rules were not relaxed until the 1930s. The traditional home was also divided into two sections: the *sarangchae* for men and the *anchae* for women. In larger homes, these comprised different buildings, surrounded by walls and gates. In the *anchae*, the women of the family raised children, did the cooking and ran the household. The *sarangchae* housed the library, an ancestral shrine and rooms in which to receive guests, who seated themselves on comfortable low cushions and enjoyed a tea service.

One of the programs of the National Trust of Korea (www.nationaltrust.or.kr), an NGO charged with helping to protect the country's environment and national relics, focuses on the preservation of *hanok*.

With South Korea's modernisation, desire to live in *hanok* waned. Their thin walls prevented privacy. There was no easy space to install indoor toilets. Rooms were small, and living on the floor had its inconveniences. In

Olympic Park (p121)

Books

Hanok – Traditional Korean Houses (various authors; 2015)

Joseon Royal Court Culture (Shin Myung-ho; 2004)

Seoul's Historic Walks (Cho In-Souk & Robert Koehler; 2008)

City as Art: 100 Notable Works of Architecture in Seoul (Yim Seock-jae; 2011)

comparison, Seoul's modern high-rises offered amenities galore. Recently, however, Seoul has seen a revival of interest in traditional homes, with increased efforts to preserve their unique character.

Bukchon has Seoul's largest concentration of *hanok*, mostly dating from the 1930s. To see larger-scale *hanok* in a more traditional setting, visit Namsangol Hanok Village at the foot of Namsan.

Early Modern & Colonial Architecture

In the late 19th century, Western and Japanese missionaries, traders and diplomats flooded into the Hermit Kingdom. The architecture of this period is often regarded as 'colonial', although some of it purely represents Korean attempts to modernise along Western lines.

Churches were usually designed by French, American or British missionaries, including wonderful examples of Gothic and Romanesque styles, but much of Seoul's early modern architectural heritage was built by the Japanese, who destroyed significant chunks of the capital's traditional buildings (particularly palaces) in the process.

Japanese colonial architects often emulated Western Renaissance and neo-baroque architectural styles, although you'll also find the occasional art nouveau or other modernist style thrown in.

Modern Architecture 1950s–80s

Though the needs of post–Korean War reconstruction required a focus on more utilitarian concerns, much of Korea's modern architecture is distinct, usually following one of two trajectories: either an attempt to reinterpret traditional Korean architecture in concrete and steel, or to communicate Seoul's cutting-edge technological prowess.

Lotte World Tower (p124) and Mall (p131)

First and perhaps foremost of Korea's post-independence architects was Japanese-trained Kim Swoo-geun, whose early work reflected the influence of Le Corbusier and Kenzo Tange. He is responsible for the curving lines of the Olympic Stadium and the ivy-clad Kyungdong Presbyterian Church (1981). Among other local architectural greats are Kim Chung-up, whose work includes the soaring Peace Gate at Olympic Park, and Kim Joong-up, responsible for the 31-storey smoked-glass Samil Building (1969), Seoul's first international-style skyscraper.

Contemporary Architecture

Spurred by its winning bid to be the World Design Capital in 2010, the city government and major construction firms went on a building spree, hiring such luminaries as the late Zaha Hadid for the Dongdaemun Design Plaza and Park, and US architecture firm Kohn Pedersen Fox for the 123-storey Lotte World Tower – Korea's highest building.

The work of these celebrated international architects shouldn't overshadow that of local talents, who have imposed their creative visions on a series of small- and large-scale projects adding to Seoul's built beauty. The shopping complex Ssamziegil in Insa-dong (designed by Choi Moon-gyu and Gabriel Kroiz) and Bae Dae-young's Why Butter building in Hongdae (housing KT&G SangsangMadang) are both fine examples of contemporary buildings with a strong point of view.

Top Early Modern & Colonial Buildings

Cheondogyo Temple (p70)

Myeong-dong Catholic Cathedral (p85)

Bank of Korea Money Museum (p84)

Culture Station Seoul 284 (p84)

Seodaemun Prison History Hall (p145)

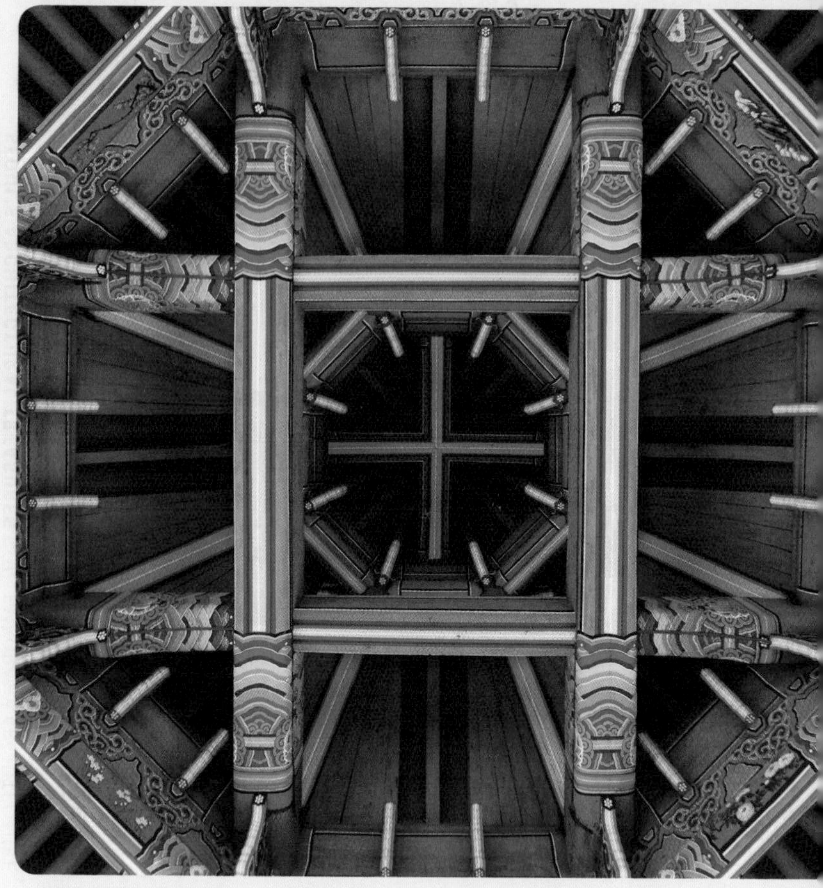

A City of the Arts

Seoul has long been the nexus of Korea's spectacular range of arts. Colourful costumes set the scene for traditional *pansori* operas. Folk dances such as *samulnori,* with its whirling dervish of dancers, seamlessly meld the cacophonous and melodic. Artisans preserve the ancient art of calligraphy with their silken strokes. Seoul takes national pride of place in the modern arts, too. Korea's film directors are regularly feted at international festivals, and the city's art museums and galleries burst with contemporary works.

Visual Art

Traditional

Above: Tapgol Park (p69) pagoda

Stone Buddhist statues and pagodas such as the one in Tapgol Park are among the oldest artworks in Seoul. Some marvellous examples of cast-bronze Buddhas can be seen in the National Museum of Korea. Zen-style Buddhist art can be seen inside and outside the temples Jogye-sa and Bongeun-sa, and you'll find stone and wooden effigies of shamanist spirit guardians outside the National Folk Museum in the grounds of the main palace, Gyeongbokgung.

Chinese influence is paramount in traditional Korean painting. The basic tools (brush and water-based ink) are those of calligraphy, which influenced painting in both technique and theory. The brush line, which varies in thickness and tone, is the most important feature. Traditional landscape painting is meant to surround the viewer, and there is no fixed viewpoint as in traditional Western painting. A talented artist who painted everyday scenes was Kim Hong-do (1745–1816). Court ceremonies, portraits, flowers, birds and traditional symbols of longevity – the sun, water, rocks, mountains, clouds, pine trees, turtles and cranes – were popular subjects.

A fascinating traditional Korean art form is *hanji* (handmade paper). Often dyed in soft colours, *hanji* can be pressed and lacquered so that it can serve as a waterproof cup or plate.

Modern & Contemporary

Within Seoul's thriving contemporary-art scene, local artists frequently mix Korean motifs and themes, and sometimes traditional techniques, with a modern vision. Insa-dong, Bukchon, Samcheong-dong and Tongui-dong are all packed with small galleries, often with free shows; you'll also find major galleries south of the river in Cheongdam.

There's a healthy street-art scene too in Seoul. Particularly in Hongdae near Hongik University subway (exit 4) with its backstreets and alleys full of cool stencils, murals, graffiti and paste-ups. Mullae Arts village and HBC Art Village (in Haebangchon) also have plenty of urban art to check out. You'll also find several mural villages where artists are commissioned to beautify downtrodden gritty neighbourhoods. Most well-known is Ihwa Maeul, now a hugely popular tourist sight. Another emerging area for street art is Seongsu-dong, commonly referred to as 'Seoul's Brooklyn'.

Ceramics & Pottery

Archaeologists have unearthed Korean pottery that dates back some 10,000 years, although it wasn't until the early 12th century that the art form reached a peak, with skilled potters turning out wonderful celadon pottery with its characteristic green tinge. Visit the National Museum of Korea for one of the best displays. Original celadon fetches huge sums at auctions, but modern copies are widely available.

Major modern Korean artists include Nam June Paik (1932–2006), whose new-media installations can be seen at Nam June Paik Art Center and the National Museum of Contemporary Art, and Kim Tschang Yeul (1929–), whose work can be seen at the Leeum Samsung Museum of Art.

Music

Korean traditional music *(gugak)* is played on stringed instruments, most notably the *gayageum* (12-stringed zither) and *haegum* (two-stringed fiddle) as well as on chimes, gongs, cymbals, drums, horns and flutes. Court music *(jeongak)* is slow and stately, while folk music such as *samulnori* is fast and lively. In recent years there's been a revival of traditional Korean music among the younger generation, with audience numbers tripling to watch *gugak* performances. Young talents such as Song So-hee, and Luna Lee (who plays covers of Western hits on the *gayageum*) have played a part in popularising *gugak*.

Similar to Western opera, *changgeuk* can involve a large cast of characters. An unusual type of opera is *pansori*. It features a solo storyteller (usually female) singing to the beat of a drum, while emphasising dramatic moments with a flick of her fan. The singing is strong and sorrowful: some say if *pansori* is done correctly, the performer will have blood in her mouth upon finishing. Only a few *pansori* dramas have survived; *Chunhyang*, the story of a woman's faith and endurance, is the most popular.

Musician playing a *gayageum* (12-stringed zither)

At the park in front of Jongmyo you may see pensioners dancing to 'trot' music. Short for 'foxtrot', this musical form combines Korean scales with Western harmonies and sounds similar to Japanese *enka* music.

K-Pop

Dating back to 1990s boy bands in Seoul, Korean pop (K-Pop) has been at the forefront of the Korean Wave (aka *hallyu*) well before Psy started busting out his crazy moves. The popularity of K-Pop has reached fanatical levels among devotees in Korea, China and Japan, and this has extended into a worldwide phenomenon with fans from the Middle East to Latin America.

But it was in 2012, with Psy's smash hit 'Gangnam Style', that things really exploded. Topping the charts in nearly 30 countries, the song single-handedly thrust K-Pop into the spotlight of Western countries and was one of the first Youtube videos to exceed a billion views.

Fans of K-Pop will have ample opportunity to enjoy tunes – both recorded and live – by their favourite singers and bands in Seoul. Other than Psy, among solo singers few have attained the commercial success of BoA and her male counterpart Rain. Among the current-day K-Pop acts, popular groups include BTS, EXO, Wanna One, BTOB, Bigbang, SHINee, the 13-member group Super Junior, Wonder Girls and Girls' Generation.

K-Indie

Seoul is home to Korea's independent music scene. Known locally as K-Indie, it's an all-encompassing genre that includes bands playing original music ranging from indie, punk, garage and metal to shoegaze, electronica and hip-hop.

Hongdae is the home of Seoul's K-Indie scene, with dive-y venues catering to bands. The scene has flourished in recent years, with many bands receiving international recognition. Some to watch out for include Jambinai, a post-rock band who combine traditional instruments with

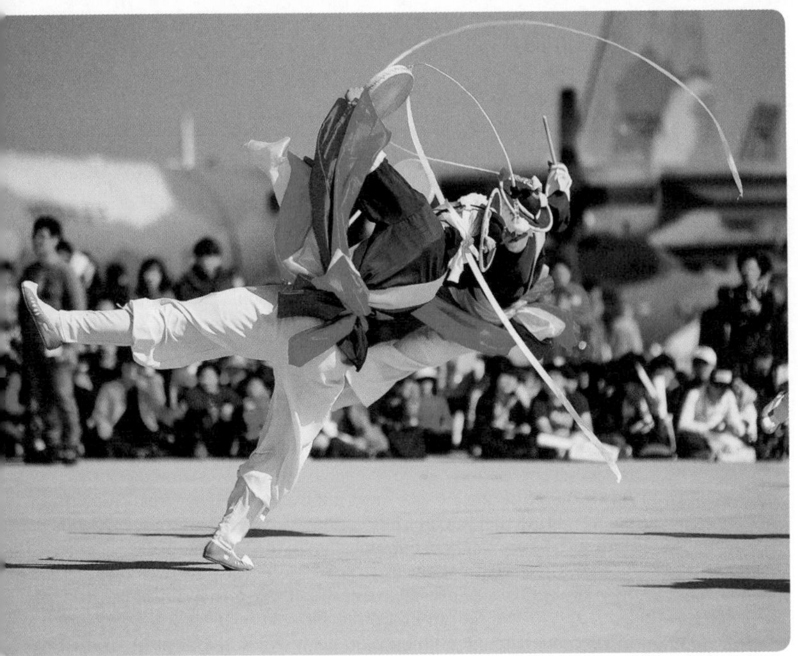

Samulnori dancer (p204)

heavy guitar riffs; alt-indie bands the Dead Buttons and the Koxx; punk rockers the Patients and Yellow Monsters, and electronica act Idiotape. All are regulars on the international festival circuit.

Cinema

Seoul's Chungmuro neighbourhood has long been the heart of the nation's vibrant and critically acclaimed film industry, which has been a major component of *hallyu* or the Korean Wave of popular culture sweeping across Asia and the world.

Directors haven't shied away from major issues, such as the Korean War with *Taegukgi* (2004) and its turbulent political aftermath in *The President's Last Bang* (2005). Pervasive social issues in modern Seoul – such as the blistering pace of city life and the shifting notion of family – are tackled in films like *The Way Home* (2002) and *Family Ties* (2006), both quietly touching. The horror films *Memento Mori* (1999) and *A Tale of Two Sisters* (2003) provide gruesome shocks for the genre aficionado, as do Seoul-based monster movies *The Host* (2006) and *Train to Busan* (2016), which also offer a satirical critique of social issues in Korea. For an action-revenge flick – something Korea excels at – nothing tops the jaw-dropping *Old Boy* (2003), a regular contender for Korea's best film of all time. *Pieta* (2012) by arthouse director Ki-duk Kim became the first Korean movie to win a best international film award, taking the Golden Lion at the Venice Film Festival.

Filmmaking used to be a boys club. No longer: superb films by female directors are receiving greater recognition. These include Jeong Jae-eun's *Take Care of My Cat* (2001), the story of five girls in the suburbs outside Seoul, and Yim Soon-rye's *Waikiki Brothers* (2001), a sobering exploration of those left behind by Korea's economic rise. Yim's *Forever*

Koreanfilm.org is a useful resource covering all aspects of the industry and featuring numerous reviews.

Elegant court dances, accompanied by an orchestra and dating back 600 years, are performed in front of Jongmyo on the first Sunday of May.

the Moment (2008) follows the Korean women's handball team into the 2004 Olympics.

Theatre & Dance

Seoul's thriving theatre scene is based mainly around Daehangno, where more than 50 theatres of varying sizes stage everything from rock musicals and satirical plays to opera and translations of Western classics. Nearly all shows are in Korean, although a handful of nonverbal shows include the excellent Nanta (p88) and Jump.

Korean folk dances include dynamic *seungmu* (drum dances), the satirical and energetic *talchum* (mask dances) and solo improvisational *salpuri* (shamanist dances). Most popular are *samulnori* dance troupes, who perform in brightly coloured traditional clothing, twirling a long tassel from a cap on their heads as they dance and beat a drum or gong.

Gig Guides

Korean Indie (www.koreanindie.com)

Groove (www.groovekorea.com)

10 Magazine (www.10mag.com)

Korea Gig Guide (www.koreagigguide.com)

Seoul in Literature

Seoul has always been a city of writers. Part of the Joseon-era government-service exam *(gwageo)* involved composing verse. During the Joseon dynasty, literature meant *sijo,* short nature poems that were handwritten (using a brush and ink) in Chinese characters, even after the invention of *hangeul* (the Korean phonetic alphabet) in the 15th century.

In the 20th century, however, there was a sharp turn away from Chinese (and Japanese) influence of any kind. Western ideas and ideals took hold, and existentialism and other international literary trends found footing, but through a unique and pervasive Korean lens. A fascinating example is *Three Generations* (1931), a novel by Yom Sang-seop that follows the soap opera-ish and ultimately tragic lives of the wealthy Jo family under the Japanese occupation of the time.

More recent is Kim Young-ha's *I Have the Right to Destroy Myself* (2007), which delves into alienation in contemporary Seoul, and *The Vegetarian* (2015) by Han Kang, a dark and disturbing Kafkaesque account of a woman's fantasy to turn into a tree.

Survival Guide

Transport

ARRIVING IN SEOUL

Most likely you'll arrive at Incheon International Airport. If you're travelling from within Korea, your arrival point could also be Gimpo International Airport, or Seoul or Yongsan train stations, or one of the long-distance bus stations. Ferries to Incheon, west of Seoul, connect the country with China. Flights, cars and tours can be booked online at www.lonelyplanet.com/bookings.

Incheon International Airport

The main international gateway is **Incheon International Airport** (www.airport.kr; 🛜), 52km west of central Seoul on the island of Yeongjongdo. Regularly ranked as one of the world's best airports, this top-class operation was enhanced even further in 2018 with the opening of Terminal 2 in time for the 2018 Winter Olympics.

Korean Air (www.koreanair.com), the nation's biggest airline, serving 123 countries worldwide, operates out of Terminal 2.

Bus

Two types of bus run from the airport to downtown Seoul. The **city limousine buses** take at least an hour to reach destinations around Seoul (₩9,000 to ₩15,000, 5.30am to 10pm, every 10 to 30 minutes) depending on traffic. The deluxe **KAL limousine buses** (www.kallimousine.com; ₩14,000) run along four routes, dropping passengers at over 20 major hotels downtown.

Taxi

Regular metered taxis charge around ₩60,000 to ₩80,000 for the 70-minute journey to central Seoul. From midnight to 4am regular taxis charge 20% extra.

Train

There are two types of **A'REX Airport Express** (Airport Railroad Express; www.arex.or.kr; express train 1-way adult/child ₩9000/7000, all-stop train basic 1-way adult ₩4150, to terminal 2 ₩4950) trains from the airport to Seoul station. The **express train** (43 to 48 minutes) departs every 30 minutes. The more frequent **all-stop trains** take 55 minutes from Terminal 1 and an hour from Terminal 2. Trains run from 5.20am to 11.45pm.

Gimpo International Airport

The bulk of domestic flights (and a handful of international routes) touch down at the more centrally located

CLIMATE CHANGE & TRAVEL

Every form of transport that relies on carbon-based fuel generates CO_2, the main cause of human-induced climate change. Modern travel is dependent on aeroplanes, which might use less fuel per kilometre per person than most cars but travel much greater distances. The altitude at which aircraft emit gases (including CO_2) and particles also contributes to their climate change impact. Many websites offer 'carbon calculators' that allow people to estimate the carbon emissions generated by their journey and, for those who wish to do so, to offset the impact of the greenhouse gases emitted with contributions to portfolios of climate-friendly initiatives throughout the world. Lonely Planet offsets the carbon footprint of all staff and author travel.

Gimpo International Airport (☎02-1661 2626; www.airport.co.kr), 18km west of the city centre.

Local airline **Air Busan** (☎02-1666 3060; www.airbusan.com; Gimpo International Airport) operates from here.

Bus

City/KAL limousine buses run every 10 minutes to central Seoul (from ₩5000/7000, around 40 minutes, depending on traffic).

Subway

Lines 5 and 9 connect the airport with the city (₩1450, 35 minutes).

Train

A'REX (Airport Railroad Express; www.arex.or.kr; express train 1-way adult/child ₩9000/7000, all-stop train basic 1-way adult ₩4150, to terminal 2 ₩4950) trains run to Seoul station (₩1300, 15 minutes).

Taxi

A taxi costs around ₩35,000 to the city centre and takes from 40 minutes to an hour.

Seoul Station

Seoul Station is the hub of the domestic rail network operated by **Korean National Railroad** (www.letskorail.com). Tickets can be bought up to one month in advance at many travel agents, as well as at train stations or online. Booking ahead is advised. If you plan to travel by train a lot over a short period, consider buying a 'KR pass' (see the website for details).

The fastest train is the KTX (Korea Train Express), which operates at speeds of 300km/h. A grade down are *saemaeul* services, which only stop in major towns. *Mugunghwa* and other commuter trains are comfortable and fast, but stop more often.

CITY AIR TERMINALS

If you're flying Korean Air, **Asiana** (☎02-2669 8000; www.flyasiana.com) or Jeju Air, you can check in your luggage and go through immigration at the **City Airport Terminal** (Map p238; www.arex.or.kr; Seoul Station; ⊙check in 5.20am-7pm; Ⓢ Line 1 or 4 to Seoul Station) inside Seoul Station, then hop on the A'REX train to Gimpo or Incheon. If you're south of the river, a similar service operates from **CALT** (City Airport; Map p252; ☎02-551 0077; www.calt.co.kr; COEX Mall, 22 Teheran-ro 87-gil; 1 way ₩15,000; ⊙bus 4.15am-9.30pm; Ⓢ Line 2 to Samseong, Exit 5), which allows check-ins for most major airlines, before transferring by limousine bus to Incheon (₩16,000, 65 minutes) or Gimpo (₩7500, 45 minutes) airports.

Bus & Taxi

City buses and taxis depart from the east side of the station.

Subway

Lines 1 and 4 connect Seoul station with the rest of the city.

Yongsan Station

Some long-distance trains from the south of Korea terminate at Yongsan station; many others pass through on their way to Seoul station.

Bus & Taxi

City buses and taxis depart from the east side of the station.

Subway

Line 1 and the Jungang Line connect Yongsan station with the city.

Cheongnyangni Station

Some trains servicing Eastern Korea terminate at Cheongnyangni station, including those from Chuncheon, Andong, Gangneung and Wonju.

Subway

Subway Line 1 connects Cheongnyangni station with the city.

Seoul Express Bus Terminal

Long-distance buses arrive at the major station **Seoul Express Bus Terminal** (Map p250; ☎02-536 6460-2; 194 Sinbanpo-ro; Ⓢ Lines 3, 7 or 9 to Seoul Express Terminal), split across two separate buildings: **Gyeongbu Line Terminal** (www.kobus.co.kr) serves mainly the eastern region, and **Central City Terminal** (www.hticket.co.kr) serves the southwestern region.

It's only necessary to buy tickets in advance for holidays and weekends. Deluxe-class buses have more leg room and cost more than ordinary buses. Buses that travel after 10pm have a 10% surcharge and are generally deluxe. Children aged six to 14 go half price.

Subway

Lines 3, 7 and 9 connect the bus terminal with the city; use exit 1 for Gyeongbu Line Terminal, exit 7 for Central City Terminal.

Dong-Seoul Bus Terminal

This **terminal** (Map p252; ☎02-1688 5979; www.ti21.co.kr; 50 Gangbyeonnyeok-ro; Ⓢ Line 2 to Gangbyeon, Exit 4) in Jamsil services destinations east of Seoul.

Subway

Line 2 to Gangbyeon, Exit 4.

Nambu Bus Terminal

Located in Gangnam, this **terminal** (Map p250; ☎02-521 8550; www.kobus.co.kr; 292 Hyoryeong-ro; Ⓢ Line 3 to Nambu Bus Terminal, Exit 5) serves destinations south of Seoul.

Subway

Line 3 to Nambu Bus Terminal, Exit 5.

Incheon Port

Ferries connect Incheon, west of Seoul, with a dozen port cities in China. Journey times vary from 12 to 24 hours. One-way fares start at ₩115,000 to most destinations but prices double for the more private and comfortable cabins. To reach Incheon's port (ferries leave from Yeonan Pier or International Terminal 2), take subway Line 1 to Incheon station and then take a taxi (around ₩6000).

Ferries to a number of Japanese cities leave from the southern city of Busan. See www.korail.com for details of a Seoul–Japan rail-and-ferry through ticket.

GETTING AROUND SEOUL

You'll definitely want to purchase a T-Money card (also called CITYPASS+) for discounts on bus, subway, taxi and train fares as well as for general convenience. Handy apps for interactive mapping and real-time journey planning across Seoul's transport network include **Subway Korea, Kakao Metro/ Kakao Bus** and **Seoul Topis** (http://topis.seoul.go.kr).

Subway The best way to get around, with an extensive network, frequent services and inexpensive fares.

Bus Handy for routes around Namsan and Northern Seoul, and for short hops in bad weather.

Taxi Best for short trips; the basic fare starts at ₩3000 for the first 2km.

Bicycle Seoul Bike, the city's public-bike scheme, can be used by visitors.

Car hire Useful only for long trips out of the city; budget from ₩80,000 per day.

Bicycle

In 2015 Seoul Bike was implemented by the city. This bike-sharing scheme, much like those in London and Paris, can be used by visitors. The green-and-white bikes and their similarly coloured docking stations can be found at over 150 locations across the city.

To use, first purchase a voucher at www.bikeseoul.com to obtain an unlock code, which is then keyed in on the bike itself (selecting the 'Foreign Tourist' option).

The bikes cost ₩1000 per hour for up to two hours, and ₩1000 every half-hour after that. A deposit of ₩50,000 is taken from your credit card and refunded within 24 hours of the bike being re-docked.

The Seoul Bike website also has a handy live map of all Seoul docking stations and available bikes.

Bicycles can also be rented at several parks along the Han River including on Yeouido, Ttukseom Resort, Seoul Forest Park and Olympic Park. Rental is around ₩3000 per hour, and you'll need to leave some form of ID as a deposit.

Bus

Seoul has a comprehensive and reasonably priced bus system (http://bus.go.kr) that runs from 5.30am to midnight. Some bus stops have bus route maps in English, and most buses have their major destinations written in English on the outside. There is a taped announcement of the names of each stop in English, but few bus drivers understand the language. When used in conjunction with certain travel apps and online maps, however, the bus system really comes into its own.

Using a T-Money (also called CITYPASS+) card saves ₩100 on each bus fare and transfers between bus and subway are either free or discounted, depending on the amount of time between transfers. Remember to swipe your T-Money card as you get off the bus as well as when you get on, just as you do on the subway.

BUS JOURNEYS FROM SEOUL

DESTINATION	EXPRESS/DELUXE (₩)	DURATION (HR)
Busan	23,000/34,200	4¼
Buyeo	11,600	2½
Chuncheon	8000	1¼
Gongju	8000/9000	1¾
Gwangju	17,00/26,100	3¼
Gyeongju	19,100/28,300	3¾
Jeonju	12,800/18,700	2½
Mokpo	20,500/30,400	3¾
Sokcho	13,800/17,900	2½

Red buses Long-distance express buses go to the outer suburbs with few stops.

Green buses These link subways within a district.

Blue buses All-stop buses going to outer suburbs.

Yellow buses Short-haul buses that circle small districts.

Car & Motorcycle

Driving is on the right, but we recommend first-time visitors to Seoul give driving a miss. Traffic jams, impatient road users and the lack of street names, directional signs and parking are not a recipe for an enjoyable holiday, particularly when the city's public transport is one of the world's best.

Hire

To rent a car, you must be over 21 and have both a driving licence from your own country and an International Driving Permit. The latter must be obtained abroad as they're not available in Korea. Incheon International Airport has a couple of car-rental agencies, including **Avis** (☎032-743 3300; www.avis.com; Incheon International Airport). Daily rates start from around ₩80,000.

Subway

Seoul has an excellent, user-friendly **subway system**, which connects with destinations well beyond the city borders, including Suwon and Incheon. The minimum fare of ₩1350 (₩1250 with a T-Money card) takes you up to 12km, and the system runs from 5.30am to midnight. In central Seoul the average time between stations is just over two minutes, so as a rough guide it takes around 25 minutes to travel 10 stops. Some top-end hotels and a few sights are up to a 15-minute walk from a subway station, but you can usually hail taxis or hop on a bus.

Most subway stations have lifts or stair lifts for wheelchairs. Escalators are common, but you'll do a fair amount of walking up and down stairs and along corridors, especially when changing lines. Neighbourhood maps inside the stations, including ones with digital touch screens, help you figure out which of the subway exits to take. The closest station and exit number is provided for all listings.

T-MONEY CARD

Bus, subway, taxi and train fares can all be paid using the rechargeable touch-and-go **T-Money card** (also called CITYPASS+), which gives you a ₩100 discount per trip and means that you can connect subway and bus as a single fare, providing less than 30 minutes has elapsed between transfer. The basic card can be bought for a nonrefundable ₩2500 from machines at most subway stations, as well as bus kiosks and convenience stores displaying the T-Money logo. Reload it with credit at any of the aforementioned places and get money refunded that hasn't been used (up to ₩20,000 minus a processing fee of ₩500) at subway machines and participating convenience stores before you leave Seoul.

Taxi

Regular orange- or grey-coloured taxis are a good deal for short trips. The flagfall for 2km is ₩3000 and rises ₩100 for every 144m or 35 seconds after that if the taxi is travelling below 15km/h. A 20% surcharge is levied between midnight and 4am. Deluxe taxis are black and cost ₩5000 for the first 3km and ₩200 for every 164m or 39 seconds, but they don't have a late-night surcharge.

Few taxi drivers speak English, so it's a good idea to have your destination written down in Korean. Most taxis have a free interpretation service whereby an interpreter talks to the taxi driver and to you by phone.

International Taxi (☎02-1644 2255; www.intltaxi.co.kr) has English-speaking drivers; these can be reserved in advance for 20% extra on the regular fare and can be chartered on an hourly or daily basis for longer journeys. All taxis are metered, and tipping is not required.

Tours

Hands down the cheapest way to tour the city is with **Seoul City Walking Tours** (☎02-6925 0777; http://dobo.visitseoul.net) FREE, which offers a wide program of free, themed walks in different city neighbourhoods, conducted by local English-speaking volunteer guides. These tours generally need to be booked online a few days in advance.

There are several Seoul-based tour companies available to take tourists out to the DMZ. One of the most well respected is **Koridoor Tours** (Map p246; ☎02-6383 2570; www.koridoor.co.kr; 251 Hangangdae-ro, Yongsan-gu; S Line 1 to Namyeong, Exit 1), which runs excursions on behalf of the USO (United Service Organizations) and employs US military guides.

Many of the major museums and palaces in Seoul have either daily or weekly free English-language guided tours.

Directory A–Z

Accessible Travel

Seoul has taken big strides in catering for travellers with disabilities. Most subway stations now have elevators and accessible toilets. A few hotels have specially adapted rooms. Tourist attractions, especially those run by the government, offer generous discounts or even free entry for disabled guests and a helper. Download Lonely Planet's free Accessible Travel guides from https://shop.lonelyplanet.com/categories/accessible-travel.com.

Customs Regulations

Visitors must declare all plants, fresh fruit, vegetables and dairy products that they bring into South Korea. Meat is not allowed without a certificate. Log on to www.customs.go.kr for further information. Antiques of national importance are banned from export.

Discount Cards

Korea Pass (www.lottecard.co.kr/app/html/koreapass/IHKPAZZ_V100.jsp) is a prepaid card, available in denominations from ₩50,000 to ₩500,000, that provides discounts on a range of goods and services. It can be bought at Lotte Mart and 7-Eleven branches in Seoul as well as at the A'REX booth at Incheon International Airport.

Discover Seoul Pass (www.discoverseoulpass.com) If you're planning on cramming an awful lot of sights into a short of space of time, Seoul's official tourist discount card is just about worth the outlay. Available in 24-hour, 48-hour or 72-hour versions (₩39,900/55,000/70,000), it gets you free or discounted entry into dozens of attractions all over the city. It also works as a rechargeable transport card on subways and buses. Buy it from CU convenience stores inside Incheon Airport, or from Tourist Information Centers throughout the city. You can also purchase it from the website as a mobile app.

PRACTICALITIES

Smoking Seoul has strict antismoking laws, meaning it is forbidden to smoke in all bars, restaurants, hotels and public buildings. It is also forbidden to smoke while walking along the street, or outside subway stations or bus stops. Generally, smokers duck into a side road or alleyway for a quick puff.

Daily newspapers Pick up English editions of the *Korea Times* (www.koreatimes.co.kr), *Korea Herald* (www.koreaherald.com) and *Korea JoongAng Daily* (http://koreajoongangdaily.joins.com).

Monthly magazines Print magazines in English include *Seoul Magazine* (http://magazine.seoulselection.com), *10 Magazine* (www.10mag.com) and *Groove Korea* (http://groovekorea.com).

TV and radio TV programs in English are aired on Arirang (www.arirang.co.kr). KBS World Radio (http://world.kbs.co.kr) broadcasts news and features programs in English as does TBS (www.tbsefm.seoul.kr) which also features music.

Electricity

Type F
220V/60Hz

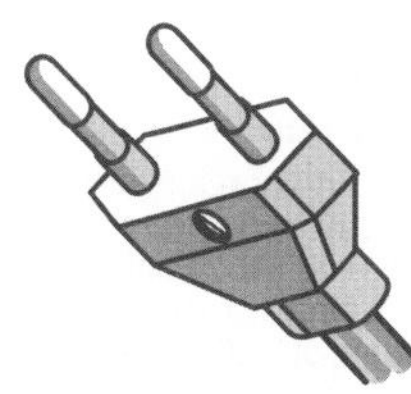

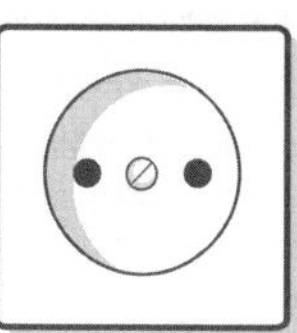

Type C
220V/60Hz

Embassies & Consulates

Australian Embassy (Map p232; ☎02-2003 0100; www.southkorea.embassy.gov.au; 19th fl, Kyobo Bldg, 1 Jong-ro; ⏲9am-5pm Mon-Fri; Ⓢ Line 5 to Gwanghwamun, Exit 4)

Canadian Embassy (Map p238; ☎02-3783 6000; www.canadainternational.gc.ca/korea-coree; 21 Jeong-dong-gil; ⏲9am-5pm Mon-Fri; Ⓢ Line 5 to Seodaemun, Exit 5)

Chinese Embassy (Map p238; ☎02-738 1038; www.chinaemb.or.kr; 27 Myeong-dong 2-gil; ⏲9am-6pm Mon-Fri; Ⓢ Line 4 to Myeongdong, Exit 5)

French Embassy (☎02-3149 4300; www.ambafrance-kr.org; 43-12 Seosomun-ro; ⏲9am-noon Mon-Fri; Ⓢ Line 2 or 5 to Chungjeongno, Exit 3)

German Embassy (Map p238; ☎02-748 4114; www.seoul.diplo.de; Seoul Sq, 8th fl, 416 Hangang-daero; ⏲9-11.30am Mon, Tue & Thu, 2-4.30pm Wed, 8.30-11am Fri; Ⓢ Line 1 or 4 to Seoul Station, Exit 8)

Irish Embassy (Map p232; ☎02-721 7200; www.embassyofireland.or.kr; 13th fl, Leema Bldg, 2 Jong-ro 1-gil; Ⓢ Line 5 to Gwanghwamun, Exit 2)

Japanese Embassy (Map p232; ☎02-739 7400; www.kr.emb-japan.go.jp; 64 Yulgok-ro; ⏲9.30am-noon & 1.30-5.30pm Mon-Fri; Ⓢ Line 3 to Anguk, Exit 6)

Netherlands Embassy (Map p238; ☎02-311 8600; http://southkorea.nlembassy.org; 10th fl, Jeongdong Bldg, 21-15 Jeongdong-gil; ⏲9am-12.30pm & 1.30-5.30pm Mon-Fri; Ⓢ Line 5 to Seodaemun, Exit 5)

New Zealand Embassy (Map p238; ☎02-3701 7700; www.nzembassy.com/korea; 8th fl, Jeong Dong Bldg, 21-15 Jeongdong-gil; ⏲9am-12.30pm & 1.30-5.30pm Mon-Fri; Ⓢ Line 5 to Seodaemun, Exit 5)

UK Embassy (Map p238; ☎02-3210 5500; www.gov.uk/world/organisations/british-embassy-seoul; 24 Sejong-daero 19-gil; ⏲9am-12.30pm & 1.30-5pm Mon-Fri; Ⓢ Line 1 or 2 to City Hall, Exit 3)

US Embassy (Map p232; ☎02-397 4114; https://kr.usembassy.gov; 188 Sejong-daero; ⏲9am-5pm Mon-Fri; Ⓢ Line 5 to Gwanghwamun, Exit 2)

Emergency & Important Numbers

Tourist helpline	☎1330
Fire and ambulance	☎119
Police	☎112

Health

The World Health Organization (www.who.int/ith) publishes the annually revised booklet *International Travel & Health*, available free online.

Health Insurance

If you already have health insurance, check with your provider to see if you are covered when you are in Korea. If not, make sure that your travel-insurance policy includes medical coverage. Ideally, any policy should cover all costs if you are admitted to hospital and provide emergency evacuation to your home country if needed.

Recommended Vaccinations

There are no special vaccination requirements for visiting Korea, but you should consider vaccination against hepatitis A and B.

Internet Access

➡ Wi-fi is universal, and you can log in at many hot spots throughout the city using Seoul's free public wi-fi network. Hotels generally offer free wi-fi, too, and you can get online in most cafes and many restaurants.

➡ If you need a computer, look for places with a 'PC 방' sign, which charge a few thousand won per hour and are invariably packed with online gamers.

➡ The major phone companies offer USB wi-fi dongles to rent, in the same way as mobile phones, to connect to the internet anywhere around Korea.

LGBTIQ+ Travellers

Korea is a sexually conservative society, and although the country has never outlawed homosexuality, gay and lesbian travellers who disclose their sexual orientation should be prepared for some less-than-positive reactions. For more information and context, log on to Chingusai (www.chingusai.net), a human rights group for gay Korean men with a detailed website.

Attitudes are changing, however, especially among young people. The annual **Seoul Queer Culture Festival** (www.kqcf.org; ⏲Jun or Jul) organises a range of activities, including a gay-pride parade and film festival. In 2017 an estimated 50,000 people took part in the parade.

Seoul has a healthy queer bar scene, although not all are foreigner friendly. Travelgay Asia (www.travelgayasia.com) has a detailed Korea section with maps and reviews to gay bars, clubs and services.

Maps

The **Korean Tourism Organization** (KTO; http://english.visitkorea.or.kr) and Seoul Metropolitan Government publish numerous free brochures and maps of Seoul, which are fine for most purposes. Especially good are maps and brochures on hiking the Seoul City Wall, available from the **Seoul City Wall Museum** (한양도성박물관; Map p247; ☎02-724 0243; 283 Yulgok-ro, Jongno-gu; ⏲9am-7pm Tue-Sun; ⓈLine 1 or 4 to Dongdaemun, Exit 1) FREE and other places.

Medical Services

Seoul has medical-care standards equal to those of other developed countries. You need a doctor's prescription to buy most medications, and it may be difficult to find the exact medication you use at home, so take extra. A letter from your physician outlining your medical condition and a list of your medications (using generic names) could be useful.

Hospitals normally require cash upfront, which you should be able to claim back from your insurance company, if you have appropriate cover.

Pharmacies

Almost all pharmacies stock at least some Western medicines. Pharmacists often know some English, but it may help them if you write down your symptoms or the medicine you want on a piece of paper. If you have a language problem and a mobile phone, dial 02-1330, explain what you want in English, and ask the interpreter to explain in Korean to the pharmacist.

Money

ATMs are widely available, and credit cards are accepted by most businesses, although not everywhere can handle overseas cards, so carry local currency too.

ATMs

ATMs that accept foreign cards are reasonably common: usually among a row of three or four in a bank at least one will have a 'Global ATM' sign or the logo of your credit-card company. Note that convenience-store ATMs tend not to accept foreign cards. Restrictions on the amount you can withdraw vary from place to place.

Changing Money

Many banks in Seoul offer a foreign-exchange service. There are also licensed moneychangers, particularly in Itaewon, that keep longer hours than the banks and provide a faster service, but may only exchange US dollars.

Credit Cards

Hotels, shops and restaurants accept foreign credit cards, but plenty of places, including budget accommodation and stalls, require cash.

Currency

The South Korean unit of currency is the won (₩), with ₩10, ₩50, ₩100 and ₩500 coins. Notes come in denominations of ₩1000, ₩5000, ₩10,000 and ₩50,000.

Opening Hours

Banks 9am to 4pm Monday to Friday, ATMs 7am to 11pm

Bars 6pm to 1am, longer hours Friday and Saturday

Cafes 7am to 10pm

Post offices 9am to 6pm Monday to Friday

Restaurants 11am to 10pm

Shops 10am to 8pm

Post

For postal rates refer to the website of Korea Post (www.koreapost.go.kr). Post offices are fairly common and have a red/orange sign.

Public Holidays

Eight Korean public holidays are set according to the solar calendar and three according to the lunar calendar, meaning that they fall on different days each year. Restaurants, shops and tourist sights stay open during most holidays, but may close over the three-day Lunar New Year and Chuseok (Thanksgiving) holidays. School holidays mean that beaches and resort areas are busy in August.

New Year's Day 1 January

Lunar New Year 1 February 2022, 21 January 2023, 9 February 2024

Independence Movement Day 1 March

Children's Day 5 May

Buddha's Birthday 8 May 2022, 26 May 2023, 15 May 2024

Memorial Day 6 June

Constitution Day 17 July

Liberation Day 15 August

Chuseok from 10 September 2022, 28 September 2023, 17 September 2024

National Foundation Day 3 October

Christmas Day 25 December

Responsible Travel

Overtourism

➡ People seated at alleyway corners in Bukchon Hanok Village hold placards reading 'Please talk quietly' to remind visitors that it is a real neighbourhood of 7500 residents.

➡ Seoul International Fair and Sustainable Tourism Forum (SIFT; http://seoulfairtourismforum.net) partners with cities such as Barcelona for joint solutions to overtourism. Their website has links to actions taken by small groups in Seoul to curb overtourism.

Support Local & Give Back

➡ Seoul Global Center (http://global.seoul.go.kr) has volunteer opportunities in the city. Leave a light footprint

➡ Seoul Bike (www.bikeseoul.com), the city's public-bike scheme, can be used by visitors.

Safe Travel

➡ Motorists can be impatient with pedestrians, so take extra care when crossing the road.

➡ Drunks in Seoul tend to be better behaved than elsewhere; there's always an exception, of course, so it's best not to antagonise people who have been drinking.

➡ Police in full riot gear, carrying shields and batons, are a not-uncommon sight in central Seoul. Student, trade-union, anti-American, environmental and other protests can occasionally turn physical. Keep well out of the way of any confrontations.

➡ Follow your home government's guidelines on Covid-19 and travel, such as Smart Traveller (www.smartraveller.gov.au/destinations/asia/south-korea-republic-korea) for Australian citizens; and the CDC (wwwnc.cdc.gov/travel/notices/covid-2/covid-19-south-korea) for US citizens.

Telephone

Mobile Phones

South Korea uses the CDMA digital standard; check compatibility with your phone provider. Phones can be hired at the airport and elsewhere.

Phone Codes

Gyeonggi-do code (031) This province surrounds Seoul.

Incheon city and airport code (032)

International access code KT (001)

Seoul code (02) Omit the zero if calling from outside Korea.

South Korea country code (82)

Phone Hire

➡ Mobile-phone and SIM hire is available from KT Olleh, SK Telecom and LGU+, all of which have counters at Incheon International Airport arrivals floor and branches throughout the city. SIM cards are also available from Evergreen Mobile (www.egsimcard.co.kr/ENG) and SIMCard Korea (www.simcardkorea.com).

➡ Each company offers similar but not identical schemes, so compare before buying or signing a rental contract if cost is an issue.

➡ Prepaid SIMs are also available from Evergreen Mobile, SIMCard Korea and vendors in Itaewon.

Phone Numbers

Korean mobile-phone numbers have three-digit codes, always beginning with 01, eg 011 1234 5678. You'll also come across internet phone numbers (also known as VoIP), which begin with 070. When you make a call from your mobile phone, you always input these initial codes or area codes, even if you're in the city you're trying to reach. For example, in Seoul, when calling a local Seoul number you would dial 02-123 4567.

> **TAP WATER**
>
> Most people don't drink the tap water in Seoul, but those who do seem to come to no harm. Filtered water is served free of charge in almost all restaurants.

Public Phones & Phonecards

➡ Public payphones are rare; the best places to look are subway stations. Ones accepting coins (₩50 or ₩100) are even rarer.

➡ Telephone cards usually give you a 10% bonus in value and can be bought at convenience stores. There are two types of cards, so if your card does not fit in one type of payphone, try a different-looking one. A few public phones accept credit cards.

➡ Local calls cost ₩70 for three minutes.

Time

South Korea is nine hours ahead of GMT/UCT (London) and does not have daylight saving. When it is noon in Seoul, it's 7pm the previous day in San Francisco, 10pm the previous day in New York and 1pm the same day in Sydney.

Toilets

➡ There are plenty of clean, modern and well-signed *hwajangsil* (public toilets) in Seoul.

➡ Toilet signs read 숙녀 for female; 신사 for male.

➡ Virtually all toilets are free of charge.

➡ Toilet paper is usually available, but it's wise to carry a stash around with you just in case.

➡ There are still a few Asian-style squat toilets around. Face the hooded end when you squat.

Tourist Information

There are scores of tourist information booths around the city. In major tourist zones such as Insa-dong and Namdaemun Market, look for red-jacketed city tourist guides, who can also help with information in various languages.

KTO Tourist Information Center (Map p232; ☎02-1330; www.visitkorea.or.kr; 2nd fl, 40 Cheonggyecheon-ro; ⏰9am-8pm; 🚻; Ⓢ Line 1 to Jonggak, Exit 5) The best of Seoul's many tourist centres, offering knowledgable staff, free internet, ample brochures and maps, and free experiences include trying on *hanbok* (traditional clothing) and cooking and craft classes.

Visas

Tourist Visas

Korea requires most visitors to apply for an electronic travel authorisation before travel, similar to the USA's ESTA and Canada's eTA.

The Korea Electronic Travel Authorization (K-ETA) costs ₩10,000 and is valid for two years. Eligible visitors are generally those who would have been on the permit-on-arrival list in the past, such as citizens from the UK and USA. Apply and pay online, at least 24 hours before travel, through the official K-ETA website (www.k-eta.go.kr).

Work Visas

➡ Applications for a work visa can be made inside South Korea, but you must leave the country to pick up the visa. You can also apply for a one-year work visa before entering South Korea, but it can take a few weeks to process. Note that the visa authorities will want to see originals (not photocopies) of your educational qualifications. This is a safeguard against fake degree certificates.

➡ You don't need to leave South Korea to renew a work visa as long as you carry on working for the same employer. But if you change employers, you are usually obliged to apply for a new visa which you have to pick up outside Korea.

➡ If you are working or studying in South Korea on a long-term visa, it is necessary to apply for an alien registration card (ARC) within 90 days of arrival, which costs ₩10,000. In Seoul this is done at the **Omokgyo** (☎02-2650 6212; www.immigration.go.kr; 319-2 Sinjeong 6 dong; ⏰9am-6pm Mon-Fri; Ⓢ Line 5 to Omokgyo, Exit 7) immigration office south of the Han River, or the **Anguk** (Map p234; ☎02-732-6220; www.immigration.go.kr; 2nd fl, SK Hub Bldg, 461, Samil-daero; Ⓢ Line 3 to Anguk, Exit 5) office, north of the river.

TRANSLATION & COUNSELLING SERVICES

Tourist Phone Number Call ☎1330, or ☎02-1330 from a mobile phone; if you need interpretation help or information on practically any topic, any time of the day or night.

Seoul Global Center (Map p234; ☎02-2075 4180; http://global.seoul.go.kr; 38 Jong-ro; ⏰9am-6pm Mon-Fri; Ⓢ Line 1 to Jonggak, Exit 6) This comprehensive support centre for foreign residents in Seoul is also very useful; it has volunteers who speak a range of languages as well as full-time staff who can assist on a range of issues. Language and culture classes are also held here.

➡ **Seoul Global Center** (Map p234; ☎02-2075 4180; http://global.seoul.go.kr; 38 Jong-ro; ⌚9am-6pm Mon-Fri; Ⓢ Line 1 to Jonggak, Exit 6) can also help with issues related to work visas.

Volunteering

The **Seoul Global Center** (Map p234; ☎02-2075 4180; http://global.seoul.go.kr; 38 Jong-ro; ⌚9am-6pm Mon-Fri; Ⓢ Line 1 to Jonggak, Exit 6) is a good place to start looking for volunteer possibilities.

Work

➡ The biggest demand for work in Seoul is for English teachers, although those who also have Korean language skills will have more opportunities.

➡ Native English teachers on a one-year contract can expect to earn around ₩2.5 million or more a month, with a furnished apartment, return flights, 50% of medical insurance, 10 days' paid holiday and a one-month completion bonus all included in the package. Income tax is very low (around 4%), although a 4.5% pension contribution (reclaimable by some nationalities) is compulsory.

➡ Most English teachers work in a *hagwon* (private language school), but some are employed by universities or government schools. Company classes, English camps and teaching via the telephone are also possible, as is private tutoring, although this is technically illegal. Teaching hours in a *hagwon* are usually around 30 hours a week and are likely to involve split shifts, as well as evening and Saturday classes.

➡ A degree in any subject is sufficient as long as English is your native language. However, it's a good idea to obtain some kind of English-teaching qualification before you arrive, as this increases your options and you should be able to find (and do) a better job.

➡ Some *hagwon* owners are less-than-ideal employers and don't pay all that they promise. Ask any prospective employer for the email addresses of foreign English teachers working at the *hagwon*, and contact them for their opinion and advice. One important point to keep in mind is that if you change employers, you will usually need to obtain a new work visa, which requires you to leave the country to pick up your new visa. Your new employer may pick up all or at least part of the tab for this.

➡ The best starting point for finding out more about the English-teaching scene is the Korea Association of Teachers of English (KATE; www.kate.or.kr).

Language

Korean belongs to the Ural-Altaic language family and is spoken by around 80 million people. The standard language of South Korea is based on the dialect of Seoul.

Korean script, *hangeul*, is simple and accessible, as each character represents a sound of its own. There are a number of competing Romanisation systems in use today for *hangeul*. Since 2000, the government has been changing road signs to reflect the most recent Romanisation system, so you may encounter signs, maps and tourist literature with at least two different Romanisation systems.

Korean pronunciation is pretty straightforward for English speakers, as most sounds are also found in English or have a close approximation. If you follow our coloured pronunciation guides, you should be understood just fine. Korean distinguishes between aspirated consonants (formed by making a puff of air as they're pronounced) and unaspirated ones (pronounced without a puff of air). In our pronunciation guides, aspirated consonants (except for s and h) are followed by an apostrophe ('). Syllables are pronounced with fairly even emphasis in Korean.

BASICS

Hello.	안녕하세요.	an·nyŏng ha·se·yo
Goodbye. (if leaving/ staying)	안녕히 계세요/ 가세요.	an·nyŏng·hi kye·se·yo/ ka·se·yo
Yes.	네.	né
No.	아니요.	a·ni·yo
Excuse me.	실례합니다.	shil·lé ham·ni·da
Sorry.	죄송합니다.	choé·song ham·ni·da
Thank you.	고맙습니다./ 감사합니다.	ko·map·sŭm·ni·da/ kam·sa·ham·ni·da
You're welcome.	천만에요.	ch'ŏn·ma·ne·yo

How are you?
안녕하세요? — an·nyŏng ha·se·yo

Fine, thanks. And you?
네. 안녕하세요? — ne an·nyŏng ha·se·yo

What is your name?
성함을 여쭤봐도 될까요? — sŏng·ha·mŭl yŏ·tchŏ·bwa·do doélk·ka·yo

My name is ...
제 이름은 ...입니다. — che i·rŭ·mŭn ...·im·ni·da

Do you speak English?
영어 하실 줄 아시나요? — yŏng·ŏ ha·shil·jul a·shi·na·yo

I don't understand.
못 알아 들었어요. — mot a·ra·dŭ·rŏss·ŏ·yo

ACCOMMODATION

Do you have a ... room?	... 룸 있나요?	... rum in·na·yo
single	싱글	shing·gŭl
double	더블	tŏ·bŭl
twin	트윈	t'ŭ·win

How much per ...?	...에 얼마예요?	...·é ŏl·ma·ye·yo
night	하룻밤	ha·rup·pam
person	한 명	han·myŏng
week	일주일	il·chu·il
air-con	냉방	naeng·bang
bathroom	욕실	yok·shil
internet	인터넷	in·t'ŏ·net
toilet	화장실	hwa·jang·shil
window	창문	ch'ang·mun

Is breakfast included?
아침 포함인가요? — a·ch'im p'o·ha·min·ga·yo

KEY PATTERNS

To get by in Korean, mix and match these simple patterns with words of your choice:

When's (the next bus)?
(다음 버스) 언제 있나요? (ta·ŭm bŏ·sŭ) ŏn·jé in·na·yo

Where's (the train/subway station)?
(역) 어디예요? (yŏk) ŏ·di·ye·yo

I'm looking for (a hotel).
(호텔) 찾고 있어요. (ho·t'el) ch'ak·ko iss·ŏ·yo

Do you have (a map)?
(지도) 가지고 계신가요? (chi·do) ka·ji·go kye·shin·ga·yo

Is there (a toilet)?
(화장실) 있나요? (hwa·jang·shil) in·na·yo

I'd like (the menu).
(메뉴) 주세요. (me·nyu) ju·se·yo

I'd like to (hire a car).
(차 빌리고) 싶어요. (ch'a pil·li·go) shi·p'ŏ·yo

Could you please (help me)?
(저를 도와) 주시겠어요? (chŏ·rŭl to·wa) ju·shi·gess·ŏ·yo

How much is (a room)?
(방) 얼마예요? (pang) ŏl·ma·ye·yo

Do I need (a visa)?
(비자) 필요한가요? (pi·ja) p'i·ryo·han·ga·yo

DIRECTIONS

Where's a/the ...?
... 어디 있나요? ... ŏ·di in·na·yo

What's the address?
주소가 뭐예요? chu·so·ga mwŏ·ye·yo

Could you please write it down?
적어 주시겠어요? chŏ·gŏ ju·shi·gess·ŏ·yo

Please show me (on the map).
(지도에서) 어디인지 가르쳐 주세요. (chi·do·e·sŏ) ŏ·di·in·ji ka·rŭ·ch'ŏ ju·se·yo

Turn left/right.
좌회전/우회전 하세요. chwa·hoé·jŏn/u·hoé·jŏn ha·se·yo

Turn at the ...	...에서 도세요.	...·e·sŏ to·se·yo
corner	모퉁이	mo·t'ung·i
pedestrian crossing	횡단 보도	hoéng·dan·bo·do

It's ...	... 있어요.	... iss·ŏ·yo
behind ...	... 뒤에	... dwi·é
in front of ...	... 앞에	... a·p'é
near ...	... 가까이에	... kak·ka·i·é
next to ...	... 옆에	... yŏ·p'é
on the corner	모퉁이에	mo·t'ung·i·é
opposite ...	... 반대 편에	... pan·dae·p'yŏ·né
straight ahead	정면에	chŏng·myŏ·né

EATING & DRINKING

Can we see the menu?
메뉴 볼 수 있나요? me·nyu bol·su in·na·yo

What would you recommend?
추천 해 주시겠어요? ch'u·ch'ŏn hae·ju·shi·gess·ŏ·yo

Do you have any vegetarian dishes?
채식주의 음식 있나요? ch'ae·shik·chu·i ŭm·shik in·na·yo

I'd like ..., please.
... 주세요. ... ju·se·yo

Cheers!
건배! kŏn·bae

That was delicious!
맛있었어요! ma·shiss·ŏss·ŏ·yo

Please bring the bill.
계산서 가져다 주세요. kye·san·sŏ ka·jŏ·da ju·se·yo

I'd like to reserve a table for ...	... 테이블 예약해 주세요.	... t'e·i·bŭl ye·ya·k'ae ju·se·yo
(eight) o'clock	(여덟) 시	(yŏ·dŏl)·shi
(two) people	(두) 명	(tu)·myŏng

Key Words

bar	술집	sul·chip
bottle	병	pyŏng
bowl	사발	sa·bal
breakfast	아침	a·ch'im
chopsticks	젓가락	chŏk·ka·rak
cold	차가운	ch'a·ga·un
dinner	저녁	chŏ·nyŏk
fork	포크	p'o·k'ŭ
glass	잔	chan
hot (warm)	뜨거운	ddŭ·gŏ·un
knife	칼	k'al
lunch	점심	chŏm·shim
market	시장	shi·jang
plate	접시	chŏp·shi
restaurant	식당	shik·tang
snack	간식	kan·shik

SIGNS

영업 중	Open
휴무	Closed
입구	Entrance
출구	Exit
... 금지	... Prohibited
금연 구역	No Smoking Area
화장실	Toilets
신사용	Men
숙녀용	Women

spicy (hot)	매운	mae·un
spoon	숟가락	suk·ka·rak

Meat & Fish

beef	쇠고기	soé·go·gi
chicken	닭고기	tak·ko·gi
duck	오리	o·ri
fish	생선	saeng·sŏn
herring	청어	ch'ŏng·ŏ
lamb	양고기	yang·go·gi
meat	고기	ko·gi
mussel	홍합	hong·hap
oyster	굴	kul
pork	돼지고기	twae·ji·go·gi
prawn	대하	tae·ha
salmon	연어	yŏ·nŏ
seafood	해물	hae·mul
tuna	참치	ch'am·ch'i
turkey	칠면조	ch'il·myŏn·jo
veal	송아지 고기	song·a·ji go·gi

Fruit & Vegetables

apple	사과	sa·gwa
apricot	살구	sal·gu
bean	콩	k'ong
capsicum	고추	ko·ch'u
carrot	당근	tang·gŭn
corn	옥수수	ok·su·su
cucumber	오이	o·i
eggplant	가지	ka·ji
fruit	과일	kwa·il
legume	콩류	k'ong·nyu
lentil	렌즈콩	ren·jŭ·k'ong
lettuce	양상추	yang·sang·ch'u
mushroom	버섯	pŏ·sŏt
nut	견과류	kyŏn·gwa·ryu
onion	양파	yang·p'a
orange	오렌지	o·ren·ji
pea	완두콩	wan·du·k'ong
peach	복숭아	pok·sung·a
pear	배	pae
plum	자두	cha·du
potato	감자	kam·ja
pumpkin	늙은 호박	nŭl·gŭn ho·bak
spinach	시금치	shi·gŭm·ch'i
strawberry	딸기	ddal·gi
tomato	토마토	t'o·ma·t'o
vegetable	야채	ya·ch'ae
watermelon	수박	su·bak

Other

bread	빵	bbang
cheese	치즈	ch'i·jŭ
egg	계란	kye·ran
honey	꿀	ggul
noodles	국수	kuk·su
rice (cooked)	밥	pap
salt	소금	so·gŭm
soup	수프	su·p'ŭ
sugar	설탕	sŏl·t'ang

Drinks

beer	맥주	maek·chu
coffee	커피	k'ŏ·p'i
juice	주스	jus·sŭ

QUESTION WORDS

how	어떻게	ŏt·tŏ·k'é
what (object)	무엇을	mu·ŏ·sŭl
what (subject)	뭐가	mwŏ·ga
when	언제	ŏn·jé
where	어디	ŏ·di
which	어느	ŏ·nŭ
who (object)	누구를	nu·gu·rŭl
who (subject)	누가	nu·ga
why	왜	wae

milk	우유	u·yu
mineral water	생수	saeng·su
red wine	레드 와인	re·dŭ wa·in
soft drink	탄산 음료	t'an·san ŭm·nyo
tea	차	ch'a
water	물	mul
white wine	화이트 와인	hwa·i·t'ŭ wa·in

EMERGENCIES

Help!	도와주세요!	to·wa·ju·se·yo
Go away!	저리 가세요!	chŏ·ri ka·se·yo
Call ...!	... 불러주세요!	... pul·lŏ·ju·se·yo
a doctor	의사	ŭi·sa
the police	경찰	kyŏng·ch'al

I'm lost.
길을 잃었어요. ki·rŭl i·rŏss·ŏ·yo

Where's the toilet?
화장실이 어디예요? hwa·jang·shi·ri ŏ·di·ye·yo

I'm sick.
전 아파요. chŏn a·p'a·yo

It hurts here.
여기가 아파요. yŏ·gi·ga a·p'a·yo

I'm allergic to ...
전 ...에 알레르기가 있어요. chŏn ...·é al·le·rŭ·gi·ga iss·ŏ·yo

SHOPPING & SERVICES

I'm just looking.
그냥 구경할게요. kŭ·nyang ku·gyŏng halk·ke·yo

Do you have (tissues)?
(휴지) 있나요? (hyu·ji) in·na·yo

How much is it?
얼마예요? ŏl·ma·ye·yo

Can you write down the price?
가격을 써 주시겠어요? ka·gyŏ·gŭl ssŏ ju·shi·gess·ŏ·yo

Can I look at it?
보여 주시겠어요? po·yŏ ju·shi·gess·ŏ·yo

Do you have any others?
다른 건 없나요? ta·rŭn·gŏn ŏm·na·yo

That's too expensive.
너무 비싸요. nŏ·mu piss·a·yo

Please give me a discount.
깎아 주세요. ggak·ka·ju·se·yo

There's a mistake in the bill.
계산서가 이상해요. kye·san·sŏ i·sang·hae·yo

ATM	현금인출기	hyŏn·gŭ·min·ch'ul·gi
internet cafe	PC방	p'i·shi·bang
post office	우체국	u·ch'e·guk
tourist office	관광안내소	kwan·gwang an·nae·so

TIME & DATES

What time is it?
몇 시예요? myŏs·shi·ye·yo

It's (two) o'clock.
(두) 시요. (tu)·shi·yo

Half past (two).
(두) 시 삼십 분이요. (tu)·shi sam·ship·pu·ni·yo

At what time ...?
몇 시에 ...? myŏs·shi·é ...

NUMBERS

Use pure Korean numbers for hours when telling the time, for counting objects and people, and for expressing your age.

1	하나	ha·na
2	둘	tul
3	셋	set
4	넷	net
5	다섯	ta·sŏt
6	여섯	yŏ·sŏt
7	일곱	il·gop
8	여덟	yŏ·dŏl
9	아홉	a·hop
10	열	yŏl

Use Sino-Korean numbers for minutes when telling the time, for dates and months, and for addresses, phone numbers, money and floors of a building.

1	일	il
2	이	i
3	삼	sam
4	사	sa
5	오	o
6	육	yuk
7	칠	ch'il
8	팔	p'al
9	구	ku
10	십	ship

At (five) o'clock.
(다섯) 시에. (ta·sŏs)·shi·é

morning	아침	a·ch'im
afternoon	오후	o·hu
evening	저녁	chŏ·nyŏk
yesterday	어제	ŏ·jé
today	오늘	o·nŭl
tomorrow	내일	nae·il

Monday	월요일	wŏ·ryo·il
Tuesday	화요일	hwa·yo·il
Wednesday	수요일	su·yo·il
Thursday	목요일	mo·gyo·il
Friday	금요일	kŭ·myo·il
Saturday	토요일	t'o·yo·il
Sunday	일요일	i·ryo·il

January	일월	i·rwŏl
February	이월	i·wŏl
March	삼월	sa·mwŏl
April	사월	sa·wŏl
May	오월	o·wŏl
June	유월	yu·wŏl
July	칠월	ch'i·rwŏl
August	팔월	p'a·rwŏl
September	구월	ku·wŏl
October	시월	shi·wŏl
November	십일월	shi·bi·rwŏl
December	십이월	shi·bi·wŏl

TRANSPORT

Public Transport

A ... ticket (to Daegu), please.	(대구 가는) ... 표 주세요.	(tae·gu ka·nŭn) ... p'yo chu·se·yo
1st-class	일등석	il·dŭng·sŏk
one-way	편도	p'yŏn·do
return	왕복	wang·bok
standard class	일반석	il·ban·sŏk
standing room	입석	ip·sŏk

When's the ... (bus)?	... (버스) 언제 있나요?	... (bŏ·sŭ) ŏn·jé in·na·yo
first	첫	ch'ŏt
last	마지막	ma·ji·mak

Which ... goes to (Myeongdong)?	어느 ...이/가 (명동)에 가나요?	ŏ·nŭ ...·i/·ga (myŏng·dong)·é ka·na·yo
boat	배	pae
bus	버스	bŏ·sŭ
metro line	지하철 노선	chi·ha·ch'ŏl no·sŏn
train	기차	ki·ch'a

platform	타는 곳	t'a·nŭn·got
ticket machine	표 자판기	p'yo cha·pan·gi
timetable display	시간표	shi·gan·p'yo
transportation card	교통카드	kyo·t'ong k'a·dŭ

At what time does it get to (Busan)?
(부산)에 언제 도착하나요? (pu·san)·é ŏn·jé to·ch'a·k'a·na·yo

Does it stop at (Gyeongju)?
(경주) 가나요? (kyŏng·ju) ka·na·yo

Please tell me when we get to (Daejeon).
(대전)에 도착하면 좀 알려주세요. (tae·jŏn)·é to·ch'a·k'a·myŏn chom al·lyŏ·ju·se·yo

Please take me to (Insa-dong).
(인사동)으로 가 주세요. (in·sa·dong)·ŭ·ro ka·ju·se·yo

Driving & Cycling

I'd like to hire a ...	... 빌리고 싶어요.	... pil·li·go shi·p'ŏ·yo
4WD	사륜구동	sa·ryun·gu·dong
car	차	ch'a

I'd like to hire a bicycle.
자전거 빌리려고요. cha·jŏn·gŏ pil·li·ryŏ·go·yo

Do I need a helmet?
헬멧 써야 하나요? hel·met ssŏ·ya ha·na·yo

Is this the road to (Donghae)?
이게 (동해) 가는 길인가요? i·gé (tong·hae) ka·nŭn ki·rin·ga·yo

(How long) Can I park here?
(얼마 동안) 여기 주차해도 되나요? (ŏl·ma·dong·an) yŏ·gi chu·ch'a·hae·do doé·na·yo

Where's a petrol station?
주유소가 어디있나요? chu·yu·so·ga ŏ·di in·na·yo

I need a mechanic.
자동차정비사가 필요해요. cha·dong·ch'a chŏng·bi·sa·ga p'i·ryo·hae·yo

I'd like my bicycle repaired.
자전거 고치려고요. cha·jŏn·gŏ ko·ch'i·ryŏ·go·yo

Behind the Scenes

SEND US YOUR FEEDBACK

We love to hear from travellers – your comments keep us on our toes and help make our books better. Our well-travelled team reads every word on what you loved or loathed about this book. Although we cannot reply individually to your submissions, we always guarantee that your feedback goes straight to the appropriate authors, in time for the next edition. Each person who sends us information is thanked in the next edition – the most useful submissions are rewarded with a selection of digital PDF chapters.

Visit **lonelyplanet.com/contact** to submit your updates and suggestions or to ask for help. Our award-winning website also features inspirational travel stories, news and discussions.

Note: We may edit, reproduce and incorporate your comments in Lonely Planet products such as guidebooks, websites and digital products, so let us know if you don't want your comments reproduced or your name acknowledged. For a copy of our privacy policy visit lonelyplanet.com/privacy.

AUTHOR THANKS

Thomas O'Malley

Thanks to my esteemed co-authors and editors, to Yoon (ique Universe), to Mr & Mrs Kim for their hospitality and gourmet breakfasts, Leo, Paris Baguette's coffee, all the beers at Magpie Brewing, and most of all, to Ophelia.

Phillip Tang

A huge thanks to Octavio Nájera for making Seoul dance and sing, *ganando como siempre*. Mariah Lee and friends for workshopping Seoul tips and the *dakgalbi* city escape. Thanks to Félix Barría and Jules Thivent for *makgeolli*, *galbi* and blossom flavoured chips, and Da Sel Lee and Jenny for Korean hospitality. Thank you to the co-writers for being patient and great virtual workmates. Thank you Vek Lewis, Fiona Ross and Francisco Vargas for additional virtual support.

ACKNOWLEDGEMENTS

Climate map data adapted from Peel MC, Finlayson BL & McMahon TA (2007) 'Updated World Map of the Köppen-Geiger Climate Classification', *Hydrology and Earth System Sciences*, 11, 1633–44.

Cover photograph: Bukchon Hanok Village, Noomna nakhonphanom/Shutterstock ©

THIS BOOK

This 10th edition of Lonely Planet's *Seoul* guidebook was researched and written by Thomas O'Malley and Phillip Tang. Tom and Phillip also wrote the previous edition; Trent Holden and Simon Richmond wrote the 8th edition. This guidebook was produced by the following:

Senior Product Editor Sandie Kestell
Product Editor Angela Tinson
Cartographer Anthony Phelan
Book Designer Catalina Aragón
Assisting Editors Andrea Dobbin, Samantha Forge, Jennifer Hattam, Ali Lemer, Charlotte Orr, Sarah Stewart, Simon Williamson
Cover Researcher Gwen Cotter
Thanks to James Appleton, Claire Glanville, Karen Henderson, Kirsten Rawlings, Adela Shin

Index

See also separate subindexes for:
EATING P225
DRINKING & NIGHTLIFE P225
ENTERTAINMENT P226
SHOPPING P226
SPORTS & ACTIVITIES P227
SLEEPING P227

Sights 000
Map Pages **000**
Photo Pages **000**

DRINKING & NIGHTLIFE

EATING

☆ ENTERTAINMENT

SHOPPING

SLEEPING

SPORTS & ACTIVITIES

Seoul Maps

Sights

- Beach
- Bird Sanctuary
- Buddhist
- Castle/Palace
- Christian
- Confucian
- Hindu
- Islamic
- Jain
- Jewish
- Monument
- Museum/Gallery/Historic Building
- Ruin
- Shinto
- Sikh
- Taoist
- Winery/Vineyard
- Zoo/Wildlife Sanctuary
- Other Sight

Activities, Courses & Tours

- Bodysurfing
- Diving
- Canoeing/Kayaking
- Course/Tour
- Sento Hot Baths/Onsen
- Skiing
- Snorkelling
- Surfing
- Swimming/Pool
- Walking
- Windsurfing
- Other Activity

Sleeping

- Sleeping
- Camping
- Hut/Shelter

Eating

- Eating

Drinking & Nightlife

- Drinking & Nightlife
- Cafe

Entertainment

- Entertainment

Shopping

- Shopping

Information

- Bank
- Embassy/Consulate
- Hospital/Medical
- Internet
- Police
- Post Office
- Telephone
- Toilet
- Tourist Information
- Other Information

Geographic

- Beach
- Gate
- Hut/Shelter
- Lighthouse
- Lookout
- Mountain/Volcano
- Oasis
- Park
- Pass
- Picnic Area
- Waterfall

Population

- Capital (National)
- Capital (State/Province)
- City/Large Town
- Town/Village

Transport

- Airport
- Border crossing
- Bus
- Cable car/Funicular
- Cycling
- Ferry
- Metro/MTR/MRT station
- Monorail
- Parking
- Petrol station
- Skytrain/Subway station
- Taxi
- Train station/Railway
- Tram
- Underground station
- Other Transport

Routes

- Tollway
- Freeway
- Primary
- Secondary
- Tertiary
- Lane
- Unsealed road
- Road under construction
- Plaza/Mall
- Steps
- Tunnel
- Pedestrian overpass
- Walking Tour
- Walking Tour detour
- Path/Walking Trail

Boundaries

- International
- State/Province
- Disputed
- Regional/Suburb
- Marine Park
- Cliff
- Wall

Hydrography

- River, Creek
- Intermittent River
- Canal
- Water
- Dry/Salt/Intermittent Lake
- Reef

Areas

- Airport/Runway
- Beach/Desert
- Cemetery (Christian)
- Cemetery (Other)
- Glacier
- Mudflat
- Park/Forest
- Sight (Building)
- Sportsground
- Swamp/Mangrove

Note: Not all symbols displayed above appear on the maps in this book

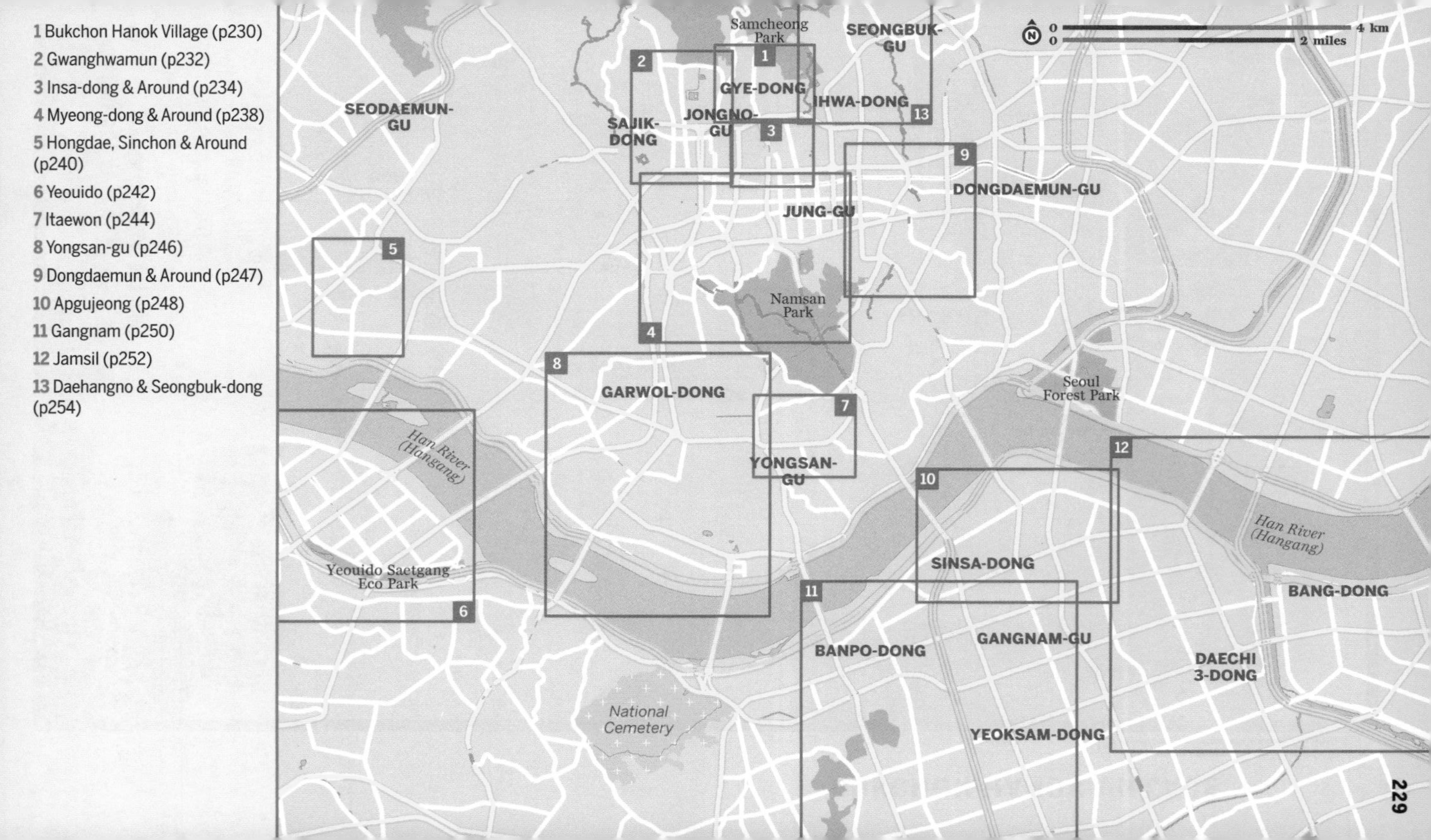
1 Bukchon Hanok Village (p230)
2 Gwanghwamun (p232)
3 Insa-dong & Around (p234)
4 Myeong-dong & Around (p238)
5 Hongdae, Sinchon & Around (p240)
6 Yeouido (p242)
7 Itaewon (p244)
8 Yongsan-gu (p246)
9 Dongdaemun & Around (p247)
10 Apgujeong (p248)
11 Gangnam (p250)
12 Jamsil (p252)
13 Daehangno & Seongbuk-dong (p254)
0 4 km
0 2 miles
Samcheong Park
SEONGBUK-GU
GYE-DONG
IHWA-DONG
SEODAEMUN-GU
SAJIK-DONG
JONGNO-GU
DONGDAEMUN-GU
JUNG-GU
Namsan Park
GARWOL-DONG
Seoul Forest Park
Han River (Hangang)
YONGSAN-GU
SINSA-DONG
Yeouido Saetgang Eco Park
BANG-DONG
BANPO-DONG
GANGNAM-GU
DAECHI 3-DONG
National Cemetery
YEOKSAM-DONG

BUKCHON HANOK VILLAGE

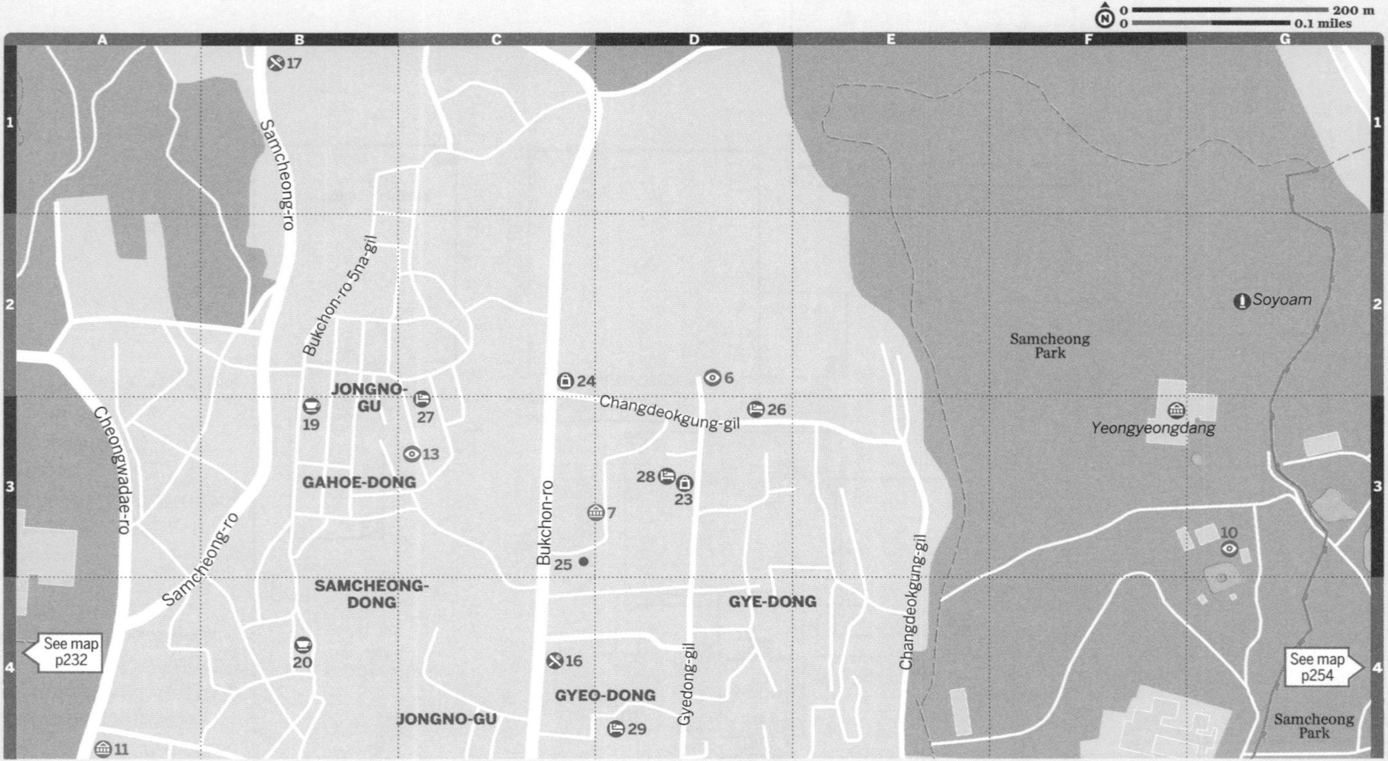

0 200 m
0 0.1 miles

A B C D E F G
1 2 3 4

17
Samcheong-ro
Bukchon-ro 5na-gil
JONGNO-GU
19
27
13
GAHOE-DONG
Cheongwadae-ro
Samcheong-ro
SAMCHEONG-DONG
20
11
24
6
Changdeokgung-gil
26
28
23
7
Bukchon-ro
25
GYE-DONG
16
GYEO-DONG
JONGNO-GU
29
Gyedong-gil
Changdeokgung-gil
Samcheong Park
Soyoam
Yeongyeongdang
10
Samcheong Park

See map p232
See map p254

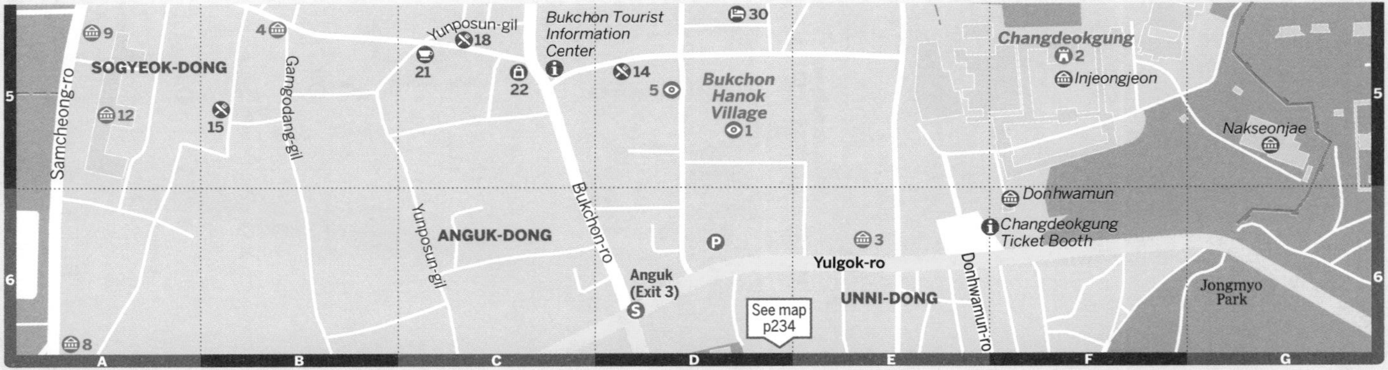

BUKCHON HANOK VILLAGE

Top Sights **p60**
1 Bukchon Hanok Village ... D5
2 Changdeokgung ... F5

Sights **p66**
3 Arario Museum in SPACE ... E6
4 Artsonje Center ... B5
5 Bukchon Traditional Culture Center ... D5
6 Choong Ang High School ... D2
7 Gahoe Minhwa Workshop ... D3
8 Gallery Hyundai ... A6
9 Hakgojae ... A5
10 Huwon ... G3
11 Kukje ... A4
12 MMCA Seoul ... A5
13 Simsimheon ... C3

Eating **p71**
14 2046 Pansteak ... D5
15 Chosun Gimbap ... B5
16 Dejangjangi HwadeogPijajip ... C4
17 Seoureseo Duljjaero Jalhaneunjip ... B1
18 Wood and Brick ... C5

Drinking & Nightlife **p73**
19 Cha Masineun Tteul ... B3
20 Kopi Bangasgan ... B4
21 Tea Therapy ... C5

Shopping **p76**
Gallery Art Zone ... (see 12)
22 Jonginamoo ... C5
23 Mik ... D3
24 Yido ... C2

Sports & Activities **p78**
25 Dong-Lim Knot Workshop ... C3

Sleeping **p168**
26 Bukchon Maru ... D3
27 Chi-Woon-Jung ... C3
28 Doo Guesthouse ... D3
29 Rak-Ko-Jae ... D4
30 Wwoof Korea Guesthouse ... D5

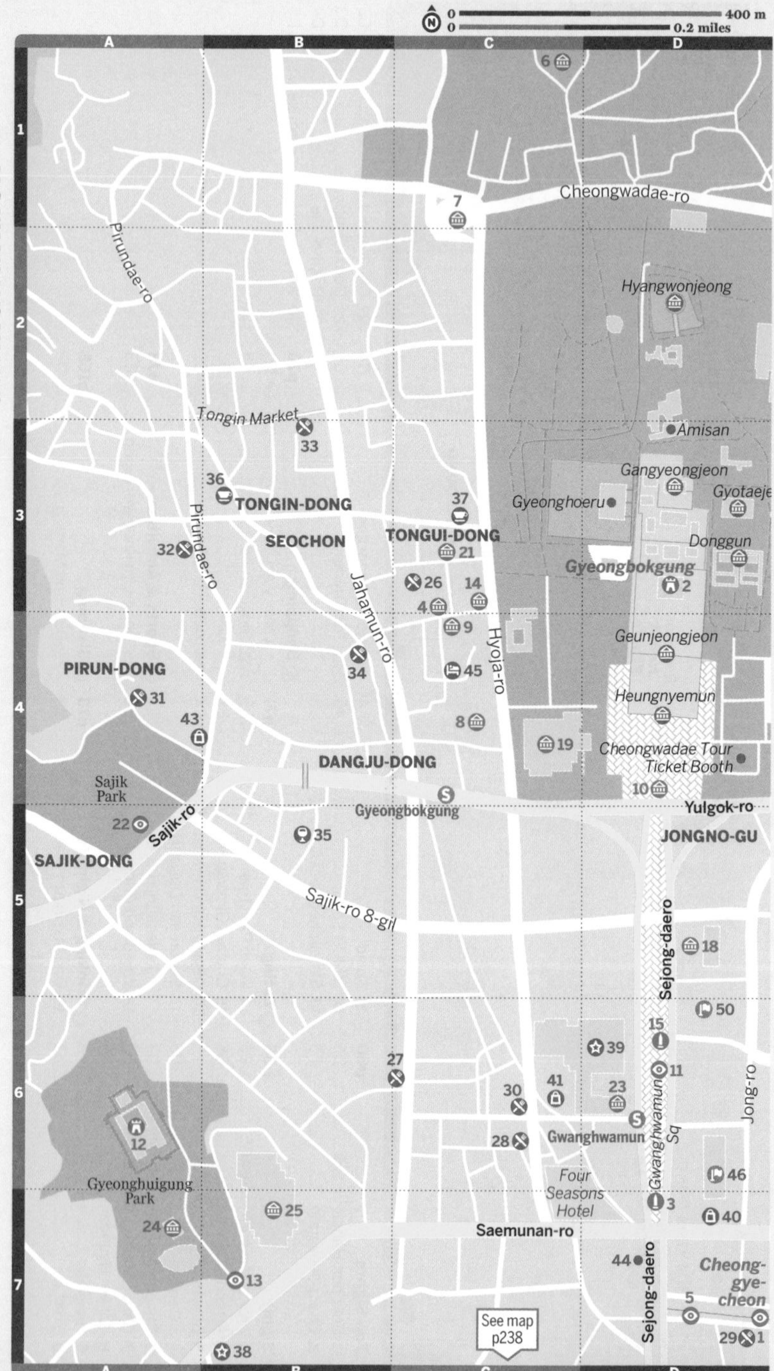
0 400 m
0 0.2 miles
A
B
C
D
1
2
3
4
5
6
7
Cheongwadae-ro
Pirundae-ro
Hyangwonjeong
Amisan
Tongin Market
Gangyeongjeon
Gyotaeje
TONGIN-DONG
Gyeonghoeru
SEOCHON
TONGUI-DONG
Donggun
Gyeongbokgung
Jahamun-ro
Hyoja-ro
Geunjeongjeon
PIRUN-DONG
Heungnyemun
Cheongwadae Tour Ticket Booth
DANGJU-DONG
Sajik Park
Gyeongbokgung
Yulgok-ro
Sajik-ro
JONGNO-GU
SAJIK-DONG
Sajik-ro 8-gil
Sejong-daero
Jong-ro
Gwanghwamun
Gwanghwamun Sq
Four Seasons Hotel
Gyeonghuigung Park
Saemunan-ro
Sejong-daero
Cheong-gye-cheon
See map p238

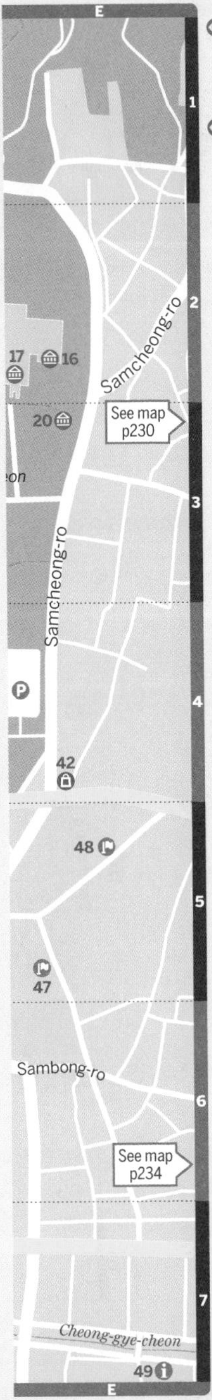

Samcheong-ro

See map p230

Samcheong-ro

Sambong-ro

See map p234

Cheong-gye-cheon

Top Sights **p58**

1 Cheong-gye-cheon ... D7
2 Gyeongbokgung ... D3

Sights **p65**

3 Admiral Yi Sun-Sin Statue ... D7
4 Artside ... C3
5 Cheong-gye Plaza ... D7
6 Cheongwadae ... C1
7 Cheongwadae Sarangchae . C1
8 Daelim Contemporary Art Museum ... C4
9 Gallery Simon ... C4
10 Gwanghwamun ... D4
11 Gwanghwamun Square ... D6
Gwanghwamun Square Underground Exhibition ... (see 15)
12 Gyeonghuigung ... A6
13 Heunghwamun ... B7
14 Jean Art Gallery ... C3
15 King Sejong Statue ... D6
16 National Children's Museum ... E2
17 National Folk Museum of Korea ... E2
18 National Museum of Korean Contemporary History ... D5
19 National Palace Museum of Korea ... C4
20 Open Air Exhibition ... E3
21 Ryugaheon ... C3
22 Sajikdan ... A5
23 Sejong Gallery ... D6
24 SeMA Gyeonghuigung Museum of Art ... A7
25 Seoul Museum of History ... B7

Eating **p70**

Euro Gourmet ... (see 26)
26 GastroTong ... C3
27 Gwanghwamun Dduckam ... C6
28 Gwanghwamun Jip ... C6
29 Hanmiri ... D7
30 Ogawa ... C6
31 Rogpa Tea Stall ... A4
32 Song's Kitchen ... A3
33 Tongin Market Box Lunch Cafe ... B3
34 Tosokchon ... B4

Drinking & Nightlife **p73**

35 Cobbler ... B5
36 Daeo Sochom ... B3
37 MK2 ... C3

Entertainment **p76**

38 Jump ... B7
39 Sejong Center for the Performing Arts ... D6

Shopping **p76**

40 Kyobo Bookshop ... D7
Mono Collection ... (see 37)
41 Sejong Art Market SoSo ... C6
42 Seoul Selection ... E4
43 Yuimaru ... A4

Sports & Activities **p78**

44 Seoul City Tour Bus ... D7

Sleeping **p168**

45 Hide & Seek Guesthouse ... C4

Information **p211**

46 Australian Embassy ... D6
47 Irish Embassy ... E5
48 Japanese Embassy ... E5
49 KTO Tourist Information Center ... E7
50 US Embassy ... D6

Key on p236

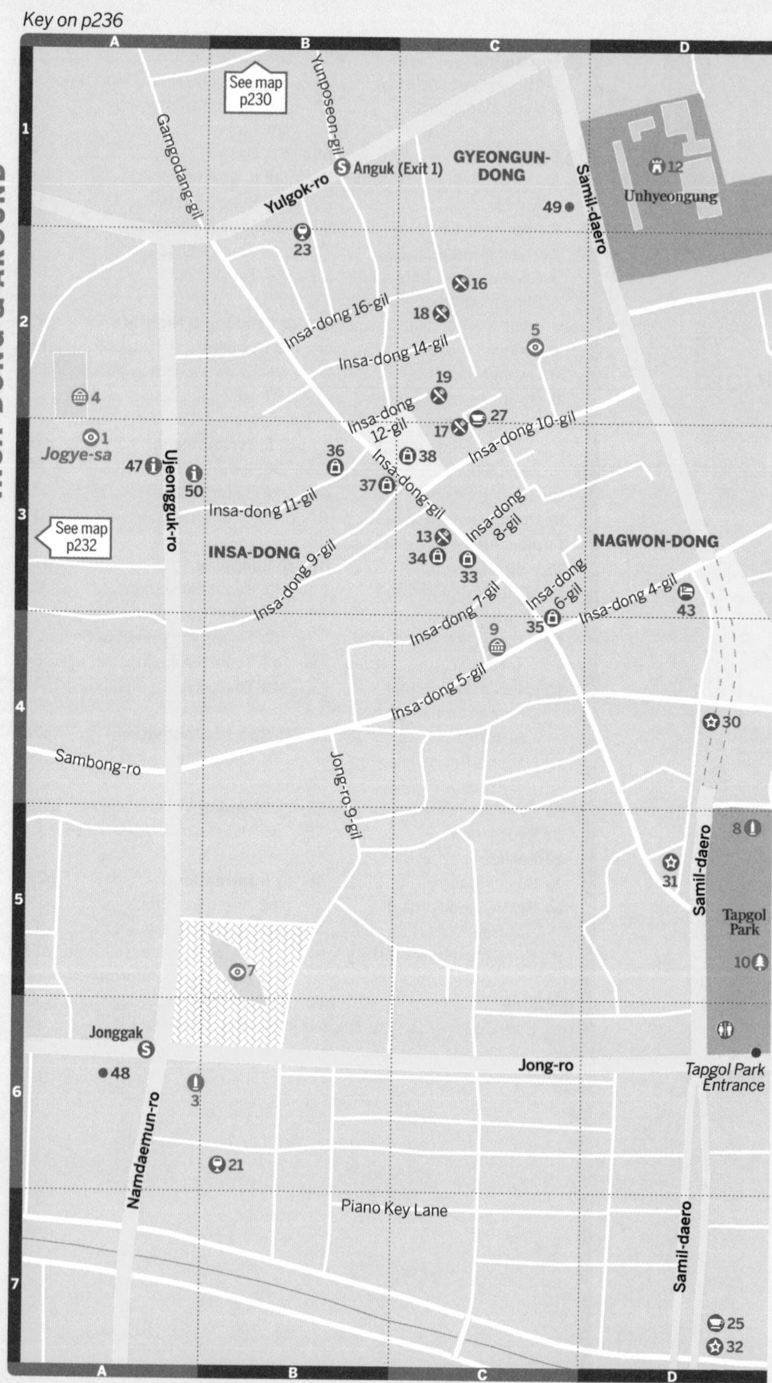

A
B
C
D
1
2
3
4
5
6
7
See map p230
See map p232
Gamgodang-gil
Yunposeon-gil
Anguk (Exit 1)
GYEONGUN-DONG
Yulgok-ro
Samil-daero
Unhyeongung
12
49
23
16
18
Insa-dong 16-gil
Insa-dong 14-gil
5
19
4
1
Jogye-sa
47
Ujeongguk-ro
50
Insa-dong 12-gil
17
27
Insa-dong 10-gil
36
38
37
Insa-dong-gil
Insa-dong 11-gil
Insa-dong 8-gil
13
34
33
INSA-DONG
NAGWON-DONG
Insa-dong 9-gil
Insa-dong 7-gil
Insa-dong 6-gil
35
Insa-dong 4-gil
43
9
Insa-dong 5-gil
30
Sambong-ro
Jong-ro 9-gil
8
31
Tapgol Park
10
7
Jonggak
48
Jong-ro
Tapgol Park Entrance
3
Namdaemun-ro
21
Piano Key Lane
25
32

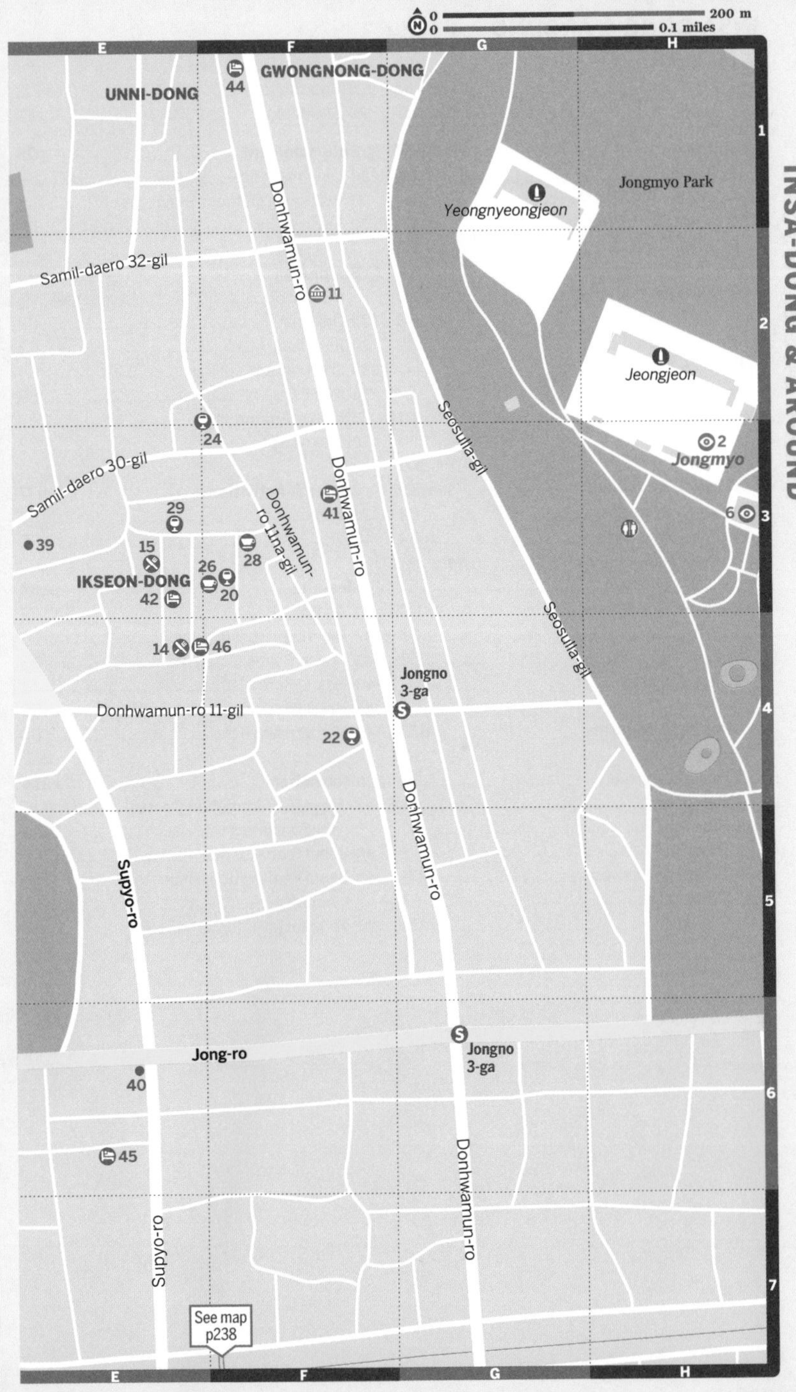
0 200 m
0 0.1 miles
E
F
G
H
1
2
3
4
5
6
7
UNNI-DONG
GWONGNONG-DONG
44
Jongmyo Park
Yeongnyeongjeon
Jeongjeon
Jongmyo
2
6
Samil-daero 32-gil
Donhwamun-ro
11
Samil-daero 30-gil
24
Seosulla-gil
Donhwamun-ro
Donhwamun-ro 11na-gil
41
29
39
15
28
26
20
IKSEON-DONG
42
14
46
Jongno 3-ga
Donhwamun-ro 11-gil
22
Supyo-ro
Jong-ro
40
45
See map p238

INSA-DONG & AROUND *Map on p234*

MYEONG-DONG & AROUND *Map on p238*

Key on p237

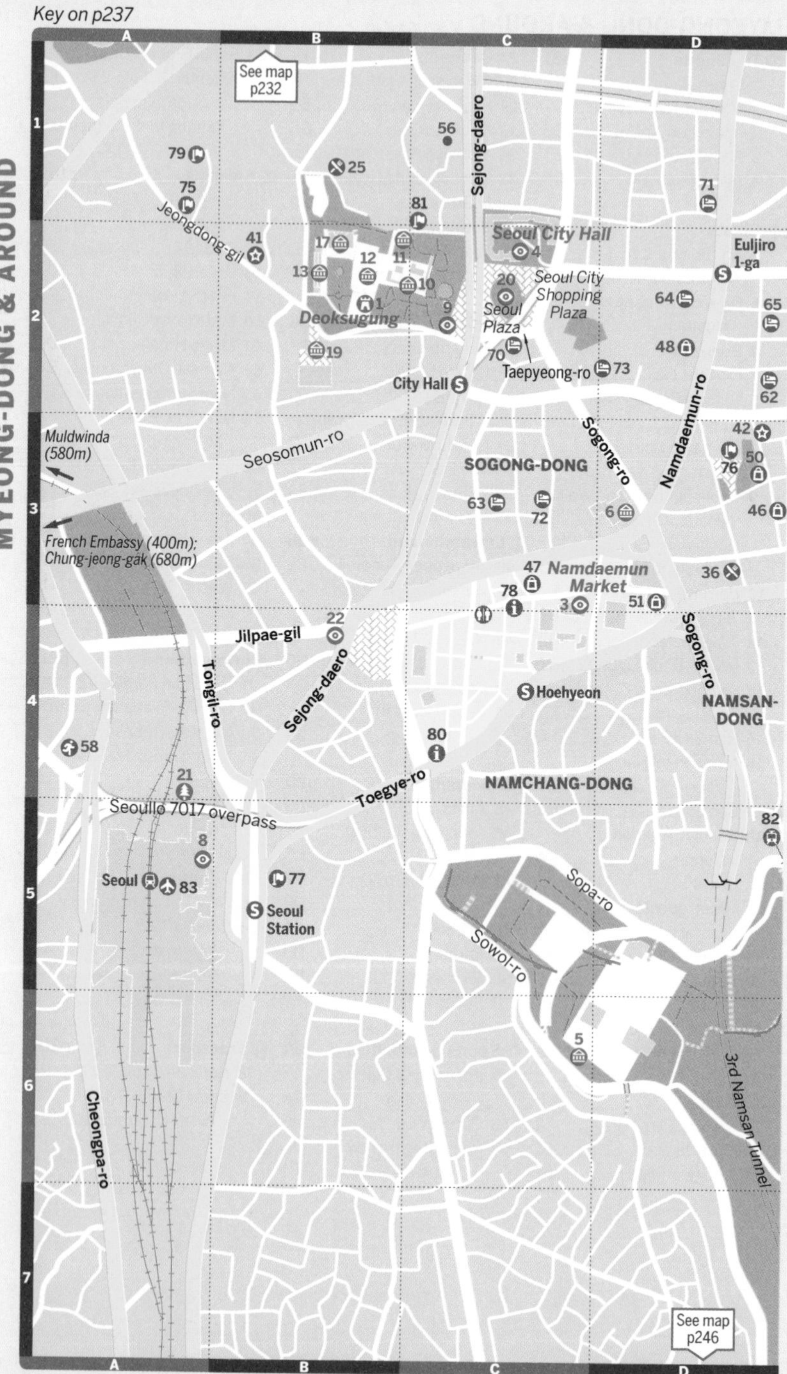
See map p232
Sejong-daero
Seoul City Hall
Euljiro 1-ga
Jeongdong-gil
Seoul City Shopping Plaza
Seoul Plaza
Deoksugung
City Hall
Taepyeong-ro
Namdaemun-ro
Muldwinda (580m)
Seosomun-ro
SOGONG-DONG
Sogong-ro
French Embassy (400m); Chung-jeong-gak (680m)
Namdaemun Market
Jilpae-gil
Tongil-ro
Sejong-daero
Hoehyeon
NAMSAN-DONG
Toegye-ro
NAMCHANG-DONG
Seoullo 7017 overpass
Seoul
Seoul Station
Sopa-ro
Sowol-ro
Cheongpa-ro
3rd Namsan Tunnel
See map p246

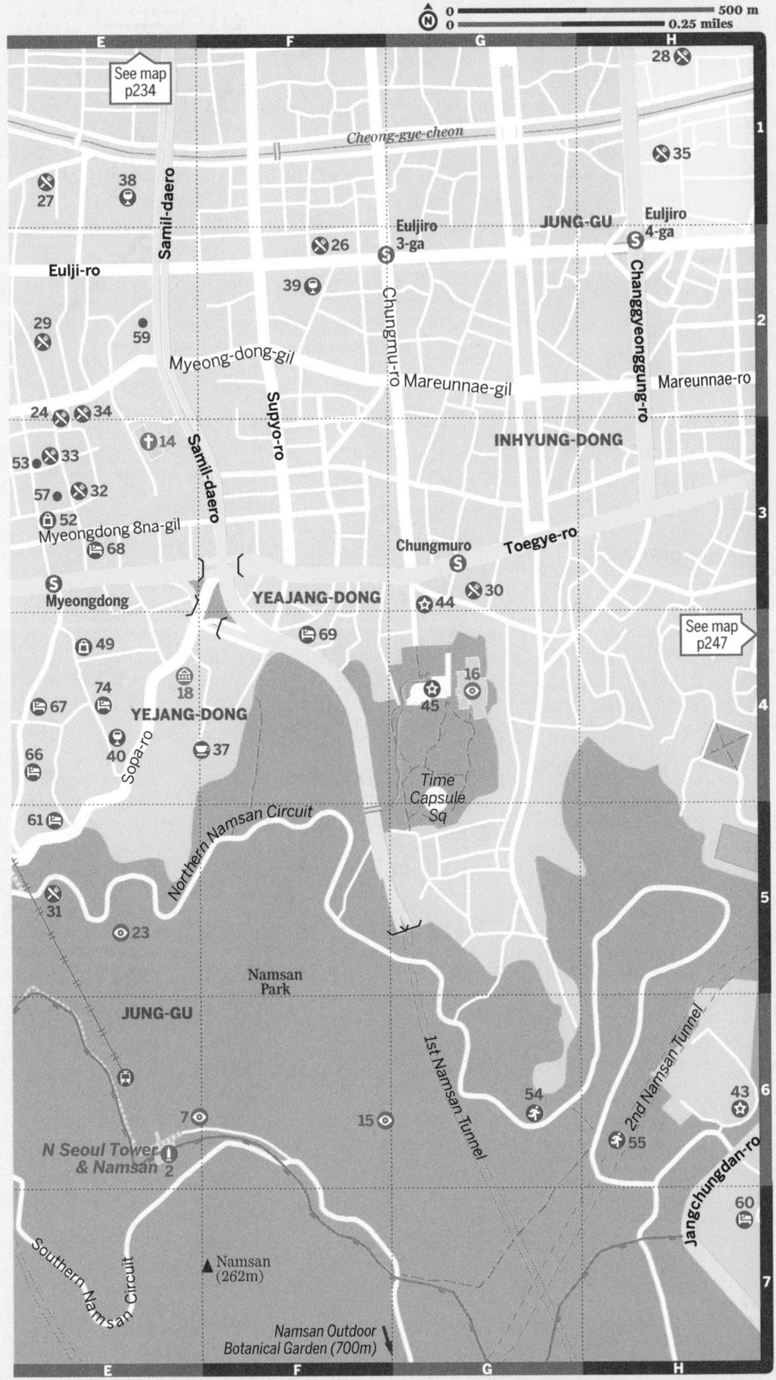
0 500 m
0 0.25 miles
E
F
G
H
See map p234
Cheong-gye-cheon
Samil-daero
Eulji-ro
Euljiro 3-ga
Euljiro 4-ga
JUNG-GU
Chungmu-ro
Changgyeonggung-ro
Myeong-dong-gil
Mareunnae-gil
Mareunnae-ro
Supyo-ro
INHYUNG-DONG
Samil-daero
Myeongdong 8na-gil
Chungmuro
Toegye-ro
Myeongdong
YEAJANG-DONG
See map p247
YEJANG-DONG
Sopa-ro
Time Capsule Sq
Northern Namsan Circuit
Namsan Park
JUNG-GU
1st Namsan Tunnel
2nd Namsan Tunnel
N Seoul Tower & Namsan
Jangchungdan-ro
Namsan (262m)
Southern Namsan Circuit
Namsan Outdoor Botanical Garden (700m)
1
2
3
4
5
6
7

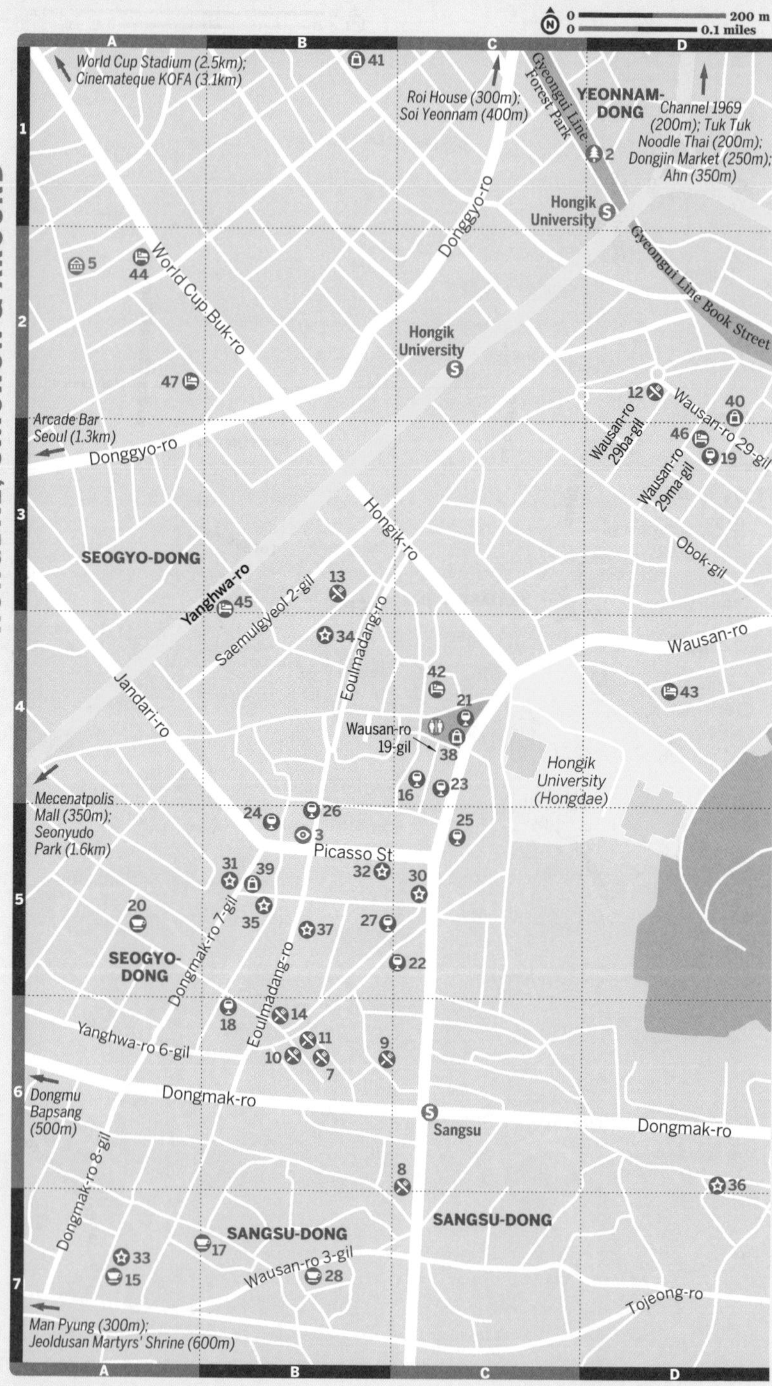
0 200 m
0 0.1 miles
A
B
C
D
1
2
3
4
5
6
7
World Cup Stadium (2.5km); Cinemateque KOFA (3.1km)
Roi House (300m); Soi Yeonnam (400m)
Channel 1969 (200m); Tuk Tuk Noodle Thai (200m); Dongjin Market (250m); Ahn (350m)
YEONNAM-DONG
Gyeongui Line Forest Park
Hongik University
Gyeongui Line Book Street
World Cup Buk-ro
Donggyo-ro
Hongik University
Arcade Bar Seoul (1.3km)
Donggyo-ro
Wausan-ro 29ba-gil
Wausan-ro 29-gil
Wausan-ro 29ma-gil
Hongik-ro
Obok-gil
SEOGYO-DONG
Yanghwa-ro
Saemulgyeol 2-gil
Eoulmadang-ro
Wausan-ro
Jandari-ro
Wausan-ro 19-gil
Hongik University (Hongdae)
Mecenatpolis Mall (350m); Seonyudo Park (1.6km)
Picasso St
SEOGYO-DONG
Dongmak-ro 7-gil
Eoulmadang-ro
Yanghwa-ro 6-gil
Dongmu Bapsang (500m)
Dongmak-ro
Sangsu
Dongmak-ro
Dongmak-ro 8-gil
SANGSU-DONG
SANGSU-DONG
Wausan-ro 3-gil
Tojeong-ro
Man Pyung (300m); Jeoldusan Martyrs' Shrine (600m)

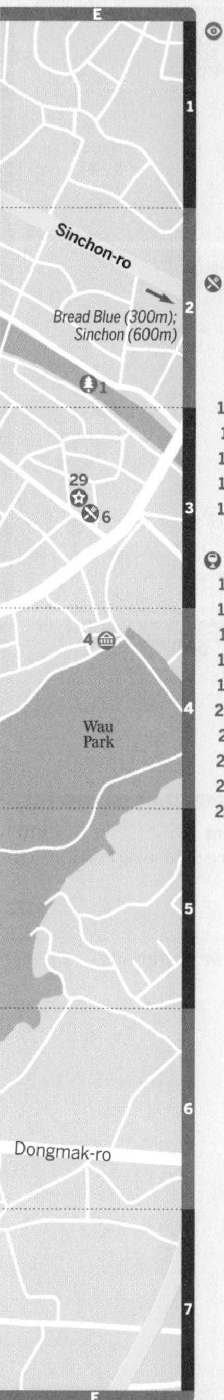
E
1
2
3
4
5
6
7
Sinchon-ro
Bread Blue (300m);
Sinchon (600m)
1
29
6
4
Wau
Park
Dongmak-ro
E

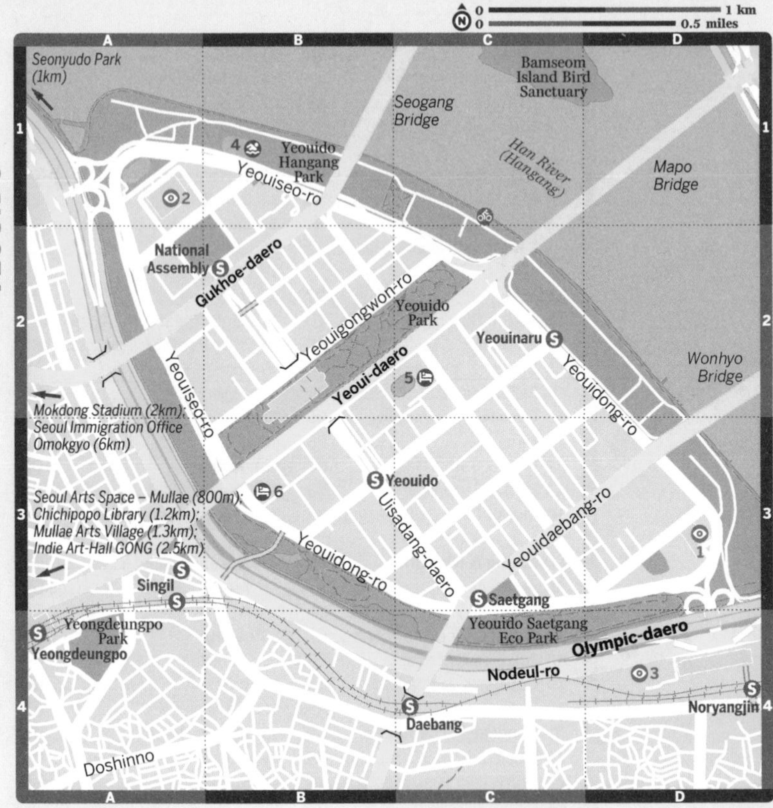

Sights p96

Eating p99

Sports & Activities p103

Sleeping p172

ITAEWON *Map on p244*

Key on p243

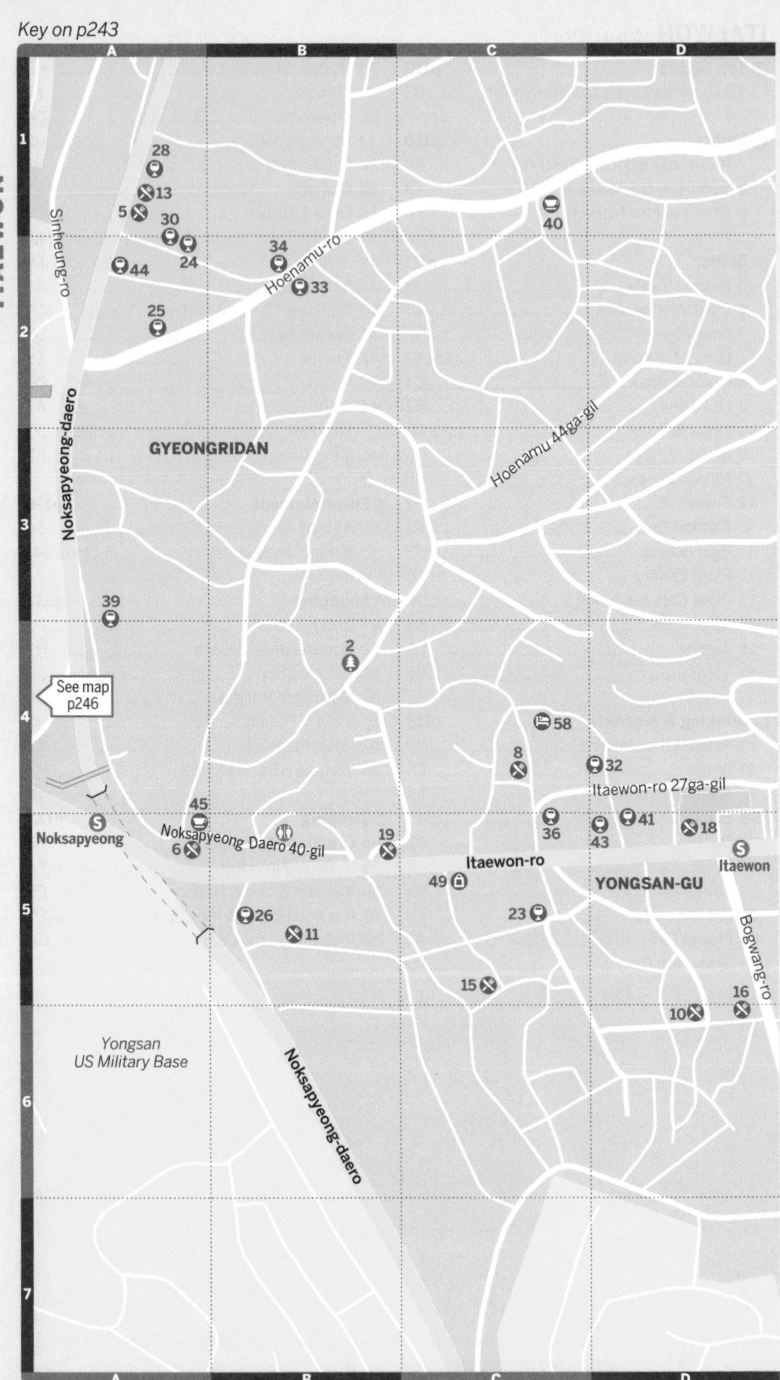

A
B
C
D
1
2
3
4
5
6
7
28
13
5
30
24
44
25
34
33
40
Hoenamu-ro
Sinheung-ro
Noksapyeong-daero
GYEONGRIDAN
Hoenamu 44ga-gil
39
2
See map p246
58
8
32
Itaewon-ro 27ga-gil
45
Noksapyeong
Noksapyeong Daero 40-gil
6
19
36
43
41
18
Itaewon
Itaewon-ro
49
YONGSAN-GU
26
23
11
Bogwang-ro
15
16
10
Yongsan US Military Base
Noksapyeong-daero

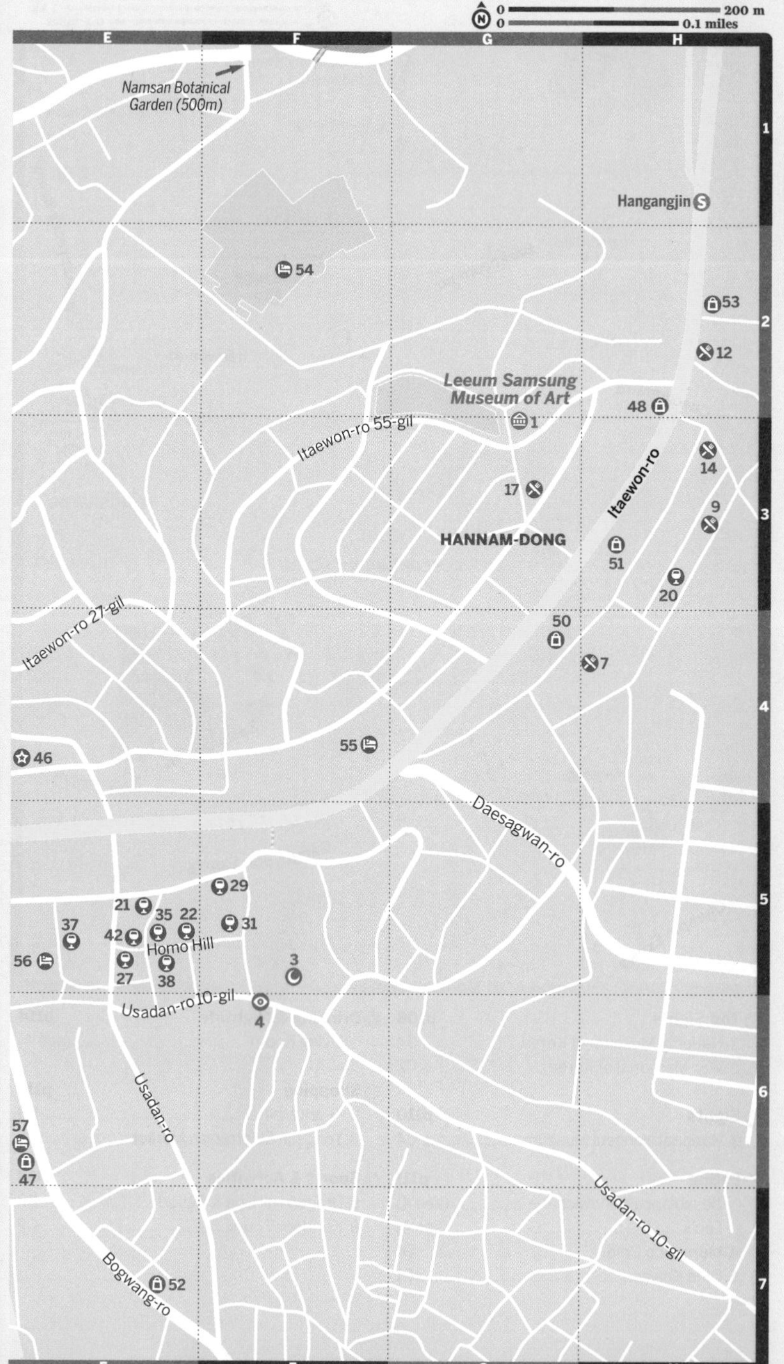

0 200 m
0 0.1 miles
E
F
G
H
1
2
3
4
5
6
7
ITAEWON
Namsan Botanical Garden (500m)
Hangangjin
54
53
12
Leeum Samsung Museum of Art
48
1
Itaewon-ro 55-gil
Itaewon-ro
14
17
9
HANNAM-DONG
51
20
Itaewon-ro 27-gil
50
7
55
46
Daesagwan-ro
29
21
35
22
31
37
42
Homo Hill
56
27
38
3
Usadan-ro 10-gil
4
Usadan-ro
57
47
Usadan-ro 10-gil
Bogwang-ro
52

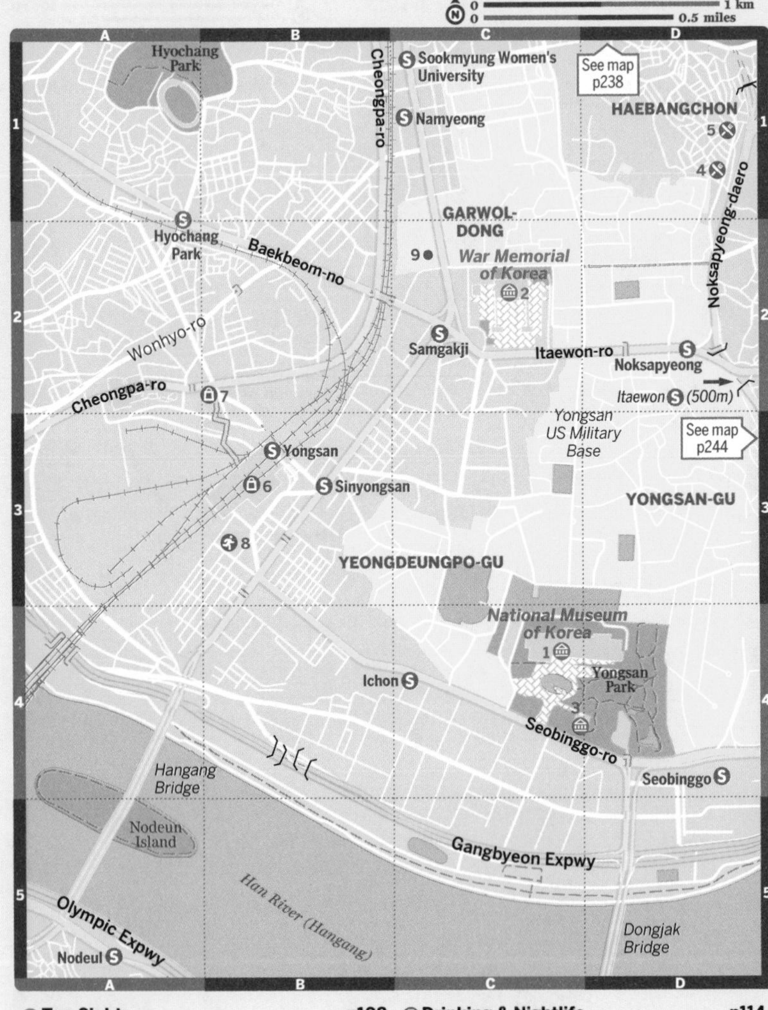

0 1 km
0 0.5 miles
Hyochang Park
Cheongpa-ro
Sookmyung Women's University
See map p238
HAEBANGCHON
Namyeong
Noksapyeong-daero
GARWOL-DONG
Hyochang Park
Baekbeom-no
War Memorial of Korea
Wonhyo-ro
Samgakji
Itaewon-ro
Noksapyeong
Cheongpa-ro
Itaewon (500m)
Yongsan US Military Base
See map p244
Yongsan
Sinyongsan
YONGSAN-GU
YEONGDEUNGPO-GU
National Museum of Korea
Yongsan Park
Ichon
Seobinggo-ro
Seobinggo
Hangang Bridge
Nodeun Island
Gangbyeon Expwy
Han River (Hangang)
Olympic Expwy
Dongjak Bridge
Nodeul

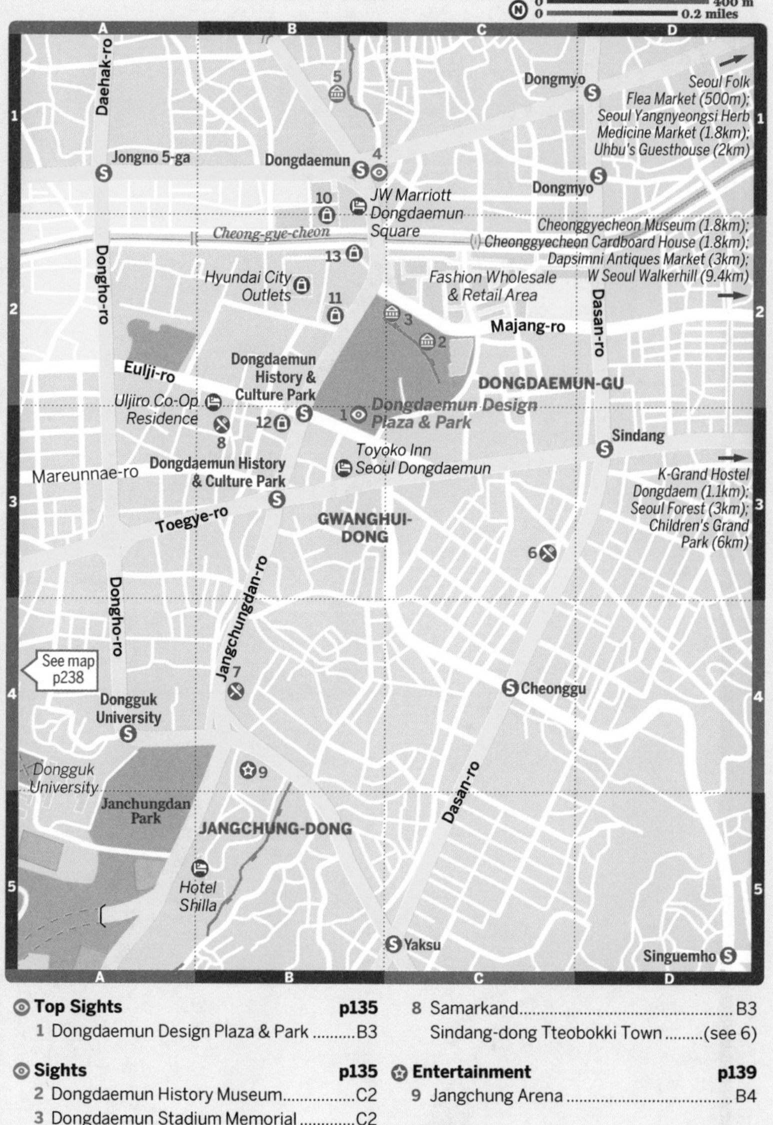

Top Sights **p135**

1 Dongdaemun Design Plaza & Park B3

Sights **p135**

2 Dongdaemun History Museum................ C2
3 Dongdaemun Stadium Memorial C2
4 Heunginjimun B1
5 Seoul City Wall Museum B1

Eating **p137**

Dongdaemun Market .... (see 10)
6 I Love Sindangdong................................ C3
7 Pyeongando Jokbal Jip B4
8 Samarkand B3
Sindang-dong Tteobokki Town ....(see 6)

Entertainment **p139**

9 Jangchung Arena B4

Shopping **p139**

Dongdaemun Market.......................(see 10)
10 Dongdaemun Shopping Complex............ B2
11 Doota B2
12 Lotte Fitin B3
13 Pyounghwa Clothing Market B2

APGUJEONG

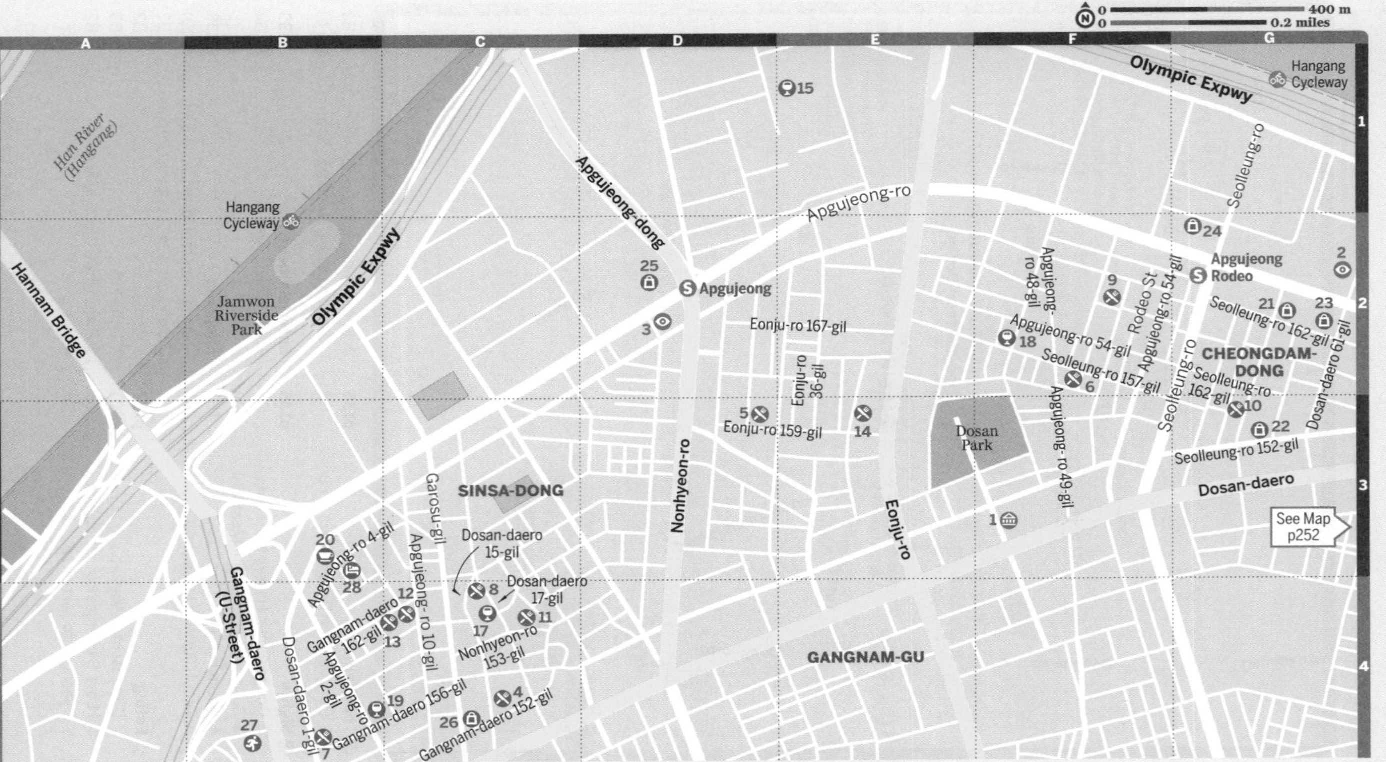
0 — 400 m
0 — 0.2 miles
A
B
C
D
E
F
G
1
2
3
4
Han River (Hangang)
Hangang Cycleway
Jamwon Riverside Park
Olympic Expwy
Hannam Bridge
Apgujeong-dong
25
Apgujeong
3
15
Apgujeong-ro
Eonju-ro 167-gil
Eonju-ro 36-gil
5
Eonju-ro 159-gil
14
Nonhyeon-ro
Eonju-ro
Dosan Park
1
Olympic Expwy
Hangang Cycleway
Seolleung-ro
24
Apgujeong Rodeo
2
Apgujeong-ro 48-gil
9
Rodeo St
Apgujeong-ro 54-gil
21
23
Seolleung-ro 162-gil
Apgujeong-ro 54-gil
18
Seolleung-ro 157-gil
6
Seolleung-ro
CHEONGDAM-DONG
Seolleung-ro 162-gil
10
Dosan-daero 61-gil
22
Apgujeong- ro 49-gil
Seolleung-ro 152-gil
Dosan-daero
See Map p252
SINSA-DONG
Garosu-gil
Dosan-daero 15-gil
Dosan-daero 17-gil
8
11
17
Nonhyeon-ro 153-gil
20
Apgujeong-ro 4-gil
28
Apgujeong- ro 10-gil
12
Gangnam-daero 162-gil
13
Gangnam-daero (U-Street)
Dosan-daero 1-gil
Apgujeong-ro 2-gil
19
Gangnam-daero 156-gil
4
26
Gangnam-daero 152-gil
27
7
GANGNAM-GU

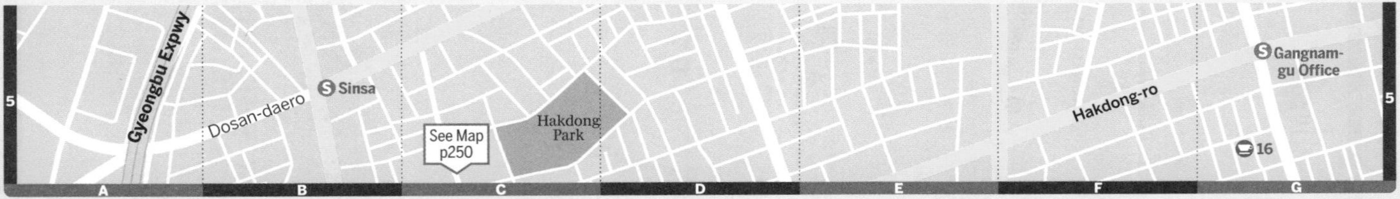

Gyeongbu Expwy
Dosan-daero
Sinsa
See Map p250
Hakdong Park
Hakdong-ro
Gangnam-gu Office
16

Sights p125
1 313 Art Project ... F3
2 K-Star Road ... G2
3 K-Wave Experience ... D2

Eating p126
4 Brooklyn the Burger Joint ... C4
5 Cine de Chef ... D3
6 Coreanos Kitchen ... F2
7 Gati ... B4
8 Gilbert's Burgers & Fries ... C4
9 Haru ... F2
10 Jungsik ... G3
11 Lay Bricks ... C4
12 Normal by Ryunique ... C4
13 Ryunique ... C4
14 Samwon Garden ... E3

Drinking & Nightlife p128
15 Art C Company ... E1
16 Greenmile Coffee ... G5
17 Mikkeller Bar ... C4
18 Moon Jar ... F2
19 Pongdang ... B4
20 Steamers Coffee Factory ... B3

Shopping p130
21 10 Corso Como Seoul ... G2
22 Boon the Shop ... G3
23 Boon the Shop Men's ... G2
24 Galleria ... G2
25 Hyundai Department Store ... D2
26 Pleasure Lab ... C4

Sports & Activities p132
27 Spa Lei ... B4

Sleeping p173
28 La Casa Garosugil ... B3

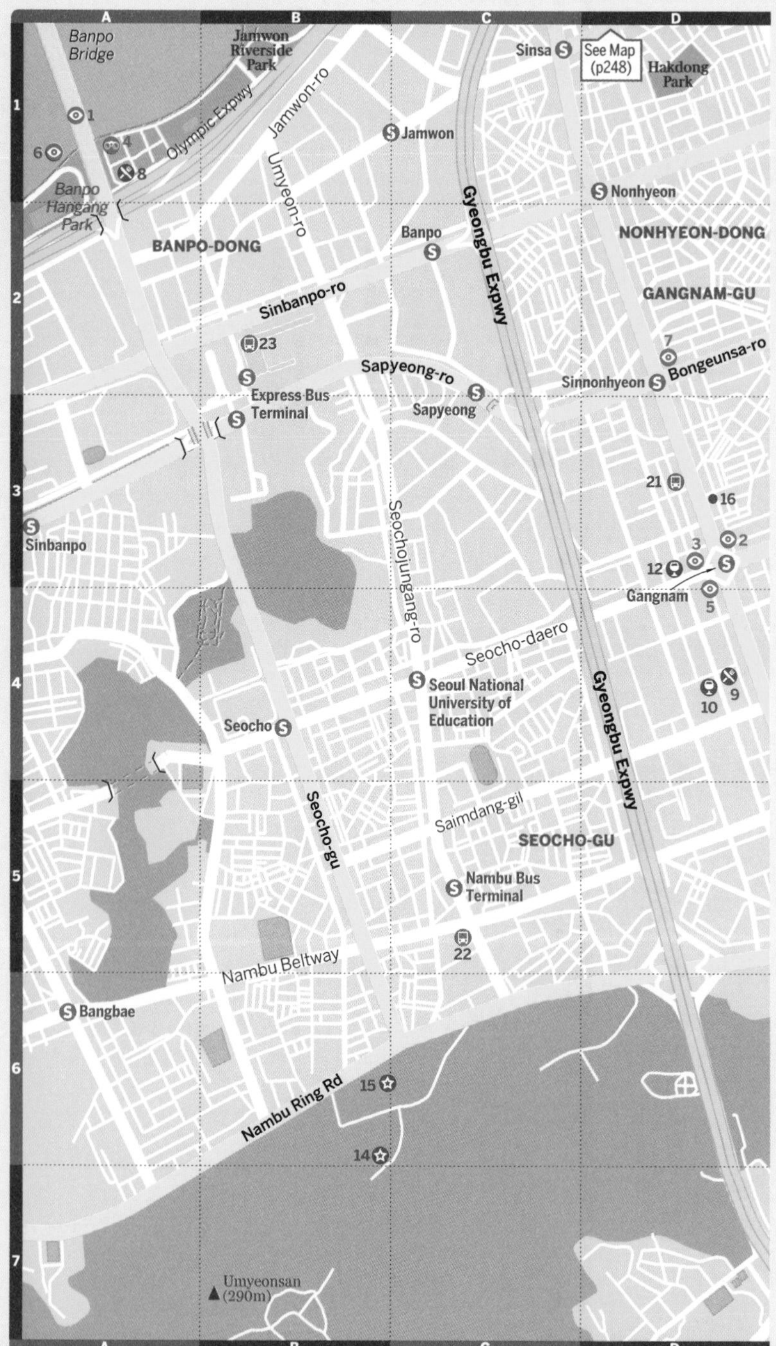
A
B
C
D
1
2
3
4
5
6
7
Banpo Bridge
Jamwon Riverside Park
Olympic Expwy
Jamwon-ro
Sinsa
See Map (p248)
Hakdong Park
Jamwon
Banpo Hangang Park
Umyeon-ro
Nonhyeon
NONHYEON-DONG
BANPO-DONG
Banpo
Gyeongbu Expwy
GANGNAM-GU
Sinbanpo-ro
Bongeunsa-ro
Sinnonhyeon
Sapyeong-ro
Express Bus Terminal
Sapyeong
Sinbanpo
Seochojungang-ro
Gangnam
Seocho-daero
Seoul National University of Education
Seocho
Seocho-gu
Saimdang-gil
SEOCHO-GU
Nambu Bus Terminal
Nambu Beltway
Bangbae
Nambu Ring Rd
Umyeonsan (290m)
1
2
3
4
5
6
7
8
9
10
12
14
15
16
21
22
23

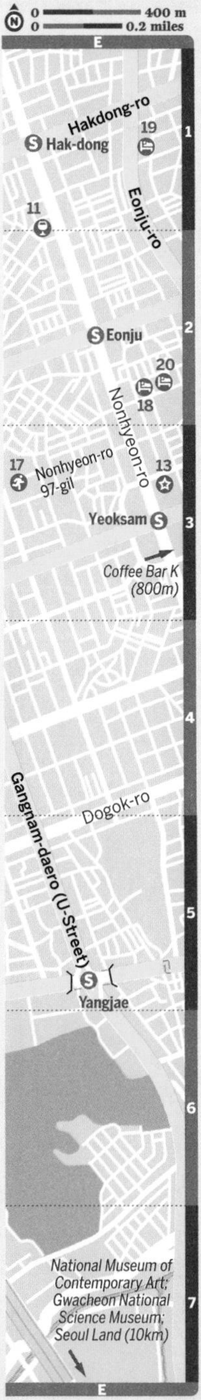
0 400 m
0 0.2 miles
E
1
2
3
4
5
6
7
Hakdong-ro
19
Hak-dong
11
Eonju-ro
Eonju
20
18
Nonhyeon-ro
17
Nonhyeon-ro 97-gil
13
Yeoksam
Coffee Bar K (800m)
Gangnam-daero (U-Street)
Dogok-ro
Yangjae
National Museum of Contemporary Art; Gwacheon National Science Museum; Seoul Land (10km)
E

Sights p124
1 Banpo Bridge Rainbow Fountain ... A1
2 Gangnam Style 'Horse Dance' Stage ... D3
3 GT Tower East ... D3
4 Moonlight Rainbow Fountain Viewpoint ... A1
Museum of Gugak ... (see 14)
5 Samsung D'Light ... D3
Seoul Arts Center ... (see 15)
6 Some Sevit ... A1
7 Urban Hive ... D2

Eating p126
8 Banpo Romantic Moonlight Market ... A1
9 Gangnam Gyoja ... D4

Drinking & Nightlife p128
10 Booth ... D4
11 Club Octagon ... E1
12 Neurin Maeul ... D3

Entertainment p130
13 LG Arts Center ... E3
14 National Gugak Center ... B6
15 Seoul Arts Center ... B6

Sports & Activities p132
16 Gangnam City Tour Bus ... D3
17 Kukkiwon ... E3

Sleeping p173
18 H Avenue Hotel ... E2
19 Imperial Palace Hotel ... E1
20 Tria Hotel ... E2

Transport p207
21 Bus Stop for Everland Amusement Park ... D3
22 Nambu Bus Terminal ... C5
23 Seoul Express Bus Station ... B2

JAMSIL

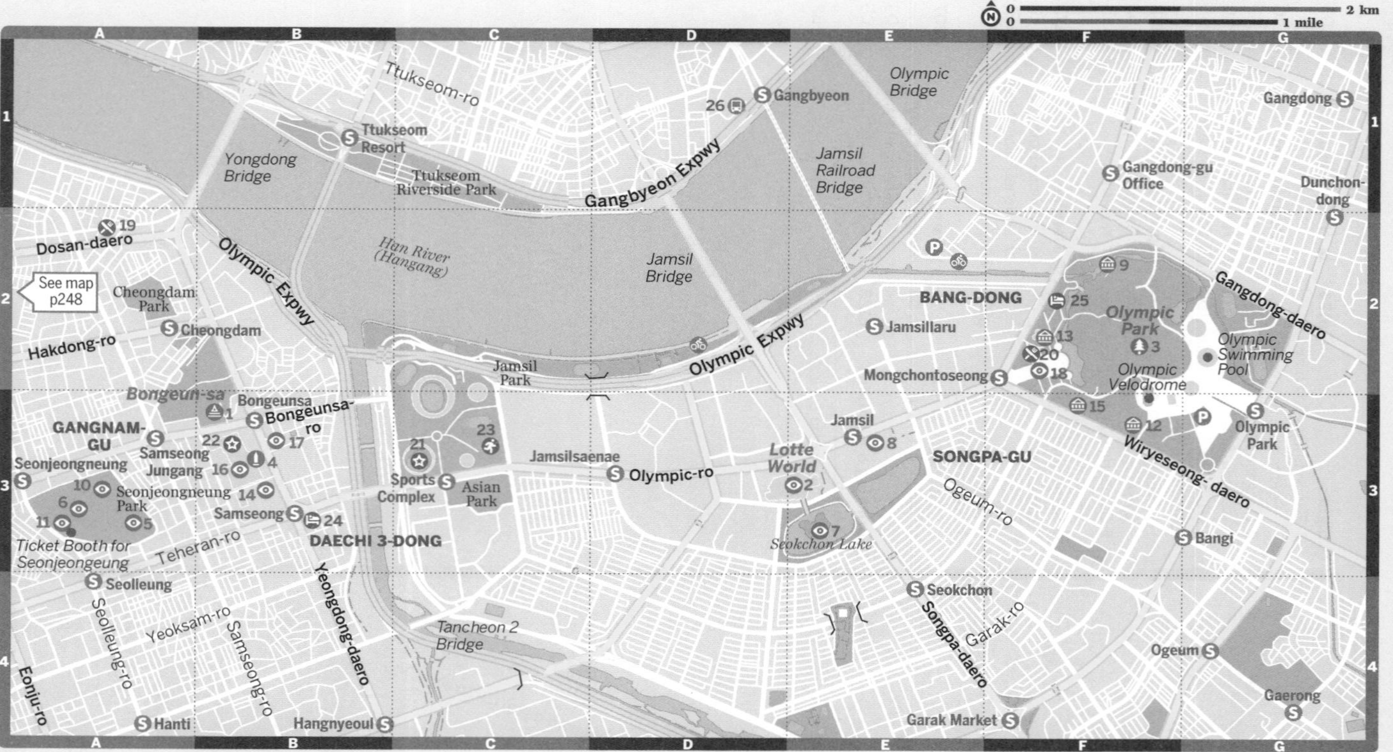

0 — 2 km
0 — 1 mile
N
See map p248
Ttukseom-ro
Gangbyeon
Olympic Bridge
Gangdong
Ttukseom Resort
Yongdong Bridge
Ttukseom Riverside Park
Gangbyeon Expwy
Jamsil Railroad Bridge
Gangdong-gu Office
Dunchon-dong
Dosan-daero
Olympic Expwy
Han River (Hangang)
Jamsil Bridge
Cheongdam Park
Cheongdam
Hakdong-ro
BANG-DONG
Jamsillaru
Olympic Park
Gangdong-daero
Olympic Swimming Pool
Olympic Velodrome
Jamsil Park
Mongchontoseong
Bongeun-sa
Bongeunsa
Bongeunsa-ro
GANGNAM-GU
Samseong
Jungang
Seonjeongneung
Seonjeongneung Park
Jamsil
Lotte World
SONGPA-GU
Wiryeseong- daero
Jamsilsaenae
Olympic-ro
Sports Complex
Asian Park
Ogeum-ro
Ticket Booth for Seonjeongeung
Teheran-ro
DAECHI 3-DONG
Seokchon Lake
Bangi
Seolleung
Seokchon
Seolleung-ro
Yeoksam-ro
Samseong-ro
Yeongdong-daero
Tancheon 2 Bridge
Songpa-daero
Garak-ro
Ogeum
Eonju-ro
Hanti
Hangnyeoul
Garak Market
Gaerong

JAMSIL

Top Sights — p121
1 Bongeun-sa ... B3
2 Lotte World ... E3
3 Olympic Park ... F2

Sights — p124
4 Gangnam Style Sculpture ... B3
5 King Jeongjong's Tomb ... A3
6 King Seongjong's Tomb ... A3
7 Lotte World Adventure & Magic Island ... E3
Lotte World Folk Museum ... (see 2)
8 Lotte World Tower ... E3
9 Mongchon Museum ... F2
10 Queen Jeonghyeon Wanghu's Tomb ... A3
11 Seonjeongneung ... A3
12 Seoul Baekje Museum ... F3
13 Seoul Olympic Museum ... F2
14 SMTown coexartium ... B3
15 SOMA ... F3
16 Starfield Library ... B3
17 Tangent ... B3
18 World Peace Gate ... F2

Eating — p126
19 Jilhal Bros ... A2
20 Seasons Table ... F2

Entertainment — p130
21 Jamsil Baseball Stadium ... C3
22 Megabox COEX ... B3

Shopping — p130
COEX Mall ... (see 16)
Lotte World Mall ... (see 8)

Sports & Activities — p132
Lotte World Ice Skating Rink ... (see 2)
23 Seoul Sports Complex ... C3

Sleeping — p172
Lotte Hotel World ... (see 2)
24 Park Hyatt Seoul ... B3
25 Seoul Olympic Parktel ... F2

Transport — p207
CALT ... (see 16)
26 Dong-Seoul Bus Terminal ... D1

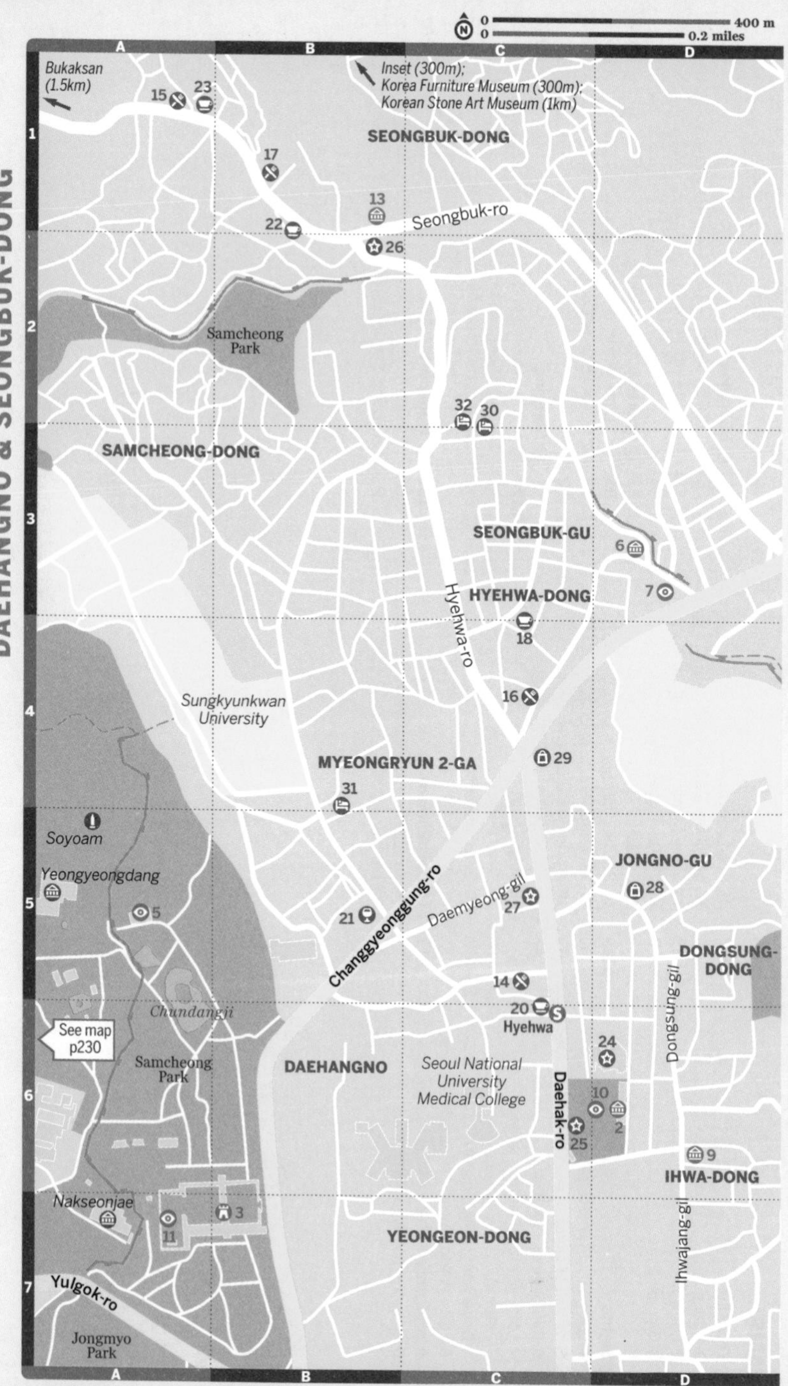
0 400 m
0 0.2 miles
A
B
C
D
1
2
3
4
5
6
7
Bukaksan (1.5km)
Inset (300m); Korea Furniture Museum (300m); Korean Stone Art Museum (1km)
SEONGBUK-DONG
Seongbuk-ro
Samcheong Park
SAMCHEONG-DONG
SEONGBUK-GU
HYEHWA-DONG
Hyehwa-ro
Sungkyunkwan University
MYEONGRYUN 2-GA
Soyoam
Yeongyeongdang
Changgyeonggung-ro
Daemyeong-gil
JONGNO-GU
DONGSUNG-DONG
Dongsung-gil
Chundangji
See map p230
Samcheong Park
Hyehwa
DAEHANGNO
Seoul National University Medical College
Daehak-ro
IHWA-DONG
Nakseonjae
YEONGEON-DONG
Ihwajang-gil
Yulgok-ro
Jongmyo Park
1
2
3
5
6
7
9
10
11
13
14
15
16
17
18
20
21
22
23
24
25
26
27
28
29
30
31
32

E
F
Daesagwan-ro
1
Korea Furniture Museum
SEONGBUK-GU
Seonjam-ro 5-gil
Seonjam-ro 5ga-gil
Seonjam-ro
4
0 200 m
0 0.1 miles
Inset
Dongsomun-ro
Hangsung University
Samseongyo-ro
Samseongyo-ro 16-gil
SAMSEONG-DONG
Seoul City Wall
Naksan Park
12
Naksan-gil
Naksanseonggwak-gil
Changsin-gil
19
CHANGSIN-DONG
8
1
2
3
4
5
6
7

Our Story

A beat-up old car, a few dollars in the pocket and a sense of adventure. In 1972 that's all Tony and Maureen Wheeler needed for the trip of a lifetime – across Europe and Asia overland to Australia. It took several months, and at the end – broke but inspired – they sat at their kitchen table writing and stapling together their first travel guide, *Across Asia on the Cheap*. Within a week they'd sold 1500 copies. Lonely Planet was born.

Today, Lonely Planet has offices in the US, Ireland and China, with a network of over 2000 contributors in every corner of the globe. We share Tony's belief that 'a great guidebook should do three things: inform, educate and amuse'.

Our Writers

Thomas O'Malley

Dongdaemun & Eastern Seoul, Itaewon & Yongsan-gu, Northern Seoul, Gyeonggi-do & Incheon A British writer based in Beijing, Tom is a world-leading connoisseur of cheap eats, dive bars, dark alleyways and hangovers. He has contributed travel stories to everyone from the BBC to *Playboy*, and reviews hotels for the *Telegraph*. Under another guise, he is a comedy scriptwriter. Follow him by walking behind at a distance.

Phillip Tang

Jeju-do, Gangnam & South of the Han River, Gwanghwamun & Jongno-gu, Myeong-dong & Jung-gu, Western Seoul Phillip Tang grew up on a typically Australian diet of pho and fish'n'chips before moving to Mexico City. A degree in Chinese- and Latin-American cultures launched him into travel and then writing about it for Lonely Planet's *Canada*, *China*, *Japan*, *Korea*, *Mexico*, *Peru* and *Vietnam* guides. Writing at hellophillip.com, photos @mrtangtangtang, and tweets @philliptang.

Published by Lonely Planet Global Limited
CRN 554153
10th edition – December 2021
ISBN 978 1 78868 039 4

10 9 8 7 6 5 4 3 2 1
Printed in Singapore